Think It Through
Reasoning in Everyday Life

Think It Through
Reasoning in Everyday Life

Moira Kloster
University College of the Fraser Valley

Anastasia Anderson
University College of the Fraser Valley

THOMSON

NELSON

Australia   Canada   Mexico   Singapore   Spain   United Kingdom   United States

THOMSON
NELSON

Think It Through: Reasoning in Everyday Life
by Moira Kloster and Anastasia Anderson

**Associate Vice President,
Editorial Director:**
Evelyn Veitch

**Publisher, Social Sciences
and Humanities**
Joanna Cotton

Senior Acquisitions Editor:
Cara Yarzab

Marketing Manager:
Laura Armstrong

Senior Developmental Editor:
Mike Thompson

Permissions Coordinator:
Terri Rothman

Senior Production Editor:
Bob Kohlmeier

Copy Editor:
Wendy Thomas

Proofreader:
Margaret Crammond

Indexer:
Dennis A. Mills

Production Coordinator:
Hedy Sellers

Design Director:
Ken Phipps

Interior Design:
Liz Harasymczuk

Cover Design:
Courtney Hellam

Cover Image:
Karen Beard/The Image Bank/
Getty Images

Compositor:
Integra

Printer:
Quebecor World

**Library and Archives Canada
Cataloguing in Publication**

Kloster, Moira, 1949–
Think it through : reasoning in everyday life / Moira Kloster and Anastasia Anderson.

Includes index.
ISBN 0-17-641535-1

1. Reasoning (Psychology)
I. Anderson, Anastasia, 1965– II. Title.

BF442.K58 2005 153.4'3
C2005-903199-9

CONTENTS

PREFACE

How do you teach critical thinking? How do you learn critical thinking? Critical thinking courses first became popular about thirty years ago, and now there are nearly as many ways of teaching as there are teachers, and probably as many ways of learning as there are students. How do you bring together the teaching and the learning?

Add in the wide diversity of contexts in which people are expected to think critically, and it becomes hard indeed to see what common threads will help tie together thinking for different purposes. The critical thinking done by nurses is almost unrecognizable as related to critical thinking done by lawyers—nurses neither give nor evaluate written arguments, as lawyers do. Lawyers do not have to examine their clients' physical condition and vital signs to design treatment plans, as nurses do. Critical thinking for nurses is now a specialized field, yet it is still called critical thinking. Even within a liberal arts education, critical thinking does not look the same in political science and theatre, history and literature.

In this book, we've built a bridge between traditions by building a bridge between our own widely divergent approaches. We teach the same course at the same institution, but we have little in common aside from the course number. One of us is unconventional, and the other is traditional. One is a "big picture" thinker, and the other is detail oriented. One is systematic, and the other does everything at once. One teaches critical thinking with an emphasis on rational belief, and the other teaches critical thinking with the emphasis on responsible action.

The book that has emerged from our debates is one that offers both a traditional core and an unconventional range of applications. The systematic approach to argument is there, and so is the practical application to non-verbal contexts such as designing a stage set or a nursing treatment plan. You can follow the strands that are of most value to you—the thread of verbal argument analysis that runs through Chapters 2, 5, 8, and 11—or the thread of practical analysis and problem-solving that runs through Chapters 3, 6, 9, and 12—or both.

We hope this blended approach will work for a wide range of Canadian students. At our institution, we have the privilege of teaching an unusually diverse student population. Our students come from rural backgrounds and from suburban homes. They come straight from high school, and they come back to college after years in the workforce. Some are single; some are raising families. They come from diverse religious backgrounds, including Sikh and Mennonite, and diverse ethnic backgrounds, including First Nations, Métis, German, Dutch, and South Asian. Most are working as well as going to school. Some juggle full-time jobs with full course loads; others attend classes part-time and finish their education over six or more years. Our reasoning courses find students in their first year side by side with students in their fourth year of studies. The students are enrolled in programs ranging from liberal arts to criminal justice, kinesiology, social work, and sciences.

This book owes much to an earlier book by one of the authors, designed for this diverse mix of students. *Constructive Critical Thinking*, by Moira Gutteridge, published by Harcourt Brace Canada in 1994, followed the principle of engaging students by drawing them into controversial topics in the news of the day. Watching students explore topics of their own choice and watching them grow in understanding through critical reflection has been one of the rewards of using that book. The spirit of applying reasoning to current public debates and to students' own lives remains in this book. Examples are taken from the news and draw on debates that continue to evolve. (What is a "family"? That debate was as much alive in 1994 as it was in 2005.)

What is new, and distinctive, in this book is the inclusion of emotions as an important part of reasoning. We have handled reason and emotion as naturally intertwined, and indeed essential to one another. We have done our best to create a flow that leads students comfortably into the full complexity of critical thinking, which includes dealing with strong feelings and with the values that can trigger these emotions. Throughout the book, we have stressed the importance of balance—doing neither too much nor too little, being neither too perfect nor too careless, feeling neither too little emotion nor too much.

The other major new element is reasoning about research and fact-checking. Students do learn research skills in many courses but often tend to treat information-gathering as an end in itself. Adding a component of critical thinking about research and fact-checking makes it possible to interweave questions about the credibility of information with the option of doing some of the investigation that is normally left out of books on assessing arguments.

In the instructor's guide that accompanies this book, sample course outlines illustrate different routes that can be taken through the book, and different emphases that can be placed on the concepts. A complete answer key and sample test questions with answers is also available.

Our thanks go to all the people who helped in the creation and production of this book. Most of all, we thank the students who participated enthusiastically in the classes where we tried out drafts of the book. Some of the exercises and examples come from student experiences. UCFV's nursing program professors, particularly Joyce Barnes and Wanda Gordon, provided invaluable insight into the links between practical reasoning and verbal reasoning. Gillian Mimmack provided help with quantitative reasoning. Wendy Watson provided examples, and insight into the reading and writing process. We also appreciate the thoughtful comments and encouragement of reviewers, listed below, who read the draft manuscript and especially Marilyn Macdonald, who provided such a thorough and encouraging student-centred critique. The book is far stronger as a result of their advice. At Thomson Nelson, thanks go to Anne Williams for her original encouragement, and to Cara Yarzab, Mike Thompson, Wendy Thomas, and Bob Kohlmeier.

The authors and editors wish to thank the following people who reviewed the manuscript during its development and offered their suggestions: Sue Adams,

Sheridan College; James Ayers, Malaspina University College; Jacqueline M. Davies, Queen's University; Victoria Digby, Fanshawe College; Jean Lachapelle, Champlain College; Colleen Mahy, George Brown College; Nina Pyne, Sault College; Linda Smithies, Humber College; and Mark Vorobej, McMaster University.

Moira Gutteridge Kloster
Anastasia Keyes Anderson

Department of Philosophy and Politics
University College of the Fraser Valley
Abbotsford, B.C.

Introduction

Getting the Best out of Reasoning

■ Perspective

Reasoning helps us to deal with what is new, unexpected, unfamiliar, or challenging. Reasoning is central to our ability to form rational beliefs and take responsible action.

This book will help you to investigate what is involved in responsible, accurate reasoning. It will show you how we form rational beliefs, and how we can act responsibly according to those beliefs. In this chapter, you will learn why reasoning is valuable, what it involves, and why it is not always easy. You'll also try some exercises to get you started.

■ Key Question

How do you decide what is rational to believe and what is responsible to do?

What Is Reasoning?

Consider the following situations. Which situation would you be most comfortable dealing with? Which situation would you be least comfortable with?

a. A young woman is sitting on the sidewalk outside a building and she seems to be crying. You can't tell if she is hurt or just upset. She does seem to be alone—no one is beside her, and passersby are avoiding her. What is going on? Can you help? Should you help?

b. You are at a big family gathering. After the meal, one of your uncles starts complaining about the behaviour of recent immigrants. He says they should never have been allowed into the country. Your father and one of your sisters start an argument with him and before long almost everyone in the room has taken sides. What will you do?

c. You have enrolled in a philosophy course because it was the only elective that would fit your timetable. On the very first day, the professor assigns you a short writing assignment: "What does it mean to be good?" The professor says, "Don't worry about trying to read the textbook before you try this assignment. I just want you to give your own argument, in a page or two." How will you deal with the assignment?

d. You are taking a psychology course, and you have been given an article from an academic journal describing an experiment. Your assignment is to critique the experiment design. You can't see anything wrong with it. The assignment asks for at least a two-page write-up. What will you say about it?

e. You were called for jury duty, and you are now serving on the jury in an assault case. All the evidence has been presented, and the jury has been sent to decide on its verdict. The foreperson of the jury does a quick poll of everyone's initial impression of the arguments presented by the lawyers on each side, and to your surprise, you are the only juror who thinks the accused person is innocent of assault. How will you deal with the difference between you and the other jurors?

The chances are you'll feel more comfortable in one or two of these situations and less comfortable in others. None of them has an easy answer. None of them is something you have trained for and can do automatically. None of them is a situation in which you can simply rely on other people to take the lead and show you what to do.

All these situations have something important in common. They all require reasoning—systematic thinking that enables you to process information carefully so you can judge accurately and act wisely. Reasoning is what we do when habit and routine cannot meet our needs. Reasoning helps us break new ground and adapt to new challenges.

If you are to deal with any of the above situations effectively, you need to reason well. They all require you to take stock of what you actually see, know, and can do. They all require you to check whether you have the information and resources you need to do the job—including deciding what job it is you have to do. They all require you to decide what is the most rational belief to hold, and they all require you to choose a way to respond appropriately. These are the elements of good reasoning: finding a path to rational beliefs and responsible actions. Sometimes reasoning is easy: we are comfortable in the situation and we know how to begin and how to tell if we've reasoned well. Sometimes reasoning is hard: we are unfamiliar with the situation and we are anxious and baffled. Yet the same skills we use in easy situations will also help in tough situations.

If you can think through one of these scenarios, you can think through all of them. The job of this textbook will be to show you how the skills you already have and use in some situations can be developed to handle a much wider range of tasks with equal confidence. You will see how to deal more effectively with challenging issues and complicated reasoning. You will be able to break reasoning into manageable steps, and you will see how to check that you are reasoning accurately at each step.

Reason and Argument

We've looked at the similarities. What are the differences between the five scenarios given above?

They all require reasoning, but they don't all involve argument. The word "argument" appears in three of the scenarios: (b), (c), and (e). In each of those scenarios, it means something a little different, and your reaction to those three scenarios may be affected by how familiar you are with different types of "argument."

If you felt strongly about scenario (b), the family argument, and chose it as your most or least comfortable scenario, that probably means you either enjoy or avoid the types of argument that involve open conflict and often heated exchanges of views. An "argument" in this sense is a disagreement between two or more people whose views clash. Some people find this kind of argument an exciting challenge, an enjoyable way to spend time with people. Other people find this kind of argument nothing but trouble, reflecting tensions between people that often are worsened, not improved, by the open disagreement. This kind of argument may involve very little reasoning—for example, when it reduces to the equivalent of "Didn't!" "Did too!" and "Oh yeah?" heard in children's clashes.

Scenario (c), in contrast, asks for an "argument" that is not going to involve any heated conversation, because it's not going to be spoken at all. It's going to be written on paper, and the professor is also likely to respond in writing with comments in the margin or at the end. If you chose this situation as the most comfortable, that often means you enjoy the type of reasoning that consists of combining your own ideas into a logical sequence to see where they lead—creating "an argument"—and presenting it without interruption so the full value of your ideas shines out. An "argument" in this sense is an exploration of ideas to support a thesis statement or belief. If you chose this situation as your least comfortable, that may mean you are not familiar with this concept of "argument" at all, and don't know where to begin.

Scenario (e) combines both of the previous concepts of argument into a very formal practice with a very specific purpose. The arguments given by lawyers in a courtroom are systematic presentations of evidence and reasons for or against the claim that the accused committed the crime with which he or she has been charged. There are strict rules as to what evidence may be used and what connections may be drawn. To this extent, legal reasoning offers the kind of reasoned "argument" you could equally well find written in an essay. But courtroom exchanges can get heated, and lawyers can use a variety of tactics and verbal moves that are deliberate, sophisticated versions of the kinds of conversational interactions used by family members who want to win an argument at all costs. To this extent, legal argument resembles the unreasonable, uncomfortable family dispute. While legal arguments have something in common with both previous types, they also have an element all their own. They are limited by rules and procedures in a way that the family and the essay writer are not. The "arguments" they give are embedded in a ritual. They cannot do whatever works or whatever they feel like creating. Similarly, as a juror, even though you have not been trained to argue as a lawyer can, the rules of courtroom process require you to engage in argument in the jury room, relying only on what you heard in court and how the judge has instructed you to weigh what you heard. There may be some evidence you must disregard, however persuasive you found it, and there are some instructions you must follow to reach a decision.

What of scenarios (a) and (d)? The first scenario, (a), is often described as "practical reasoning." It may involve no words at all, let alone anything recognizable as any type of argument. You may realize what is going on, figure out what needs doing, and go ahead and do it, all without ever stopping to express your reasoning. If you chose this scenario as the most comfortable, it often means you see yourself as a practical person, preferring hands-on activity with concrete results. "Arguing" in any form may seem to you a poor use of your time. Conversely, if you chose this situation as the least comfortable, this may mean you are not as confident in your reasoning about what you see and feel, or about dealing with a situation that is presented to you all at once, with no recognizable steps to take in a helpful order.

Scenario (d), although it does not mention the word "argument," actually introduces a fourth variant on the idea of an "argument." A "critique" is a form of analysis in which you first examine what someone else has done, often a written argument, and then evaluate it using reasoning. Where it has strengths, you point out the strengths. Where it has weaknesses, you explain the weaknesses. When you write up the results of your evaluation, you are presenting an uninterrupted argument of the same type as the essay in (c). However, like the lawyers' and jurors' arguments in (e), you are presenting the argument for a purpose and within a formal structure: academic debate. Here, the search is for truth—a search that does not end with a jury's verdict, but continues through constant refinement of reasoning. The argument receives a critique; the critique in turn may be critiqued. New evidence or per-spectives may be introduced. The aim is to identify the most rational beliefs by finding supporting arguments that stand up to the most rigorous scrutiny and critique, and this goal may not be reached in a working lifetime.

Overall, then, not all reasoning involves argument, and not all arguments involve reasoning. When you need reasoning, when your reasoning should take the form of an argument, and what type of argument is needed are all questions about "argumentation"—the reasoning practices we use in different social settings, rituals, games, and other contexts where we may or must use arguments.

Arguments and Argumentation

"Argumentation" is a convenient word to cover the different meanings and uses of argument. When we study argumentation, one thing we can do is stand outside particular arguments and examine how they are being given, why they are being given, and what counts as arguing "right" or "well." The study of argumentation gives us a better overview of what arguments are and what we are trying to do with them.

Our previous description of the multiple forms of "argument" covers far more than the most common sense of "argument." An argument does not have to occur between two or more people and it certainly doesn't have to become heated. An additional form of argument not mentioned in the scenarios is a two-sided argument with yourself playing both sides. For example, you can reason with yourself when considering whether you should change how you dress and act to conform to what employers seem to want or when deciding whether you still accept the faith you were raised in. Your purpose in presenting yourself with an argument is to decide what to believe or how to act.

Also, as noted in the discussion of scenario (d), there does not have to be a "winner" of an argument. Arguments can be good or bad, but they are not always competitive. As illustrated in scenario (d), they can be part of a continuing cycle of critical thinking, moving constantly forward as new evidence becomes available or as people reflect on what they have heard. For example, you might argue about religion with someone whose beliefs you don't share, and you might learn a great deal from a mutually respectful discussion even though neither of you changes your personal beliefs as a result. Similarly, society might engage in ongoing public debate about whether to support euthanasia. You may find your own views and everyone else's change gradually over time: as palliative care improves, as we rethink our moral reasoning, or as we learn more about the hardships people endure because of chronic disease.

From now on, in this book, when we use the word "argument" we will mean the collection of reasons put together to support a conclusion. It is the one common element in all arguments that require reasoning, and it is the one element we can pick out and work on as a component of the many different practices of argumentation. When we find, investigate, and evaluate an "argument" in this sense, we restrict our concern to its reasoning: how does it support its conclusion, and is its support enough to justify the conclusion? When we come to respond to or take action on the basis of an argument, we return to considering argumentation: what was the argument for, why were we considering it, and for what goal or practice is it being used?

The Uses and Value of Reasoning

Why is it so important to think things through? Why do employers so often say that "critical thinking" is one of the essential characteristics they look for in employees? Why is a "reasoning" or "critical thinking" course required by so many academic programs, from general arts to nursing and human kinetics?

As noted earlier, we reason when we think through something rationally, responsibly, and objectively. For example, we use reasoning when

- we think through something for ourselves,
- our friends give us wildly conflicting advice,
- there is no answer at the back of the book,
- we want to start something new,
- we finally break down and read the instruction manual and it doesn't say anything that helps.

When we reason, we can reason well or reason badly. The better we can reason, the more it helps us to

- become confident that we can deal with disagreements,
- handle situations in which the best available information still leaves us uncertain,
- show our thinking can be trusted, because we can explain why our thinking is reasonable,
- weigh competing arguments accurately and judge which is best,
- recognize and compare more options for action,
- justify our decisions so that they can withstand public scrutiny.

Good reasoning shows us what to look for in deciding if an opinion is sound or a decision is justified. It puts us in a much better position to see what we might have to do next. It makes it possible for us to deal with new situations and unforeseen circumstances, to resolve disagreements, to avoid dangers, and to recognize opportunities. We don't do it all the time, and we don't always do it easily or well, but when we need it, there is no substitute.

How We Reason

From deciding how to stretch your food budget to deciding how to prevent starvation around the globe, from deciding to restore an old car to designing a non-polluting engine, whenever we tackle a challenging problem, we combine creativity and critical judgment, individual thinking and group discussion, trying out new ideas and learning from feedback. Reasoning is a two-way street—you determine what is of value to you, and how you are of value to the discussion or situation.

For example, "Why do you want this job?" an employer asks. Thinking fast, you say exactly what you suppose the employer wants to hear: "I'm looking for a job where I can learn retail sales skills." This works so well that you get the job. You haven't done yourself or the employer any favour if you actually hate retail sales but you were so desperate for a job that you'd say anything to get one. But if you know retail sales is the right career for you, and that you are a good choice for this employer, then your thinking has produced results that you and other people can live with. And that is the heart of good critical thinking: not just to figure out how to say and do what works for the moment, but to be sure that what you say will produce satisfying results.

How can you think through and make constructive contributions to an issue or a problem that concerns you? The same basic cycle will help you in both public issues and purely personal problem-solving.

We take in information from our surroundings, and we make sense of it. We need to be responsible and reasonable in how we take in information and in how we think through and express our evaluation. Any mention of being "critical" or "evaluating" or "judging" tends to make us think first of forming our own opinions. When you are presented with something—a conversation, a piece of writing, a situation—you react to it, usually by forming an opinion or preference. But a good reasoner is concerned with all legitimate interests and needs, not only his or her own. Your own opinion may be a good guide to the benefit you can gain from what you experience, but it doesn't necessarily show you how other people might benefit. When you consider the other people in the situation, it is important to understand and work with their needs and interests as well as your own.

Your first objective is to observe what exactly you are presented with and make good sense of it. What do you see, hear, and feel? What does it mean? What are the other people doing, what are they trying to achieve, and why is that important to them? What might happen next, and what ought to happen next?

When you complete this process of observing and investigating, you have a confident, detailed understanding of what you must deal with. You know what the other people want to achieve, and you know what it will take for them and for you to achieve your goals.

Your second objective is to figure out how you can make use of what you have learned, and how you can contribute effectively. You make sure that what you do is correctly connected to what you and other people need. When you see the implications of what you have understood, you can make sure that what you do is correctly connected to what you and other people need.

When you have evaluated and responded, you will see how you can benefit from what you have learned, and how you can make the most helpful contribution to others.

The Reasoning Cycle

Critical thinking and reasoning in general flow back and forth between taking in information and expressing ideas. Think of good reasoning as a cycle, not a linear process with a clear beginning and end. It is this cycle that provides

FIGURE I.1
The Reasoning Cycle

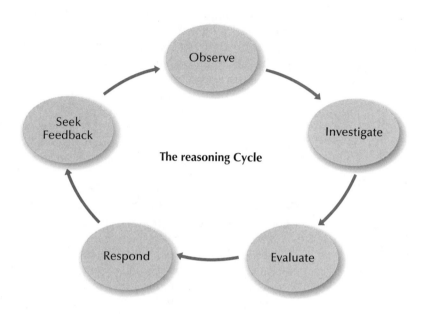

the common thread of skills and strategies we can bring to a wide variety of reasoning tasks. Reasoning requires us to look at the same things from a multitude of different perspectives, using different skills. We will approach the same material with different objectives depending on which stage of the cycle we are in at that moment.

How does this work in practice? We can't do everything at once, so we need a place to start. The general stages of reasoning are observing, investigating, evaluating, responding, and feedback (see Figure I.1).

1. *We observe carefully,* to see what we are really dealing with.

We check that we can make sense of what we are seeing, hearing, and feeling. We check that we understand what's at issue. Can we put into our own words what we think is at stake? Can we explain other people's reasoning, not just repeat it?

Using careful observation, we achieve a confident understanding of what we are actually dealing with. We have solid ground to stand on as we begin to explore further.

In Part 1—Chapters 1, 2, and 3—you will find out how to start where you are, collect all the information initially available to you, and best make sense of it.

2. *We investigate,* gathering information as it comes to us and as we need it.

Typically, each piece of information that we get will answer some questions and raise others. As we think about each piece of information, we decide what further information we'll want. So instead of gathering all the information that we can before we reflect on it, we use each new piece to help make sense of what we have and decide what else we need. We check what the expectations and goals are in this context: who is responsible for doing what, and to what standard?

As we investigate, we achieve a deeper understanding of what is involved and what is expected of us. We become aware of the options open to us. Our knowledge grows, and we see how to apply it.

In Part 2—Chapters 4, 5, and 6—you will develop your skills in investigating to search for more information and find out how it can be used to help you.

3.   *We evaluate* the reasoning.

Are we getting at the real concerns and problems? Do we have other options that have not yet been explored? Have we set the right priorities? Have we made errors or omissions in our thinking? Are our proposed solutions really going to meet our goals? We aim to improve matters, so we look for the best solutions and the most defensible reasoning. We may even realize that we need to re-define the issue and change the way in which we look at it.

Fair-minded evaluation helps us achieve a balanced perspective. We find common ground and understand what is at stake in any remaining areas of disagreement. We weigh our options and choose the most practical. We examine our beliefs and choose the most rational.

In Part 3—Chapters 7, 8, and 9—you will see how to evaluate the information you have and judge it by fair and impartial standards.

4.   *We act responsibly,* helping to make progress in the situation.

What might happen if we say or do things this way or that way? What do we expect other people will do next, and why? We plan our responses to produce the best results, by looking for contributions that are helpful, that reflect our valuable insights, and that open up new options for everyone involved.

We treat ourselves and others with respect, and turn our considered judgments into constructive actions. We achieve an outcome that meets other people's needs as well as our own.

In Part 4—Chapters 10, 11, and 12—you will see how to make the most of your judgments and constructive suggestions by developing proposals and procedures that carry you forward.

5.   *We seek and use feedback.*

There is a final step: the feedback step. In this step, we review what happens to see how well our thinking worked. We build on successes and improve on failures—we learn from experience.

In the Postscript (pages 341 to 352), you will see how to plan for feedback and how to make best use of it.

The Value of a Systematic Approach to Reasoning

What has just been described is a systematic approach to critical thinking— breaking it down into steps that can be taken one at a time.

Breaking a task down into components or steps like this is a helpful way to manage difficult tasks. It helps you focus your attention and it helps you check that you have covered everything you need to.

Each of the five steps described above is valuable in its own right. In some contexts, taking just one of these steps is all that's needed. For instance, researching what's been said can pull together an information package that helps others to learn about the issue. Coming up with a suggestion can break a deadlock and move a discussion forward. Remembering to take advantage of feedback helps you act more wisely next time. Each time you think about a particular problem, you do a little more critical thinking. You have other people's reactions and ideas to consider. Your perspective changes as new factors and new reasons appear.

Good reasoning attempts to give us a shared way of approaching problems, a way that we can trust to lead us to reliable conclusions. It isn't always a mechanical process, because it is precisely what we use when there are no pre-set rules to follow. To get the best results, we have to make the problem manageable, which usually means making several attempts to solve it and getting help from others, learning more each time and building on what we have done.

Good reasoning also helps us make good decisions in situations where we know we do not understand everything yet. Sometimes you accept an expert's advice without question; sometimes you want to question or challenge it. In either case, to feel comfortable with your decision, you use critical thinking skills to understand the explanations and decide whether the advice is likely to work in your circumstances.

Another valuable application of reasoning is in thinking about the reasoning process itself: thinking about argumentation. As we engage in reasoning with other people, we find times when we don't seem to be working in the same way. We may not agree on when and why we want to see good reasons. We must be willing to reexamine our expectations. So reasoning is also used to investigate how we go about reasoning: why we value reasons, how we want to express them, and what we will try when people do not seem to place the same value on reasoning that we do.

Why We Need Practice

Most of us find that we do some critical thinking easily in some situations and with difficulty in others. Some questions that call for critical thinking are quite straightforward. For instance, is it worth your while to read a book on critical thinking? You need to think critically to answer this question, because only you can decide how reading the book could fit usefully into your plans. But you've answered similar questions before about other books or courses, and you've juggled other demands on your time, so you can also deal with this question.

Other questions come at you fast, yank on your emotions, demand that you deal with difficult people, and generally make life very challenging. For example, should you move across the country for a job? Should you let go of your current relationship? These questions are harder to answer. We all vary as to what comes easily to us and what needs practice.

Yet even with difficult problems and issues, we can usually take at least a first run at them. One great advantage of critical thinking is that it is accessible: we can all get started. Critical thinking takes us from where we are to the next step we need to reach. We can start with nothing more than some words we've just heard and figure out what sense they make and what we should investigate further. We can start from a lifetime's experience in business and figure out how best to use a new technology that has just arrived on the scene.

To get all the way through a complicated problem, we need some way to break our thinking into manageable pieces and some way to check whether we really are getting dependable results. These ways are what this book offers you.

Try the following sample situations to see how you'd currently deal with them. You might find some more challenging than others. The best way to try them is to enlist help from one or two other people: each of you should think about the same situation and then compare your answers. The purpose of the exercise is to see how many factors you might need to take into account.

EXERCISE **I.1**

Sample Situations Calling for Good Reasoning

NOTE: Throughout this book, questions marked with an asterisk have answers provided in Appendix A. You may use these questions as self-tests.

*1. It's your first day on the job at a gardening service. The boss has shown you around and explained the procedures. Now you've been left alone at the entryway to a building to replace the plants that have stopped flowering with new plants that are in full bloom. You finish the job with thirty plants left over. Were there meant to be extra plants, or did you space them too far apart? Everyone around you is busy. What will you do? Should you interrupt someone to ask if you're doing it right, or should you reposition the plants to get them all in?

2. You're the manager of a four-star restaurant. It's a busy night. One of the patrons collapses at a table, vomiting. What do you do?

3. Your sports team has an opportunity to compete in two events in the next six months. One is a national competition and the other is a provincial competition. The team cannot afford to go to both events. How will you decide which event to compete in?

4. Your car has just broken down in a busy intersection. Now what?

5. You're travelling in a foreign country and you're getting very low on money. A local resident who made friends with you in a café has invited you to stay in the family home as long as you want. What do you do?

If you discuss your answers with other people, you are likely to see that there are differences in your approaches. We don't all have the same insights or set the same priorities. Not surprisingly, we often disagree about how to settle any differences that we have. How do we make sure that we come up with good results when we think through problems like these?

We can feel a conflict within ourselves as well. What do we do when different tendencies pull us in different directions? Can our emotions be trusted as a guide to what we should do? Sometimes, when we're angry, we believe that we should stand up for ourselves. Sometimes we believe we should bottle up the anger and let other people have their way. Sometimes we just have a gut feeling that this person or that deal cannot be trusted. Sometimes we can think and think without ever feeling that we've reached a decision we can trust. We also know that when we are judging a person's credibility, we ought not to rely on criteria such as appearance. Yet these criteria often can and should be trusted. There are times when your gut feelings are the only signals you have that something is wrong, and it is wrong—even though every scrap of information and reason you have says clearly and logically that nothing can be wrong. When should you trust your emotions or your gut feelings? Reasoning helps to see how to balance your logic with your emotions and intuitions.

EXERCISE 1.2

Opening Up Possibilities

The following scenarios describe situations where your initial reaction may not be a wise choice. Test your ability to "think it through" by describing what you might reasonably do in each situation.

*1. You're helping a friend move. As you stagger up the stairs into the apartment with the third heavy box of books, you find your friend relaxing on the floor with a cold drink. As a good reasoner, your thoughts are . . .

2. Last year, you asked for your shifts to be changed at work so you could have your birthday off. The manager said she'd see what she could do— and when the schedule came out, you were working the morning of your birthday and the morning immediately after. Other people seem to get their schedules adjusted in their favour, and you couldn't figure out why your request seemed to have been ignored. Now it's getting close to your birthday again, and you want to try again for the time off. As a good reasoner, your plan is . . .

3. Someone you've recently met seems eager to be friends, yet the last three times you've called, this person has either been too busy to get together or has cancelled on you at the last minute. As a good reasoner, you think . . .

4. You're travelling in a big foreign city where people generally seem friendly. A man asks you if you will take a picture of him and his friend, with his camera. He starts to show you how to use the camera. As a good reasoner, you watch for . . .

*5. It's been tough to find work, and your eye has been caught by an ad that says "Earn $$$$$ in your spare time! No experience necessary. Call 555-8694." As a good reasoner, you consider . . .

Reason and Intuition

Often, in thinking about the value of reason, we question whether it is really needed. Do we need it to make a decision, or only after the fact, to justify our decision to someone else? To say we should be "ruled by our heads, not our hearts" is to suggest our reasoning alone should guide us. Yet there is another "body part" that often guides us, making us think we don't always need reason, and that is "gut feeling"—our intuition.

To be guided by your "gut feeling"—your intuition—is to have a swift, confident response that something is right: the right decision, the right way to go, the right thing to do. Your intuition also gives you strong negatives—something is wrong here, this wouldn't be the right job for you, this person is not friendly, you could never live in this house. You might not even feel any particular emotion along with this confident feeling.

When your stomach is happy, your heart is often happy too: if your "gut feeling" is there, your emotions are usually within safe bounds, and you are happy to rely on the confidence your intuition gives you.

Conversely, when you feel strong emotions, you also often lose your confidence in what's right—you may feel very strongly that you cannot face doing something, or you may feel that you want very much to do something. But at the same time, you are often not sure that what you want to do is the right thing to do. You become anxious that perhaps your emotion—for example, your fear at the prospect of moving—is not a reliable indicator of what you should do.

The Interplay of Reason and Intuition

There is a traditional view that says reason and intuition are separate and should not be combined. (As we'll see in Chapter 1, there is a very similar argument for separating emotion and reason.) Intuition, almost by definition, cannot be explained. Reason can and often must be explained. Therefore, the argument goes, reason should not rely on intuition. Intuition can be wrong, can mislead you, and can make you overconfident.

However, even in this traditional view, some allowance is made for reliable intuition. If you have a good "track record" of finding your intuition does lead you in the right direction, then you can reasonably appeal to the general reliability of your intuition when you want to justify using your intuition again. You can explain that you are relying on intuition because it has guided you reliably in the past.

What is important for good reasoning is to realize that gut feelings deserve as much critical attention as any other aspect of a situation. They may be indicating that we have unconsciously absorbed some information we can't easily put into words. Our intuition that a person is unfriendly may come from some aspect of facial expression or behaviour that we didn't even realize we had noticed. Your feeling that you couldn't live in a particular house, no matter how well its layout suits your needs, might come from having sensed that it is simply too dark inside and you need more natural light to be comfortable.

Intuition, then, like emotion, deserves to be noticed for the added insight it can give. We can devote critical attention to discovering the causes of a "gut feeling," just as we do to identifying the cause of an emotion. Intuition can be factored into a decision, but should not be given so much weight that it preempts any rational discussion.

EXERCISE ## How Intuition Fits In

*You probably have an excellent sense of whether you are intuitive, and if you are, whether you can or cannot rely on your intuition. Compare yourself to someone who is either much less intuitive than you are or much more intuitive. If you do

trust your intuition, when and why do you trust it? If you don't have intuition or don't trust it, why not, and what do you rely on instead? What are the differences between you and the other person?

The Interplay of Reason and Culture

To do critical thinking, we need to be able to reason accurately. We often confuse what is right with what feels right. We make very firm decisions about what makes sense and what doesn't, what's true and what's false. Yet the strength of our conviction is not a reliable measure of what really is reasonable.

It used to be thought that, if we break down our reasoning into small enough steps, then each step will seem obvious, and we will all agree on it. It has turned out that, even for allegedly simple problems, we do not reliably agree on what is obvious. There have been many interesting studies in this area.

For example, how obvious is the answer to the following problem?

All bears in the Far North are white.
Novaya Zemlya is in the Far North.
What colour are the bears there?

A Russian study in the 1930s found that for residents of Uzbekistan, the answer was not obvious—in fact, many of the test subjects could not answer the question at all (Luria 108–09).

Here's another example. Are all the following statements true?

I am tall or I am not tall.
You are tall or you are not tall.
He is tall or he is not tall.

A study by James Hamill in the 1980s found that test subjects from the Navajo nation who spoke English and Navajo fluently gave different answers depending on which language they were using. In English, they all agreed that all three sentences were true. In Navajo, only the first and third sentences are true. "You are tall or you are not tall" is counted as obviously false in Navajo, because it is not logically possible to assert anything about the person to whom you are speaking.

What are we to make of individual and group differences in reasoning? We will discuss this further in Chapter 12 when we consider how to respond to differences. For now, as we begin our development of critical thinking, we must bear in mind that nothing is so "obvious" that everyone will agree on it. Good reasoning is a matter of seeking common ground and respectfully exploring and negotiating our differences.

Reasoning and Responsibility

Reasoning is closely linked to responsibility, the standards of performance to which you can reasonably be held, given who you are and what your role is. If you have no particular responsibilities and no one will ever challenge your choices, you don't need to think reasonably. For example, you can laugh your way through an outrageously bad movie, enjoy it thoroughly, and at the end declare, "That was the best movie ever!" All that matters is that the movie worked for you, even if you're the only one who laughed at it and everyone else found it so bad they hated it. But when someone else asks whether you'd recommend the movie, your enjoyment is no longer all that matters. Will this other person enjoy it too? At the very least, you have a responsibility to say, "Well, in my opinion, it was the best movie I've seen." You have indicated that this was your personal opinion, based on your own reaction, and you have not said the other person will enjoy it too. Making a recommendation carries with it the responsibility of thinking about what the other person would like, not just what you like.

You also have responsibilities to yourself—personal responsibilities, responsibilities to uphold your own standards and act in your own best interest. For example, imagine you're living on a tight budget, and there's a movie you've been dying to see. Will you pay full price to see it in the theatre, or will you wait until it's released in the video stores? You have a responsibility to yourself to manage your money wisely, so you'll want to avoid acting on impulse. You'll be responsible for thinking through whether you really can afford the extra cost of seeing the movie now.

When you are interacting with other people, there will generally be some level of responsibility involved—to not hurt them or their feelings, to consider their needs as well as your own, and to maintain respectful relationships. We could call this "social responsibility."

Added to that, when you are on the job, you will also have employment-related responsibilities—to get the job done, to do it to the employer's standards, and to do it on time. For some occupations, such as law, teaching, or nursing, there are even stronger requirements—professional responsibilities, where you must conform to a code of ethics and uphold the high standards of the profession even if these might clash with what your employer has asked you to do, and to perform as reliably and ethically as can reasonably be expected.

In some settings, such as academic studies and many public and community issues, you are responsible not just for your actions but also for your thinking. You need to be sure that the beliefs you hold are rational—that they can be reasonably defended—before you act on them. This is intellectual responsibility: a commitment to uncover and uphold the truth, to show where we got our information, to give other people full credit for their ideas, and to reflect critically on the information we have. Academic studies require this because their principal aim is seeking truths. Public and community issues require responsible debate and an informed vote.

Given the levels of responsibility you might have, one of the first tasks of reasoning is to figure out what context you are working in and what responsibilities and opportunities you have in that setting.

EXERCISE I.4

Thinking about Responsibility

*Look back at the sample scenarios given in Exercise I.1. For each one,

a. decide what responsibility you would have. Is that responsibility best described as a personal responsibility, a social responsibility, a professional responsibility, or an intellectual responsibility?

b. specify who else has responsibilities in this situation, and what those responsibilities are.

 EXERCISE I.5

Overview of the Critical Thinking Cycle

__Written Assignment:__ Can you remember a work-related situation that you think was handled particularly well, or one that you think was not handled well?

1. Observe: Describe the situation clearly enough that someone who did not work with you would be able to understand what happened.

2. Investigate: Based on your knowledge of the workplace, describe why you think the situation was handled that way. For example, consider the personalities involved, the time constraints, usual practices, and so on.

3. Evaluate: Explain why you think this was a particularly good or bad way to handle the situation. For example, what was missed or ignored that ought to have made a difference?

4. Respond: Suggest appropriate ways to act in future, to make sure good results happen next time something similar comes up.

Asking Key Questions

To make any complicated task more manageable, it helps to have questions to prompt us to focus on each aspect of the task. In any stage of the reasoning cycle, there will be helpful key questions you can ask to remind yourself to cover all the important aspects. Throughout this book, you will find a Key Question in each chapter. Each one will aid in focusing your attention on the aspect of reasoning covered by that chapter.

Before you start any reasoning task, it also helps to ask a few preliminary questions so that you know why you are getting involved at all.

Probably the most central prompting question for good reasoning is *"Why am I doing this now?"* Notice the multiple questions packed into one: why me, why this, why now? That's time management in a nutshell: a quick, sensible check on what your role is, what the expectations are, and what the priorities are. What exactly am I trying to do—why this? What's my role—why me? Is this the best current use of my time—why now? The question asks not only how "this"—some information, a situation, a problem, or a person—might have something useful to offer to your life and world but also how you might contribute usefully to it. If you can answer the question, you see not only why "this" is worth doing, but also how you can use your knowledge, skills, and interests to contribute to the wider world around you.

When other people's views, expectations, and needs differ from your own, the next key prompting question for good reasoning is *"How might this make good sense to that person?"* This question looks into which beliefs and what background might have shaped the person's views, into what the person might hope to see happen, and into how he or she has actually fitted together the statements that make up the position being presented. Explore this question and you will have understood the other person's position, values, and needs. Understanding the other people involved puts you in a position to work with them to see how to meet their legitimate needs as well as your own.

Asking this second question makes you step back for a moment between recognizing the difference of opinion and acting on it. It is a calming move: when you are questioning, you cannot be rushing to agree or disagree—you are asking, gathering information. And when you check that you've understood, each person who has spoken feels respected—feels heard and understood. This fosters their willingness to cooperate. Critical thinking takes place in contexts in which progress is important and cooperation is needed—yet in which people cling firmly to their positions, often in the face of strong opposition. Some people argue playfully, and some argue fiercely; these people may enjoy an equally fierce challenge from you in response. Other people argue from the heart; they believe deeply in what they say, and a challenge from you may threaten their self-confidence and view of the world. Communication skills and respect for others are important to your success at this stage. You have to use good communication skills to express your good critical thinking. This book will suggest ways in which you can communicate your insights constructively.

A third important prompting question looks ahead: *"What would be the best thing to happen next?"* What do you want to happen after you have thought everything through? This requires you to have a sense of the overall goal or destination—the big picture—and also a good sense of the immediate, concrete actions that would guide you in the right direction. You need to anticipate what might happen next, and anticipation in turn requires thinking about how other people might respond and about how you can help to make it probable that you'll get the best response. This involves being able to come up with not one but several possible options for action. You will usually not be the one with the sole responsibility for taking action, so you will often have to present your recommendations as suggestions, and you will need to have some backup suggestions in case your first one is not accepted or does not work.

EXERCISE **Starting with Questions**

*Try the three prompting questions to approach this letter, which appeared in a newspaper.

Universities are wrong, utterly wrong to complain they do not have enough funds to meet societal needs.

About one-third of university and post-secondary college course offerings consist of shallow, useless tripe, measured by intellectual or practical standards. Examples abound, most in the watery menus of social sciences and humanities (much with a leftish twist). Take a quick look at university and college calendars. Women's Studies? Peace and Conflict Studies? Many of the traditional study areas have also been degraded to simple-minded Marxism or other manifestations of malignant cant.

Brutal necessity plays a role here. About half the applicants for so-called higher education are so under-prepared in language and computational skills that secondary and post-secondary schools have created dumbed-down courses and departments to give these unfortunates a sense of worth. So now much of the post-secondary system is a day-care system for undereducated refugees from life, work and a real education. Facile fibs and simple-minded busy activities replace intellectual inquiry or skills. Math, thinking and language training are notoriously rare. The societal and economic costs of such waste are enormous.

Universities short-changed? No way. It's the taxpayers who have been ripped off, short-changed, overcharged.

I might note for credibility sake that I worked in the college and high school system in B.C. and abroad for 25 years, teaching humanities, social science and business courses, retiring undefeated.

Brian Buchanan, Vancouver

[*VANCOUVER SUN*, AUGUST 11, 2003, A7]

Key Points in Review

- Reasoning in general and critical thinking in particular help us to deal with what is new, unexpected, unfamiliar, or challenging. Reasoning and critical thinking are central to our ability to form rational beliefs and take responsible action.

- Reasoning combines creativity and critical judgment, individual thinking and group discussion, trying out new ideas and learning from feedback. It is a two-way street—you determine what is of value to you, and how you are of value to the discussion or situation.

- A valuable application of reasoning is in thinking about the reasoning process itself. Critical thinking is used to investigate how we reason: why we value reasons, how we want to express them, and what we will try when people do not seem to place the same value on reasoning that we do.

- Reasoning is closely linked to responsibility. Reasoning helps us identify and live up to our personal, intellectual, professional, and social responsibilities.

- Reasoning can be done in a cycle: observing, investigating, evaluating, responding, and learning from feedback.

- Good reasoning is a matter of seeking common ground and respectfully exploring and negotiating our differences.

We had seen no other travellers or hunters since we set off and expected no one else to be at the fishing place. In one sense, this whole landscape was "empty," a "wilderness." But all of it had been given a set of complete human shapes—names and purposes and meanings—by Inuktitut. Inugu and Willie knew this land. They could navigate, select routes that took them over hundreds of miles of sea ice. As we travelled, they named each bluff and headland, identified bays and fjords. They gave me the names of every river and told me the names of many inland lakes. Again and again Inugu took me to places where we could see far into the distance, and there he would point and name and take delight.

To move around with safety, to hunt with success, to make that land's resources available and nourishing, the hunter works with a mass of detail and the names of many, many places. Nothing could be better, for there could be no alternative: to know this particular territory is to prosper; neither the land nor the knowledge of the land can be replaced.

Hugh Brody, *The Other Side of Eden: Hunters, Farmers and the Shaping of the World,* Vancouver: Douglas and McIntyre, 2000, p. 35.

The first step in reasoning is to take stock of what you already have and what you see around you—in other words, to start with a full awareness of where you actually are. We are often so used to seeing just what we expect that we never notice anything else. We run into the room, grab our keys, and run out again—never noticing that a pan is still boiling on the stove. Our tendency to see only what we expect to see or what we think we should see is the first main obstacle to critical thinking, because it limits us to one perspective and our regular routines of responding. It makes it very hard for us to respond to new or changing circumstances.

We've called this first stage of critical thinking "observation," to emphasize that you should actively consider what is before you. You should not yet be actively drawing conclusions from what you are examining and you should not be instantly judging and evaluating it. Skilled observation is the open-minded examination of the details of a situation—the ability to note the unexpected and the ignored aspects of a situation, speech, or piece of writing while still maintaining a critical distance from it.

In this section, you will learn how to use observation skills more effectively to identify, recognize, record, and understand what you are dealing with. In Chapter 1 we will focus primarily on all the nonverbal elements of our surroundings: the sights, sounds, and feelings. Observations of the verbal elements (the written and spoken words) will be covered in Chapter 2. In Chapter 2 you will be introduced to the concept of an argument and learn how to distinguish between arguments and non-arguments. The focus of Chapter 3 is interpretation. In Chapter 3 we explore questions of meaning and the role of context when making observations.

Chapter 1

The "Big Picture" and the Details: Observing and Recording

■ Perspective

What captures your attention? Are you generally an active observer of the world around you? Do you ever look back on a decision and wish you had paid closer attention to details you ignored before acting? In this chapter you will learn the importance of objective observation and how to develop a more effective strategy for gathering and keeping track of information that is immediately accessible to you.

■ Scenario

You're standing in a public park when you notice a group of teenagers making a noise. You look more directly at them and see that one is yelling while the others seem to be laughing. Is this a group of friends at play, or is one of them being teased and bullied by the others? You'll probably want to look and listen more carefully before you decide what is going on. If one teen is being hurt by the others, you may want to call the police. What would you look and listen for in order to decide whether this is harmless play or dangerous aggression?

(This situation is a close parallel to the first scenario you saw in the Introduction. Think about how you would handle this situation. We'll show later in the chapter how you can use reasoning techniques to help you.)

■ Key Question

What exactly am I dealing with here?

The Purpose and Value of Observation

You've determined that there is a situation that calls for reasoning. That situation can range from needing to decide how to act to deciding what claims are reasonable to believe. First, you need to take stock of what you already know and what you can immediately observe. The observation stage has a threefold purpose.

- First, it makes you slow down enough to notice what is really in front of you. This reduces stress and makes it easier for you to deal with a situation.
- Second, the observation stage gives you a chance to recognize your own biases and determine how to direct your attention.
- Finally, consciously noting and recording your observations gives you an invaluable way to make your observations available for future reference and further insight.

For example, picture the scenario at the beginning of the chapter. If you do find yourself noticing that teenagers are scuffling in a park nearby, you may find that you would rather not look closely to figure out what's happening. You're scared, perhaps, and you don't want to get involved. Or perhaps you're excited at the thought that this could be a fight, because you have exactly the skills to deal with such a situation. Either way, you'll be noticing only what you want to notice, and you'll miss the information that could have helped you react more safely and responsibly. Consider, first, your own emotions. If you're scared, that is itself a valuable piece of information—it's an emotion that should be respected, because very often it means you have already recognized a problem. Your own fear is an indicator that this may be a situation where you personally would be wise not to go any closer. However, you could responsibly call 911 to bring help for anyone involved. Similarly, if you're excited, that may indicate you have already reacted to elements in the situation that stimulate your willingness to get involved. That willingness may be very helpful—so often, passersby prefer not to be involved. But you'll need more thought and observation to figure out how best to intervene. As you'll see soon, finding the right role to play requires **objective observation**—attention that acknowledges what you feel and what you can do, and also notices additional relevant information that will guide how you can best respond.

A good reasoner carefully checks what's here now, because one very basic element of good reasoning is realizing that we do tend to overlook important information. Pause a minute and make yourself look: Yes, there are my keys on the counter where I left them . . . and that's an overdue library book beside them, so I'd better take it too. And while I'm here, are the doors locked, the windows shut, and the stove elements all off? Did I leave enough dry food out for the cat? Now I'm in a much better position to leave the apartment, knowing I have what I need with me and I have left the apartment safe behind me.

Observation is an important skill, but it doesn't stop at noticing what's around you. A good observer will recognize what information cannot be accessed immediately and what will require further investigation.

In this chapter we will introduce ways to distinguish between good and poor observations. We will survey the different aspects of a situation that it might be important to note. You will also learn how your goals influence what you observe, and you'll see what it means to take an "objective" approach to material.

It is often important to record your observations for future reference. The ability to take notes and report your observations will help you keep track of what you've recognized and what you may need to go back and check. Having a good report of your observations to rely on as you go through the rest of the critical thinking cycle will help remind you of vital details and remind you to stay objective about the material once you are well into the stage of evaluating it.

Approaches to Observation

In the observation stage we should strive to be **objective.** We must try to notice what is there without worrying whether we like or dislike it, whether we need to do something about it or we can ignore it, whether we enjoy it or are bored by it. Before we begin observation, we should think critically about where we stand in relation to the world around us. It is worth pausing here for an examination of the concept of objectivity and the role of emotion in reasoning.

Whether you are working toward your own opinion or helping other people to reach theirs, it is invaluable to take time to stand outside what's being said and to look at it thoughtfully, questioningly—but not indifferently. Being objective does not mean being unemotional or uncaring. Many of the issues over which we disagree involve strong emotion, especially when they touch on principles that are important to us, for example, same-sex marriage or the right to die. To be objective is to be able to consider more than one point of view and be able to take an interest in subjects not of immediate personal value.

DEFINITION

Observation is **objective** when the observer does not allow personal bias to limit what is observed. The objective observer reserves judgment until observations are complete.

The Value of Objectivity

Objectivity protects us from acting too quickly and overlooking key information. In observation, we emphasize objectivity because we need to be sure we are noticing what really is there and not just what we would hope or expect to be there—we don't want our personal preferences to mislead us.

We need objectivity whenever there is a possibility that our instinctive or personal reactions could lead us into difficulty—for example, by making us unfair or too squeamish or too lazy to react responsibly. If I like you better than your sister, I might give you the last cookie without noticing you already had three and she only had two. If I hate the sight of blood, I might avoid looking at the cut on my face carefully enough to realize it's deep and will need stitches. If I'm bored by anything to do with money, I may not notice that I've been billed twice for the same purchase on my credit card, and I'll pay twice what I actually owe.

At the same time, many people worry that objectivity is either impossible—we'll always be selective in what we notice—or else it's a disadvantage, because we'll be too indifferent to people's needs and feelings. This is a misunderstanding. Objectivity doesn't mean we notice everything possible the first time—it means we stay willing to look again, and to check what we thought we saw. Objectivity doesn't mean caring less—it means caring enough to be willing to hear everyone's version of events.

Objectivity, Neutrality, Opinion, and Bias Contrasted

A person is objective when he or she is willing to fairly consider all points of view including reasons against his or her own point of view. As an **objective person,** you put aside temporarily your own likes and dislikes, your own needs and obligations, and your own preferences. The value of being objective is that you can see what's important to people whose views are different from your own, and you can recognize the merit in others' points of view. For example, an objective person may say, "I would personally prefer to see marijuana legalized, because I think it's less harmful than alcohol, which is legal. But I do understand that some people think it makes more sense to ban both than to legalize both. And I may not have heard all the evidence yet. So I'm still willing to listen to the reasons for banning marijuana." The person is objective because he or she is willing to take into account reasons against his or her own opinion. A person can be objective and not be neutral.

A **neutral person** has *no opinion* on the topic or has heard arguments on both sides of the topic but *does not yet favour either side*. For example, a person who is neutral on the topic of legalizing marijuana for recreational use may say, "I can see why some people want it and why some people think it's too dangerous, but personally, I could live with either decision."

A **biased person** assumes that one particular view is right and does not or cannot produce enough support to show that his or her views are any better than those that he or she criticizes. For example, a person who is strongly biased in favour of legalizing marijuana might say, "I can't imagine why they would make such a harmless, helpful drug illegal." Biased thinking typically produces "slanted" reasoning, that is, reasoning that leans so much more to one side of the issue that it glosses over or ignores the other side.

The problem with biased or slanted reasoning is that it narrows your vision to one side of an issue and cuts you off from other alternatives and other people; it closes dialogue instead of keeping it open.

It is essential to realize that even when a person has strong emotions about an issue and has definite opinions, it does not mean the person's reasoning is bad. Being reasonable or unreasonable depends on how accurate the reasoning itself is. The person who says, "Regulating marijuana is the best way to go. I can't imagine why they'd make such a harmless, helpful drug illegal. It's so obvious regulation is better than prohibition" could be right, even though he or she has not compared prohibition fairly to regulation.

EXERCISE   1.1

Reflecting on Objectivity

Comprehension

*1. Which of the following statements would you expect to be spoken by a person who is objective?
   a. "I never take a stand on any issue."
   b. "Marijuana is obviously safe. Nothing you say will make me change my mind about that. I know people who smoke it every day and they're just fine."
   c. "I would love to stay home today, but Janice phoned and explained that they need me at work. I think I'd better go in for a few hours at least."
   d. "Your essay was really interesting to read."
   e. "Your essay is clear and easy to follow."

2. Give one example of a person being objective.

3. Give one example of a person being neutral.

4. Give one example of a person being biased.

Discussion: What might contribute to making a person biased? For example, are there some types of experience or some influences that tend to produce bias?

Written Assignment: Write a short, one-act play that involves a discussion between one person who is biased, one who is objective, and one who is neutral.

The Interplay of Emotion and Reason

We have defined objectivity in a way that allows an objective person to be emotionally engaged with the issue at hand. This is because feeling and thinking are interwoven.

This may seem to go against what you have heard before. Many people do want to separate emotion and reason. For example, have you ever said or had someone say to you, "You're clearly not being reasonable—you're much too emotional"? Have you ever felt that if you can't stay calm, you won't be able to trust your own judgment? According to one traditional theory of emotion, emotions and reason stand in opposition to each other.

One version of this theory holds that emotions are feelings of physical agitation. For example, fear is the awareness of one's heart beating, palms sweating, and hands trembling. In this view, almost by definition, emotions are incompatible with thinking clearly and are irrational. Emotions cloud our judgment by allowing our bodies to overwhelm our minds. Furthermore, emotions are just physical feelings and therefore do not involve beliefs or judgments. To say emotions are rational or irrational would be like saying having a bloody nose is rational or irrational.

To see the pervasiveness of this view of the relationship between emotion and reason, consider the common stereotypes of a perfectly logical being: the unemotional computer VIKI in the movie *I, Robot,* or the android Data in the TV and movie series *Star Trek: The Next Generation.* The clearest example is probably Mr. Spock from the original Star Trek TV series and the movies. Mr. Spock is half Vulcan and half human. When his logical Vulcan side is dominant, he is cool and rational. He lacks compassion and reaches his decisions using facts alone. When his human side is dominant, he becomes passionate and unreasonable, unable to control himself. We are invited to see not only Spock but ourselves as weakest and most fallible when we are emotional.

Recently a number of philosophers and scientists have been challenging this traditional view. They ask if it is even possible to do purely unemotional thinking. They wonder how you could finish a task if you didn't care whether it got done. It would be hard to choose a career or a life partner if you really had no feelings about any of the options open to you. How would you decide what to think about?

Allowing a more robust role for emotion in reasoning, some philosophers now claim that emotions involve some sort of evaluation of the object of the emotion. For example, if you are afraid then you are evaluating what you are afraid of as being dangerous or threatening. Emotions, in this view, are not just the awareness of physical feelings, but involve some sort of belief. Some philosophers have gone so far as to claim that emotions are nothing more than certain kinds of beliefs. The more common theory, which we will use in this book, is that emotions have a cognitive component—beliefs—and a physical component—feelings. The combination of these two emotional components gives emotions a role in reasoning in at least two different ways.

First, emotions are useful indications of how we view the world because they provide us with information about our own values and beliefs as well as the values and beliefs of the people we interact with. We can sometimes use this information as good reasons to act or to form a belief.

Second, through their physical feeling component, emotions both motivate us to act and play a role in determining what we notice and what we take as relevant to the decision-making process. If our emotions are impaired, then our everyday reasoning and decision-making are severely limited.

Antonio Damasio has been using neurological research to establish the role of emotion in decision-making. In his book, *Descartes' Error: Emotion, Reason, and the Human Brain,* he describes work he has done with subjects who have brain damage that causes them not to experience emotions. These people can reason logically and consistently in test situations, but have great difficulty applying reasoning skills in the real world. The reason, it is speculated, is that emotional feelings are what cause us to pay attention to particular aspects of a situation we happen to be faced with. Damasio talks about emotions as "somatic markers"—physically felt reminders or indicators of important judgments and past experiences. Emotions act like highlighters marking certain passages of your experience so that they stand out and get extra attention. Emotions provide us with the motivation that creates our goals and orientation toward the world. They let us know when decision-making is called for and also motivate us to do what has been decided.

Take the following example. Imagine you are walking down the street on a sunny day. Lots of people are strolling by, there are interesting things for sale in the stores around you, and cars are zooming along the road next to you. In the middle of the sidewalk is a small child standing still and alone with no adult near him. If you are like most people, you will notice this child and feel worried about him. You have evaluated this situation as being potentially dangerous for the child. In this situation, there are so many perceptions, so much data to be processed, that if you were unable to focus in on this scenario as requiring decision-making—if the situation had not been highlighted by your feeling—you would just walk on by. It is the emotion that leads us to notice this scene as one that calls for a decision and most likely will motivate us to act on that decision. We are tuned in to the world, and we focus on what we do, because of the emotional makeup we possess.

Similarly, the scenario at the beginning of the chapter expects that you won't simply fail to notice the teenagers in the park. You won't react to them as if they were simply another piece of scenery. Any of several emotional reactions will draw your attention to the scene. You might feel concern for the youth who is yelling. You might remember fondly what it was like to be a teenager enjoying yourself at top volume. In some situations you might even feel concern for your own safety. While none of these possible emotions indicates that you have correctly judged the situation, all the emotional reactions are equally helpful in making sure you notice it and you are in a position to take further action if needed.

So, we may need emotions to draw our attention toward an issue as a problem to be considered. And perhaps we could extend our view of emotion in a way that allows us to say that on occasion strong emotions give us insight into a problem because of the way they draw our attention to details that might otherwise pass unnoticed. Someone who loves you can pick up on nuances of your behaviour and notice when you are feeling bad about something. No one else may notice, but the one who loves you can tell there is something wrong. Because of your partner's emotional involvement, he or she looks more closely, or notices little things no one else pays attention to.

But if emotions have the power to direct our attention, it is easy to see how emotions might also cause us to become obsessed with our own point of view and become blind to opposing arguments. As reasoners, we don't want to become blinded in this way.

If emotions are a part, perhaps even an essential part of reasoning and yet can sometimes interfere with our thinking about a subject, how should emotions fit into our critical thinking? The observation stage is an invitation to note our own emotions and the emotions of others who may be involved in the situation and to remind ourselves that we are human and what we do matters to ourselves and others. In later stages of the cycle we will be considering how emotions should fit into our decision-making and how we might evaluate emotions as good or poor reasons for belief or action.

Types of Observation

To understand, you must first observe—what is there to be understood? The aim of observation is to find out exactly what is there and therefore what exactly you have to deal with.

Let's turn our attention back to the scenario from the beginning of the chapter, and picture again a group of teenagers doing something in the park near you. You have already noticed whether you feel scared, nostalgic for your own teenage good times, or excited by the challenge. What else might you notice as an open-minded observer?

There will be a wealth of information available to you, everything from how many teenagers you can see to how warm the air is today. What will you pay attention to?

If you focus only on the teenagers and how they are behaving, you might miss something very important in the surroundings that changes the whole situation. Perhaps there's a camera operator off to the side, and a couple of big trailers parked nearby. Perhaps, like one of the authors, you live near where the TV series *Smallville* is filmed, and what you're seeing is a scene for the TV show in which you certainly should not intervene.

If you try to take in everything, you risk becoming distracted or slowing down so much you can't respond in time. How warm the air is won't likely influence your interpretation of what is going on. How loud the teenagers' voices are will matter.

Critical attention in this situation needs to be purposeful or directed observation.

Purposeful Observation

Purposeful observation has specific goals. For example, a nurse does purposeful observation of patients in order to be sure that their medical needs are being met. The nurse might ask, "Is this patient's condition deteriorating?" This is a question the nurse can answer only by careful observation of skin colour, temperature, pulse rate, and other indicators of health. Similarly, a teacher might ask, "Is this child ready to start kindergarten in the fall?" To make a decision, the teacher observes the child's play, coordination, and behaviour and listens to the parents' descriptions of the child's abilities. The teacher needs to know whether this child's needs can be met in a regular classroom setting. Based on the answer to the questions, the nurse can adjust the treatment plan for the patient, and the teacher can recommend that the child start school in the fall.

When we have a purpose in mind, some details can safely be ignored. For example, to give the correct medication, the nurse doesn't need to know what colour gown the patient has on or whether there are flowers at the bedside. The nurse must not be distracted by the extra detail, because the key purpose is to make sure the dose of medicine is given correctly. The teacher doesn't need to notice the colour of the child's hair in estimating mental development. We need to focus our attention on observing the details that are relevant to our purpose.

However, staying alert to other details can still be useful. The nurse might notice the gown and realize the patient is still wearing yesterday's hospital issue. That means the patient hasn't had a clean gown today. The medicine dose remains the priority, but staying open to additional observations helps maintain better overall patient care. As you'll see later, there is a type of observation that takes advantage of additional details that happen to catch your eye.

What is important in purposeful observation is that we must keep our priorities straight and be sure we do notice each of the details that matter, whether or not we have time to notice other things as well.

Checklists as an Aid to Observation

In purposeful observation, we often rely on checklists and other prompts to make sure we remember everything we must look for. The classic example is a pilot making a pre-flight check: every detail that might affect safety in the air is checked before the plane leaves the ground. Checklists are a practical way to balance priorities: it is important to keep your eyes open to every detail, in case something unexpected comes up, but it is also important to be able to cover all the most important elements in a timely manner.

Here's a sample checklist for people doing loading or rigging of stage scenery and equipment:

✔ Are you sure you are within the safe working load of the equipment and tackle being used?

✔ Have you determined the load weight before rigging it?

✔ Have you examined all hardware, equipment, tackle, and slings before using it and destroyed all defective components? (It is not enough to discard defective equipment since it might be used by someone unaware of the defects.)

✔ Have you made sure that there are no hazards to personnel, property, or the public due to weather conditions? (For example, large loads with a broad surface can catch the wind and cause the operator to lose control of the load.)

✔ Is there a competent signal person stationed at all times within view of the operator to warn when any part of the load is approaching the minimum safe distance (three to six metres) from a power line? (The most frequent cause of death among riggers and load handlers is electrocution caused by contact of a boom, load line, or load of a crane with power lines.)

[Adapted from D. E. Dickie, *Rigging Manual,* Construction Safety Association of Ontario, revised edition, 2000]

This checklist shows how important it is to observe carefully what you are doing. The safety of yourself and others may be at stake even in a job that only requires large items to be moved from place to place. This checklist highlights what you would need to observe, and shows you why it matters.

It is useful to create your own checklist while observing, as a way of making sure that you have noted the relevant details. Drawing up a checklist is one good way to decide what details should count as relevant. A checklist can also help you realize what you cannot observe directly and will have to investigate further. Your checklist should contain questions that prompt you to gather the information you will need to make a reasonable decision. The more experience you have, the better and more comprehensive your checklist will be. For example, an experienced parent may know better than a babysitter what behaviour to look for when trying to decide whether his child is ill: the child's face will be flushed, she won't be hungry, and her cry will sound "different."

This is why we often rely on checklists created for us by more experienced people to guide us through an unfamiliar task. If you've never jump-started a car, you'd be wise to follow carefully the checklist in the car owner's manual or the instructions attached to the jumper cables. However, some tasks don't have established procedures, so you also need to be able to construct your own checklists for new situations.

Here's an example of a checklist for the scenario of the teenagers in the park:

✔ Can you hear what's being said? If so, do the words or tone indicate whether someone needs help?

✔ Who is in the group and what exactly are they doing? What is their body language?

✔ How long have you been observing the situation? Has it changed for the better or worse while you've watched?

✔ Are there any other observers nearby? What do their reactions indicate?

✔ What is your emotional state? Can you tell what's making you react that way?

✔ Are you in a position to help? If so, what can you do?

It's almost always a good idea to add questions about your own emotional state when creating your checklist. If our observations are to be accurate, we must recognize the role our own biases and emotions play in determining what strikes us first and how we interpret what we observe. It is through recognizing the force of our own preconceptions that we can note the role they play in our observations and attain the objective observations we aim for.

Elements of Good Purposeful Observation

Observation can be done well or poorly. It is done well if it includes the details you need. It is done poorly if it overlooks or misrecords important details. How do we decide if observation has been done well? Relevance is one factor. The idea of some observations being relevant to the goal of your thinking and others being irrelevant gives us one way to distinguish between good observations and poor observations. Good observation should provide you with details related to what you need to begin your investigation and evaluation of the situation. Poor observation will provide you with irrelevant details that might stop you from reaching your goal.

Good observation should provide sufficient detail. It should include not just some but all of the details relevant to your goal. Are the teenagers screaming as they fight? Is there a microphone picking up the screams for the benefit of a camera crew filming them? Good observation will include a check for any detail that might change your interpretation of what you observe.

Another element of good observation is accuracy and awareness of how reliable your observations are. You may think you see a gun in the hand of one of the teenagers. You need to note how certain you are in this observation. Have you simply seen an object that slightly resembles a gun, or are you certain that you have observed a gun? Describe your observations so that they clearly represent what you're able to observe.

Open-Ended Observation

The observations we have practised so far are directed: they are aimed at identifying key details to answer a specific question. For example, to separate emergencies from non-emergencies, you need to look for key details. Is that smoke from a house fire or from a backyard barbecue that's under control? You need to look at the base of the column of rising smoke to see where it's coming from, and whether someone is nearby keeping watch. Is that person lying in the bus shelter a homeless man asleep for the night, or an addict who has passed out and needs medical care? You need to look for details that suggest the person has deliberately gone to sleep—a sleeping bag or other covers, a position that seems sheltered enough.

There is another type of observation that is equally useful but not as directed. It has no specific goals in mind and generates questions rather than answers them. It is used to "see with fresh eyes"—to look at the familiar as if for the very first time. For example, when artists sketch a scene, they pay attention to shadows and highlights, shapes and textures. They are copying what they see without even thinking about what it "really is," because they want to be sure they notice all the subtle details of shape and colour that make the scene what it is. Another example is what can be called "walking meditation"—you take a walk, paying attention to the sounds, the sights, and the smells around you as if you are seeing your neighbourhood for the very first time. You are focusing on the here and now because you want to unwind, to free yourself from your current cares and concerns and remind yourself you are part of a much bigger world. We'll call this type of observation **open-ended observation**—you really are free to notice anything and everything, from the people around you to the temperature of the air and the feel of the breeze on your skin.

The aim of staying open, not just directed, is to free yourself to discover, not just to answer. For instance, you look into your clothes closet, suddenly aware of the overall effect of what's there, and find yourself wondering, "Why do I have so many black clothes when I actually prefer bright colours?" This may in turn lead you to wonder whether your clothes reflect who you were five years ago, not who you are now. On a geography field trip to Mexico, you might notice the vegetation and wonder whether it is native to the area, or if some of it has been introduced by colonizers. This will lead you to further questions about patterns of human habitation.

Purposeful and open-ended observation overlap in a third kind of observation that is often needed in problem-solving and research. For example, an extra person has turned up for dinner and you have to solve the problem of how to stretch the food somehow. Or, as another example, a biology lab assignment says, "Plant one bean sprout in unfertilized sterile soil, and one in soil to which nitrogen has been added. Observe the growth of the bean plants after one week." What would you look for in these situations? In the first case, if you look only at the food you've already prepared, and for more of the same type in the fridge, you may not realize that you have cans of vegetables in the cupboard that would make a good side dish so everyone eats less of the main dish. In the second case, if you look only at the roots of the plant because you know that was the main purpose of the biology experiment, you may miss the extra stem growth that indicates something else interesting is going on as well.

Whether your observations are purposeful or open-ended, keep reminding yourself that there is a difference between observation and formation of opinions or inferences about what you observe. In this stage of the reasoning cycle, you should be observing and not drawing conclusions or forming opinions about what you are observing. Keeping this distinction in mind is often a difficult task—but an essential one for an accomplished reasoner.

Observing without Judging

Because you want to be careful and accurate in reporting your observations, in this stage of reasoning you should not be drawing conclusions. You should simply report what you observe. Whichever type of observation you are doing, the aim is to identify exactly what is around you or presented to you and therefore what exactly you have to deal with—to note details of the situation and not to rush to judgment.

For example, you notice your co-worker's car as he pulls up to give you a ride to work. Your observation: His vehicle is an old blue van that needs body work and spews blue smoke out of the exhaust pipe. You probably won't stop there—you'll go on to form an impression of him based on his van. You draw a conclusion: "From the look of his van I'd say he doesn't have a lot of money or else doesn't really care about driving expensive or well-tuned vehicles." Your observation remains accurate even if your conclusion is mistaken. Perhaps, as you get in the van, he says, "Sorry about the old clunker. It's a loaner while my own car's in the shop." It is still true that he is driving an old blue van that needs body work and spews blue smoke.

The art we will be practising in this chapter is that of separating the observation from the judgment. Rushing to judgment is one of the most common mistakes we make in reasoning, because it closes off options and blinds us to details that don't fit our preconceived ideas.

EXERCISE 1.2

Observations or Judgments?

Which of these statements report observations and which statements draw conclusions or make judgments?

*1. He was driving way too fast.

*2. The jury brought in its verdict at 9:45 a.m.

*3. I feel very happy and excited about your visit.

*4. They were standing very close together, so they must have known each other.

*5. Given the events of 9/11, life must have changed drastically for New York firefighters.

6. He spoke with a British accent—he must be English.

7. The clothes they wore suggested that they had lived a poor and difficult life.

8. They wore old and ragged clothes.

9. Judging by the state of his house, he was a conscientious housekeeper.

10. I heard the child shrieking with joy as she was being tickled.

Recording Your Observations

Recording is what preserves the value of observations for the future. We all think we'll remember much better than we actually do. Making a record of what we observe as we observe it will at least help us to remember accurately. How many times have you read something interesting while you were researching for an essay, only to find you couldn't use it in the final essay because you'd never recorded the citation and you couldn't find it again? A record for yourself alone needs only to have enough detail to jog your memory. If your records are going to be clear enough to be helpful to others as well as to yourself, then they must be clear enough to make complete sense even when you are not there to interpret them. One reason professors ask for clear citations in a consistent format, such as MLA style or APA style, is so they can find your sources if they have any questions.

In creating a record of your observations, your checklists will help— a written and completed checklist is itself a record. Checklists remind you what details you want to remember for the future.

In all reporting, you are preserving what you noticed so you can remember it later, share it with others, and think about it further. The form of reporting you use should be chosen so it will work for these purposes. This requires some judgment. It may take more time than you have to report every detail. Which details must you note down, and how might you best record them?

Good recording has to have the following:

- all relevant information
- clear detail
- consistent format

For example, suppose you are recording how long it takes you to get to work. Relevant information will include not only the days and the length of time you took, but all the factors that might affect the length of time: the route, the mode of transport, the time of day, perhaps the weather, and any unusual events such as an accident. You may also need to record why you're tracking this information—are you more concerned about how to plan your commute to spend the least time travelling, or are you more concerned about whether you're getting enough exercise? For clear detail, you'll need times recorded to the nearest minute, routes described well enough to retrace your steps if needed, mode of transport specified—which parts are on foot? cycle? bus? own car? carpool? subway? A consistent format will require that you list all these details in the same order each day, so you don't leave anything out and so you can make comparisons or add up totals easily.

EXERCISE **1.3**

Practising Purposeful and Open-Ended Observations

The goal of this exercise is to compare purposeful and open-ended observation.

*1. Describe what you see around you. Move systematically from one side of your field of view to the other.

Purposeful observation

Imagine you are listing the contents of a room for insurance purposes.

Now imagine you are getting ready to paint a picture of it.

Compare your lists. How are your two descriptions different from each other? Now compare your lists to the actual scene. How well have you recorded the details relevant to your purpose? Would you be able to draw a picture or submit an accurate insurance claim?

Open-ended observation

Now that you have looked at your surroundings, what strikes you as curious, noteworthy, or distinctive about what you are seeing?

2. Listen to and watch the lead item in a TV newscast.

Purposeful observation

Take notes as you listen, then read them back as if you are a court reporter reading back what you have just recorded.

Describe the appearance and body language of the anchorperson, as if you are a curious anthropologist or sociologist arriving in this culture for the first time.

Compare your lists. How are the descriptions different from each other? How well can you anticipate what will happen in the next news broadcast?

Open-ended observation

Now that you have listened to and looked at this news broadcast, what strikes you as interesting or unexpected?

What to Look For: Images, Sounds, Quantities, and Words

We typically start observation with what we can directly perceive: the words that are spoken or written, the sights and sounds around us.

Those of us who are "big picture" observers will tend to form a general impression of the overall scene, but we may not even notice some of the details. We know that was a car accident we drove past, but we have no idea what colour the wrecked car was or even if those people belong to that car.

Those of us who are "detail" observers will have our eyes caught by a series of interesting details, but may not get any sense of how the details relate to each other. We notice the car stopped at the side of the road, and the two people standing beside it, but we couldn't say if it was an accident or just a breakdown.

To become better observers, we need the advantages of both big picture and detailed observation. We need to notice all the key details and to get a sense of how they fit together.

Whether our observation is purposeful or open-ended, it helps to have prompting questions to remind us of the many different types of details we might need to notice, and to remind us why they matter—how they relate to the "big picture."

Think of the scenario at the beginning of the chapter: a group of teenagers in a park. You might have noticed the group of teenagers scuffling without even wondering if they were fighting or playing. You might have formed the impression they were fighting without being sure why you had that impression. As you look more closely, you start to shape your observation by asking questions.

For example, you might ask *detail questions*. Is the teenager who is yelling doing anything else that would signal distress? Can you see any hitting or weapons?

You might also ask "big picture" questions, about the scene as a whole and your overall impressions. Do other bystanders seem concerned, or are they treating this as normal? Is the situation changing as you watch, so the teenager who was yelling begins to laugh instead?

Both types of questions help you to form a more accurate impression of what is happening, so you can decide what action you ought to take.

The following sections will give you an idea of how you might direct your attention.

Images: Visual Information

What do you see as you look around? Everything from the room around you to the pictures on the wall to the movie you watch to the ads you see when flipping through a magazine is imagery. "Images" is the term we will use for all types of visual information.

Paying critical attention to visual information helps you orient yourself in your environment and get information that will later allow you to draw conclusions and also recognize the impact of the details of the image. For example, consider what you see as you walk in to a job interview. How is the room furnished? How do the people dress? What is their body language? Where are they positioned in the room? Are your clothes similar to theirs? Your observations may allow you to draw conclusions about what type of company this is, and how well you will fit in. You know they are sizing you up the same way, so you should have looked carefully in the mirror before you left home: what impression do you create by your posture, your appearance, and your clothing? Will you come across the way you hope to?

Critical attention notices both the "big picture"—the overall impression—and the details. When you are observing visual images, look for

- Details: Colours, shapes and sizes, people's appearance, body language, etc.
- Big Picture: Placement and groupings, overall impression

Soundscape: Auditory Information

What sounds do you hear, other than words spoken? The soundscape is everything audible around you, all the sounds from all the different sources. Do you hear something in a person's tone of voice that reveals their feelings or even changes the meaning of their words? Are there background noises, music, birds or animals? What does that say about the kind of place this is? Is there suddenly a silence, and does that indicate that something has changed for the better or for the worse? Is there music in the background of the television commercial, and is it affecting your impression of the product?

Paying critical attention to sounds brings information about mood, and about whether things are functioning as they ought to. Are there birds singing or is the field unnaturally silent? Could pesticides have ruined the birds' food source or is a predator nearby? Should your car be making that funny rattling sound that seems to come from under the driver's seat? Could it mean the transmission's going? Does your stepmother sound cheerful or worried? Could there be a problem with your father's health?

When you pay critical attention to the soundscape you will notice both the overall atmosphere and the important details of what's making each sound and why. Listen for

- Details: Natural sounds, mechanical noises, music tempo
- Big Picture: Tones of voice, mood, atmosphere, music style

Quantities: Estimates, Measurements, and Relationships

When you pay critical attention to quantities, you will notice not only how many and how big or small, but also how fast or slowly the quantities might be changing, how frequent or common an occurrence is, and how quantities compare to one another. Size is one example of a quantity that can be expressed numerically—other examples are weight, duration, and frequency.

"Detail" observations focus on the actual quantity, either by measuring it or by estimating it. For example, you estimated your groceries would cost $40 just by counting the items and estimating $2 per item, but when you got to the checkout, the register showed the actual cost was $55.60. Both the estimate and the exact figure are useful observations. Your estimate gives you a good idea of whether you have enough money with you to cover the bill. The exact figure is a useful record of what you spent, to compare with other bills.

"Big picture" observations focus on the relationships between quantities. Is that gift-wrapped box big enough to contain the present you're hoping for? How much is the cost of groceries going up from year to year?

You will be able to use observations and comparisons of quantities to determine risks more accurately, assess studies more reliably, and be better able to translate ideas into specific actions. For example, you probably know that West Nile virus has spread across Canada, but what exactly is your chance of catching it? Is it high enough to justify staying out of your backyard this summer? Similarly, you probably know whether your bedroom is big, small, or in between. But if you want to paint it, you'll need to know the dimensions of your room accurately. It is inconvenient to buy too little paint and have to go back for more. It's expensive and environmentally unwise to buy too much paint, because the leftovers are hazardous to store and must be disposed of safely.

Here are some useful prompting questions to help guide quantitative observations.

- Details: How many? How high/wide/deep? How fast? How often?
- Big Picture: What is the relative position or size of one item compared to another? How are the numbers changing over time, and what might that indicate?

Feelings: Emotional Information

As we discussed earlier in this chapter, emotions are essential to critical thinking and can be relevant factors in decision-making. They can provide essential information about people's motivations, personalities, and values. Our own emotions are often signals that we have noticed something important without being otherwise consciously aware of it. We need to consider our emotions and the emotions of others so we can make use of the information they are providing to us. Then we can evaluate that information along with all the other factors that we rationally judge as relevant to the issue at hand.

Identifying Your Own Emotions

To notice what emotions you are feeling, try out some of the possibilities by asking yourself, "Am I . . . angry? sad? relieved? happy? fearful? anxious or worried?

For example, you don't know whether to laugh or cry when you're told you've been laid off. You didn't like the job that much, but the paycheque was essential. As you pay more critical attention to your reaction, you may discover that you are feeling a mixture of emotions. The temptation to laugh might indicate anger that they could spring this on you with so little warning. The need to cry might indicate worry because you have so little money saved. You may be feeling both emotions more strongly than you initially admitted, which in turn may indicate that your job is not just a paycheque, it's also an important source of your confidence and self-esteem. Putting a name to the emotions is not only part of observing how you are feeling, but also a very helpful step in making your emotions manageable.

Identifying Emotions in Other People

To notice emotions in others, we look at body language and listen to tone of voice. Some of us read others very well; others of us need practice in paying attention to more than just the words spoken. When someone says, "It's fine with me," do you hear only the words and just go ahead with what you're planning? Or do you also hear the lack of enthusiasm in the tone of voice, see the downcast eyes and slumping shoulders, and realize it's anything but fine? If you know the person well, and remember to notice the extra details, you can probably identify emotions correctly. If you don't know the person well, you will probably need to ask. That fleeting frown might mean the person disagrees with what you've just said, or it might mean the person is concentrating because that particular point was thought-provoking.

Studies by Paul Ekman have suggested that the ability to recognize emotions from facial expressions is shared by humans from various cultures and that as a species we are quite adept at identifying basic emotions in others. Try to use this ability consciously during the observation stage of critical thinking. As we will see in later chapters, noting your emotions and the emotions of others can provide you with a good source of information that can lead to valuable insights—ones that will later help you to evaluate and respond to the situation at hand.

Another good reason to take note of the emotional reactions in a situation is that they can be affecting your thinking about an issue and your approach to solving a problem. How might emotions bias or alter observation?

For example, if you are angry because of the tone taken by a letter to the editor, you may find you have focused your observations on the offensive language or insults in the letter and neglected to observe the reasons given by the writer to defend her point of view. If you have noted your emotion, you can later determine if it has affected your other observations.

When you pay attention to emotions, observe their impact as well as the emotions themselves.

- Details: What emotions are you feeling? What emotions do you detect in others? Are your emotions similar to the emotions of others you are interacting with?

- Big Picture: Is there a general emotional atmosphere (for example, tense, fearful, relaxed, enthusiastic)? Are your emotions affecting your ability to make observations?

EXERCISE **1.4**

Generating Accurate Observations

*1. For the following estimates or measurements, decide whether the given quantity is likely to be an accurate or mistaken observation.
   a. Two soft-drink cans would be enough to hold a litre of milk.
   b. My two-year-old daughter is already 2.5 metres tall.
   c. Bus fare for a month would cost $45.

2. Make your own quantitative observations and decide what you can learn from them.
   a. Observe your own spending for a week. How does it change from day to day?
   b. Measure your weight at eight different times over two days. Does it vary, and if so, how?

The purpose of the following exercises is to practise observational skills. Be careful to note only what you observe. Do not draw any conclusions from your observations or compare your observations to past experience. Simply note what you have paid attention to.

3. Stand at an intersection. Describe it as accurately as you can just as the light turns green in one direction. Which cars or other vehicles are stopped on the red light? Which vehicle was last through the intersection before

the red light, and which was first through on the green? In which direction was each vehicle travelling, and how fast was each one going? You should be able to see how this observation would apply to witnessing a traffic accident. Draw a diagram of what you saw as if you were recording your observations for someone investigating an accident.

4. Watch three different television commercials. Note every detail you can about the sounds used in the commercials. Record your observations in a format which will allow you to compare the commercials easily.

5. The next time you have an experience that evokes an emotion in you, pause to think about what emotion you are feeling. Later, make notes about what the situation was that evoked the emotion. Did you clearly observe what triggered the emotion? For example, if you were angry, who was the target of your anger? If other people were involved, note their emotional reactions.

Written Assignment: For one of the following options, record your observations in a format that can easily be followed by another reader: include all relevant information, give clear details, and use a consistent format.

1. Read one short illustrated magazine article from each of two different magazines that interest you. Approach them with the attitude of open-ended observation. What information is in words that isn't in pictures? Make observations about the picture choice, word choice, and structure of each article.

2. Watch a pet—your own or someone else's—for twenty minutes. Choose a purpose to your observation (for example, with the goal of seeing how the animal responds to humans or the goal of later comparing its behaviour to that of another animal). Create a checklist first to record your observations easily and quickly.

3. Look at a car engine—your own, or someone else's if you already know your own very well. Draw the battery and its connections. Can you see or feel the starter and alternator? Draw a picture as if you were going to show a novice driver how to attach jumper cables to charge this battery.

4. In a cafeteria or restaurant where you can see people choose their drinks, watch fifty people select drinks. Create a checklist first to record your observations easily. What is the most popular choice? Do your observations indicate any correlation between the type of drink and the person who chooses it?

Words and Ideas: Observing Verbal Information

So far, we have looked at nonverbal information available to you—the sights, sounds, and feelings. The other main type of information available to you is the words you hear or read. Words are usually your first clear evidence of what another person is thinking. Observation of words requires not just observation but a particular type of comprehension.

Most of the next two chapters will cover observations about verbal communications and how to interpret them. But it is important to emphasize that any use of words should also first be noticed as a choice that has been made: words have been used rather than some other form of communication. The person who says, "I can't stand this any more!" and the person who simply gets up and leaves the room have both communicated their displeasure. The first person communicated by words, and the second communicated by action. Might this mean that the person who used words is more willing to continue to discuss the situation, while the person who left the room is ending all possibility of discussion?

The next step in basic observation of words is to observe the words themselves: what has been said or written and how the words have been used. One person says, "I can't stand this any more!" while another person says, "You're driving me crazy!" What does the choice of words indicate about differences between the two speakers? Might it mean that the second person sees you as the cause of the problem, while the first person is not judging you at all?

Observe the word choice and phrasing of the sentences. Is the word choice formal? Have slang or swear words or technical terminology been used? Is there anything that is unusual about the phrasing of the communication?

Observe the structure or format of the communication. Are the words in prose or poem form? Is it a story, newspaper article, book review, personal communication, or some other form? Is there a rhythm or cadence of language that should be noted?

As described above, the purpose of your observation should guide what you take note of. If you are preparing a critical analysis of a poem, you may need to note the meter and form of the poem. If you are analyzing a historical text of philosophical importance, you may need to note the exact words used so that you can later compare the usage of the same word or words in various contexts.

Depending on the goal of your observation, it may or may not be important to be able to repeat the exact wording of the communication. For example, when someone you know meets you on the street and greets you with friendly enthusiasm, it would usually be enough to note that she greeted you verbally before beginning a conversation. Whether she said "Hi" or "Hello" or "How are you doing?" would usually not be worth special note. However, if you are being given information by a government official or are in the midst of a legal battle with the author or speaker it might be very important to observe exactly what was said and which words were used in which order. For example, the person whose car hit yours in the supermarket lot might say, "I'm so sorry!" or "How unfortunate!" The first phrasing suggests the speaker feels responsible, the second does not.

Here are some useful prompting questions to help guide your observations.

1. What sort of language, terminology, and phrasing have been used?
2. Are there any unusual word choices? What are they?
3. What is the structure and length of the verbal communication?
4. What else besides the words might be important to understanding the meaning of the communication?

EXERCISE **1.5   Observing Word Choices**

For each of the following pairs of phrases or gestures, decide what important differences the use of these words might indicate.

*1.   a. "That makes me mad!" b. The person pounds the table with a fist.

*2.   a. "The sky so clear, the sun set, green flash—rare wonder." b. "As the sun set, we saw a green flash."

*3.   a. "It's completely unnecessary." b. "It's nugatory."

4.   a. "You should have known better." b. "Why did you do that?"

5.   a. "I was only joking." b. "Can't you take a joke?"

Written Assignment

*Part A: Look back at the letter by Brian Buchanan you saw in the Introduction (page 18). Rewrite the letter in neutral language.

Next, try writing a passage of your own, using strongly emotional language. Trade your passage with another person or group. Rewrite the passage in neutral language.

Part B: Choose one of the following articles. Imagine your goal is to determine whether you should agree with the author of the article. Create a checklist for your observations. Explain why each item should be on the checklist. For example, item 1 on your checklist might be "Who is the author?" This item should be on the checklist to remind you that it may be important later to investigate the author's credibility or expertise in this area.

Make the observations suggested by your checklist. Remember to record only your observations; do not add any judgments.

The first piece is the letter to the editor that was reproduced in the Introduction. The second piece is an editorial.

Re: The other threat facing our universities, Peter McKnight

Universities are wrong, utterly wrong to complain they do not have enough funds to meet societal needs.

About one-third of university and post-secondary college course offerings consist of shallow, useless tripe, measured by intellectual or practical standards. Examples abound, most in the watery menus of social sciences and humanities (much with a leftish twist). Take a quick look at university and college calendars. Women's Studies? Peace and Conflict Studies? Many of the traditional study areas have also been degraded to simple-minded Marxism or other manifestations of malignant cant.

Brutal necessity plays a role here. About half the applicants for so-called higher education are so under-prepared in language and computational skills that secondary and post-secondary schools have created dumbed-down courses and departments to give these unfortunates a sense of worth. So now much of the post-secondary system is a day-care system for undereducated refugees from life, work and a real education. Facile fibs and simple-minded busy activities replace intellectual inquiry or skills. Math, thinking and language training are notoriously rare. The societal and economic costs of such waste are enormous.

(Continued)

Re: The other threat facing our universities, Peter McKnight   *(Continued)*

Universities short-changed? No way. It's the taxpayers who have been ripped off, short-changed, overcharged.

I might note for credibility sake that I worked in the college and high school system in B.C. and abroad for 25 years, teaching humanities, social science and business courses, retiring undefeated.

Brian Buchanan, Vancouver

[*VANCOUVER SUN*, AUGUST 11, 2003, A7. REPRINTED WITH PERMISSION OF BRIAN BUCHANAN.]

You Say Crusade, I Say Lost Cause

Ah, a crusade. That's what Premier Danny Williams promised Tuesday night in a fundraising speech at a $500-a-plate dinner in St. John's.

If Prime Minister Paul Martin does not do the right thing and agree to the oilfield deal this province already had, then Williams promised to launch a speaking tour, "a crusade" across the country, selling Newfoundland and Labrador's case to the infidels (i.e., the mainlanders).

Now, crusades are the stuff of marvellous and heroic tales.

There's the epic loss by the crusaders at the Horns of Hattin at the tail end of the fourth crusade—the beginning of the end for the Christians.

Or the heroic victory at Antioch in the first crusade, where crusader Peter Bartholomew had visions of St. Andrew and found what other crusaders believed was the Holy Lance, inspiring the warriors to defeat the infidel armies—and, as a byproduct, put every last Turk in the fortress city to death.

There were knights in armour, and prisoners who suffered great privation; there were evil ungodly enemies and pious religious figures like the hermit St. Leonard, who was, to failed crusaders, a great comfort as the patron saint of prisoners.

It is wonderful sound and fury, but in the end, at least as far as the cause of freeing the Holy Lands goes, the crusades were a failure.

On to more earthly crusades: this province has a long history of premiers setting out to right great wrongs by going across the country to state this province's case.

They've spoken out on the Upper Churchill contract and on French codfishing in 3PS, they've spoken out about our place in Confederation and on the structure of the federal union itself.

Then-premier Clyde Wells, for example, set out for points west on a crusade to explain why the Meech Lake Accord was fatally flawed. He set out not with the Holy Lance, but with plenty of extra copies of his speech—copies that the province spent extra cash on so they could be sent with him on the airplane. When Wells returned, so did the copies of the speech—extra air freight once again.

But what none of the provincial crusades has ever done is actually outline our cause persuasively enough to have other Canadians grasp the fact that we are not trying to get more than our fair share.

This may well be an argument where Premier Williams is truly right: the province's argument is clear, and it certainly looks as if Paul Martin is trying to pull a fast one on a commitment clearly given—that this province would receive 100 per cent of its offshore oil revenues.

But, unfortunately, it's not enough that the cause be true and its upholders just. The original crusaders obviously thought their crusades were right, just and necessary. That didn't mean it was a successful strategy—it was foreign lands, long supply lines, different cultures and complicated languages where plain English fell on deaf ears.

A crusade is no route to success, and it is the last and least-likely of efforts.

The Saracens don't care, Premier Williams. They just don't care.

And you will not win your battle there.

[*TELEGRAM* (ST. JOHN'S), NOVEMBER 4, 2004, A6. REPRINTED WITH PERMISSION]

We will look at further details of interpretation in Chapter 3. Here we will focus on how you can best follow and understand the content of the communication. Two useful techniques help ensure you understand fully: one is active listening, when the words are being spoken, and the other is careful reading, when the words are written down.

Comprehension and Reporting: Active Listening and Careful Reading

The next step in observing words and ideas involves a shift in the type of observation. Although you remain objective and non-judgmental, you become an active participant in constructing an interpretation of the words being communicated. You interact, in speech or writing, with the person communicating these words. You show that you have understood by reporting your observations.

Showing that you've understood is a basic courtesy to the speaker. It shows that you care enough to have listened attentively. When you can report accurately what you have heard or read, you also help other people to understand, and you help more people become involved.

Active Listening

Active listening is listening to collect a full and accurate picture of another person's thinking. Your aim is to understand the person's main points and all the key phrases and details. Like the other forms of observation discussed so far, it is objective. You do not offer your own opinions, information, or solutions.

The listening becomes "active" when you go one crucial step beyond simply hearing and remembering the words. As the listener, you use critical comprehension to deduce the person's main concerns and values. When the person raises his or her voice, or speaks faster, or sounds more emotional, these are clues to what the person feels most strongly about. You can follow up on these clues later to gain greater insight.

The final step in active listening is to report what you have heard. You organize what you remember and repeat it clearly.

The Value of Active Listening

Most of us can't easily keep track of our points while we are speaking— hearing them reflected back to us gives us a chance to consider what we said and often allows us to develop deeper insights. The more controversial or sensitive the topic, the more important it is to do active listening before you open up any discussion or debate. Active listening is very useful both to you and to the person to whom you are listening. Consider these benefits:

■ The person will feel safe enough to explore his or her own thinking in your presence. Reacting to your ideas feels like dealing with opposition, even if it is not intended that way.

■ The other person can develop his or her own thinking. Reacting to your ideas is a distraction. Trying to understand and respond to your ideas takes the person's concentration away from developing his or her own thoughts.

- You can collect complete and accurate information, so you know your eventual response will be based on a full understanding. You don't have to divert your concentration into deciding how to respond. In fact, it would be premature for you to decide what response you'd like to give, because you don't have enough information to work from.

- When you report what you heard, everyone has an equal chance to check the key points and be sure everything has been covered.

Reporting Active Listening

To show that you have listened actively, you report as much detail as needed to convey the full flavour of what was said. You want to strike a suitable balance between showing you did hear exactly what was said and showing you fully understand what it meant.

Checklist for Active Listening

✔ Give the main point and all the key details of what the speaker said. Use your own words as much as possible, but quote important points or phrases.

✔ Ask if you have got it right and if you missed anything. If you did miss or misunderstand something, the person can correct you. If you have got it right, the person will feel understood, and you will both be in a position to explore further.

✔ Point out what seemed to stand out most or to concern the other person most. This will give the other person, and you, a chance to reflect on what is really at issue here. You will be able to continue a discussion that has real insight.

EXERCISE ## Oral Report of Active Listening

Discussion: Find a partner.

1. Ask for your partner's view on a topic that he or she doesn't mind discussing with you. Have your partner explain his or her thinking. Do not interrupt.

2. Report to your partner what you remember he or she said. Can you identify the main concerns?

3. Ask if your report was correct, and rephrase it if necessary until your partner agrees that you've understood.

4. Give your partner a chance to reflect and perhaps come up with some new ideas.

Switch roles—and switch topics: this exercise should not turn into a debate. Let your partner report your thinking on the new topic. See what happens when you have heard your words repeated to you. Do you have any new insights or further thoughts?

Reading Carefully

This may not seem as interactive as active listening, where the person who is communicating is right there with you. Yet careful reading does still involve your playing an active role in turning another person's words into a form that makes sense to you, and then reflecting it back in words that can shed new light on what was said. The process is different than reading for pleasure or information.

When you read, you normally read for sense. You read to make best sense of what's being said, and in the process you usually don't stop to puzzle over unfamiliar words or to worry about ungrammatical sentences.

If you are asked to "read carefully," you need a different reading process. To see the difference between reading for sense and reading carefully, think of "reading the fine print" in a contract or an advertisement. When you check the fine print, you are not just seeing if it makes sense—it usually does. You are looking for potential problems, trying to see how the language might be interpreted in ways that are not favourable to you. Are you committing yourself to something you don't want to do? Is the deal that seemed so good so full of restrictions that you'll never actually get the special price or the free flight? Is the cellphone contract full of hidden charges? You are trying to be sure that the language contains nothing to your disadvantage. "Reading carefully" is judged by its results—will you find any problems that can occur as a result of what's said?

To do this kind of reading, you need to approach it as if you were listening to the author read aloud. As with active listening, you want to do more than just make sense of what you read. You want to be able to capture and reflect all the main points, and you want to recognize and report which particular details are used to support the points. You need this level of detail in reading carefully in order to prepare yourself to look for problems and mistakes. Knowing exactly what is said helps pin down what has not yet been mentioned. Knowing which details are included prepares you to see whether they are the kinds of details you would expect or need.

Checklist for Reading Carefully

✔ First, develop the "big picture" by reading for sense as you normally would, to get the overall sense of the piece.

a. Use any skills you have for examining headings and first sentences of paragraphs to see what to expect.

b. After you have read it, cover the text so you can't see it and try to write out the main points from memory. This is an important "digestion" step—if you cannot write down at least the main points, you have not yet understood the text.

c. Check the text again for any important points you may have missed the first time.

d. Aim to have the equivalent of at least one sentence per paragraph of the original.

(Continued)

✔ Next, observe details accurately. With the text visible beside you, go through it again looking for key details:

- names
- quotes
- numbers
- studies
- definitions
- references

✔ Finally, report in your own words what you have read. Start with the main points and see where the key details fit in to explain or support those points.

The Value of Careful Reading

■ You see both the big picture and the details. In reading for sense, you tend to remember one or the other—the main point, or some of the salient details. When you know you have to report it in organized detail, you have to pay attention to the details and to how they fit into the big picture.

■ You have an opportunity to put your own reactions on hold and see both the strengths and the weaknesses of the writing. Because careful reading and reporting slow you down and make you re-read passages, you have a much better chance of noticing which points seem really strong and which points seem questionable. This is excellent preparation for analysis.

Reporting Careful Reading

To report your careful reading, you need more than a summary or précis. You need to set out what you've read clearly and completely. It's a written version of "active listening," and it involves the same principles as reporting observations in general.

1. Identify the writer (or the principal person quoted, if the ideas are being reported by someone else) and include the details of the source— the full citation. This is essential so we know exactly whose words are being examined. It gives proper credit to the person who originated the ideas.

2. Indicate what you take the main point or conclusion to be.

3. Include all the exact details and all the points the writer made, and set them out as clearly as possible. That is, repeat everything that is relevant, and reorganize it for clarity. Just as with active listening, you want to give the writer and your reader the best chance to develop their thinking on this issue by seeing it reflected to them as clearly as possible.

EXERCISE	1.7	**Careful Reading and Written Reporting**

*Read carefully and report one of the following short articles.

Give no notice of cataclysmic asteroid, scientists told

Asteroid heading to Earth? Please, just don't ask. Forget Bruce Willis, daring space missions and Hollywood high explosives. If a real life Armageddon-style asteroid were discovered on a deadly collision course with the Earth politicians would be better off doing nothing and telling no one, scientists heard Friday.

According to Geoffrey Sommer, of the Rand Corp., an American think tank, advance warning of the end of the world would bring chaos to the streets, rioting in the shopping malls and send the economy spiraling out of control.

Rather than spread "unnecessary" panic, politicians might be wise to keep it dark, he said.

There are still no plans for civil defense in the event of the sudden discovery of a doomsday asteroid and no studies of how it could be deflected out of harm's way, he said at the American Association for the Advancement of Science meeting.

Of the 2,000 or so asteroids orbiting the sun close to the Earth, around 1,100 are thought to be at least two thirds of a mile long, big enough to pose a serious threat to mankind.

Over the last few years, the international collaboration of asteroid watching scientists, Spaceguard, has tracked 650 possible threats. So far it has found none on target to hit the Earth within the next couple of hundred years.

However, if an asteroid big enough to wipe out mankind was found to be on a collision course—and if nothing could be done—governments should keep quiet, Sommer said. "If an extinction type impact is inevitable, ignorance for the population is bliss."

[DAVID DERBYSHIRE, *DAILY TELEGRAPH* REPRINTED IN *VANCOUVER SUN*, FEBRUARY 15, 2003, A10. © TELEGRAPH GROUP LIMITED 2003. REPRINTED WITH PERMISSION OF TELEGRAPH GROUP LIMITED.]

Pacific Rim, Asian countries meet to discuss food safety

SEREMBAN, Malaysia—Bird flu, SARS and other health threats are on the agenda for officials from 40 Asian and Pacific Rim countries opening a four-day meeting on food safety today.

Government regulators, food industry officials and consumer activists attending the United Nations-backed conference will discuss ways to improve food safety and strengthen regional co-operation in investigating food-

borne diseases, the World Health Organization said.

According to WHO estimates, about one in three people worldwide suffer from food-borne diseases each year, and 1.8 million die annually from severe food- and water-caused diarrhea.

Several recent regional health emergencies, including bird flu and severe acute respiratory syndrome, have been closely linked to food.

Bird flu is transmitted by chickens, and scientists suspect that SARS was passed to humans from civet cats and other mongoose-like animals sold in live food markets in southern China.

British Columbia is suffering the effects of a bird flu outbreak in poultry farms in the Fraser Valley. The Canadian Food Inspection Agency has killed about 19 million chickens, turkeys and ducks to stem the spread of the disease.

(Continued)

Pacific Rim, Asian countries meet to discuss food safety *(Continued)*

A UN official said today countries must try to ensure food is produced, handled and distributed more safely to prevent hundreds of thousands of deaths worldwide each year from food-borne illnesses.

Recent reports of toxic maize that is believed to have killed dozens of people in Kenya and the possibility of salmonella in raw almonds exported by a U.S. company have underscored fears about how contaminated food can threaten people's health and disrupt international trade, said Hartwig de Haen of the UN Food and Agriculture Organization.

"From the farm to the final consumer, the risk of food-related outbreaks needs to be reduced," de Haen told government regulators, food industry officials and consumer activists from 42 Asian and Pacific Rim countries at the launch of the food safety conference.

De Haen, the FAO's assistant director general, noted that the U.S. Food and Drug Administration has in the past week recalled 13 million raw almonds distributed by California-based Paramount Farms Inc. because of the possibility of salmonella.

The almonds were distributed nation-wide and in Britain, France, Italy, Japan, Korea, Malaysia, Mexico, and Taiwan.

De Haen said the death toll of food-borne diseases globally was "staggering," especially in developing countries where poor governments lack funds to monitor food safety and people's choices of food sources are often limited.

Severe diarrhea kills 1.8 million people annually, de Haen said. High casualties can also surface from smaller, sporadic outbreaks such as a suspected mould contamination of maize in eastern Kenya that is believed to have killed up to 40 people so far.

The four-day conference in Seremban, 60 kilometers south of Kuala Lumpur, is aimed at planning measures for countries to create effective food safety systems.

Hockey sticks deter elk

Finally there's a safe way to keep the elk that wander into Banff from knocking down the people who live there: Raise a hockey stick over your head.

Elk wander into town to forage and get away from wolves. But when they lose their fear of humans, they can be dangerous.

No one wants to fire guns in town to kill the elk or scare them off—tactics that tourists especially don't approve of.

But now, University of Alberta biologists say lifting a hockey stick high in the air makes the elk think humans are bigger, and scares them away.

"They initially tried what they had tried some years ago—aggression and firecracker-type things. But they found that just making yourself bigger was the key," said Suzanne Bayley, a biology professor and colleague of the team that did the research. (The researchers themselves couldn't be reached.)

"The reason they used a hockey stick was that the people didn't mind. It didn't have anything to do with the elk," she said.

Prof. Colleen Cassady St. Clair and her student Elsabe Kloppers spent three years testing ways to scare the elk and keep them a safe distance from humans. Several things worked, like chasing them with border collies, but the hockey stick was the least obtrusive and silent.

Over the past decade, elk in the town have become relaxed around people. By 2001, Banff National Park staff were recording seven incidents per year where an animal had made physical contact with a human, sometimes causing broken bones or other injuries.

There was another possible threat: If elk came to town, wolves might follow.

The elk researchers suggest the same hockey stick trick might work with other wild animals that get too close to humans—maybe even bears.

Alzheimer's drug eases the daily strain

Re: Major study pans Alzheimer's drug, June 26

Can you imagine yourself going through your day wearing one of those suits for deep diving? The kind that have airhoses and cables attached to a ship somewhere on the ocean surface. Now imagine having to wear that suit 24/7 and perform your daily tasks. This is how I feel most days.

Some days are easier than others, but only because I take a drug called Aricept. A recent British study said that Aricept doesn't work. I'm here to tell you that it does. And I think if you ask anyone else in the early stages of Alzheimer's, they would agree with me.

I admit it might not work for some people: Not all medications work for all people. Just ask anyone with a life-threatening illness if the first medication prescribed was the one that allowed them to function normally.

So shame on the British researchers and double shame on B.C. Health Services Minister Colin Hansen because he would sooner believe a study involving 565 people and not take the word of thousands of people who might say something different.

Robin Kilburn, Abbotsford

[*VANCOUVER SUN*, JULY 2, 2004, A11. REPRINTED WITH PERMISSION OF ROBIN KILBURN.]

Key Points in Review

- Observation makes you slow down enough to notice what is really in front of you. The activity of observing slows and calms your mind, giving you the best chance to think clearly.

- Emotions are essential to critical thinking and should be observed as potentially relevant factors in decision-making.

- Observation is objective when the observer does not allow personal bias to determine what is observed. The objective observer reserves judgment until observations are complete.

- Observations should not be judgmental, and you should avoid drawing conclusions from your observations at this stage.

- Having a good report of your observations to rely on as you go through the rest of the critical thinking cycle will remind you of vital details and remind you to stay objective about the material.

Chapter 2

Recognizing Arguments

■ Perspective

In thinking critically about an issue or a problem, we try to react as fairly, reasonably, and helpfully as possible to the opinions and information that are presented to us. When we use reason, we typically have to express the reasoning in words. To share reasoning with others, we must be able to understand how words work to convey reasoning. In this chapter you will see how to develop the critical observation of words from Chapter 1 into critical comprehension of arguments—understanding the words well enough to recognize the purpose of the communication, and seeing how the sentences are put together to convey reasoning.

■ Scenario

You have enrolled in a philosophy course because it was the only elective that would fit your timetable. On the very first day, the professor assigns you a short writing assignment: "What does it mean to be good?" The professor says, "Don't worry about trying to read the textbook before you try this assignment. I just want you to give your own argument, in a page or two." You're not even sure what an argument means in this context. How will you deal with the assignment?

■ Key Question

What is the goal of this communication?

Reasoning and Verbal Expression

The principal use of reasoning is to determine what to believe and how to act. Should I quit that job? Should I call the doctor? Should I support the legalization of marijuana? Whenever we want to understand the decisions of other people, or when we need to justify or come to our own decisions, we give, and get, reasons. The verbal defence of a point of view or justification of an action requires argument.

Arguments and Reasoning

A **claim** is a thought expressed as a declarative sentence. For example, "The rate of childhood obesity in Canada is increasing" or "I am concerned about global warming" are claims. In contrast, "Give your children more exercise" or "Why don't we do something about global warming?" are not claims because they are not declarative sentences. An **argument** is the attempt to defend a claim by offering one or more other claims as support for it.

The function of an argument is to establish—or prove—the acceptability of its conclusion. In other words, arguments are supposed to prove that a certain claim is accurate. The short argument below is designed to prove its conclusion—"You are unhealthy"—by offering two additional claims that show why we might believe you are unhealthy. To construct an argument, we need to be able to find information that we can offer as supporting premises for the belief we wish to defend.

Given our definition of argument, all arguments are verbally expressed. For example, sticking your tongue out at someone could not be considered a claim in an argument and neither can a picture of a starving child.

An argument is composed of a conclusion and at least one premise. The **conclusion** is the claim defended in the argument. The **premises** are the claims that are offered as reasons supporting the conclusion.

For example: "You get less than thirty minutes of exercise each day. All people who get less than thirty minutes of exercise each day are unhealthy. Therefore you are unhealthy."

Conclusion: You are unhealthy.

Premise 1: All people who get less than thirty minutes of exercise each day are unhealthy.

Premise 2: You are a person who gets less than thirty minutes of exercise each day.

Reasons in General

A good argument for an action or belief will make it reasonable to hold that belief or act in that way. But not all reasoning involves argument, and there can be good reasons to believe or do something that we would not call the premises of an argument.

For example: Your seeing a child drowning in a pool coupled with your ability to swim give you good reasons to jump into the pool to save the child.

DEFINITION

An **argument** is the attempt to defend a claim by offering one or more other claims as support for it. (Notice that our definition does not require that an argument be a successful attempt at defending a claim. A bad argument is still an argument.)

DEFINITION

A **reason** is anything that motivates, explains, causes, or acts as a rationale.

This is a case where your view of the child and your swimming ability are not premises, but are reasons. A **reason** is anything that motivates, explains, causes, or acts as a rationale. Premises are reasons, but not all reasons are premises. Premises are, by definition, claims that support a conclusion. Reasons, on the other hand, do not have to be claims. "Reason" is a very broad term that covers *anything* that motivates, explains, causes, or acts as a rationale. Images, music, and feelings can count as reasons, but not as premises. When we try to decide whether an act or belief is reasonable, we can take into account not only any arguments that the person believing or acting considered, but also the motivating reasons that are not in the form of an argument. We distinguish not only between good arguments and bad arguments, but also between good reasons and bad reasons in general. Your reasons for jumping into the pool to save the child in the example above would normally be considered good reasons, making your action reasonable. (In Chapter 9 you will find ways in which we can distinguish between good and bad reasons when those reasons are numerical, visual images, sounds, or emotions.)

You could maintain that what makes seeing the child and knowing your swimming ability reasons is the fact that we could take the situation and express the reasons alternatively as premises.

For example: You see the child is drowning. You can swim. All people who can swim and see a child drowning should try to save that child. Therefore, you should try to save that child.

In this book, we are going to leave open the question of whether all reasoning could be expressed in terms of premises and conclusions. If we have to express our reasoning to someone else, we would certainly try to put the reasons in the form of an argument or explanation. However, it is enough for our present purposes to note that by "reason" we mean not just premises but an entire range of different things that may play a role in making one's belief or action reasonable or unreasonable.

Our focus in this chapter is not on reasons in general, but on identifying and reporting arguments. The ability to identify and understand arguments is tremendously valuable given the vast number of different contexts in which arguments occur.

Facts and Opinions

When people first encounter a task such as "Present your own argument about the meaning of the word 'good,'" they'll often think they are supposed to present only opinions because the word "argument" can imply differing opinions. For example, they might think all that is needed for an argument is to say, "In my opinion, being good means being responsible, careful, loving, and honest." Once people hear the definition of "argument" presented above, they'll often switch to thinking of arguments as presenting only facts because the words "proof" or "support" imply factual evidence. For example, they might think all that is needed for an argument is to say, "Being good is defined in the dictionary as 'well-behaved.'" As it turns out, the distinction between fact and opinion is not of much use in the identification of arguments because arguments can be composed of all facts, all opinions, or a combination of both. Arguments are composed of claims, and both opinions and facts can be claims. So you cannot rely on a fact/opinion distinction to determine whether you are being given an argument.

Facts inform us about the world—we tend to use the word "fact" to imply truth, or what is claimed to be true. Opinions inform us about a person's individual perspective or preferences. For example, it is a fact that the tsunami that swept the Indian Ocean on December 26, 2004, caused destruction and loss of life. Everyone who knows that the tsunami swept away fishing villages in eleven countries from Indonesia to Madagascar and who remembers that at least 160,000 native and foreign people were known dead and more were missing can agree on that. In contrast, an "opinion" is typically thought of as a personal impression or a subjective judgment—many people can have completely different opinions based on exactly the same information. For example, it is an opinion that the tsunami on December 26, 2004, was the greatest tragedy in recent history. Opinions differ about what is the greatest tragedy in recent history. By themselves, the statements expressing opinions are simply opinions and not arguments. But now suppose that the person who believes the tsunami was the greatest tragedy offers a justification for that opinion, as follows. At least 160,000 people died, towns and villages in eleven countries were destroyed—all facts. Furthermore, the loss of life and livelihood is going to make it extremely difficult for survivors to carry on, it will take years to rebuild their economy, and the world community is going to be as inconsistent and unlikely to follow through properly on its offers of aid as it has been for past earthquakes and natural disasters—all opinions. This combination of fact and opinion creates an argument.

Arguments are needed when a claim is not so obvious that everyone agrees with it. It is not obvious that the tsunami on December 26, 2004, was the greatest disaster in recent history. We will want to hear the premises that could justify this conclusion. We are also likely to find that there are arguments offered to support competing conclusions. For example, another person may accept all the facts of the destruction caused by the tsunami, but may still consider the deaths in the World Trade Center on September 11, 2001, a greater tragedy. This person may support this opinion with an argument that human-caused deaths are more tragic than deaths caused by impersonal natural forces. Because the World Trade Center deaths were caused by terrorists deliberately flying passenger planes into office buildings, these deaths are more tragic than deaths caused by an ocean wave. Yet another person may agree that human-caused deaths are more tragic, but consider the genocide in Rwanda far worse than the World Trade Center because there were more deaths and because the rest of the world was so reluctant to sympathize or help. This too is an argument, relying on yet another set of facts.

Arguments can have opinions as their premises to support other opinions. A person might argue that the genocide in Rwanda was the worst disaster in recent history, therefore more action should be taken by other nations to ensure that similar incidents cannot happen in the future.

Arguments, then, are not just a set of facts or just a series of opinions. They can be composed of a combination of both, and they have characteristics of both. Like facts, arguments can be tested and challenged, using evidence from various sources to confirm the truth of the statements. Like opinions, arguments can be disagreed with and can lead to further debate and to changes in opinion.

Our definition of argument captures what most uses of the word "argument" have in common—expressing reasons to support or defend a claim. As we discussed in the Introduction, this definition differs from the common use of the word "argument" to mean only a heated debate, quarrel, or passionate piece of writing or speech. A wide variety of reasoning processes involve some form of argument. Remember that an argument does not have to occur between two or more people, and it certainly doesn't have to become heated. You can present yourself with an argument when trying to decide what to believe or how to act. For example, you can present an argument to yourself to decide if it is reasonable to believe in ghosts, or if you should risk taking a shortcut through that dark alley.

Contexts and Uses of Arguments

When we use the word "argument," we will mean a collection of claims that work together as premises and a conclusion. We will use the words "arguing" or "**argumentation**" to cover all the different social practices that involve the presentation of arguments. For example, a lawyer who presents a case in court is arguing, because she is delivering arguments meant to show that the accused is innocent or guilty. A psychology professor who publishes a paper showing that readers do not easily detect contradictions in what they read is arguing, with the goal of contributing to our understanding of how people read and think. Union and management negotiators at the bargaining table are arguing in an attempt to get their demands met.

People will present arguments in different contexts with different goals. In some contexts, the goal will be to win a debate or get someone to back down from their position. But there does not have to be a "winner" of an argument. Although "arguing" means more than just fighting, you can argue during a quarrel as well as argue in an essay.

Arguments can be used to justify or explain, by showing how a claim could be understood and supported. For example, you might offer an argument to explain why it was reasonable for you to leave work early. Arguments can be used to evaluate and critique. For example, your supervisor may offer an argument to show why your reasons for leaving work early are not as good as you thought they were. Arguments can be used to explore ideas in more depth, working forward to see where an idea leads, or working backward to understand how the idea made sense. For example, the scenario at the beginning of the chapter invites you to explore a topic you may never have considered in detail: what does it mean to "be good"? Arguments can be used in a search for common ground, as people test each other's claims to see what they can all agree to. For example, parents might use arguments to decide which parenting techniques they will use with their children. Arguments can be used to inform; for example, an environmentalist may give an argument to show exactly why pollution from cruise ships should concern us all. And arguments can be used to persuade; for example, the environmentalist may use an argument to persuade you to sign a petition for better anti-pollution legislation.

Given our definition, arguing does not have to be, but can be, part of a continuing cycle of critical thinking, moving forward as new evidence becomes available or as people reflect on what they have heard. For example, what does it mean to be a person? There was a time when Canadians would have accepted that women were not persons, because under the law women were defined as being subordinate to their fathers, legal guardians, or husbands. As a result, women were denied the vote, and even when voting privileges were extended to women in 1916, a distinction was drawn between white women and others. Women of Asian or First Nations descent were denied the vote until after 1945. In the famous "Persons Case" of 1929, the government had argued that women could not serve in the Senate because only "persons" could serve in the Senate and in that context "persons" clearly meant "men." Nellie McClung and others challenged this conclusion, and the Supreme Court accepted their argument. The definition of a person has evolved through argument.

Recognizing Non-arguments in Speech and Writing

During the observation stage, it is just as important to note when an argument has not been presented as it is to note when an argument has been presented. "Non-argument" is a term that describes any form of communication that does not provide premises supporting a conclusion. Non-arguments include narratives, instructions, propaganda, data offered "for your information," and many other forms of communication. Sometimes we can easily distinguish arguments from non-arguments. However, in many cases, we need a careful examination of the context and the communication itself to be sure whether we are being presented with an argument or a non-argument, because either the context or the form of the communication allows for non-arguments as well as arguments.

An example where the form of the communication might present a problem is a narrative. Suppose I tell you a vivid story of what happened to me the last time I went outside when it was forty below zero. Am I expecting you to admire my fortitude—a non-argument—or am I using my story as evidence that I am tougher than you are—an argument? A narrative can be offered purely as entertainment, or it can have a "moral" or be used to make a point—that is, it can be offered as support, as you'll see when we discuss anecdotal evidence in Chapter 7 (page 221).

As we noted earlier, arguments can be used for different purposes including information and persuasion. Arguments are not the only types of communication used to inform or persuade. Two common settings in which non-arguments are mistaken for arguments are contexts in which someone offers a neutral presentation of information and contexts in which someone attempts persuasion without relying on reasons.

Non-arguments That Are Neutral Presentations of Information

You will frequently find newspaper articles and websites that offer a **neutral presentation of information**. The author's goal is neither to convince you to believe one side of an issue nor to prove that a conclusion is true; the goal is to inform the reader in an objective, nonpartisan fashion. When the goal is to inform or describe only, you often cannot tell what the writer's personal opinion is about the information. The author is not presenting an argument. Even if the writer or speaker is offering a personal opinion, he or she is not necessarily presenting an argument. The goal of stating your opinion can simply be to tell people what you believe and not to persuade them that you are right.

You will also find neutral reports of arguments in speeches or pieces of writing where the goal is simply to present information. The writer of the article is merely informing, but the information includes reports of what people said when their goal was to establish a conclusion. If there is enough quoted from what a particular person said, it may be worth examining that piece of the article by itself in order to evaluate the argument that is reported.

For example, look back at item 2 in Exercise 1.7: "Pacific Rim, Asian countries meet to discuss food safety." The first six paragraphs are communicating information:

Bird flu, SARS and other health threats are on the agenda for officials from 40 Asian and Pacific Rim countries opening a four-day meeting on food safety today.

Government regulators, food industry officials and consumer activists attending the United Nations-backed conference will discuss ways to improve food safety and strengthen regional co-operation in investigating food-borne diseases, the World Health Organization said.

According to WHO estimates, about one in three people worldwide suffer from food-borne diseases each year, and 1.8 million die annually from severe food- and water-caused diarrhea.

Several recent regional health emergencies, including bird flu and severe acute respiratory syndrome, have been closely linked to food.

Bird flu is transmitted by chickens, and scientists suspect that SARS was passed to humans from civet cats and other mongoose-like animals sold in live food markets in southern China.

British Columbia is suffering the effects of a bird flu outbreak in poultry farms in the Fraser Valley. The Canadian Food Inspection Agency has killed about 19 million chickens, turkeys and ducks to stem the spread of the disease.

In fact, the overall goal of this article is only to convey information. However, the next paragraph introduces what appears to be an attempt by one of the people interviewed to prove to us that there is a concern here: a UN official is reported as wanting countries to take action to improve food safety:

A UN official said today countries must try to ensure food is produced, handled and distributed more safely to prevent hundreds of thousands of deaths worldwide each year from food-borne illnesses.

As the article continues, we hear more of this one person's view, and we hear how he supports his belief that food safety must be improved. We are not just given his personal opinion—we are given the reasoning he uses to show that his belief is justified.

"From the farm to the final consumer, the risk of food-related outbreaks needs to be reduced," de Haen told government regulators, food industry officials and consumer activists from 42 Asian and Pacific Rim countries at the launch of the food safety conference.

De Haen, the FAO's assistant director general, noted that the U.S. Food and Drug Administration has in the past week recalled 13 million raw almonds distributed by California-based Paramount Farms Inc. because of the possibility of salmonella.

The almonds were distributed nation-wide and in Britain, France, Italy, Japan, Korea, Malaysia, Mexico, and Taiwan.

De Haen said the death toll of food-borne diseases globally was "staggering," especially in developing countries where poor governments lack funds to monitor food safety and people's choices of food sources are often limited.

Severe diarrhea kills 1.8 million people annually, de Haen said. High casualties can also surface from smaller, sporadic outbreaks such as a suspected mould contamination of maize in eastern Kenya that is believed to have killed up to 40 people so far.

These five paragraphs, together with the paragraph before that introduced his concern, are a report of how the UN official, de Haen, attempts to argue in support of the claim that food is not safe enough worldwide and we should do something to make it safer. He has offered an argument.

In the final paragraph, we return to pure information:

The four-day conference in Seremban, 60 kilometers south of Kuala Lumpur, is aimed at planning measures for countries to create effective food safety systems.

This final paragraph confirms that the overall purpose of the article was to convey information.

Taken as a whole, then, this article is a neutral report of information. However, as part of the information, the article includes a report of one person's argument. If we are interested simply in information, we treat the article as a whole as a neutral presentation of information. If we are interested in the argument, we lift out just the six-paragraph piece reporting de Haen's view for examination.

Non-arguments That Are Attempts at Persuasion

You'll find that arguments are often presented to you in an attempt to persuade you to believe or do something. Arguments are a common form of communication in which the purpose is to persuade an audience. However, you should be alert for other forms of persuasion that are not arguments.

There are many ways people try to convince others to believe what they say. Think about the various methods of persuasion used by politicians during political speeches. Politicians will choose their words carefully. They will also dress differently for different audiences. They will carefully position themselves for the camera so that the right image is in the background. They will stand behind a podium on some occasions and walk toward the audience on others. They will take measures to ensure that they are seen with people who will lend them credibility or at least interest. All these strategies are attempts to persuade—to influence and impress, in order to draw people toward a particular position or point of view, without presenting an argument.

When a piece of writing has the goal of persuading you to accept a particular viewpoint, you should be able to see a clear overall direction to the piece, and you should be able to tell what the writer's own opinion is by the end of the article.

There are two types of persuasion, and as we move forward in understanding and investigating reasoning, it will be important to be able to distinguish the two. They are argumentative persuasion and non-argumentative persuasion.

- **Argumentative persuasion** seeks to persuade by offering arguments. These arguments can be evaluated and assessed based on their merits.

- **Non-argumentative persuasion** seeks to persuade without presenting an argument. It might sidestep argument by appealing only to your emotions, by using powerful language or images, or by appealing to your prejudices. It attempts to persuade you to accept a claim without presenting any claims to support it. Pieces of writing aimed at persuading you to believe a claim can be beautifully written and have great literary merit, but still be non-argumentative because there are no premises offered as support for that claim.

Types of non-argumentative persuasion in speech and writing include describing something in slanted language in an attempt to foster a certain attitude toward that thing. For example:

> Should the demonic, card-manufacturing sadists who thought up Valentine's Day be lined up and shot? Apparently, more and more people every year are ready to sign up to be on that firing squad.

In this example, it is clear that the author wants you to have a negative attitude toward Valentine's Day, but no argument has been presented to support the idea that Valentine's Day is a bad thing. Instead, the word choice communicates the idea, and in some instances word choice alone can be very persuasive.

In some situations, non-argumentative persuasion might provide you with good reasons to act or believe in the way that is being promoted. For example, if someone holds a gun to your head and points toward the locked safe, you'll probably have good reason to be persuaded to open the safe. It is not the threat that is a good reason—holding a gun to someone's head is unreasonable coercion. However, your concern for your own safety is a good reason to open the safe instead of arguing with the person holding the gun. We'll also see in Chapter 9 that persuasion that relies on appealing to a reader or listener's emotion can be non-argumentative and yet provide good reasons for a belief or action. However, non-argumentative persuasion is also used as a way to stop you from thinking about what is reasonable and unreasonable and can lead you to form a belief or act in a way that is ill-considered and foolish.

Writing style can be used as non-argumentative persuasion. Be careful to separate the persuasive effect of a well-written piece from the reasoned persuasion of an argument within that piece. An argument can be well written or poorly written. It can be poorly organized and have an unappealing style, but as long as it contains premises that are offered to support a conclusion, it is considered an argument. Bear in mind that an argument can be disorganized, poorly written, and unstylish yet still be an excellent argument.

EXERCISE **Argumentative vs. Non-argumentative Persuasion**

Written Assignment

1. Write a play in which two characters have opposing views on an issue. Have each character try to persuade a third character over to his or her side of the issue. One person uses only non-argumentative persuasion. Another uses only arguments to persuade. Try to construct a situation in which it is likely that the character who uses only non-argumentative persuasion will win the debate.

2. Write one paragraph in which you use an argument to persuade your reader to take one side of the issue on whether gun control is necessary in Canada. Write a second paragraph in which you use no argument, but still try to persuade your reader to take one side of the gun-control issue.

Recognizing Arguments

You've already seen that the function of an argument is to establish the acceptability of a claim. This section shows you how to pick a written argument out from the context in which it is found. You can recognize the structure of an argument by identifying its components. The work of understanding an argument ensures that you can explain the details of the reasoning and see how it is intended to work. Taking the time to show that you understand also demonstrates respect for the arguer.

The first step in picking out the details of an argument is to be sure that you have correctly identified the conclusion.

Picking Out Conclusions

DEFINITION

A **conclusion** is a claim supported by other claims.

As we have already noted, the conclusion is the statement that is being supported by other statements. If there is an argument in what you hear or read, you should be able to discern a focus or destination to the argument. For example, what point is the arguer trying to prove? What are the premises leading us toward? Is there a viewpoint this arguer strongly opposes? The conclusion may be an opinion, an explanation, or a proposed course of action—anything that the arguer tries to establish. Someone might argue for the conclusion that "Canada's the best country to live in"—which is an opinion. A person might conclude, "It's time I started getting in shape by walking an hour a day"—a proposed course of action.

The conclusion may represent the arguer's own position on an issue being discussed, it may be a rejection of an opposing position the arguer strongly disagrees with, or it may be a position that the arguer just wants to explore in order to see how it makes sense. For example, an arguer may ask, "How could somebody believe that it is fair to sit and have a cool drink while a friend is carrying heavy boxes upstairs?" and then proceed to figure out reasons that will support the conclusion that it is fair. The arguer personally thinks it isn't fair, but is willing to see how the other person could come to the opposite conclusion.

Identifying the conclusion is similar to identifying the main point of a passage. It may not be explicitly stated, so you may have to figure it out from what is said—but if it is, it is often at the beginning or the end. If the conclusion is not clearly stated, you should report the conclusion in a way that is neither too broad nor too narrow to capture the ideas expressed in the argument. For example, the conclusion of de Haen's argument in "Pacific Rim, Asian countries meet to discuss food safety" is neither "we must reduce salmonella outbreaks" (too narrow) nor "we must increase safety in general" (too broad). The conclusion is "countries must try to ensure food is produced, handled, and distributed safely."

If you are having trouble identifying conclusions you can look for **conclusion indicator words.** These words signal that the speaker or writer believes a point has been proven. Conclusion indicator words include

- therefore
- so
- hence
- thus

and phrases such as

- which establishes that
- I conclude that

Not every conclusion is signalled by a conclusion indicator word, so it can be helpful to add a conclusion indicator word yourself as a way of testing whether the conclusion you've identified is correct.

In conversation, you have the advantage that the arguers are there in person: you can hear disagreement, and you can ask questions to help ensure that you are correctly identifying the different positions people are taking and what their conclusions are. Sometimes, in conversation, you will hear a position but not hear any reason for it. You may be able to draw out the argument by asking the person, "Can you explain?" (This question is preferable to a direct "Why?" which can be too challenging.)

To identify conclusions in conversation,

- listen carefully to opening statements: many people start with their position or recommendation
- think about what the speaker is trying to convince you to believe
- check any questions asked with obvious emphasis: would the intended answer to the question be a conclusion?

- take advantage of asking directly: if the person stops speaking without seeming to indicate a conclusion, ask what he or she concludes
- listen for conclusion indicator words

To identify conclusions in written material

- think about what the speaker is trying to convince you to believe
- look for conclusion indicator words
- locate quotes: brief quotes may report conclusions
- check the headline or heading: would a full-sentence version of it work?
- check any questions asked with obvious emphasis: would the intended answer to the question be a conclusion?

If you cannot see any overall emphasis or trend in the article, check whether you have a combination type of article—a debate, which presents two or more different arguments without favouring one side over the other. If you can see at least two different arguments, you can treat each conclusion that you find as part of a separate argument. In a conversation, it's best to assume that each speaker offers a different argument, even if the conclusions are similar.

Picking Out Premises

A premise is one of the claims provided as support in an argument to justify a claim, an explanation, or a position. All the premises, taken together, are meant to establish that a claim is correct.

Premises can be facts, opinions, or conclusions from earlier arguments—whatever helps the claim or explanation or position make good sense.

For example, "Why do you want this job?" the interviewer asks. You do want the job: the claim you want to support is that you are the best choice for the job. You'd like to be able to say, "I'm the best candidate" and have the interviewer agree. But the interviewer doesn't find that claim nearly as obvious as you do, and that's why the interviewer asks why you want the job: what reasons do you have for thinking you would be good at this job? How can you back up the claim that you are the best candidate? You try to make it more obvious you are the best choice. Each bit of backup support that you give is a premise for your argument: "Because I've trained for it." "Because it will use my best skills." "Because it's a people job, and I'm a people person." "Because you need a person who can do customer support and web page design, and I have experience in both." "Because . . ."

If it helps to show why, it's a premise. Notice that in the example above, "Because I've trained for it" is a fact, while "Because it will use my best skills" is an opinion, yet they are both premises. Both of them help show why you would be a good choice for the job. "Just because" is not a premise: it adds no information that helps us to see why your position makes good sense. (Remember how frustrated you felt as a child when your parent said, "Because I said so"?)

Questions are not premises, though they may clearly hint at or disguise them. Some questions can be considered indirect premises or conclusions. For example, a rhetorical question can be interpreted as a statement that may be a premise, and some questions are so clearly meant to express a belief that it can be acceptable to interpret them as claims. However, in general, "Why not?" or "What if . . . ?" are not reasons: they offer puzzlement, not information. You've said that you'd like to see tougher penalties for young offenders. When I ask you why, you reply, "What if they just let kids off with a slap on the wrist?" You have not given me a reason yet, because I might not answer the question the same way that you do. Perhaps I'm uninformed and have no idea what will happen if they do. Perhaps I disagree with you and think that harsh punishment hurts more than it helps, so we'd do better if the kids get off lightly. Your question only opens the way to disagreement; it does not direct me toward your position. But the answer that you'd give to your own question might very well be a reason. When you say, "Kids don't learn from a slap on the wrist; it takes a serious punishment for them to change their attitude," you've given me a reason. I may still not agree, but I can see more clearly why you take the position that you do. And that is the purpose of reasons: they are intended to help show why a statement, position, or conclusion is believable and worth accepting.

Just as there are conclusion indicator words, there are **premise indicator words** that signal a reason is about to be stated. Premise indicator words and phrases include

- because
- since
- for
- given that
- for the reason that

Some languages, such as French, are careful to include all the linking words that reveal connections between ideas. In English, however, it is becoming less common to use indicator words, so you might see instead an indirect signal of premises—a list of "ands." For example, "She's been on city council for five years and she's always been active in the community and she clearly has people's best interests at heart." This could be a set of premises to support the conclusion "We should support her as a candidate for Parliament for this riding."

Another signal is a numbered or bulleted list of points, or the equivalent in words: "First, second, third," and so on. For example, "It makes sense to adopt an animal from a rescue shelter. First, you'll give the animal a better home with you. Second, you'll be helping to reduce the number of strays and unwanted pets. Third, you won't be paying the high costs of a pedigreed animal."

To identify premises, look for all information offered as reasons in defence of the conclusion:

- premise indicator words
- multiple "ands" linking facts or opinions
- bullet points, which may be marshalling evidence
- numerical sequence words: first, second, third

For disputes accessible through the news media, you will need to be able to pick arguments out of the background of information and entertainment. Generally, in newspapers, the letters, the editorials, and most columns by regular columnists are arguments. In magazines, the editorial, some articles, and some letters may be arguments. Other sources may contain only fragments of arguments and only part of the information about who gave an argument and in what context. Arguments also turn up in advertising, when an advertiser gives you reasons for the product or service being a good choice. Internet sources vary considerably and include non-argumentative persuasion as well as arguments and information. Academic sources such as journals tend to be mostly arguments, even when expressed in very neutral terms.

EXERCISE 2.2

Identifying Arguments and Non-arguments

For each of the following passages, decide whether the passage contains a neutral report of information, an argument, or non-argumentative persuasion. Defend your answer.

*1. They said it would happen, and it has. Researchers in South Korea have taken a donated human egg, squeezed the DNA out of its nucleus, replaced it with a cell from the ovaries of the egg's donor, and induced the egg to develop into an early-stage embryo that was, as a result, a genetic clone of its donor. They then destroyed the embryo in order to harvest its stem cells—the building blocks of life, with the potential to become blood, nerves, bone or any other part of the body.

[*GLOBE AND MAIL*, FEBRUARY 14, 2004, A24]

*2. Re: Seven parks go to dogs all day
Extending off-leash hours at city parks is not the solution to the growing dog problem in Vancouver. The solution is to make dog owners earn that privilege by demonstrating they can use parks responsibly. That has not happened to date.

[JACQUI UNDERWOOD, "IRRESPONSIBLE DOG OWNERS OVER-RUN PARK,"
VANCOUVER SUN, FEBRUARY 14, 2004, C7]

*3. Is obesity really about individual "choice"? Not really. First, obesity often begins in childhood, and children's "choices" are highly constrained by their family structure and income level. For example, children from single-parent families are more likely to be obese. As well, children are systematically targeted by sophisticated advertising for unhealthy foods and sedentary activities (movies, video-games). Second, obesity is an issue of poverty. Research shows that poor children and adults are more likely to be obese—not primarily because they are poorly educated, but because purchasing and preparing healthy food and accessing recreational opportunities costs more (both in terms of time and money). Moreover, poor people are more likely to experience stress—a third key aspect of obesity.

[MICHAEL POLANYI, "POVERTY BEGINS IN CHILDHOOD," *LEADER-POST*, FEBRUARY 13, 2004, B8. REPRINTED WITH PERMISSION OF MICHAEL POLANYI.]

4. Ottawa—I just don't buy Michael Polanyi's argument (letter—Feb. 13) that poverty is a cause of obesity because poor people can't afford healthy food. After graduating, when I was at my poorest, my diet was based on rice, beans, broccoli, sweet potatoes, canned tomatoes and oatmeal. All healthy, all dirt cheap. I was putting together a week's worth of meals for under $15 and I was in the best shape of my life. The other secret to my svelte form was not buying a car; this remains the best fitness and financial plan I've ever committed to. Rich or poor, people get fat for the same reasons—bad food choices and not enough exercise.

[ADAM SCOTT, LETTER TO THE EDITOR, *LEADER-POST*, FEBRUARY 14, 2004, A24]

5. The fact that NHL general managers want to change the rules, stating that goalies cannot play the puck behind the net, is ridiculous. It creates less of a scoring chance for the opposing team, and Canucks' goalie Johan Hedberg is right by saying the proposed rules are "stupid." Currently, the goalie is more involved in the game. Changing this would drastically change the game. Please don't change it.

[CANDICE RIDYARD, LETTER TO THE EDITOR, *VANCOUVER PROVINCE*, FEBRUARY 15, 2004]

6. Responses to a **macleans.ca** question: Should trans fats be banned?
   a. Trans fats should be banned, but the ban should be phased-in to allow the businesses and the taste buds of the consumers time to adjust. Having said that, I will miss my hamburger and fries, let alone the cookies and pies! Well, the sacrifice is well worth it, if it makes my quality of life better.
      Ravi Sharma, Calgary, Alberta. Reprinted with permission.
   b. I've seen raw trans fats. It's the most disgusting thing I've ever seen. It hardens in a matter of minutes . . . maybe even seconds. Banning trans fats would help Canadians overcome their weight and heart problems and there sure would be fewer people visiting the hospitals.
      Randy Gibson, Sudbury, Ontario
   c. Anything we can do to stop kids from eating foods high in trans fats and sugar should be done. Kids eat what we provide to them and bad eating habits start at school cafeterias, fast food restaurants and "convenience meals" served at home. Stopping trans fats may be the cheapest prevention of medical problems in the future.
      Darek Kluza, Vancouver, British Columbia
   d. Ban? No! What would "ban" mean? Every trace, down to parts per million levels? That would be virtually impossible to do. And what

would you ban next, chocolate? Education plus labelling is *all* that is needed. Then it's a matter of personal choice. I don't want anyone trying to legislate my diet.

David Newman, Sarnia, Ontario. Reprinted with permission.

e. Ban trans fats from processed foods? Sure . . . and while we're at it, why don't we make a list and ban everything else out there proven not to be healthy for consumption. Of course, that list seems to change depending on the day!

Pam McInnes, Ariss, Ontario

f. I don't believe that Canada should ban trans fats from foods, as it would be a logistical nightmare and probably cost a fortune. However, the Canadian government should require all foods to list the amount of trans fats in a serving of food effective immediately. Those of us who are inclined to read the labels will make our consumer decisions based on these values.

Megan Chemesky, Calgary, Alberta

g. Listing trans fats on the labels assumes that the labels will be read, can be read, are understood or are being read by someone who cares. My teens will not read a label; my elderly father cannot understand the labels; my spouse needs his reading glasses to see the labels. Further, if there is a cookie to be had, trans fats or not, my spouse and teen children will consume it. If the dangers posed by trans fats are as alarming as being reported, then this threat must be met with an adequate response. Remove the fat and you decrease health risks for all persons regardless of their capacity to understand the risks.

E. Groves, Sudbury, Ontario. Reprinted with permission.

[WWW.MACLEANS.CA/SWITCHBOARD/ARTICLE.JSP?CONTENT=20040212_170535_1628]

7. Look back at Chapter 1, Exercise 1.7, Examples 1, "Give no notice of cataclysmic asteroid, scientists told" and 3, "Hockey sticks deter elk." Are they arguments or non-arguments? Explain your decision on each one.

Creating Arguments

We've looked at how you can recognize an argument generated by someone else. Now let's look at the creation of arguments: how you can construct your own premises to support a conclusion. For example, consider the scenario at the beginning of the chapter. How might you generate an argument on the topic "What does it mean to be good?" Often, an assignment like this is challenging because people don't even know where to begin.

As we've suggested in Chapter 1, the best first move is to start where you are. What do you already know, and what can you already do? You probably could list a number of things you'd count as good, and you know how to use a dictionary to find meanings of words. You can start there and work toward finding a statement that you could put forward as a conclusion.

Suppose you look up "good" in the dictionary, and it says, "*adj.* having suitable or desirable qualities; promoting health, welfare or happiness; virtuous; pious; kind; benevolent; well-behaved; not troublesome; of repute; doughty; able; worthy; commendable; suitable; adequate; thorough; competent; sufficient; valid; sound; serviceable; beneficial; genuine; pleasing; favourable; of a shot or play in tennis, golf, etc. made accurately" (*Chambers Dictionary,* 720–21). This dictionary then continues for more than a page, defining "good" as a noun, and continuing to list and explain a wide variety of expressions using the word "good," such as "good morning," "goodwife," and "good grief." You could use that in your essay and probably meet the length requirements for the paper, but quoting the dictionary simply states a fact: that is how the word is defined.

You know now that any fact, by itself, is not an argument. The fact must be one in a set of claims that has at least one premise and a conclusion. The professor who asks for an argument is asking you to create an argument of exactly the type we have defined. For an argument, we need the ideas to connect together so that they will lead toward a destination—a conclusion.

To create an argument, we might already have a conclusion in mind, or we might discover a possible conclusion simply by examining ideas to see what they suggest. What kind of statement might be a conclusion for an argument for the assignment topic, "What does it mean to be good?" When a question like this is asked as a test of your comprehension, it asks you to remember and repeat a definition you have already been given. When the question is asked as an open question, it asks you to explore on your own, to create a possible definition, and see how it might be defended.

When you do not already know what you want to argue, you might try some mind-mapping to help you. At this stage, you are seeking insights—you need to gather information and ideas that are relevant to your topic. Mind-mapping is a technique used to generate ideas and see how they fit together. So for this topic you might start with the word "good" in a circle at the centre of a blank page and generate as many ideas as you can that somehow connect with "good" (see Figure 2.1). For example, you might think, "Good, better, best." That will go on your diagram in one cluster. Then you might imagine a parent saying to a child, "Be good!" Then you might think of a good person, someone you know, or someone who is often mentioned as an example—Terry Fox, perhaps, or Mother Teresa. Thinking about people might make you think of good athletes—Olympic skiers, NHL hockey players, friends you know on a soccer team. Each of these ideas seems like a different type of example, a different line of thought, and as your mind-map builds, it will branch in different directions to show these different lines.

Notice that what we have here is a spray of ideas branching off in many directions from the central point. This is not an argument—it's still just a collection of ideas. The mind-map is a diagram showing where the ideas seem to connect to each other and where they don't.

To go from a collection of ideas or information to an argument requires you to choose something important that stands out for you and formulate it as

FIGURE 2.1

Example of a Mind-Map

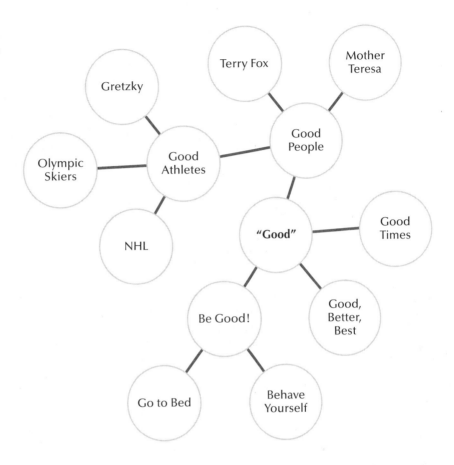

a conclusion. For example, you might have an insight based on the dictionary definition you read—you see that many of the definitions seem to convey a sense of approval, of human judgment. Perhaps you hadn't thought of it quite that way before, but now you wonder if "being good" is really nothing more than being "something people like." You can put this as a thesis statement: "To be good means to be approved of." That's a conclusion you could support by showing how each component of the definition fits with the idea of approval.

Now, you need to organize the remaining ideas as premises to show how they lead toward the conclusion.

Perhaps your own examples, such as those in the mind-map, will suggest the idea that "when we call something 'good,' we mean it has qualities we should admire, or copy, or value." This again is a thesis statement: a conclusion you can support by organizing the ideas from the mind-map into premises that will support this statement. Here is a very short written argument that might be generated from just the examples mentioned in the mind-mapping example.

When we call something "good," we mean it has qualities we should admire, or copy, or value. For example, there are good people such as Terry Fox, or Mother Teresa. We call these people "good" because we admire what they did for others. Terry Fox raised money for cancer research by running partway across Canada after he had lost one of his own legs to cancer. Mother Teresa helped the homeless in Calcutta. We also call people "good" for their skill as athletes—for example, Olympic skiers and NHL hockey players are good athletes. Their skills are the skills that weekend skiers and recreational hockey players admire and would like to be able to copy. We say "Good work!" to someone who has produced something we admire or value, such as a great tennis shot or a beautiful painting. If a parent says, "Be good, now," to a child, it means the parent wants the child to do only things the parent values, such as saying "Please" and "Thank you," finishing homework, and going to bed in time to get enough sleep. These represent values the parent would like the child to copy: good manners, hard work, and healthy habits.

If we represent this short argument in a diagram, we can see what makes it an argument: unlike the mind-map, which leads outward in several directions, the argument all leads in a single direction: toward its conclusion.

Diagrams can be a very useful way to represent your own argument or any argument. Representing ideas on a diagram forces you to make decisions about how the statements are connected. Figure 2.2 shows how the ideas in the short argument are grouped into clusters by similarity, and it indicates by arrows how each cluster of ideas is meant to point toward the conclusion.

At this point, you can meet the minimum goal of the assignment, which was to create an argument. What more might be needed? It's time to look at the big picture: what would be the point of asking for an argument on this topic? Is it just to see how you write, or is there something more? We step back to the wider context—not just the particular course and assignment, but the topic itself as a topic of interest. The professor is inviting you into the discipline, showing you what topics are discussed in philosophy. The key question to ask yourself is why the topic matters—when and why might we care about what it means to "be good"? This question should lead you to realize that we do care about the topic in a wide range of situations, not just in a philosophy class. We want our partners and friends to be good people. We want laws to enforce good behaviour in society. We want banks and businesses to do good things with the money we entrust to them. Which partners and friends shall we choose? Which behaviour should be illegal? Where will we spend our money?

Now you are in a position to see how your own argument could make a contribution to the topic, and see if you want to develop or change the argument so that it makes the contribution you want to make. So far, you have argued that to "be good" means to be approved of. One consequence of this might be that different people approve of different qualities, so any given person, or law, or business might be good in some people's judgment, but bad in others'. That might not be a problem in choosing friends or partners, but it is going to make it difficult to agree on laws or business practices. As you think about the impact and the consequences of your argument, you may decide that you need to expand on your original version and work in more points.

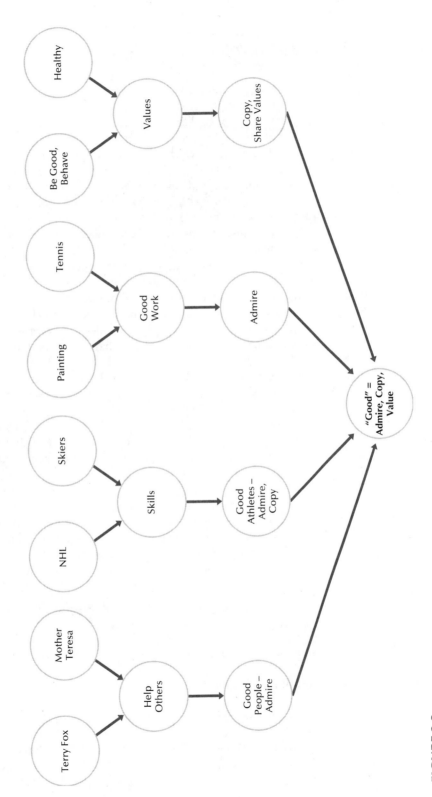

FIGURE 2.2
Diagram of an Argument

Developing Arguments: Increasing Complexity

Arguments are not our most natural form of speech, so it can be challenging to organize thoughts and words in this structured way. An argument needs to make sense to you and to anyone else to whom you present it. As we combine our attempts to construct an argument with our skills in a variety of forms of personal expression, we create prose that works less directly toward what are the conclusion than the examples you have seen so far.

Recognizing arguments requires disentangling them from the questions, anecdotes, and detours that may have worked to create a comfortable flow of ideas. It also means recognizing when an arguer is offering a premise to support a conclusion, and when an arguer is mentioning a premise just to acknowledge or explain how people defend the opposite conclusion. Creating arguments means bringing out into the open the connections that made intuitive sense to you as you thought about them. It means explaining points that were obvious to you, but not at all obvious to anyone who didn't experience the thinking that you did. Recognizing and creating arguments require you to realize why the argument is given at all—what is the potential opposition or what are the alternative viewpoints that would lead to different conclusions?

For example, an "argumentative essay" often calls for you to present opposing points of view, in order to show you have understood why your own conclusion needs support. Using our example of arguing about what it means to "be good," why might someone disagree with the conclusion that to call something "good" just means it has qualities we should admire, or copy, or value? As noted earlier, you may have already realized that this conclusion would leave us in a difficult position when we try to agree on good laws. There are other alternatives as well. Some people think that to "be good" is to aspire to a fixed ideal, such as to be a good Christian or Muslim, or to have a "healthy mind in a healthy body." They may think being good is not in any way connected to mere personal judgment about what seems good.

You can now see what you might have to add to your own argument if you have to strengthen its support for the conclusion. As your argument deals with opposing points or adds support, its structure becomes more complicated.

Layered Arguments, Indirect Arguments, and Recognizing Opposition

An argument example that has been quoted for centuries is this classic:

All men are mortal. Socrates is a man. Therefore, Socrates is mortal.

This is a clear example of an argument because it is so simple. Each sentence is either a premise that directly supports a conclusion or the conclusion itself. Each sentence is in the form of a declarative sentence. The example is straightforward, but as just noted above, it isn't a very good representation of the type of argument you'll usually come across.

It is rare that someone will speak or write in a way that states nothing but clearly expressed premises that directly support a conclusion. All the following ways of presenting an argument are more common:

- Arguments can be expressed indirectly.
- Arguments can build on established conclusions to draw further conclusions.
- Arguments can be wholly concerned with disproving someone else's conclusion.
- Arguments can recognize opposing points that in fact count against the conclusion.

Indirect Arguments

To make a point indirectly, an arguer may ask questions, hint at a point, omit points that seem too obvious to include, or use humour or sarcasm instead of plain statements; these are known as **indirect arguments.** When arguments are expressed indirectly, in questions or by humour, we must translate their reasons into clear claims that work as premises.

Here is an example of an argument presented in indirect phrasing that would need to be converted to declarative sentences. Joe Taylor was born in England to a Canadian father and English mother. Taylor talked to reporter Daphne Bramham about his loss of Canadian citizenship in 1968 due to changed regulations:

"In 1952, the Canadian government passed regulations to remove Canadian nationality from unsuspecting children of Canadian servicemen who had been born abroad. This was to apply to any minors who, for whatever reason, had left Canada.

"There were two escape clauses. You could return to Canada to live before you were 21 or you had to wait until you were 21 and, within 3 years, apply for retention of your nationality status."

Nobody bothered to tell . . . Joe. In fact, the Canadian government didn't contact anybody affected by the regulation.

"So, on my 24th birthday 5,000 miles away, I lost my birthright without knowing about it. Is that fair or just?"

[DAPHNE BRAMHAM, "SOLDIER'S SON SECRETLY STRIPPED OF HIS BIRTHRIGHT," *VANCOUVER SUN,* JULY 3, 2004, C7. REPRINTED WITH PERMISSION OF THE PACIFIC NEWSPAPER GROUP.]

Although the conclusion of the argument is "The regulations are unjust," this conclusion is actually expressed in the form of a question, "Is that fair or just?" A question invites you to take a step in support of the speaker, by filling in the intended answer. Look for questions in arguments: they can indicate that the speaker already has a particular answer in mind that is supposed to be obvious to you, and the answer to the question is the actual conclusion (or premise).

Among the hardest arguments to understand and report are those in which the arguer is being humorous, sarcastic, or indirect in some other way. To understand such an argument, you first have to recognize that it is humorous or sarcastic, and then, since it is indirect, you have to construct what the direct, serious argument would be.

For instance, consider this editorial:

Cellphones hit a new low

Oh no! First it was cellphones as a trigger for an epidemic of brain cancer.

Then it was cellphones as a cause for the early onset of Alzheimer's disease. Next it was cellphones as a traffic hazard in the hands of drivers too dumb or lazy to pull over to make a call. That was followed by warnings that cellphones can interfere with aircraft instruments and human sleep patterns.

Just for the record, Health Canada, the agency responsible for regulating the public's exposure to radiation, concludes that there's no conclusive evidence of any biological risk from using cellphones—although it points out that driving and using the phone is definitely a danger to yourself and other drivers.

But now we have new research suggesting that carrying a cellphone weakens men's sexual potency.

Last week the *Sunday Times of London* reported a study suggesting that men packing their units in belt holsters or trouser pockets can reduce their chances of conception by 30 per cent.

Gosh, and we thought it was just their boorish telephone manners.

[EDITORIAL, *VANCOUVER SUN*, JULY 3, 2004, C6. REPRINTED WITH PERMISSION OF THE PACIFIC NEWSPAPER GROUP.]

Shorn of its playful phrasing and indirect route, this argument simply concludes that we should not be too quick to worry about risks that may be very low. Accidents caused by thoughtless use of cellphones are a real risk; harm to the body from carrying a cellphone is not a plausible risk because Health Canada has claimed that there is no evidence of biological risk from using a cellphone. The last two paragraphs in particular just make the point that a man's impolite telephone behaviour may be much more likely to reduce his chance of getting into a relationship that could lead to children than his cellphone itself is likely to reduce his fertility.

Notice that humour is not being used here simply to catch your eye or to entertain you. The humour is also working as an aspect of the argument: it is intended to show that there is something wrong with what it is poking fun at. Humour and satire are often used to convey the view "This is absurd." If the idea that something is absurd is an indirect premise or conclusion, then the humour is part of the argument.

One of the reasons it can be difficult to recognize humour being used as a premise is that humour is also often used to make a point without argument. If the humour cannot be seen as indicating a premise or conclusion, then it is a non-argumentative persuasive device. For example, consider the following comment heard on the radio: "Just days after the recent controversy over claims that SpongeBob SquarePants is gay, a major U.S. network is coming out with a new program called 'Square Pants for the Straight Guy.'" This statement is intended as a joke, poking fun at the idea that it makes sense to see SpongeBob as gay and suggesting that even if he is, it should make no difference to how popular he and his show are. The statement may be attempting to persuade you that it is silly to protest the use of a cartoon character by claiming he is gay, but it doesn't present you with an argument to that effect.

The identification of indirect arguments depends on the reader or listener interpreting the argument in a particular way. You will see in Chapter 3 that we need to be careful in how we interpret arguments and that there are some guidelines to follow. Legitimate disagreements can occur.

Recognition of the Opposition: Counter-Considerations and Counter-Arguments

An argument may pause to acknowledge, discuss, and dismiss points that work against its conclusion; such claims are known as **counter-considerations**. For example, consider this statement made by Kilburn in "Alzheimer's drug eases the daily strain" (Exercise 1.7, Example 5, on page 49): "A recent British study said that Aricept doesn't work." This statement doesn't help to support Kilburn's conclusion, because she believes Aricept does work and concludes that it should be available for Alzheimer's patients. So she immediately counters the statement by saying, "I'm here to tell you that it does. And I think if you ask anyone else in the early stages of Alzheimer's, they would agree with me."

Then she notes another counter-consideration that she acknowledges does not favour her conclusion: "I admit it might not work for some people."

In mentioning and perhaps discussing these counter-premises, the arguer acknowledges that there are points to be made against the conclusion. The arguer may accept, reject, or not know how to respond to these points.

If the arguer acknowledges counter-premises without discussing them, it is obvious that he or she has heard the opposing points but either does not know what to do about them yet or considers them to be less important than the supporting premises. The arguer might well think that his or her premises simply outweigh the counter-consideration.

If the arguer discusses and dismisses the counter-considerations, he or she is explicitly indicating that they are not considered strong enough to count against the conclusion. (This move is usually advocated in argumentative essays.) For instance, an argument against keeping wolves in captivity might include the statements "Advocates of captivity point out correctly that wolves are hunted in the wild and are no safer there. But we could act to protect the wolves in the wild by patrolling the areas and by refusing to issue licences for trapping wolves." Here the arguer is not accepting the statement that wolves are hunted in the wild as a good point: he or she believes that it is possible to get around this objection.

When an arguer responds to counter-considerations by giving reasons within the argument to show why the counter-considerations are unconvincing, the arguer constructs one form of a counter-argument. The counter-argument is a sub-argument within the main argument. A counter-argument recognizes an opposing point but produces evidence against it and leads us back to the original point.

How do we deal with points that the arguer recognizes do not directly support the conclusion? In understanding the argument, we see that the arguer has anticipated some possible objections to his or her position, so when we report the argument to anyone new, we should indicate that the arguer acknowledges these points. When we come to evaluating the argument, one of the aspects we will need to look at is how well the arguer has countered the counter-considerations: Do the counter-considerations really weigh more heavily? Are the reasons given for dismissing the non-supporting premises good enough?

Another way an opposing view is recognized is by constructing a new argument that works as a counter-argument. This argument stands alone, but its entire purpose is to prove some previous argument wrong. You saw an example of this earlier. Peter McKnight had written an article arguing that universities were under-funded. Brian Buchanan, responding to this argument, offers his own argument to show why he think McKnight is wrong. (See "Re: The other threat facing our universities," page 41) Buchanan's conclusion is the opposite of McKnight's: universities are not under-funded. Buchanan's counter-argument aims to show that universities could easily have enough money to meet social needs. He does this by arguing that they are wasting money on the courses Buchanan considers to be useless. Buchanan considers a wide range of courses in social sciences and humanities, such as Peace and Conflict Studies, to be "shallow, useless tripe." He also claims that applicants to university are under-qualified in basic skills, and that the universities have simplified courses to suit them instead of training the students to meet course demands. The overall effect of this argument is not to establish what Buchanan thinks should be done, but only to counteract McKnight's conclusion that universities do need funds.

Many academic arguments are of this type. In counter-arguments, all the supporting evidence is used to show where some earlier argument was inadequate—perhaps because some of its premises were unacceptable, or its reasoning did not work, or its conclusion was wrong. To understand these arguments, we need to be able to recognize what the original arguer said that this arguer disagrees with. We also need to recognize whether this arguer's conclusion is the opposite of the original arguer's or whether the arguer just decides that we cannot conclude anything on this topic yet.

EXERCISE 2.3

Identifying Indirect or Counter-Premises and Conclusions

Look ahead to the articles in Chapter 8 (pages 253–257) or Chapter 11 (pages 320–324). See if you can identify indirectly stated premises, counter-premises, and counter-arguments in any of the articles.

Layered Arguments

Premises and conclusions can be difficult to spot in some arguments because there will be more than one conclusion. Some arguments are **layered arguments**. Each argument will support a conclusion that will then in turn be used to support a further conclusion. When a conclusion is used as a premise in a further argument, that conclusion is called a **sub-conclusion**. The argument that supports the sub-conclusion is called a **sub-argument**.

As a simple example, consider this one:

1. The kids would love to have a pet.
2. We don't mind getting them one as long as they take care of it.
3. They've said they'll take care of it,
4. so we could have a pet.
5. Sandra is allergic to cats and dogs.
6. Hamsters are very messy,
7. so the pet has to be something other than a cat, a dog, or a hamster.
8. A bird would entertain the children.
9. It wouldn't be too hard to take care of.
10. Therefore, let's get a bird as a pet.

This set of statements, 1 to 10, is a complex argument with two sub-arguments; 1, 2, 3, and 4 are a sub-argument, with 1, 2, and 3 supporting the sub-conclusion 4. Similarly, 5, 6, and 7 are a sub-argument, with 5 and 6 supporting the sub-conclusion 7. These two sub-conclusions, together with the additional statements 8 and 9, build up to the overall conclusion 10.

As a more complex example, suppose you have improved your original argument about what it means to be good. You have decided to drop the example of good athletes because it seems unrelated to issues about choosing friends or agreeing on laws. You have decided that you should deal with the question of whether we need to agree on what counts as good. Your short argument now reads this way:

> When we call something "good," we mean it has qualities we should admire, or copy, or value. For example, there are good people such as Terry Fox, or Mother Teresa. We call these people "good" because we admire what they did for others. Terry Fox raised money for cancer research by running partway across Canada after he had lost one of his own legs to cancer. Mother Teresa helped the homeless in Calcutta. We say, "Good work!" to someone who has produced something we admire or value, such as a great tennis shot or a beautiful painting. If a parent says, "Be good, now," to a child, it means the parent wants the child to do only things the parent values, such as saying "Please" and "Thank you," finishing homework, and going to bed in time to get enough sleep. These represent values the parent would like the child to copy: good manners, hard work, and healthy habits.
>
> Some people might say that this definition causes problems, because it appeals only to our personal standards of what is admirable or valuable. For example, not everyone thinks that a great tennis shot or a beautiful painting is worthwhile. They may be entitled to their opinion, but it is going to make it difficult for everyone to agree on whether schools should receive more money for tennis programs or art classes.

However, we can allow for these differences and still base our definition of "good" on what is admirable and valuable. We are not all so far apart on what we value that we each have completely different ideas. There will be many areas in which we do share at least some core values, such as respect for life and freedom from suffering. We can discuss and possibly resolve differences in values, such as whether we value life much more than suffering, so that it is good to use whatever medical means are necessary to keep a person alive.

Therefore, to "be good" is to be valued by a significant majority of people, for reasons that everyone can understand.

Now you have a more complex argument that makes a more effective contribution to the topic: you have provided a counter-argument to deal with one possible line of opposition, and you have opened up a direction for future discussion, about why we value things.

In an oral discussion, the best way to see connections in a layered argument is to pause during the discussion and ask if you're following it correctly: offer what you think are the conclusions and the reasons, and see if the speakers agree.

For written arguments, one good way to identify structure in a layered argument is to read the argument, set it aside out of sight, and try to reconstruct it from memory. What was the conclusion? What were the main points that the arguer made to back up the conclusion? What details were added to make those points plausible?

EXERCISE 2.4

Understanding Structure

1. In groups, agree on the conclusion in the argument below. Identify and label the premises.

2. Put the argument aside and have each person write down the argument as he or she remembers it. Compare notes: do you agree on the argument?

*3. Prepare a diagram showing the structure of the argument. Group together the premises that are related to one another.

Another fur flap that need not fly

When urban people start making emotional decisions about life in rural Canada, it seems the decisions are almost always the wrong ones.

An animal-rights group is taking on the RCMP over the force's continued use of the muskrat hat, the famous headpiece with flaps that has been official cold-weather gear since 1933. The Fur-Bearer Defenders, a B.C. group, is concerned about the trapping of muskrats. And the RCMP is at least reviewing its use of hats, taking a look at a synthetic alternative.

We're more concerned about the health and welfare of our federal police officers who can spend hours at a time out on a highway in rural Canada in a minus-30 C storm, and who swear by the muskrat hats. What about the thousands of Canadians who make a living trapping, many of them aboriginal? Some people think muskrats are cute and need to be protected. Actually, they are a rural rodent found in marshes across Canada, as common as squirrels in Ottawa.

Another example of misguided urban sentimentality applied to rural Canada is the cancellation of the spring bear hunt in Ontario. Out of the blue, then premier Mike Harris cancelled the hunt in 1999, under intense pressure from the anti-hunting lobby. The result has been disastrous. Some of Ontario's 150,000 black bears are roaming into cities and towns. Some rural residents have been afraid to walk in the woods and Ontario's police chiefs recently complained that bear nuisance calls are all too common. As Derek Nighbor, the Liberal candidate in Renfrew-Nipissing-Pembroke recently noted, anti-hunting sentiment comes from people who think of Winnie-the-Pooh, not a large bear, with cubs, running by an Eganville elementary school.

Let's not permit knee-jerk urban sentimentality to shape decisions that have dramatic effects on the people who live in this huge, cold country.

[EDITORIAL, *OTTAWA CITIZEN*, SEPTEMBER 25, 2003, A14. REPRINTED WITH PERMISSION OF THE OTTAWA CITIZEN.]

Reporting Arguments

Once you have identified an argument, you need to be able to convey your understanding to others. A **report of an argument** sets out, briefly and objectively, the structure of the argument: what the conclusion of the argument is, and what reasons are offered to support that conclusion.

In reporting an argument, you confirm that you have understood it, and you make it possible for someone new to the discussion to understand it and independently to assess its reasoning.

Putting other people's ideas into your own words is the "digestion process" in which you connect what you've heard or read to what you already know and translate it into personally meaningful terms. Even if the person's ideas are so cleverly expressed that you feel you shouldn't try to change them, it is still important to be able to say them in your own way, because your own words show that you really did follow the clever original.

In the report, you will often have to reorganize what is said in the argument in order to make it clear how the argument works. You are not simply repeating what is said—you are rearranging it so that the main point the arguer wants to make is clear, as is the evidence that supports this point. In doing so, you provide a service to your readers by making sure that the argument is easy for them to follow.

You will also have to maintain the trust of your audience and of the original arguer: a report that imposes your impressions or is not offered respectfully is immediately damaging. For instance, if you start your report with "So all you're really saying is . . ." it won't matter how objective and accurate it is from that point on: you've already belittled the argument (and, by extension, the arguer) by showing that you think there is not very much of value in the argument. You'll have an uphill struggle to rebuild the arguer's willingness to cooperate and the audience's trust. In contrast, if you start with "If I understand you correctly, you're saying . . ." you have signalled that you want to do your best to understand before you react; you are visibly trying to cooperate and to put your own agenda on hold. Consequently, it is best to speak neutrally at this stage. If you stay neutral in tone and do not mention which side you favour, you are more likely to get the cooperation of supporters of both sides. You are more likely to be seen as open-minded and really willing to listen.

Reporting Orally

If you're debating an issue with someone, you should put what you've heard into your own words. Putting someone else's ideas into your own words and asking if you've got the argument right has two important purposes: it shows that you can make sense of it and that you really did listen to the arguer. The guidelines presented in Chapter 1 for active listening can be followed in reporting an argument.

Reporting in Writing

Reporting in writing has a slightly different function than reporting in person. You're in a different role because your words may be read by people new to the topic; you want to enable them to begin to understand it. You are building an additional type of cooperation between the original arguer, yourself, and new readers. If your tone in the report is impartial, readers can be confident that they are following what the original writer thought rather than your interpretation.

A good report identifies the conclusion clearly and organizes the reasons. It preserves factual details and data that help to show how specific the original writer's evidence was. It stays close enough to the wording of the original to preserve its tone and meaning. It is objective: there is no indication at all of the report writer's opinion, and the use of quotation marks signals any specific wording that occurred in the original. A clear indication of the source tells readers that what follows is a report and allows them to locate the original argument if there is any question about the accuracy of the report.

In drafting the report, you may find it most helpful to begin by writing without looking at the original, to be sure that you can put it into your own words, and then going back to check and to fill in details.

Checklist for Written Reports of Arguments

To be sure that you are giving an accurate and objective report, check that you do the following:

✔ *Report objectively:* Avoid evaluative words or phrases such as "This well-thought-out argument" or "It mistakenly concludes." Where the original uses strong or unusual language, report it in quotes so that it is clear the original writer, not you, chose that language.

✔ *Include the complete citation:* The citation is all the bibliographical information on the source in which you found the argument. Such details are important indicators of the reliability of the information and its availability for independent checking.

> ✔ *Identify the conclusion:* Set out the conclusion very clearly and report who makes it. Often the conclusion is indicated only indirectly and may even be unstated. The person who writes an article may be the reporter, not the arguer.
>
> ✔ *Clarify the structure:* If necessary, reorganize the reasoning so that it follows a more logical order.
>
> ✔ *Include specific names, numbers, or other details:* This information will provide support for the general points. These specific details are often crucial evidence. For brevity, you can omit minor details or reasons if they make no apparent difference to the conclusion.

Sample Written Report

A written report of de Haen's argument in "Pacific Rim, Asian countries meet to discuss food safety" (page 47) might look like this:

> In "Pacific Rim, Asian countries meet to discuss food safety" (*Vancouver Sun*, May 24, 2004, p. F8), the FAO's assistant director general, de Haen, concludes that countries must try to ensure food is produced, handled, and distributed more safely. He believes that this will prevent hundreds of thousands of deaths worldwide each year from food-borne illnesses. The death toll of food-borne diseases globally is, he says, "staggering," especially in developing countries where poor governments lack funds to monitor food safety and people's choices of food sources are often limited. Severe diarrhea kills 1.8 million people annually. He gives two specific examples. High casualties can surface from small, sporadic outbreaks such as a suspected mould contamination of maize in eastern Kenya that is believed to have killed up to 40 people so far. Casualties can also result from widespread distribution of a food. In the previous week, the U.S. Food and Drug Administration recalled 13 million raw almonds distributed by California-based Paramount Farms Inc. because of the possibility of salmonella. The almonds had been distributed nationwide and in Britain, France, Italy, Japan, Korea, Malaysia, Mexico, and Taiwan. "From the farm to the final consumer, the risk of food-related outbreaks needs to be reduced," de Haen says.

The report omits the parts of the original article that were simply information about the conference. However, it includes all the relevant details from the portion of the article that reported de Haen's argument. (It could be compressed if the context made it necessary.) The full citation is there, woven into the first sentence. The argument has been slightly rephrased and reorganized to show understanding without losing clarity. The tone stays objective—the writer's own opinions cannot be identified.

In the article in Exercise 2.5, more than one person's view is reported, and the article as a whole does not favour any side. When you summarize it, pay particular attention to who holds what view.

EXERCISE 2.5

Distinguishing Separate Arguments

*Identify and report each of the arguments in "Academics drawn into Klein essay controversy," below. You should be able to pick out two separate short arguments, by Oberg and by Amrhein. You should also be able to recognize a non-argument—an attempt to persuade using emotion alone, by Vanderleer.

Academics drawn into Klein essay controversy

Alberta's learning minister gets university presidents writing letters

Alberta's four universities have become entangled in a growing political turmoil over an essay written by Premier Ralph Klein.

Learning Minister Lyle Oberg confirmed Wednesday that he called the universities last week after Klein was criticized for taking large passages of his essay directly from the Internet without properly attributing them.

"I suggested that they write a letter to the editor about this issue because it's a very, very serious issue," Oberg told reporters who staked out his office. Oberg said he felt compelled to ask the universities to get involved after questions were raised about the integrity of the Athabasca University professor who gave Klein a grade of 77 per cent for his essay on the events leading up to the 1973 coup in Chile.

"This was a direct challenge to our post-secondary institutions," said Oberg, his voice trembling.

Carl Amrhein, provost of the University of Alberta, issued a brief statement confirming Oberg's call last Friday.

He said he and officials at the province's three other universities—Calgary, Athabasca and Lethbridge—held a conference call to discuss it.

"We discussed issues around academic freedom, confidentiality between students and teachers and the autonomy of university policy from outside influences," said Amrhein.

"We agreed that it was not appropriate for us to comment on any issue related to another university. Rather, we decided that each of us would consider penning a letter to the editor celebrating the importance of lifelong learning."

Roderick Fraser, President of the University of Alberta, wrote in his letter to the editor: "I am writing to say that an important issue has been over-looked, and that is the premier's commitment to lifelong learning."

Fraser's letter drew an immediate outcry from academics and students, who countered with a barrage of their own letters.

"Shame on Klein and his poor and inexcusable academic laziness," wrote Russ Vanderleer of Edmonton. "Shame on University of Alberta President Roderick Fraser for skirting the issues of plagiarism and sloppy academic practice which many students are disciplined for each year."

Other letters to the editor in Wednesday's editions targeted Klein for the way he sourced his paper. "My own (junior high) students could have done a better job citing their sources than the premier did," wrote Khrysty Greif, a social studies teacher in Edmonton.

[JIM MACDONALD, CANADIAN PRESS, REPORTED *IN VANCOUVER SUN*, MAY 20, 2004, F10. THE CANADIAN PRESS.]

EXERCISE 2.6

Reporting a Written Argument

Find an article on a topic that interests you. Make sure the article contains an argument. Alternatively, choose an argument from Chapter 8, pages 253–257. Report the argument given in the article. Use the checklist on pages 78–79. You may also want to use the Checklist for Reading Carefully in Chapter 1, pages 45–46.

EXERCISE **2.7**

Giving a Written Argument

Give an argument in support of a conclusion you personally hold, on a topic of your choice. Use the checklist as a guideline to structure your argument so that it is clear to read and easy to understand. Ask someone else to read your argument and report it to you. Has your reader grasped your argument correctly? If not, how could you make it clearer?

DEFINITION

A **standard form** report of an argument is a *point-form* arrangement of the premises, with *each premise numbered* and placed *on a separate line* and the conclusion placed at the bottom of the list.

Reporting an Argument in Standard Form

Sometimes you need to report an argument in a way that lets each premise stand out so we can see how the argument builds to its conclusion. A useful way to clarify an argument is to put the argument into **standard form.** "Standard form" is a phrase used to describe a point-form arrangement of an argument that makes it easy to see how the premises are meant to build up to the conclusion.

An argument in standard form sets out each premise and the conclusion on its own numbered line. After all the premises have been written, a line is drawn and the conclusion is written under the line.

The purpose of putting arguments into standard form is to clarify the basic structure of the argument and highlight each premise. The numbers make it easy to refer to the premises when evaluating an argument.

Simple Arguments in Standard Form

A simple argument is one in which there is only one conclusion, and all the premises directly support the conclusion.

We've seen the argument "All men are mortal and Socrates is a man, so Socrates is mortal."

Here is that argument converted to standard form:

1. All men are mortal.

2. Socrates is a man.
    _____

3. Socrates is mortal.

Each premise in the standard form of an argument should be one declarative sentence. A declarative sentence is a descriptive sentence. "The cat is on the mat" is a declarative sentence. Examples of non-declarative sentences are questions and commands.

The conclusion in standard form is similarly a single sentence. You saw an example of indirect phrasing on page 71, in Joe Taylor's "So, on my 24th birthday 5,000 miles away, I lost my birthright without knowing about it. Is that fair or just?" His conclusion is given there as a question. Turned into a declarative sentence, it would be "It is not fair that I lost my birthright when I turned 24."

If the wording of the original text is clear and straightforward, you can use exactly the same wording when putting the argument into standard form. However, you do have the option of rephrasing the premises and conclusion in order to clarify them. You can put premises and conclusions into your own words as long as the intended meaning remains the same. In fact, it is often best not to use quotations when putting an argument into standard form unless you feel uncertain about the meaning of a term used in the argument. When you paraphrase the original, you show that you have been able to understand it and you are less likely to include slanted language or irrelevant details. When you paraphrase you can often capture the meaning of the original sentence with a shorter, clearer, sentence.

As another example of putting an argument into standard form, let's take a look at de Haen's argument. The argument, in its original form, reads:

A UN official said today countries must try to ensure food is produced, handled and distributed more safely to prevent hundreds of thousands of deaths worldwide each year from food-borne illnesses.

"From the farm to the final consumer, the risk of food-related outbreaks needs to be reduced," de Haen told government regulators, food industry officials and consumer activists from 42 Asian and Pacific Rim countries at the launch of the food safety conference.

De Haen, the FAO's assistant director general, noted that the U.S. Food and Drug Administration has in the past week recalled 13 million raw almonds distributed by California-based Paramount Farms Inc. because of the possibility of salmonella.

The almonds were distributed nation-wide and in Britain, France, Italy, Japan, Korea, Malaysia, Mexico, and Taiwan.

De Haen said the death toll of food-borne diseases globally was "staggering," especially in developing countries where poor governments lack funds to monitor food safety and people's choices of food sources are often limited.

Severe diarrhea kills 1.8 million people annually, de Haen said. High casualties can also surface from smaller, sporadic outbreaks such as a suspected mould contamination of maize in eastern Kenya that is believed to have killed up to 40 people so far.

Here is the argument's structure, set out in standard form:

1. By ensuring that food is produced, handled, and distributed more safely, countries could prevent hundreds of thousands of deaths worldwide each year from food-borne illnesses.

2. The U.S. Food and Drug Administration has in the past week recalled 13 million raw almonds distributed by California-based Paramount Farms Inc. because of the possibility of salmonella.

3. The almonds were distributed across the United States and in Britain, France, Italy, Japan, Korea, Malaysia, Mexico, and Taiwan.

4. Globally, large numbers of deaths are caused by food-borne disease.

5. Death tolls from food-borne disease are highest in countries where governments lack funds to monitor food safety and poverty limits people's choice of food sources.

6. Severe diarrhea kills 1.8 million people annually.

7. High casualties can also surface from smaller, sporadic outbreaks such as a suspected mould contamination of maize in eastern Kenya that is believed to have killed up to 40 people so far.

8. The risk of illness and death due to contaminated food needs to be reduced.

9. Countries must try to ensure food is produced, handled, and distributed more safely.

Arguments with Sub-arguments

Putting layered arguments into standard form can help you keep track of what each part of the argument is doing. A quick way to keep track of sub-arguments is to put the numbers of the premises that support a conclusion next to that conclusion. This can be used as an alternative to a diagram, or it can be used in preparation for drawing a diagram. Here is an example:

1. All men are mortal.

2. Socrates is a man.

3. Socrates is mortal. (1, 2)

4. All mortals like cheesecake.

5. Socrates likes cheesecake. (3, 4)

In the above example, the claim in premise 3 (Socrates is a man) has been established by premises 1 and 2. Premise 3 is a sub-conclusion. To indicate that 3 is a sub-conclusion that has been proven by premises 1 and 2, the numbers 1 and 2 are written in parenthesis beside premise 3. The final conclusion (5) is directly supported by premises 3 and 4, so the numbers 3 and 4 are written next to statement 5.

Here is another example:

Original version: You should not rent the suite that costs $850 per month because rent that high will leave you with no money for food. If you shouldn't rent that suite, your only choice is to take the basement suite at $600 per month. So you'd better take the basement suite.

Standard form:

1. Rent of $850 per month will leave you with no money for food.

2. You should not rent the suite that costs $850 per month. (1)

3. If you shouldn't rent the suite that costs $850 per month, you should take the basement suite at $600 per month.

4. You should take the basement suite at $600 per month. (2, 3)

By putting (1) beside the second premise, we've indicated that premise 2 is supported by 1. In other words, premise 2 is a sub-conclusion based on 1. Then premise 2 is used along with premise 3 to prove that 4 is correct.

De Haen's argument is also a layered argument. Once the sub-conclusions are indicated, the structure of the argument is clearer.

1. By ensuring that food is produced, handled, and distributed more safely, countries could prevent hundreds of thousands of deaths worldwide each year from food-borne illnesses. (5)

2. The U.S. Food and Drug Administration has in the past week recalled 13 million raw almonds distributed by California-based Paramount Farms Inc. because of the possibility of salmonella.

3. The almonds were distributed across the United States and in Britain, France, Italy, Japan, Korea, Malaysia, Mexico, and Taiwan.

4. Globally, large numbers of deaths are caused by food-borne disease.

5. Death tolls from food-borne disease are highest in countries where governments lack funds to monitor food safety and poverty limits people's choice of food sources.

6. Severe diarrhea kills 1.8 million people annually.

7. High casualties can also surface from smaller, sporadic outbreaks such as a suspected mould contamination of maize in eastern Kenya that is believed to have killed up to 40 people so far.

8. The risk of illness and death due to contaminated food needs to be reduced. (2, 3, 4, 6, 7)

9. Countries must try to ensure food is produced, handled, and distributed more safely. (1, 8)

Once you have put an argument into standard form, you can also easily diagram the argument by using arrows to link premise numbers to sub-conclusions and conclusions. A diagram gives you a visual representation of the structure of the argument, which may help you see more clearly how the premises are meant to work together. An arrow points from a premise toward a conclusion.

When premises work independently, we can indicate this in the diagram by drawing a separate arrow from each premise to the conclusion it supports. When premises work together, we can indicate this in the diagram by adding a plus sign between the premises that work together and then drawing a single arrow from those premises to the conclusion (see Figure 2.3).

FIGURE 2.3

Premises Supporting a Conclusion

A. You should rent the basement suite at $600 per month.

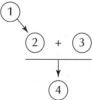

B. Countries must try to ensure food is produced, handled, and distributed more safely.

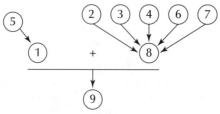

Counter-Considerations

If an argument contains counter-considerations that are not discussed or are explicitly rejected, those counter-considerations should not appear in the standardized version of the argument. Only the premises that are meant to support the conclusion should appear in the standardization of the argument.

For example, consider this short argument with one counter-consideration:

Original version: Although I have to admit that the Biology professor is very interesting, I think I should take the English class because it is a requirement for my degree and it will help me write better essays.

Here's how we would put this argument into standard form:

1. The English class is a requirement for my degree.
2. The English class will help me write better essays.
   _____
3. I should take the English class.

The counter-premise, "I have to admit that the Biology professor is very interesting" is not included because it does not support the conclusion "I should take the English class." The conclusion stands or falls based on the premises that do support it, so it is only those premises we want to look at when we consider whether the premises provide enough support for the conclusion.

Counter-Arguments

If a piece of writing contains not only a pro-argument that supports a conclusion, but also a counter-argument against an opposing position, the pro-argument and counter-argument should be put into standard form separately. This indicates that there are two different arguments presented by the speaker or writer: one in support of a conclusion and one rejecting arguments against that conclusion.

For example, consider the following short argument:

"I have chosen to reject Hans's argument for the immortality of the soul because he claims that television psychics prove the existence of life after death. But television psychics are notorious fakes. I think the soul is mortal because the soul is nothing other than the body. If the body can die, the soul can die right along with it."

Counter-argument:

1. Television psychics are fakes.
2. Television psychics don't prove the existence of life after death. (1)
3. Hans's argument for the immortality of the soul relies on the claim that psychics prove the existence of life after death.
   _____
4. Hans's argument for the immortality of the soul is poor. (2, 3)

Pro-argument:

1. The soul is the same as the body.
2. If the body can die, the soul can die with it. (1)
   _____
3. The soul is not immortal. (2)

EXERCISE **2.8** Converting Arguments to Standard Form

1. Put the following arguments into standard form:
   *a. My parents don't like John. I could only marry a person my parents like. So I obviously can't marry John.
   *b. I'll tell you why marijuana should be legal. My best friend has smoked pot every day for twenty years. He is a hard worker, a good father, and a good friend.
   c. Only rich people belong to that yacht club. Sasha belongs to the club. That means Sasha is rich!
   d. When I was a little girl my grandmother used to say that worrying is a waste of time. I believe that she was right because worrying is not trying to solve a problem and it is not accomplishing anything.
   e. It is such a beautiful night tonight that I think I should walk to the supermarket instead of driving. It's probably also a good idea given that by walking I'll get some exercise and some fresh air after spending all day studying. Besides, Raj is down the street watering the lawn and I had a question I wanted to ask him.

2. Put the following arguments into standard form. Make sure to indicate any sub-arguments by writing the number of the premise that supports a sub-conclusion next to that sub-conclusion.
   *a. I either pay back the money I owe my brother or I pay my phone bill. The thing is that I can't pay the money I owe my brother because my sister will find out and then I'll have to pay the money I owe her. So I'll have to pay my phone bill.
   b. French immersion is a good choice for my children because becoming fluent in a second language will give them an advantage in the work-place. Therefore, it's best to move to a neighbourhood where there is a well-respected French immersion program for my kids.
   c. The black dog looks friendlier than the white dog. So I'll walk on the side of the road where the black dog is sitting. Every time I walk on the side of the road where the black dog is sitting I have to stop and talk to old Mrs. Andrechuk. So I'll have to stop and talk to old Mrs. Andrechuk.
   d. They found him with blood on his hands and the murder weapon at his feet. So it's a safe bet that he is the murderer. But if he is the murderer, he couldn't have been the man I saw at the movies the night of the murder. I guess I'm forced to conclude that he was not the man I saw at the movies that night. But if that's the case, then I don't have a very good memory because I do remember seeing him there. Therefore, I don't have a good memory!
   e. If euthanasia is destined to become socially acceptable, murder will also become socially acceptable. However, murder will never become socially acceptable so we must conclude that euthanasia will never become socially acceptable. Yet we are a society concerned with the well-being of people in acute pain and distress. So either we will find new ways to comfort people in acute pain and distress or the

impossible will happen and euthanasia actually will become socially acceptable. Ultimately all these considerations lead me to conclude that we will indeed find new ways to comfort people in acute pain and distress.

f. Even though you hate the colour I've chosen to paint the living room, it's the best choice because it is bright and cheerful, and besides the paint was free.

g. Of course trains are noisy and expensive to run, but a commuter rail system is environmentally friendly and will solve traffic problems on the highway. So the government should support a commuter rail program.

The Connection between Structure and Quality

An argument gives reasons to support a claim, but that doesn't guarantee that it gives good reasons. Bad reasoning makes bad arguments, yet bad arguments are still arguments. What makes a collection of statements an argument is that some of those statements are intended to prove that a conclusion is reasonable to believe. The arguer may succeed or fail in meeting this goal. We will be investigating more closely what makes the difference between a good argument and a bad argument in Chapter 5, and we will be seeing how to recognize good and bad arguments in Chapter 8. For now, we simply need to acknowledge that just because a statement is offered as a reason, that does not make the statement obviously true, and just because an argument is presented to support a conclusion, that does not mean the conclusion is true.

Key Points in Review

- An "argument" is the attempt to support a claim by offering one or more other claims as support for it.

- Arguments can be used to justify and explain, to evaluate, to explore ideas, to inform, or to persuade.

- Arguments must be distinguished from neutral presentations of information and from non-argumentative forms of persuasion.

- Arguments are built up from premises offered as reasons to support the conclusion of the argument.

- Arguments may have a simple structure, where all the premises connect directly to each other and to the conclusion. Arguments may have a layered structure, using several lines of reasoning.

- Arguments can be expressed indirectly using humour or questions.

- Some arguments will recognize opposing positions by mentioning counter-considerations or composing counter-arguments.

- Reporting arguments clearly and accurately is a constructive contribution to the discussion because it helps more people to become involved.

Chapter 3

Interpretation: Clarity and Uncertainty

■ Perspective

In Chapter 1, you noticed and recorded what you already had around you. In Chapter 2, you saw how to use what you already know and can do in creating and recognizing arguments. The results of both of these observations may generate questions: What exactly does something mean? How are you to interpret it? One of the most important skills in recognizing what we are dealing with is realizing what we don't know for sure. We need to acknowledge our doubts as well as our confidence, what's fuzzy or hidden as well as what's in plain view. In this chapter you will see how to use contextual clues to fine-tune your interpretation—how to clarify meaning and how to keep going even when you are not sure what you are dealing with.

■ Scenario

Your job was increased from part-time on-call to full-time. When it became full-time, you moved closer to work in order to be able to get there on time every day. When you're doing your income tax, you discover that you might qualify for a deduction of your moving expenses if you "moved more than 45 kilometres to take a new job." You moved exactly 45 kilometres, but does your job count as a "new job"? Should you be entitled to this deduction?

■ Key Question

What is the most reasonable interpretation?

Interpretation

When we have recognized that we are not sure what we're seeing, or we're not sure what something means, we also need to take at least the first basic steps to check whether we can settle the uncertainty. Interpretation resolves uncertainty by choosing a meaning that makes sense in the context. Part of interpretation is being properly cautious and recognizing when we can see two or more equally workable interpretations. On occasion, contextual clues will help us choose. Sometimes we will be able to make an educated guess. However, if we have no information that will help us choose among the various options, it is best to investigate further or admit we are stuck.

We've heard someone say, "Stop right there!" but what did he mean—are we to stop what we're doing, or are we to stand still on this spot? How have things developed to this stage, and what might happen next? We're here, but where do we fit in?

Once you've recognized uncertainty, you'll see how you can use **context**—the background and setting against which a communication or other event takes place—and questions to see more clearly what is uncertain and how you might handle it. Is the hat on the washing machine because that was a convenient place to leave it? Should you take it with you? Or is it covering up a bad scratch on the washing machine lid, so you should leave it right where it is? What were we doing when "Stop right there" was yelled? Were we about to throw something on the fire? Were we walking toward a live wire? Was it our action that was the problem, or our position?

Whether our observation is purposeful or open-ended, we must always carefully make note of context. The context must be taken into account because it affects the meaning of the words, gestures, sounds, and images that we've observed.

Is it okay to leave my car here while I dash into the store? I can already see that it looks as if it's safe to park here at the curb, but no other cars are parked in this block. I'd better admit I'm not sure. If there's a post behind me with a sign on it, I'd better go back and check. Perhaps this is residents' parking only; perhaps the curb lane is an express lane in rush hour, with no parking after 3 p.m.

The context includes not only the details we've observed, but also when and where and how we've observed those details. The context includes our goals and our values as well as the observable goals and values of others involved. The context is the background and setting against which a communication takes place; it makes what is being observed unique and yet still part of a larger whole.

For example, when we note that a newspaper article has appeared in *The Globe and Mail* but not the *National Post*, or that a particular hand gesture was in response to being cut off in traffic, we are noting context. We note that the newspaper article may reflect a particular newspaper's priorities, or the hand gesture means something aggressive.

If we are reading or listening to verbal expressions, we must try to understand what is being expressed so we can ultimately evaluate the sentences as being true or false. If you cannot understand a sentence, you cannot determine its accuracy. For example, is it true or false that "Van Gogh was a poor artist"? Before you answer, you need to figure out whether being a "poor artist" means Van Gogh was an incompetent painter, or Van Gogh was impoverished, or Van Gogh is to be pitied. Is it true or false that "people are sensible"? It's not even clear what this means, so we don't know what to look for in deciding what is true or false.

Interpretation is also needed to decide on our own role in a situation. Part of understanding a situation is recognizing the nature of our task. Why are we involved? Why do we need to think about this at all?

Interpretation in context involves

- clarifying the meaning of words, gestures, and feelings
- clarifying what the task is

When we have interpreted our observations in context, we are in a position to know what we will need to investigate further, which will be the next step in the reasoning cycle.

Interpreting in General: The Principle of Charity

We've spoken so far as if it's quite easy to identify what we see, hear, and read. Unfortunately, it is not always easy, not even when we allow the context to guide us.

The **principle of charity** should be a guiding principle in interpreting claims and arguments in general.

Why Use the Principle of Charity?

> **DEFINITION**
>
> When there is more than one possible interpretation of a word, phrase, gesture, or claim, you should use the interpretation that makes the best sense of the word, phrase, gesture, or claim given the context. When more than one interpretation of an argument is possible, the **principle of charity** requires that you use the interpretation that makes the argument the strongest and most reasonable.

The principle of charity expresses exactly the key principle we want to follow in clarifying meaning: we want to narrow the areas of uncertainty where we can, and we also want to recognize where we still aren't sure and will need more information. The principle of charity is a way of ensuring that you are approaching the situation in a fair and open-minded way. You basically give other people involved the benefit of the doubt—unless the context (for example, past history) gives you good reason not to. So, for example, if someone says, "Children love to stay up late," you interpret them as meaning "Most children love to stay up late" because it is obviously false that all children love to stay up late. If someone mistakenly uses the wrong word, but the correct word is clear from the context, the person should be interpreted as if he or she had used the correct word. If you are having a pleasant conversation with someone who points at something with her middle finger, the principle of charity ensures you do not immediately interpret the gesture as an insult.

Part of interpretation is being properly cautious and recognizing when you can see two or more equally workable interpretations. On occasion, you will have contextual clues that will help you choose. Sometimes you will be able to make an educated guess. However, if you have no information that will help you choose among the various options, it is best to investigate further or admit you are stuck.

The principle of charity does not mean that you always choose the most favourable interpretation. For example, imagine that you are a teacher or a parent who wants to know if a child has done today's homework, so you ask, "Have you done your homework?" The child replies, "No, I haven't finished it yet." The sentence could be true in a wide variety of situations, including when the child is almost finished—and, at the opposite extreme, when the child hasn't even begun. The principle of charity does not expect you to give the child the benefit of the doubt, letting you assume that the homework's almost done and you have no reason for concern. In the context, you know the child and the child's work habits. You can make an educated guess as to whether the child is almost done, partway through, or not even started. You can ask the appropriate follow-up question: "How much do you still have to do?"

Clarifying the Meaning of Words

In Chapter 2, we looked at how to recognize arguments and distinguish between premises and conclusions. In order to understand the argument fully, it is often important to check what a word, a phrase, or a sentence is intended to mean in the context in which it is used.

In disagreements about meaning, the disputed word, phrase, or sentence will almost always have an accessible dictionary meaning, but that dictionary definition is usually too **abstract**—that is, removed from particular and specific examples—for us to see how to interpret it in the specific context. The definition may involve concepts we understand—"love," "busy," "important"—but it doesn't connect these concepts clearly enough to what we are expected to observe around us. Will we know it when we see it? For example, you're sitting at the computer, but you're not even looking at the screen. You're staring off into space. Can I ask you something or are you busy? What counts as "busy"? What we understand in the abstract and what we recognize in the here and now have to be linked before we can fully understand a situation or take action.

We must have a clear understanding of what a sentence means because when we reach the stage of evaluating information and arguments we will have to decide whether the sentence is acceptable. If it has no clear meaning, it is **vague**, or imprecise—we won't be able to see how the argument works at all. If it has more than one meaning, it is **ambiguous**—there will be two or more ways that the argument might work, and we'd have to consider both. If the sentence uses controversial or offensive vocabulary, it is employing **loaded words**—words which convey a problematic or offensive message.

When faced with sentences that are vague or ambiguous or use loaded terms, look to the context to see whether you can clarify the meaning of the words. If the meaning cannot be clarified, you should note the lack of clarity and investigate the meaning further by doing some research, speaking with others, or presenting reasons for adopting one interpretation rather than another. If there are two or more equally plausible interpretations of a claim, both should be investigated for acceptability and relevance to the argument.

The bottom line is that if you are faced with a sentence that is unclear, you should not immediately shrug your shoulders and give up. You should not simply assume that the lack of clarity means the acceptability of the claim made in the sentence is just a matter of opinion. As a reasoner, you need to approach unclear sentences by recognizing the source of the lack of clarity, checking the context for clues to the meaning, and ultimately deciding if there are numerous possible meanings that must be discussed and investigated.

Vagueness

Vague words and sentences do not provide us with clear enough or detailed enough information for our purposes. When a word or phrase is vague, we are not sure what the word or phrase really means in the context.

Awareness of context is essential when interpreting verbal expression because a sentence that is vague in one context may be acceptably precise in a different context. For example, if we are fellow students (but virtual strangers) and happen to be waiting for the same bus, I might casually ask you, "So, how are you doing in Math 100?" You reply, "I'm doing quite well." Given the context, that answer would probably not be too vague. If I'm just expressing general interest to get a sense of whether you are finding the course hard or easy, that answer would be precise enough given the context.

On the other hand, if we are sitting in an admissions office where I am interviewing you for admission to a program that requires Math 100 and I need to have the exact grades that you've received in the math class, then your answer would be too vague for that context. The answer "I'm doing quite well" is imprecise, given the goal of having an accurate record of your grades.

When we use abstract words or phrases, like "kindness" or "a fair chance," we can be vague even when we think we know the meaning of the words or phrases. We may understand the concept of kindness or a fair chance well enough, but we may not entirely understand how to apply these concepts. Was it kind of the boss to let you have the day off, or was it only standard practice for this business? Did you have a fair chance to get a ticket for a show if people have been lining up for the tickets all night but you work nights and couldn't join them? The problem arises when we cannot agree on how to apply the word or phrase to particular cases, even though we think we understand it—and, indeed, agree on its dictionary meaning. Is it true that "there are only a million people living in poverty in Canada"? We will not be able to decide whether this statement is true until we agree on what "living in poverty" means. Until we agree on what counts as "poverty," we do not know whom to place in the category. In a context in which "poverty" has already been defined—for example, as having an annual income below

$20,000—this sentence would not be vague. However, if there has been no previous agreement as to the meaning of "poverty," we could find the wording too imprecise to evaluate.

Abstract terms such as "cruelty," "abuse," or "cheating" are problematic in exactly this way. We can agree that pulling the wings off flies is cruel, that chaining a child to a bed is abusive, and that having an affair with another person while swearing absolute fidelity to one's spouse is cheating. But difficulties arise in the less obvious cases. Is it cruel to withhold a promised treat? Is it abusive to spank a child in public? Is it cheating to have lunch with an ex-girlfriend and then kiss her goodbye? When we disagree on terms, we are also going to disagree on what we can conclude: should the parent who spanks a child in public be treated as an abuser? The context should affect how you answer these questions and thus how you interpret the crucial word. For example, how you answer these questions may vary depending on whether you are asking them from the perspective of a social worker, a police officer, or a friend.

The context includes details of the particular situation. If the statement is being made in response to a particular set of circumstances, those details can affect whether the word is too vague for it to be reasonable for us to accept or reject the statement.

Is it cruel to withhold a promised treat when the child has misbehaved, or when the child has behaved perfectly but you cannot afford the treat, or when you think it is funny that you fooled your child?

Is it cheating to have lunch with an ex-girlfriend and then kiss her goodbye when your current partner has told you it offends her when you do so, or when your ex-girlfriend has just told you she's getting married, or when your ex-girlfriend has just told you she has cancer?

Another source of vagueness is not indicating how general we mean a sentence to be. When we say, "Mother bears attack if you get too near their young," we might mean that this is an absolute law—any time you get too close to a bear cub, the mother will definitely attack you—or we might mean that it is probable but not inevitable. It is what you should expect, though it doesn't always happen. The problem is a lack of "quantifiers" in the sentence. A **quantifier** is a word that tells you "how much." The expression is vague because it could mean "all mother bears" or "most mother bears." "All" and "most" are quantifiers that indicate how many bears you mean. Without interpreting which quantifier was intended, we cannot say whether the sentence is true or false.

A more complicated example is "Anyone who is worried about polluting the environment by driving twenty kilometres to work can always ride a bike instead." This sounds as if it might mean "all people who worry about polluting the environment" could ride bikes, yet we know there are many people who drive but who could not possibly cycle twenty kilometres no matter how fit they are. So perhaps it means "Most people could become fit enough to cycle twenty kilometres." However, there is another possible meaning, especially if we know the speaker actually does cycle that distance— it might just mean "I do it, so it can be done" and have the effect of indicating that people would rather complain about the problems of driving than actually do what it takes to reduce car usage.

Again, context will affect whether the use of abstract terms is too vague to be analyzed as truthful or as giving you the information you need to respond reasonably.

Ambiguity

A sentence, phrase, or word is ambiguous when it has more than one meaning. Note that the difference between ambiguity and vagueness is that the ambiguous sentence is not imprecise. Instead it gives us a choice of two (and sometimes more) possible interpretations.

When we say, "You can have ice cream or pie," we might mean you can have only one of the two, or we might mean you can have both if you want to. "Or" can mean "one but not the other" and it can mean "at least one and maybe both." It is not always clear from the context which we mean. If your host says, "Would you like ice cream or pie?" you cannot assume you could have both—perhaps there isn't enough to go round if everyone has both.

Another example is "These days, non-steroidal anti-inflammatory drugs (NSAIDs) are what doctors use first for migraine headaches" (Making Migraines 1). This is ambiguous. Does it mean that doctors themselves prefer NSAIDs for their own migraine headaches, or does it mean they prescribe NSAIDs as the first choice for their patients? It could mean either one, since we know that often an advertisement will encourage us to choose a medication because doctors use it themselves. We need to know that doctors do prescribe NSAIDs for their patients before we interpret this as a recommendation.

There are many examples of ambiguous sentences that are used deliberately, usually to create a funny misunderstanding. For example, this exchange came in a recent Austin Powers movie:

"How dare you break wind before me!"
"Sorry. I didn't know it was your turn."

Usually, a careful look at context can resolve ambiguity in sentences. For example, in a restaurant you are often asked if you'd prefer soup or salad. Given the context, we can safely interpret the sentence as meaning that we must choose one dish and cannot have both.

What we need to be particularly aware of are cases in which ambiguity leads to genuine lack of clarity and cases in which the ambiguous word is hidden and relied on in an argument. For example, "The patient complained about pains last night." This sentence is ambiguous because it is unclear whether the patient complained last night or complained today about last night's pains. The difference in interpretation may make a difference to what the pain indicates.

Again, we must look at context to see if we can resolve the ambiguity using the principle of charity. If we cannot clarify the sentence, the ambiguity and both of its possible meanings should be noted.

Problems Caused by Ambiguity: Equivocation

We will be looking at mistakes in reasoning in Chapter 5 and Chapter 8. For now, notice that ambiguity in arguments is one source of faulty reasoning. **Equivocation** occurs when the bad reasoning in an argument is hidden because an ambiguous term is used in two different senses in the same argument. The same word is used in one sense in one premise and in a different sense in a different premise or conclusion.

For example, consider the following argument:

1. All killing of human beings is wrong.
2. Abortion is the killing of a human being.
3. Abortion is wrong.

Compare that challenging example to the following simpler example.

1. Avril Lavigne is cool.
2. All cool things have a temperature below 20°C.
3. Avril Lavigne has a temperature below 20°C.

In the simple example, the word "cool" is used differently in premises 1 and 2, and we can see that it's at best a joke to move from the combination of 1 and 2 to the conclusion 3. In the first, challenging example, the ambiguity is much more subtle.

It has been argued that the argument on abortion uses "human being" in two different senses. In the second premise the phrase "human being" is used in the sense of creatures of a certain biological type who possess a particular type of DNA. In the first premise, "human being" is used to indicate a certain moral status rather than a biological status.

Is this the only interpretation possible? Of course not. We would need to discuss which interpretation makes best sense, and why. In the abortion debate, and in debates about many other issues such as euthanasia, same-sex marriage, and intelligent design, interpretation of the key words and phrases is a significant challenge that deserves considerable attention. When we interpret unclear claims or even when we interpret claims *as* unclear, we must defend our interpretations by presenting reasons. This, in turn, allows others to engage in debate by presenting different interpretations with different reasons. Reasoning about interpretation is a significant part of many disciplines in the humanities, such as philosophy, literature, theatre, and anthropology.

Loaded Words

The choice of a word can cause offence or reveal attitudes that generate an additional argument, if the listener interprets the word differently than the speaker or if the listener disagrees with an assumption implied by the word. When a choice of words reveals a debatable or dubious assumption or attempts to persuade you to believe or do something without presenting an argument, we call that word "loaded." The exact meaning, or "unloaded" meaning, of the term must be determined in the context.

For example, can I "help" you with the housework when we both live in the house? Even if I agree that the task needs doing and that I should do it, we may get into a separate argument about whether I am revealing dubious attitudes just because I used the word "help." Some people will say that using the word "help" implies that the task is really yours to do and that I think I'm graciously giving assistance I don't have to provide. But if sharing the house means that we share responsibility for keeping it clean, then I do have to do the work: "help" may not be the right word for me to use.

Word choices that raise the issue of dubious assumptions can often qualify as ambiguous or vague. What makes a loaded word unusual is the hidden assumption the word may or may not reveal, the emotional impact of the word, and the fact that loaded words are often used to try to persuade you to believe a claim without actually presenting you with good reasons to believe it.

One of the reasons we are cautious in interpreting loaded terms is because they are often forms of non-argumentative persuasion. The use of loaded language can push us into doing or believing something without presenting us with good reasons or any reasons at all. Before we react too strongly, we need to be able to separate the psychological impact of the wording from the information. We do not want to be misled by our reaction to word choice. We need to distinguish between persuasive language that merely indicates the speaker's own preferences or feelings—a legitimate expression of his or her emotions— and strong language that tries to take the place of reason by pressuring the reader or listener into agreement simply through the evocative force of the words used.

Consider, for example, the difference between saying, "Those park guards are just like Nazis, the way they push you out of the park at sunset" and saying, "The government of Slobodan Milosevic acted just like the Nazis in trying to eliminate a whole category of people in Kosovo," referring to the mass killings of ethnic Albanians. Both statements invite you to share the speaker's disgust, but only the second one is a fair comparison and therefore a legitimate use of persuasion. Typically, a comparison to repressive regimes, notorious dictators, criminal acts, or morally repugnant acts is justified only when the item compared should indeed be viewed and treated just as severely because it shares precisely the offensive features that come to mind when we think of what it has been compared to.

At the opposite extreme, we get attempts to persuade that are based on vague and high-sounding ideas evoking a positive emotion but with no real grounds for it. Consider, for example, a company boss telling you there's a "bold new partnership" in the works, or a politician saying a new mental health policy will give people who have mental illnesses their "rightful place in society." Sounds wonderful. What does it mean? Listen to a speech delivered with enough enthusiasm and you'll feel warm and fuzzy, perhaps even uplifted. But should you? What is the partnership, and what exactly is bold or new about it? What is the new mental health policy, and what place in society is assured for people with mental illnesses? These great ideas stand or fall on their substance, not on our happy feelings.

To see if you are being presented with persuasive or coercive language, one test is to replace the dubious terms with neutral terms. For instance, we might replace "handicapped" with "in a wheelchair" or "legally blind," a term that describes more neutrally the person's actual condition. If we still agree with the reasoning when it is expressed in neutral terms, then we can take it seriously. We will look more closely at appeals to emotion in Chapter 9. During the interpretation stage, in spite of the strong, and sometimes undesirable, impact of emotional, persuasive, or coercive language, we do not generally criticize the choice of expression—unless

- concepts have been misused—for example, "He's stealing from the company" when all that's meant is "He was half an hour late back from lunch" (and is supposedly "stealing" that half hour's wages), or

- we cannot follow the meaning because it isn't clear what it applies to—for example, "bold new partnership" or "rightful place in society."

Loaded words are often euphemisms or dysphemisms. A **euphemism** is a positive expression used in the place of a neutral or negative expression. A **dysphemism** is a negative expression used in the place of a neutral or positive expression. For example, a person fighting a current government can be called a freedom fighter (euphemism) or a terrorist (dysphemism). When we try to clarify the meaning of loaded words, our goal is to understand a sentence well enough to be able to decide if it is true or false. It can be very difficult to decide whether a sentence is true or false when it uses a loaded word.

For example, is it true or false that "the freedom fighters who destroyed the World Trade Center buildings on 9/11 flew airplanes into the buildings"? Before deciding whether the sentence is true or false, it needs to be clarified. If you accept the sentence as true, does that mean that you agree the people who destroyed the World Trade Center were freedom fighters? One way to resolve this type of problem is to clarify the sentence by turning it into two sentences.

1. The people who destroyed the World Trade Center buildings on 9/11 were freedom fighters.

2. The people who destroyed the World Trade Center buildings on 9/11 flew airplanes into the buildings.

By turning the single sentence into two simple sentences, you have clarified that there is a loaded word hiding within the first simple sentence. Now you are free to see that the two sentences may not both be true: the second may be true while the first may be false.

EXERCISE 3.1

Resolving Vagueness and Ambiguity

Are any of the following sentences unclear? If so, identify the source of the lack of clarity. If there is more than one possible meaning, state the possible meanings.

*1. When politicians have debates they are just playing games.

*2. They hunt for criminals with no remorse.

*3.   My husband is babysitting our children tonight.

4.   Children love to be tossed in the air and tickled.

5.   Short-answer questions should be answered in no more than one or two paragraphs.

6.   Tax accountant: What was your annual income?

Client: I did well this year. I made more than $80,000.

7.   Sam is the nerd who runs the computer club at the local high school.

8.   Ignorance maintains the cycle of poverty.

9.   "There's a little McDonald's in everyone."—TV ad for McDonald's restaurants

10.   The Olympic long jumper takes his jump and is short.

Problems of Definition

In order to clarify expressions that are vague or ambiguous or that contain loaded words, we often need to find a clear definition for the words or phrases that are the source of the problem.

Limitations of Dictionary Definitions

Dictionaries are of limited use in this clarifying process. A dictionary may seem like a good place to start when you are involved in a dispute over the meaning of a word. However, dictionaries only report what the word normally means; if there is more than one typical usage of the word, each meaning is reported in the dictionary. As a result, dictionaries are not helpful when what is at issue is whether the word can be extended to cover a new situation or what two words mean in combination.

For example, consider the expression, "good grief," mentioned in Chapter 2 as one of the expressions included in a dictionary definition of "good." Your dictionary might not include this expression—it's not very common in Canada. If you try to figure out what it means by looking up "good" and "grief" separately, you won't find it easy to figure out. "Good" is favourable, effective, sufficient, and so on. "Grief" is sorrow, distress, feelings of loss, mourning, and so on. How can you have "favourable or sufficient feelings of distress and loss"? "Good grief" is simply an expression of surprise or dismay. The word "good" here might even be like "good" in expressions like "goodbye"—a way of saying "God," as in "God be with you" (goodbye) or "God's grief" (good grief).

The limitation of a dictionary definition is that it does not show us which real things or situations will fall within that definition. What can be described as "good"? If what is good is anything "promoting health, welfare, or happiness," what actually does promote health, welfare, or happiness? Would a low-carb diet count? If to be "good" is to be "virtuous," then what is it to be virtuous? Would I be virtuous if I told the truth about not having bothered to do my homework?

From Abstract to Concrete

To deal with most problems of definition we need to find a way to move accurately from the abstract to the concrete. We need to understand what the arguer might mean by the word so we can see how the argument is intended to work. We will also need to question that meaning when we evaluate the argument, in order to decide whether it is reasonable to apply the word to particular cases and examples; then we can see if we agree with the way in which the arguer uses the word.

It is not enough to formulate a general definition that seems to cover what's being said. The definition itself may contain expressions as unclear as those in the original, or the words may be stretched to cover situations beyond their usual application.

We also need to use one of the most effective ways to analyze a concept: looking for examples that we can picture. When the meaning of a word is in dispute, the clearest route to agreement about meaning is to see if we can agree on at least some real, concrete examples to which the word can definitely be applied.

For instance, a concrete example of sexism is refusing to hire women for firefighting positions even when they have qualifications equal to those of male applicants. Similarly, a clear case of cheating is copying a fellow student's original essay word for word and then handing it in with the name changed to your own.

Specific examples help us to see what is normally meant by the word or phrase. We can then determine the limits of its application by looking for examples that are similar in some ways, but to which it cannot be applied.

For instance, it is not sexist to refuse to hire a woman for a face-shaving commercial: women don't grow beards of the right texture to demonstrate the effectiveness of blades or shaving foam. Similarly, it is not cheating to quote other people's ideas in an essay if you give proper credit to the person who originated each idea you quote.

Then, to establish if the words and phrases are being used appropriately in the context we are concerned with, we check if they apply equally well to the examples or situations being described.

For example, let's say that as part of an argument you have read the sentence "A person who kills an animal for food when other food is available commits murder." The meaning of this sentence is not entirely clear. The sentence is not vague because it is not imprecise, but the word "murder" is either being used as a loaded term to generate a particular effect or may be ambiguous if there are different meanings of the word "murder." A competent English speaker will generally understand the word "murder" and might not usually think of it as having more than one meaning. But "murder" is being used in an unusual way in this sentence and we need to think about the definition of the word before the sentence can be interpreted.

How we understand this sentence and whether we agree with it turns on the definition of "murder." Again, we can start by looking in the dictionary. The *Longman Dictionary of Contemporary English* defines murder as

1. the crime of killing a man unlawfully; 2. pointless death especially caused by carelessness; 3. a very difficult or trying experience. Notice how different the third definition is from the other two. You can clearly see here how the dictionary does not solve all our problems with meaning.

We now know what the possible common uses are for the word "murder," but we still need to consider the context: this author's intended meaning. What could the author of the sentence mean by "murder"? What is the best way to interpret that use of the word given the context of the rest of the sentence? Using the principle of charity, we wouldn't say that the author meant that killing an animal was the crime of killing a man unlawfully or a difficult or trying experience. Perhaps the second definition works. "Murder" in this context might mean a pointless death. But it also seems to have other connotations.

What are some central examples of murder that we can agree on? We can probably agree that a robber who kills a bank teller in the middle of a robbery commits murder. We can also agree that a person who is minding her own business and then is randomly killed is also murdered. We might think that lawful killings such as deaths caused by war or state executions are murder. One element that all these examples have in common is that the killing is morally wrong and the killing involves people. In the context of the original sentence, we are reasonably sure it is a loaded word. "Murder" is being used to express outrage. In that case, the sentence would be interpreted as "A person who kills an animal for food when other food is available commits a morally wrong act on a par with the wrongful killing of a human being."

Our application of the principle of charity has helped us narrow down the possible meanings. Our exploration of concrete examples has helped us unpack the loaded word to find its neutral equivalent.

Clarifying General Concepts with Specific Examples: Exploratory Definitions

Even after investigation, we may still not be sure how the use of a word or phrase affects the acceptability of what is being said. As with the concept of "murder" discussed above, whole arguments may stand or fall on what is really meant by the key terms used.

For example, should same-sex couples have the same benefits as opposite-sex couples? Legislation permits this in Canada and in the Netherlands, but in 2004 the United Nations was sharply divided over whether that applied to same-sex couples working for the United Nations. Normally, United Nations employees who live in partnerships legally recognized by their home country do receive family benefits for their partners. The disagreement between member nations focused on the definition of a "family." Some countries considered that paying benefits to the same-sex spouse of a United Nations employee was an indirect way of legitimizing same-sex marriage. The countries that oppose same-sex marriage in principle claim that only heterosexual marriages create a "family." Are they correct? The United Nations had not as a whole discussed this issue. If they did, how could they decide? Again, they would have to examine what is important to each nation about a "family" and how well it fits the various patterns of love, dependence, and living together that we see around us.

Any definition of family that claims to be "traditional" or "historical" but restricts itself to a man and a woman or two parents and their children overlooks other traditions and historical meanings. Muslim traditions permit one man to have up to four wives. So do some African traditions, including a tradition in which a man symbolically marries his brother's wives if his brother dies, so that the wives are guaranteed support. In other traditions, grandparents are as central to the family as parents; one woman may have several husbands; the mother's brother may be more important in raising the children than their biological father. In some periods of time in Europe, "family" meant the blood relatives and the unrelated servants—the entire household.

Definitions of terms like "family" or "marriage" may vary according to the dispute they are expected to resolve. For example, between 1992 and 2002, disputes about the rights of same-sex couples shifted from an emphasis on the right to equal benefits under the law to an emphasis on equal access to marriage. To see how the definition of family can vary according to the context, try a quick mental exercise. First, list the people you would count as members of your family in the sense that you are related to them by blood or legalities. This is your family in genealogical terms—your kinship, in anthropological terms. Now think about who you would want put on the list to visit you in hospital if you were seriously ill and you could be visited by family members only. This is your family in the sense of "the people who are most concerned about you, the people you count as your support system." On this list, you might actually want to include friends who are not related to you by blood or marriage but who have become closer and more important to you than some of your relatives. They feel like family. For many of us, our lists will not be the same in both cases. Our own definition of family does not even necessarily centre on who is married to whom.

Consequently, any attempt to single out one definition of family and put it forward as the real or traditional one will not succeed unless it can show why one definition should win out over all others in contemporary society. This doesn't mean we cannot settle the question or decide what our laws should be. It just means that we must debate which definition makes best sense in the circumstances. No definition from any single dictionary, religion, culture, or historical source will be enough by itself to stop debate.

To limit problems caused by definitions, testimony in court is required to be specific and concrete rather than abstract. When we rely on what was actually observed, without interpreting it, we ensure that we are not being misled by a difference in interpretation of abstract terms. "The car was being driven very dangerously." Does that mean the car was swerving all over the road or just that it was travelling ten kilometres per hour over the speed limit? Perhaps the speaker is a driver who considers the speed limits already too high for safety. "The driver was tailgating the car ahead of it, and when he swung out to pass on the right, he nearly struck the car coming up in that lane." This concrete description makes it clear what we might have seen at the scene, and it allows us to decide independently whether the driving was dangerous or not. The careful observations described in Chapter 1 help us report without relying on controversial definitions.

As we contemplate questions of how to decide on a reasonable definition, we also face the issue of whose voices must be counted. We are often happy to accept a "majority" decision, and so we are correspondingly concerned when only a "minority" is in favour of something. But who is in the minority? Ethnic and religious groups who oppose same-sex marriage object to Canadian law and social practice being driven by a minority, usually meaning the minority of Canadians who are gay or lesbian. The implication is that everyone else is part of a majority that either opposes same-sex marriage or whose members have no need of it themselves. However, we might define minority and majority here on the basis of opinion rather than personal need. It may be a minority of Canadians who strongly oppose same-sex marriage for any reason, and a majority of Canadians who either approve of it or don't mind one way or the other.

Let's look at one example in more detail. A great deal hangs on the definition of "terrorism" today. How many terrorists are operating in Canada? How do we define the term clearly enough so we know whom to count in? News media have to be very careful when they choose to describe an act as a terrorist act or a person as a terrorist. As the saying has it, and as we saw earlier when discussing loaded words, "One man's terrorist is another man's freedom fighter." Is terrorism defined by the acts the person commits, or by whether the person supports a political cause? One definition of terrorism is "the deliberate targeting of civilians in pursuit of a political goal" (Spector A17). Another states that terrorists are "groups or individuals who use violence against the innocent public, or the threat of it, to achieve political ends. . . . We do not use this term to describe raids on military and police personnel or installations" (Spector A17).

To think about how we might decide when it is legitimate to use the word "terrorism," it helps to look at specific examples, especially examples that are not part of any current controversy. Consider an example that is not too close to home. In Kenya in the 1950s, the Mau Mau campaigned to win their land back from control by the British. In the course of their campaign, they forced members of their own tribes to swear binding oaths of loyalty. Failure to swear allegiance to the Mau Mau was punishable by killing cattle—their source of wealth—or by death. Many of their own people died because they resisted. A number of white settlers were also killed, in some cases by trusted servants who had been compelled to join a cause they did not believe in. Eventually, Kenya became an independent nation, and a man who had been imprisoned for allegedly having a leadership role in the Mau Mau, Jomo Kenyatta, became the country's president, well-respected by whites and blacks. Were the Mau Mau terrorists or were they freedom fighters? How you decide this case will help you see which elements of this particular situation have influenced your choice. In turn, this should help you see which elements would help you decide other cases.

We want to defy terrorists, no matter their cause, but we might support freedom fighters, depending on their methods. You can see the power of a definition—who is going to count as a terrorist? How will that affect Canada's approach to dealing with people such as the Air-India bombers, who were linked to the campaign to create a separate Sikh homeland in India, or Canadians known to have contact with al-Qaeda, the organization that claimed responsibility for destroying the World Trade Center in New York on September 11, 2001? You can see the usefulness of concrete examples. We can compare the campaign to create a separate Sikh homeland in India with other struggles for local or national independence. We might look at the Mau Mau, or at the FLQ, the Front de libération du Québec, which was responsible for kidnappings and a murder in the 1970s, or at the IRA, the Irish Republican Army, which carried on an active campaign of bombings in Ireland and in England. We can compare the cause and the methods of al-Qaeda with the Taliban, the religious leadership that ran Afghanistan according to strict Islamic law, or with the Mormon group that runs the community of Bountiful, B.C., on polygamist principles.

The key idea here is that definitions are not just opinions and not just objective records of common usage. Definitions have powerful implications for attitudes and actions. A comparable example of the struggle to define fairly words that carry powerful implications is the challenge of defining "genocide." If we count a massive loss of life as genocide, it carries the connotation that it is a crime against humanity, not legitimate warfare, and other countries should step in. Canadian General Roméo Dallaire was unable to persuade the United Nations that what he was seeing in Rwanda in 1994 was genocide, yet in the years afterward, the massacres in Rwanda became regarded as a clear example of genocide. New, more than a decade later, the example of Rwanda could help decide if the deaths in the Darfur region of Sudan count as genocide that calls for international intervention or simply as a humanitarian crisis, which calls for more effort by international aid agencies.

By dealing with specific comparisons, we have the best chance of seeing where we can most helpfully draw the boundaries that determine our response.

EXERCISE **3.2**

Constructing Definitions with Examples

How would you define each of the following terms? Give several concrete examples to illustrate your definition, including at least one example where you do not think the term can be correctly applied. In the first two exercises, would you agree with the interpretation given to the word in the quote provided?

*1. *Accident:* Writing about accidents in which young drivers or their passengers have been killed, Paul Willcocks says, "We need to quit calling car crashes 'accidents.' That implies an act of fate or external force. In every case police have investigated, the crash was no accident. It happened because of a choice someone made, a mistake in judgment or performance" (Willcocks C6).

2. *Stealing:* Writing about shopping carts used by homeless people to push their belongings with them, Bob Thompson writes, "Every cart that you see discarded on boulevards, parked in driveways, played with by children, or put to general purpose use, has cost the store about $200 each. . . . When

you take a cart home from the store, without the store's permission, in the eyes of the law you are stealing" (Thompson).

3. *News:* It's not uncommon to claim that some things "aren't news" in the sense that they don't deserve space in newspapers or on television broadcasts. Examples of the items people object to include reports of movie stars' dating or breakups, and reports of car accidents.

4. *Employable:* Who should count as employable if welfare or disability benefits are to be provided only to people who are not employable?

5. *Terrorist:* How should the law distinguish terrorists from people who commit other crimes with similar methods, such as arson, blackmail, kidnapping, or murder?

6. *Family member:* Who would be included in the family if a major inheritance is to be divided equally among the members of the family?

Practice in Interpretation: Understanding Claims

As a step toward clarifying meaning and revealing where we need to investigate further, we will expand what we have just done with words to examine sentences. One common feature of arguments is the use of claims and generalizations that may or may not be clear, and may or may not be accurate. When we clarify the meaning of "Van Gogh was a poor artist," it is the single word "poor" that needs exploring. When we clarify the sentence "People are thoughtful," it is the whole sentence that needs to be interpreted. A sentence like this usually is intended to mean "All people are thoughtful," "Most people are thoughtful," or "Some people are thoughtful," but we don't know which is meant without more interpretation of the context.

What Job Is the Claim Intended to Do?

As you read or listen to people, some sentences may stand out as claims you need to clarify. These will be claims you are not sure you would or should accept. One type of sentence that often causes us to react automatically is a **generalization**—a claim about groups of people, things, events, or characteristics. Think of the rules and laws that you are expected to live with: for example, "No one can get a loan for more than thirty percent of his or her total income"; "No refunds will be given without a receipt." Think also of the truisms that are quoted to you, such as "If it ain't broke, don't fix it" and "If it's worth doing, it's worth doing well." And think of the blunt statements that people put forward in arguments: for example, "Children should be in the custody of their natural parents wherever possible"; "People who make themselves sick should have to pay for their treatment"; "Anyone over eighty is too old to drive safely"; "No fish, no future."

These kinds of statements should make us want to clarify what is intended. We are quick to react when we think a rule is not fair or should not apply to our particular situation—but we might not be right, so we should check first. What does the rule intend to achieve, and is our own situation a legitimate exception?

Expectations

We need first to clarify what force the claim is intended to have. Some claims are meant to work like absolute rules. They assert that something must happen. Examples are rules of games, legal regulations, and "laws" of nature. For example, "If you hand your paper in late, it will not be accepted" is a rule. "If you fail to submit your payment or Notice of Dispute of a Violation Ticket, you are automatically deemed guilty of the offence described on the front of the ticket and the full ticketed amount is due and payable immediately" is a legal specification of how your ticket will be dealt with. "If you let go of that glass, it will fall" is a "law" of nature—the law of gravity. For all these types of claims, the expected force is that we are guaranteeing what will happen. There will be no escape. They are meant to show exactly what will happen in *every* case to which they apply, and for that reason they are often called universal claims. A **universal claim** is a claim about all members of a category.

In contrast, other claims are predictive in force. They don't try to guarantee a particular result, but they do claim to show how likely a particular outcome is. These are non-universal claims, because they acknowledge ahead of time that there may be exceptions. A **non-universal claim** is a claim about some but not all members of a category. For example, "Bears can move faster than I can" is best interpreted as a non-universal claim. The speaker does not usually intend to assert that you'll never find a single really slow bear or an injured bear who can't move at all, let alone move faster than the speaker.

Non-universal claims are usually claims about the way the world is, and they can indicate how probable an occurrence is, from "almost certain" to "highly unlikely." For example, "One in five new drivers, regardless of age, is involved in a crash within their first two years on the road." This claim doesn't indicate that all, or even almost all, new drivers will have an accident, and it certainly doesn't guarantee that every new driver will have an accident. It says only that based on past evidence one in five (twenty percent) of new drivers will have at least one accident within two years of getting a licence.

Not all claims are immediately clear in their force. For example, section 7 of the *Canadian Charter of Rights and Freedoms* says, "Everyone . . . has the right to life, liberty, and security of the person." In 1985, the Supreme Court of Canada had to examine the meaning of this sentence in deciding whether one man, Harbhajan Singh, had been fairly denied refugee status in Canada. To decide this, they had to decide whether "everyone" as used in section 7 of the *Charter* meant "every Canadian citizen," or "every person legally present in Canada," or "every human being" (Dixon and Bryden A23).

When a claim is still not clear in its force, we recognize that we are uncertain and we stay open to further investigation and argument.

Clarifying a Claim

Interpretation in general usually moves us toward investigation, as we realize we need more information than we have now to help us answer the questions raised by our observations and our initial attempts at interpretation. These questions of interpretation also happen with our own writing, especially when we are trying to craft an argument (as in the scenario from Chapter 2).

Again, claims provide a useful illustration. Can I say, "If an action is good, it brings benefits to someone"? Am I sure what I mean by that, and do I think it is always true or most often true? We sometimes find a claim obviously meaningful and acceptable because we have not fully recognized that there are problems with its interpretation. We sometimes don't even stop to think about what it means to say something like "If it's worth doing, it's worth doing well" because the sentence resonates so quickly and completely with our sense of duty and our desire to take pride in what we do. But problems with ambiguity, vagueness, and loaded words in general should alert us to the need to be a bit more cautious about what it means for something to be "worth doing" and what exactly is the standard for "doing well." Even when we know what we mean by "doing well," we still don't know whether we must always do well. Much as we want to do well, might we find ourselves losing sight of our priorities by putting too much energy into the wrong tasks?

This kind of problem in interpretation expands on what we did earlier with definitions, using specific examples to see when we would and would not apply the terms "family" and "terrorist." The problem in deciding whether a claim can meaningfully be applied to a particular situation is that we are not typically good at spotting exceptions. When you hear something that sounds like a generalization, a natural first reaction is to find yourself agreeing, because your first thoughts usually fit with the claim: you see where it could be true.

For instance, when you hear "People who make themselves sick should have to pay for their treatment," you might think of skiers who ski out of bounds, injure themselves, and need to be rescued, or smokers who know they should quit but don't, or motorists who don't wear seat belts. These people cause rescue and health-care costs that they could easily have prevented. But we can't stop there. All we know at this point is that the claim *could be* true. At this point, we don't even know if the claim was intended universally—all people who make themselves sick should have to pay for their treatment—or whether it was intended non-universally—there could be some exceptions, but in most cases people who make themselves sick should have to pay for their treatment. We don't even know what kinds of cases are being grouped together as "people who make themselves sick." Perhaps there is an important distinction to be drawn between people who injure themselves in accidents and people who have unhealthy habits such as smoking or overeating.

A good reasoning process will take advantage of our strengths and compensate for our weaknesses. So, to decide whether a claim can meaningfully be applied in a particular case, we might require research, but it is often possible to interpret it just with our existing background knowledge. Again, as in all good reasoning, we start from where we are and see where we need to go.

To interpret the application of universal and non-universal claims, we check how much force they have—that is, are they true in all the situations they claim to be true in? For example, will the professor sometimes accept a late paper in spite of claiming it's a firm rule that late papers will not be accepted? Is the person saying, "Bears can move faster than I can" an Olympic track star who could in fact outrace most bears over a short distance?

Interpreting isolated claims, rules, and inferences in this way is useful preparation for investigating arguments. It will help us see how we test the limits of what is being said, so we can be confident that we understand what is really meant and to what it is intended to apply.

In order for universal, rule-like claims to be true, they must be true in every single case they claim to cover (otherwise they cannot guarantee what will happen). Even one single exception shows that the rule has not been designed or understood properly. If one person gets a late paper accepted, then it isn't really a rule that no late papers are accepted. As soon as one late paper is accepted, we're not quite sure what the real rule is—"Late papers are not accepted without a really, really good excuse"? "Late papers aren't accepted unless the instructor is feeling unusually generous at the time"?

The important thing to notice here is that interpretation of either type of claim does not mean checking every possible case the claim might cover.

There are two basic kinds of examples we look for.

1. **Supporting examples:** examples that are consistent with the claim.
   For example, a late paper that has been refused supports the universal claim that no late papers are accepted, and a bear that's been timed running at twenty kilometres an hour supports the non-universal claim that bears are faster than a human.

2. **Conflicting examples:** examples that are incompatible with the claim.
   For example, a late paper that is accepted is incompatible with the universal claim that no late papers are accepted, and a human athlete who can sprint at twenty kilometres an hour is incompatible with the non-universal claim that bears are faster than humans.

If we already have supporting examples, the claim makes sense—it is at least possibly true. If we already know of conflicting examples, the claim could be possibly false. How we handle conflicting evidence to decide whether the claim can be applied in the given situation will depend on whether the claim is universal—like a rule—or non-universal, like a prediction or probability.

Consider the claim "Dogs make Donna sneeze." First, is this intended as a universal generalization? Does Donna sneeze when she's near any dog, or is she fine near poodles and other dogs that don't shed? To interpret the intention, you need to be able to draw on observations. Who is Donna? Do at least some dogs make Donna sneeze? (If not, the claim is simply not true at all.) Suppose you've seen Donna sneeze when your Shih Tzu was in the room. Now you know the claim is at least potentially true—you have confirming evidence. What you need to do as well is check the likely exceptions, so you can tell if the claim is universal or non-universal. Your most crucial test would be to see if she sneezes when one of the least allergenic dogs is around. If she doesn't, then you know it is not true that all dogs make Donna sneeze, so you know the claim will not work as a universal claim. Even without further investigation, you know you have enough evidence to confirm that "Dogs may make Donna sneeze," and you are now in a position to check for further evidence to see if "Most dogs make Donna sneeze."

Clarifying Universal Claims

For a universal claim, one piece of conflicting evidence is enough to prove the claim is false. If we find an exception, there is something wrong with the claim. Has it been stated too strongly, so it covers more cases than it really should? Should late papers be accepted in exceptional circumstances? Should refunds sometimes be given even when the customer can't produce a receipt? We won't have to check every paper the instructor accepts, just the ones that genuinely were handed in late, and see if any of them was accepted.

To prove a universal claim true, however, we have to be sure there is no conflicting evidence—there are no cases that don't fit—and that does mean checking every possible case that could prove it wrong. We really do have to check every late paper offered to the instructor to see if any one of them was accepted. This would require further investigation of the type we will do in Chapter 4.

However, we don't have to check the papers that were handed in on time—the rule doesn't say exactly what is supposed to happen to them (we assume they get marked) so we don't need to worry about them.

Sometimes, we can test universal claims by interpretation alone, just by doing "thought experiments"—we can see if we can think of a case where an instructor could hardly refuse a late paper, or we ask the instructor how he or she would handle what we think are the most challenging cases. What about a student who was in hospital on the due date for the paper, for example? We may be able to see by reason alone whether a rule will break down in some circumstances.

Note that finding *apparently* conflicting examples isn't quite sufficient by itself to show the rule is false—we also have to check that the example really does conflict. We have to see if there are any possible exceptions, and then we have to see whether these exceptions are legitimate—are they genuine examples of where the rule breaks down? Again, this is a question of interpretation.

"The exception proves the rule" is a sentence that is often misunderstood. It doesn't mean that a few exceptions are okay for any rule. The verb "proves" is being used here in its earlier sense of "tests or challenges." "The exception proves the rule" actually means that we look at possible exceptions to see if the rule really does make sense as it stands, or if it ought to be changed.

When we are trying to establish an interpretation, it often takes more than one cycle of checking and revising to be sure that a claim, a rule, or a clause in a contract says exactly what it is intended to say. If you have ever tried to draft a contract or a mission statement, you know how difficult it can be to get your words and sentences to convey exactly what you intend. Our laws and systems such as unemployment insurance and health care are examples of sets of rules that have been carefully worded, checked, and re-checked. Even then, however carefully they have been checked, new and unusual situations may call into question whether the rules really fit all the situations they are intended to fit, and they may have to be revised again. You saw this earlier, in the example from the *Charter of Rights and Freedoms,* where section 7 says, "Everyone . . . has the right to life, liberty, and security of the person" and the Supreme Court had to decide how exactly to apply the claim. Who counted as "everyone" in this context? The purpose of interpretation is to keep checking specific examples to establish the boundaries for where the rule applies and where it doesn't.

Clarifying Non-universal Claims

Non-universal claims cannot have their truth challenged by a single case, the way a universal rule can. Interpretation of our existing information is usually only enough to tell us that a claim is intended to be non-universal. However, for these claims, the interpretation stage can also at least tell us what sorts of exceptions to allow for and what kind of evidence we will need to look for. It helps us see what we don't yet know.

Producing one worn-out old bear isn't going to challenge "Bears can move faster than I can." Finding as many as a hundred drivers who had no accidents in their first two years of driving isn't going to challenge the claim that one in five new drivers will have an accident in their first two years. We need many more bears than one to show that a majority of bears are slower than a person, and we learn from the study of statistics that we'd need to check at least 1,068 drivers to have a fair chance of discovering whether there are significantly more or less than twenty percent who have accidents within two years.

Typically, non-universal claims can only be challenged by **empirical data**—that is, evidence we collect by observing, investigating, and measuring in the actual world. Many disciplines and professions now require at least a basic knowledge of statistics to learn how to gather and test empirical evidence in ways that will reliably indicate what the probabilities are. (We'll see more on this in Chapter 5 in the section on Inductive Reasoning.)

With non-universal generalizations, you have to check the facts. "Almost every cake contains eggs," "Some people eat lunch before noon," and "Most cats don't like strangers" are non-universal generalizations. They are usually intended just to predict what is most likely to happen. Make sure you have eggs on hand if you want to bake a cake. Don't be surprised if you invite someone to lunch at noon and he's already eaten. Don't expect to see your friend's cat when you go over; the cat is probably hiding under the bed until you leave. But if the cat comes out and actually comes over to you to be stroked, your friend may be surprised but not astonished—this cat is not "most cats." Similarly, "Almost every cake contains eggs" already allows for the existence of cakes that don't require eggs, such as a spice cake that uses beer in place of eggs.

To show that a non-universal claim is false, we need to see what will be enough cases to challenge the probability. "Most cats don't like strangers" is going to start to seem unlikely when you encounter five cats belonging to strangers, and four of the five come right up to you to check you out. Five is a very small sample, but four out of five is a very high percentage of the small sample.

Notice that "Some people eat lunch before noon" could put us in a tricky position when we try to check it. If we find one person who regularly has lunch at 11:30, that's a supporting example. If we can find a few more, that's even better. Suppose we find large numbers of people who do. That's fine too—it might seem a little odd to say "some" rather than "many" or "most," but we should remember that the intended force of "some" is just that it can and does happen. "Some" allows us to remain open to a wide range of possibilities, from only one to every one. However, what if we don't find anyone who eats before noon? Can we say the claim is false? Not yet—this will be the one situation in which sufficient checking really will mean we have to check every person. We can interpret the claim, and we can confirm the claim easily, but we can't easily prove it false.

Checklist for Testing Claims

✔ Understand the claim. What does it mean, and how is it intended to apply—universally or non-universally? This makes use of the natural tendency to confirm by connecting what is familiar to you—examples that come to mind—with what the person is trying to get you to believe—the generalization.

✔ Check the facts: what confirming or conflicting evidence can you come up with? Remind yourself of the wider world. What else is out there? Are there other examples that don't fit? Are there situations in which this claim ought not to be applied? Are there consequences that we would not want to see?

✔ Check whether the conflicting evidence really does show there is a problem with the claim.

✔ If the claim must be revised as a result of your investigation, check the revised version to be sure it is more accurate.

✔ If you cannot turn up reliable evidence, suspend judgment: acknowledge that the claim might be true but you cannot be sure.

EXERCISE **3.3** ## Testing Claims

For each of the following claims, (a) decide if they are universal generalizations or non-universal generalizations, and (b) if possible, test them accordingly. Are there legitimate exceptions that show the claim is not true as it stands?

*1. If it's worth doing, it's worth doing well.

2. Late papers will not be accepted by this professor under any circumstances.

3. Horses find direct eye contact threatening.

*4. Farms are unsafe workplaces.

5. If you take something, you should put it back where you found it.

Interpreting a Task

Interpretation of the tasks that you take on is also essential so you don't misdirect your effort. You have probably found yourself rushing to finish an assignment only to find that all you needed to do was have a rough draft ready to discuss that day. You may have bought school supplies for your child based on what you thought was needed, not having seen the official list your child forgot to give you. Once you've made your observations and interpreted the situation, the next element to interpret is what needs to be done and why it must be done. Before you put effort into doing something that turns out to be the right answer to the wrong question, you need to set out for yourself—and check with anyone else involved—what exactly is needed. What needs to happen, by what deadline, and to what standard?

Your task might be obvious: a class assignment you need to complete, a treatment plan you must write up for a patient, three boxes of files your boss has told you to photocopy. In these cases, you know what the goal is and how to get there. Your assignment comes with instructions, you've been trained to prepare and write up treatment plans, you know how to run the photocopier (and preferably how to fix its usual minor quirks).

Often, the task is less clearly set out: keep the customers happy, keep the children occupied for the afternoon, find a way to raise some funds. Here, you have a sense of what the goal is but not how to get there. Do the customers need a lot of attention or do they prefer to be interrupted as little as possible? Must the children do something educational or can they watch TV? Do you go with the usual fundraisers or try something new?

Again, this is a question of interpretation, and you can use the same interpretation skills you have just practised. We need to figure out what it means to "keep the customers happy"—what does this abstraction mean in concrete terms? We need to figure out which occupations are acceptable for these children—what does this generalization mean in specific terms? We need a sense of the ethical and practical boundaries—are there any ways to raise funds that would not be acceptable for the organization?

Record your answers to the questions you asked—this record will be vital in ensuring you stay on track and will help you resolve any disagreements at the end as to whether you did what was expected of you.

EXERCISE **3.4**

Interpreting a Task

From the list below, pick the task that you are most familiar with. Use your experience to draw up a checklist for all the details that would need to be checked in order to be sure the task was done properly.

Now pick another task you are not familiar with. Again, draw up a list for the details you think you would need to check in order to be sure you were ready to do the task properly.

Compare your results on these lists with people who have had experience in these tasks. What does this tell you about what you learn from experience? What does this show about the limitations of your own knowledge?

*1. Photocopying ten full boxes of reports, each about six pages long, each one stapled in the top corner.

2. Keeping your four-year-old niece and nephew busy for the afternoon while your sister and her husband are out.

3. Preparing a presentation on personal safety for a community group's annual meeting.

4. Making a booking for your sports team in accommodations convenient to an event that is to be held in a province some distance from your home.

*5. Running a small sandwich store while the manager is on vacation.

Correctly interpreting the task is essential to doing a good job. As with the other types of interpretation we have covered in this chapter, interpreting the task means clarifying what is needed and realizing what you still need to find out in order to succeed. Whenever we cannot interpret words, claims, or tasks clearly, we need to begin looking for more information to help us proceed.

Key Points in Review

- There is always a measure of interpretation in any observation.

- Interpretation in context involves clarifying meaning of words and sentences and clarifying what the task is. When we interpret our observations in context, we are in a position to know what we will need to investigate further. Interpretation is essential to avoid misdirecting our effort.

- The "principle of charity" should be a guiding principle in interpreting claims and arguments in general. When there is more than one possible interpretation of a word, phrase, gesture, or claim, you should use the interpretation that is most reasonable given your understanding of the context.

- When we interpret unclear claims or even when we interpret claims as unclear, we must defend our interpretations by presenting reasons. This, in turn, allows others to engage in debate by presenting different interpretations with different reasons.

- To interpret universal and non-universal claims, we check whether they really work with the force they are expected to have—that is, are they true in all the situations they claim to be true in? Confirming evidence shows that the claim is at least possibly true. Conflicting evidence shows that the claim has limited application or is possibly false.

Part 1
Summary

Getting the Best out of Observation

In the field of observation, chance favours the prepared mind.
— *Louis Pasteur*

Accuracy of observation is the equivalent of accuracy of thinking.
— *Wallace Stevens*

Observation Overview

Part 1 has been devoted to developing the skills of open-minded, objective observation and interpretation. The goal of observation is to take stock of what is around you without rushing to judgment. Taking the time to note and report your observations allows you to absorb the situation and attend to subtle details you might otherwise have missed. You have seen how to pause, be objective, and suspend judgment to make sure you do not overlook important information.

Observation requires attention. The observations that you make will depend on whether your observation is purposeful or open-ended. You have guidelines to help you pay particular attention to words, quantities, images, sounds, and feelings. Careful observation allows you to recognize the goal of verbal communication and to recognize when the goal is to present information or to persuade you to believe something. If the communication presents you with an argument, you can recognize the structure of the argument by picking out its conclusion and its premises. Although your observations should be non-evaluative, interpretation is a part of observation. Observation means attending to what people have said or written, but you must also understand what has been said or written before you can move on to the next stage in the critical thinking cycle: investigation.

Part-Ending Exercises
Comprehension Questions: Review

1. What are two types of observation discussed in this part?
2. How does being objective differ from being neutral?
3. What is one good way to ensure that you make all the observations needed in purposeful observation?
4. What is the definition of "argument"?
5. Give one example of an argument that contains a sub-argument.
6. What does it mean to put an argument into standard form? Why is it useful?
7. Give two examples of conclusion indicator words and two examples of premise indicator words.
8. How does a counter-argument differ from a counter-consideration?

9. What are indirect arguments?

10. What is the principle of charity and why is it a fundamental principle of interpretation?

11. Name and explain two different sources of lack of clarity.

12. What is a loaded term? Give one example.

13. How is emotion related to reasoning?

14. Explain why dictionary definitions may be inadequate when attempting to clarify terms.

Application Exercises

1. Begin a collection of arguments that you find in books, magazines, newspapers, or online. These will be used in part-ending exercises.

2. Find an article that takes a clear side on a subject you find interesting. Write a checklist of elements of the article that should be observed if your goal is to determine whether you should agree with the article. Explain why you've included each element on the list. Make observations based on that list.

3. Find an article that contains an argument. First, report the argument. Second, put the argument into standard form.

4. Take an old persuasive essay that you have written. Make sure it contains an argument. Standardize the argument.

Part 2 | *Investigation*

Do you know what you don't know?

After you have taken stock of what you already know, what you have available, and what you can already do, it is time to think about what you don't yet know.

The investigation stage of critical thinking calls for us to find out not just what is happening but what ought to be happening—the expectations—and to collect additional information to build a more complete picture.

After our initial observations, we need to know what additional information will help us understand the situation better, and we also need to know what is missing from the complete picture. We're going to check the facts, fill in the details, and build a deeper understanding. We've read the lines very carefully—now we are going to read between the lines. And we'll go further: we are going to explore the silences as well as the sounds, the backstage areas as well as the on-stage performance.

The investigation stage, therefore, has three principal aims:

1. Establish expectations: what are the standards for successful completion of the task?

2. Perform background research: gathering the additional information we need

3. Identify options and alternatives: finding out how things might turn out, figuring out what is not being said, not being shown, not being acknowledged

The investigation stage calls for a different set of skills than you have used so far. For investigation, you need research skills to uncover new information, and you also need the ability to explore with an open mind—the ability to make connections that are not obvious and to look in directions other than those you are expected to see. You need to know when to stay open to multiple possibilities. You need to know what your responsibilities are and what it will look like to meet them.

Chapter 4

Exploring behind the Scenes: Principles of Investigation

■ Perspective

In Chapters 1 to 3, we have focused on observation: careful and critical attention to what we are actually seeing, hearing, and experiencing. We have looked, listened, and thought more carefully about more details than we might ordinarily do. Now we expand our critical attention beyond what is in front of us, to investigate what is going on that we *can't* see or hear in direct observation. What do we need to know that we don't know yet? How do we find out?

■ Scenario

Your boss is responsible for putting out a trade publication in the medical field. One day, your boss asks you if you can find a way to "rent" a guinea pig for the day. The next issue of the publication is about experiments, and your boss wants to have a real guinea pig photographed for the cover. How could you find out whether it is possible to have a guinea pig for a day? (This was a request made of a reporter for a Pennsylvania diagnostic-imaging publication [Joyce E3]).

■ Key Question

How can I get the information I need?

Investigation

Investigation involves collecting additional information to expand your knowledge and increase your awareness of the possibilities open to you; it also involves checking observations for accuracy. The research skills you need to use the Internet, the library, and archives, to interview people, or to design and carry out experiments are beyond the scope of this text. Our aim here is to focus on the specific components of investigation where you need to use reasoning skills. Generally, these fall into three main stages:

- Where to begin
- Why to keep going
- When to stop

"Where to begin" involves all the questions you need to ask to set up the research task effectively. What is it you need to look for, where might you find it, and how can you phrase your questions so you will get useful answers?

"Why to keep going" covers the thinking involved in figuring out whether you have met the objectives of the investigation. Is the information you have collected enough to do the job?

"When to stop" involves setting limits on your search, so it does not become too time-consuming, too expensive, too impractical, or too overwhelming.

This chapter will prepare you for the reasoning required in each of these stages.

Where to Begin

Often the most difficult part of finding out what you don't yet know is figuring out where to start. You may never have been asked to rent a guinea pig, but you probably can think of tasks you have been given that have left you feeling equally bewildered. Think of job searches you may have made, or open-ended assignments where you had to find your own information. Where do you look? What search terms would you use to turn up results on the Internet or in a library index? Who could you ask for help? How should you phrase your request so it makes sense to the people you ask?

The research skills you learn in a postsecondary education build your skills in this area—the more research assignments you have done for different courses, the more you can confidently search for a wide range of information. But no matter how skilled you already are at research, there will always be new tasks that take you beyond your current sources and outside your comfort zone. Where do you start when you don't know where to start?

Here is where the first stage of the reasoning cycle proves its value. Once you take stock of what you have, what you know, and what you can already do, you have enough information to find a safe starting point. Simply compiling a list of what you do know can help you.

First, you do know a number of sources of information. For example, you know there are libraries, and librarians are helpful—finding information is one of their special skills. You know the Internet has search engines that will list every site containing the words in your search. You know there are telephone directories. (The would-be guinea pig renter started with the phone directory and listings for pet stores.) You may also know "someone who might know"—a person who might not be able to answer your question, but might know to whom you could go for an answer.

Next, you do know where your own knowledge begins and ends. You know what a guinea pig is, for example—you do know that they're kept as pets. You do know that there are sources to rent equipment of various kinds. If the guinea pig is needed for a photograph on a magazine cover, then there will be a photographer needed. Slight as this information seems, it is enough to get you going.

You have three possible starting points:

- Pet stores. They sell guinea pigs. They might possibly rent them, but if they don't, they may know who typically buys guinea pigs—there may be owners you could contact.

- Rental equipment stores. Rental stores don't typically rent animals, but since they do rent supplies for weddings and parties, they may get requests for unusual items. They may have an idea where you could ask about renting guinea pigs.

- Photographers. Photographers often use props of various kinds when they take pictures—backdrops, graduation robes, library books, and so on. Photographers who take portraits of children and animals might know if there is a way to arrange to get particular animals to photograph.

You still don't know if you'll succeed in your quest for a guinea pig to star on the next magazine cover, but you should feel much better able to start asking around and see what turns up. Who knows, perhaps the pet store will direct you to a kindergarten teacher who's willing to lend the class pet, or the photographer will point you toward an "animal wrangler" who handles everything from spiders to tigers for the local movie industry.

EXERCISE **4.1** ## Finding a Place to Start

To get the answers for one of the following questions, use your current knowledge to think of two or three possible starting points:

*1. Where could you get good used sports equipment, preferably free, to supply a youth drop-in centre?

2. How could you arrange an opportunity to film a live shark or moose?

3. How could you meet the best local car mechanic?

4. What regulations would you have to comply with if you wanted to put an above-ground pool in the backyard of a private house in your municipality or township?

5. Is it safe to eat food that has been on the floor for more than five seconds?

One further step is important before you get started. Before you start to seek information, you need to think about the practical, ethical, and conceptual limits on gathering information. Not all information you might want is available. It may never have been collected. It may be located in sources you cannot get to. It may be private and confidential, such as medical records or notes from counselling sessions that can be released only with consent. It may not be counted as something that people can give permission to reveal, such as jury deliberations, trade secrets, or traditional First Nations songs that are the exclusive property of the families who have the right to sing them. To protect the safety and privacy of research subjects, national policies now require that faculty and student projects—even interview projects—must be reviewed by institutional ethics committees. The ethics review ensures that sufficient care has been taken to get informed consent from participants and to safeguard the information so it cannot be released or used in unauthorized ways.

All these considerations mean that you need to prepare in advance to find out whether you can get the information you want, and if so, whether you will need permission, whether there will be costs, and whether there will be limits on what you may know.

EXERCISE **Research Ethics**

* What are the limits on collecting information about people? What are the limits on doing research with animals? One source you can check is http://www.pre.ethics.gc .ca/english/index.cfm. There are also sources at individual postsecondary institutions.

When to Keep Going

Once you've taken the first steps into your investigation, you'll need to pause and take stock again before you decide if you're done. How do you tell whether you need to keep going? By keeping an eye on the bigger picture of what the overall task is and what you need the knowledge for, you can gather information step-by-step, stopping frequently to assess what you've learned and what you need next.

And indeed the art of investigating will be to strike a practical balance between doing too little—doing only the most obvious checking, so that you never see anything new—and doing so much exploring that you never get around to doing anything with the results. How do we strike this balance?

First, we do enough background research—gathering information to help us understand the concepts—to gather needed information. Then we go just far enough beyond the obvious to see missing pieces, unspoken problems, or questionable assumptions.

In other words, just as with observation, investigation can be *purposeful*—directed toward a particular goal—or *open-ended*—collecting information as it strikes your fancy. You are not limited to checking information you already have or filling in obvious gaps. Stay open to the possibility that the search for information may take you in directions you did not expect. You may be stopped or restricted in ways you did not expect. At the same time, you may find your investigation opens up new avenues you did not anticipate.

For example, if you are researching the causes of homelessness and the best strategies for dealing with it, you may do a library or Internet search using the terms "homeless" and "poverty." You may use a newspaper index to check for stories about the homeless in your area. You may talk to people you know who have experience living in poverty, or people who have worked with the homeless. What you have just completed is a *strategic search:* you have given yourself the best chance of uncovering material that is related to your topic. In a strategic search, you may find that your choice of key words brings up too many results or too few. If so, you will adjust your search by making it narrower or broader as you need.

There is another kind of search that is also useful—one that takes advantage of chance encounters. Suppose that as you're scanning subject indexes for "poverty," you notice "pollution" as a nearby heading. On the surface, there is nothing connecting poverty to pollution. However, you might check "pollution" simply because it is another topic that generally interests you. As you check, you may find that there are articles on how pollution affects a country's economy—and how pollution might impair health or economic conditions. Now you have not only a connection between poverty and pollution, but an original thesis to explore: is it possible that pollution has an effect on poverty through its effect on the economy?

There is even a name for this kind of search: a "serendipity search." Librarians know it as a legitimate way to uncover new ideas and new connections simply by giving yourself some time to explore whatever intriguing titles or topics catch your eye. The trick to a serendipity search is to be able to see connections between apparently unconnected items.

A full discussion of what's involved in good research is beyond the scope of this text. As noted at the beginning of the chapter, you may already have had practice in this area. Most schools and postsecondary institutions offer library orientations, and many offer research skills workshops and courses. Libraries and librarians are experts on information retrieval. Whether you are looking for information on the Internet or on library shelves, libraries usually have guides as to which sources are best and how to use them. Reference librarians can help you choose the best search terms and narrow or broaden your search as needed.

Investigating the Nonverbal Aspects of the Situation

Part of an investigation is making sure we have also explored the nonverbal aspects of the context. What effects are they intended to achieve? What significance might they have that is not obvious on the surface? There is valuable information in numbers, images, and sounds as well as words.

Numbers: Quantitative Information

As you do background research, you may already have put some thought into any numbers that have been included as part of the information. If numbers have already been presented to you, you investigate them just as you would any other details: What is the source? Are there other sources that confirm the same figures? If there are different estimates, how close are they to each other?

Again, investigating the context requires us to find out what will count as relevant and sufficient in the particular context. Are the numbers relevant to the context in which they are being used? For example, in an argument, the numbers must give information that is useful in showing whether the conclusion is true. "Sixty-five percent of first marriages fail" is relevant to the conclusion "You should think very carefully about deciding whom to marry." The statistic is not relevant to the conclusion "Second marriages are unlikely to succeed." We'd have to stretch a long way to claim that, because more than half of first marriages fail, second marriages will also fail at the same rate.

To be relevant, the numbers must also be correctly compared. For example, "Over sixty-five percent of households in the Yukon own two or more guns. This is significantly more than the twenty-five percent average of households with guns in the rest of Canada. People in the Yukon must be much more violent if so many of them need guns." The numbers seem to be reasonably compared, but they are not. We generally draw a useful distinction between rifles and handguns. Rifles are used for hunting and for other purely sporting purposes. They are not associated with interpersonal violence in the same way as handguns. The guns owned in the Yukon may all be rifles and be no indicator at all of the level of violence in Yukon communities.

If the numbers have not already been noted during observation—for example, if your observation included only estimates of quantities—this is the time to measure exactly or look for data to confirm the estimates. For example, if you looked at some reading assigned to you and read the expectations of the assignment, you'll have been able to estimate how long the reading will take you given what you need to know. Responsible investigation will include pausing after you have read, say, one-quarter of the material and checking how much time it has taken. Are you on schedule, behind schedule, or ahead of schedule? This investigation allows you to adjust your planning as needed.

This is also the time to convert percentages to numbers, and numbers to percentages, so you can make fair comparisons. Sometimes a percentage will seem alarming: "There has been a 100 percent increase in cases of West Nile virus!" Wait a minute—how many cases were there before? If there were only two, a 100 percent increase is another two, for a total of four. This is not nearly as scary as finding out there were 200 cases before, and now there are 400. Conversely, a number may seem alarming where a percentage does not: there have been 5,000 motor vehicle accidents in Canada in the past year—perhaps this figure is only seventy-five percent of the total for the previous year and thus represents a significant decrease in problems on the roads.

Another type of investigation you might do with numbers is to see what further information you can extract from the numbers themselves. For example, suppose you read that in 2004, natural catastrophes around the world accounted for at least 320,781 deaths. The tsunami in the Indian Ocean accounted for all but about 16,000 of these deaths: about half of the number are known dead, and almost as many again are missing and presumed dead. The other deaths were caused by floods in Haiti in May, followed by a hurricane in September, for a total of 6,000 deaths in that country alone. The remaining deaths occurred in floods in India, Bangladesh, and the Dominican Republic; in storms in the Philippines and in Madagascar; and in an earthquake in Morocco. The Red Cross noted that the reported number of deaths from catastrophes in 2003 was 76,806, including deaths from an earthquake in Iran and a heat wave in Europe. An annual average taken over a decade for deaths from natural catastrophes is 62,000 (Associated Press A15). Investigation of these figures might involve simply checking additional sources to confirm the numbers. For example, do the United Nations and the International Red Cross give the same numbers? However, investigation here also involves thinking about what those numbers might tell you. You may be able to extract further information about disasters in general. Do the number indicate how many deaths from natural catastrophes can be expected each year? Do they indicate any consistent locations or types of disaster—for example, flooding of coastal areas? The answers to these questions might indicate the types of relief planning that could reduce the impact of disasters when they occur. How do these numbers compare to deaths from starvation or disease? Again, the comparison may help set priorities for types of aid.

Exercises and research in history, economics, and sociology can involve this kind of reflection on what the numbers might mean.

Some systematic questions can help you to extract more information from quantitative information.

- Are there *drops or increases* in sequences of numbers? What might be causing these drops or rises?

- Are the numbers *consistent* in different sources? If not, there may be differences in how the quantities have been measured or estimated.

- Are the numbers *up-to-date* (or relevant to the time we are interested in)? If not, how likely is it that they are a good guide to what is/was going on at the time?

- If the numbers are estimates, what assumptions have gone into producing the estimates? How plausible are those assumptions?

Investigating Numerical Information

*Here is an argument that gives numbers to support its conclusion.

First, read the article, and use only your background knowledge to evaluate the numbers given. Do the numbers seem plausible?

Next, do some background research: can you find information in any other sources that either confirms or conflicts with the information given here? If you can find information, does it confirm or conflict with what is given here? If you can't find further information, how does that reflect on the plausibility of the numbers?

Study reveals lefties thrive in violent societies

French scientists believe they may have discovered why left-handers are so common despite suffering disadvantages when it comes to handling tools, disease risk and historical prejudice in predominantly right-handed societies against the "cackhanded."

Since this trait is substantially inherited, and because it can be a disadvantage, scientists have puzzled for years over what it is about being left-handed that helps survival or the ability to reproduce.

Now it seems that left-handers are more likely to thrive in a violent society. A French team reported yesterday that because they are in the minority, left-handers have a strategic advantage in fights.

The reason isn't that they are innately superior but that their opponent is likely to be more used to combat with right-handers, according to Dr. Charlotte Faurie and Dr. Michel Raymond of Université Montpellier II, France.

The team was inspired to carry out the study by the observation that, in a right-handed society, left-handers have an advantage in sports such as fencing, tennis, cricket and baseball.

They reasoned that "interactive sports in western societies are special cases of fights, with strict rules, including in particular the prohibition of killing or intentionally wounding the opponent."

Thus it could be that being left-handed in a right-handed society may have offered an advantage in fights.

"If this is true, then the advantage of being left-handed should be greater in a more violent context, which should result in a higher frequency of left-handers."

They decided to test their idea. Earlier studies have shown the number of left-handers in the Kreyol people of Dominica, the Ntumu people of Cameroon, the Dioula-speaking people of Burkina Faso, Baka people of Gabon, Inuit people and the Eipo people in Irian Jaya, New Guinea.

When the team studied the rate of murder in each society, they found "a significant positive correlation between homicide rates and left-handedness frequencies."

The Dioula had a homicide rate equivalent to one-hundredth of a death per 1,000 people per year, while the Eipo had around three deaths per 1,000 people. And the percentage of left-handers was 3.4 per cent and more than 20 per cent, showing how left-handedness thrived along with aggression.

In societies, being able to win fights meant more than killing opponents, enabling warriors to gain status and impress women. A study by the same team of 600 students found that the same forces are at work today in sports, which they describe as "ritualized fights."

Competitive athletes, particularly men, have more sexual partners than their couch-potato peers. Because left-handers often have a competitive advantage in sports, they're more likely to enjoy this benefit, said Faurie.

However, left-handers face disadvantages. Statistics suggest reduced life expectancy, smaller body size and immune system disorders, she said.

"But it seems to be true that they are more frequent among some professional categories as musicians and mathematicians," said Faurie.

"Our team showed that they have some socioeconomic advantages [like a slightly higher income]."

[ROGER HIGHFIELD, *KINGSTON WHIG-STANDARD*, DECEMBER 10, 2004, 31. © TELEGRAPH GROUP LIMITED 2004. REPRINTED WITH PERMISSION OF TELEGRAPH GROUP LIMITED.]

Images: Investigating Imagery

Many visual images—advertisements and movies especially—are the products of skilled artists or sophisticated design studios. The use of colour, the vividness of the image, and the layout or camera angles have been carefully chosen to ensure that your attention is caught, held, and directed to exactly the intended features of the image. The effect is to make you ignore what lies outside the frame of the picture. This might cause you to overlook or underestimate the significance of what you are seeing.

Consequently, we need to explore beyond what we are being directed to see, and investigate two aspects that cannot be directly observed.

- What is not seen in the picture?
- What might this imagery convey to the creator or viewers?

Seeing the Unseen

What don't we see in a picture? The omissions can tell us something that is as significant as what has been included. One obvious omission is the maker of the picture—almost always, the painter, photographer, or camera operator is out of the frame of the picture. At the same time, the picture or movie is taken from that particular viewpoint. When you see the image, you are seeing it as if you were standing where the creator of the image stood. If you had been standing where the photograph was taken, or where the picture was painted from, or where the movie camera was positioned, what else would you be likely to see?

It's very common for striking landscape postcards to be taken from viewpoints that carefully exclude all the tourists, tour buses, and souvenir stalls that actually come right up to the sight. The pyramids in Egypt are just across the road from the suburbs of Cairo, but most photographs of the pyramids don't show the larger surroundings. In a similar fashion, when native masks are photographed or mounted in museums against plain backgrounds, they are being separated from all their ritual accompaniments and turned into "art objects" instead of carrying their full mythological and cultural significance.

Have the omissions made the view more romantic, more dramatic, or more unpleasant than it might otherwise be?

If you had been standing where the photographer, artist, or filmmaker stood, would the people or animals in the scene have noticed and reacted to you? Are you a "fly on the wall" seeing the scene without being noticed, or are you a participant, "one of the crowd," caught up in the action? Invisible voyeur or legitimate participant? It makes a difference to how the scene should be interpreted or judged. If you could not have been there, you are being placed in a position of apparent objectivity: you could not possibly be involved, so you couldn't possibly identify with one participant more than another.

Finally, if you had been there, could you have seen what is presented to you? If not, you are looking at an image that has been faked or altered in some way—a constructed image that shows you what the creator's vision was, but tells you nothing reliable about how the world is. Images that have been modified to construct a specific impression cannot be relied on to indicate what you would experience.

EXERCISE **4.4**

Investigating Imagery

*Investigate the image in the Rogers advertisement. What do you notice about the placement of the image? Where are you, as the viewer/photographer, positioned? Are you expected to identify with anyone in the image? What is not seen? What might this image be expected to convey to people who are interested in cell-phones?

Significance of Imagery

The significance of the imagery will probably require background knowledge or research. If you've never seen a Harley-Davidson motorcycle you won't know that the company's insignia on clothing can indicate strength and toughness. You might be able to tell which Haida figure represents Raven, but you can't tell from observation alone that Raven is the Trickster who acts as a source of disorder and mischief. Without some information about Christian imagery, you will not be likely to know that a rose in a medieval painting represents Mary, the mother of Jesus.

Developing an understanding of the significance of imagery often requires detailed study in fields such as art history, anthropology, semiotics, or media and communications. For purposes of reasoning, it is important to remember at least to check whether there may be a particular significance of the image to its creator or viewers—at least to the extent of doing some initial research into what it might mean.

Consider an example where the interpretation of an image has far-ranging effects. In the following examples, the interpretation of a picture is central to deciding whether the game of hockey originated in Canada, which in turn has a significant impact on how Canadians view hockey as a national game. Look at the first image on page 127: do you think it is reasonably interpreted as people playing hockey? Also refer to the illustration on page 128, "Winter Sports" by Henry Buckton Laurence, which is the Canadian picture mentioned in the article

below. Compare the two pictures to see if either seems to represent people playing hockey. (Note that in the Laurence picture, the "hockey players" are in the far right background, behind the people curling.)

Virginia painting depicts 1835 hockey scene

Barely a month after a Nova Scotia art gallery loudly proclaimed it had discovered the world's earliest depiction of hockey, a group of skeptical researchers has pointed to a painting 32 years older that shows stick-wielding skaters scrimmaging on a frozen river in—hold on to your toque—Virginia.

Produced in 1835 by Irish-American folk artist John Toole, *Skating Scene* playfully captures four sportsmen holding curved sticks and battling over a small, round object momentarily controlled by the figure in the foreground of the painting.

There are no nets or other goal markers, and the players—including one in the midst of a spectacular fall and another dramatically poised to check the "puck" carrier—all have cane-like sticks and curly toed skate blades.

But the scene has the same basic elements and action shown in an 1867 Henry Buckton Laurence lithograph that was unveiled with much hoopla last month by the Art Gallery of Nova Scotia.

That scene showed 10 lively skaters, each with a curved stick, in the background of a sketch focused on a curling match at Dartmouth's Lake Banook, across the harbour from Halifax.

No ball or puck is discernible in the picture, though a chase is implied in the skaters' movements. And a February 1867 newspaper article describing a "hockey match" on the lake between the Garrison and the Fleet was advanced as documentary corroboration of the lithograph's historic significance. Gallery director Jeffrey Spalding

(Continued)

Virginia painting depicts 1835 hockey scene *(Continued)*

hailed the exhibition of the Laurence sketch as "a momentous occasion for Canada and for the world" during a Feb. 12 news conference covered by national media.

"There may be another image, an earlier image, somewhere else in the world. But until that comes up, Halifax holds the hammer."

Halifax Mayor Peter Kelly also boasted the 1867 sketch was irrefutable evidence that the sport's origins could be traced to his city— another salvo in the long-running birthplace-of-hockey battle between Halifax-Dartmouth, Windsor, N.S., Montreal, Kingston, Ont., and Deline, NWT.

"A picture is worth a thousand words," Kelly said at the time. "We believe hockey started here and we'll hold to that belief until anybody else brings any other proof forward."

Cue the Society for International Hockey Research, a Canadian-based group of history buffs that had

previously weighed in on the birthplace debate (on Montreal's side) and greeted the latest claims from Nova Scotia with bemusement.

For one thing, notes SIHR Secretary Lenard Kotylo, the Laurence sketch has been known about for decades and was even reproduced in a 1987 book on hockey history by SIHR co-founder Bill Fitsell.

For another, he says, presenting an 1867 picture of sticks-and-skates action on Lake Banook as "proof" of hockey's origins in Halifax was an invitation for any number of European countries to present similar visual records including paintings more than 400 years old showing skaters with curved sticks—and lay claim to birthplace honours.

Now, the SIHR is pointing to Toole's painting as proof that neither Nova Scotians specifically nor Canadians in general can claim to have invented the idea of skaters

on ice—knocking an object around with sticks. Several nations in Europe and then several waves of European colonists to North America—English, Irish, Dutch, French—played early forms of ice hockey, the group says.

It has been argued that early European images show static skaters playing a golf-like sport. But both the Laurence and Toole pictures show skaters in hot pursuit of an object.

Kitchen argues the existence of such an early illustration from the United States should sharpen Canada's focus on the event that marked the moment hockey evolved from a rudimentary, recreational pastime with diverse roots and many names—hockey, hurley, ricket, wicket, shinny and shinty—to a bona fide sport played according to specific rules.

He says that event, according to the latest research, was a March 3, 1875, match at the

HENRY BUCKTON LAURENCE, **CURLING ON THE LAKES, NEAR HALIFAX, NOVA SCOTIA,** 1870 (CREATED IN 1870 OF AN EVENT IN 1867). TINT STONE LITHOGRAPH ON PAPER. PURCHASED WITH FUNDS FROM "THE FAMILY" IN MEMORY OF H. DONALD AND DOROTHY OYLER. COLLECTION OF THE ART GALLERY OF NOVA SCOTIA. REPRODUCED WITH PERMISSION.

Victoria Skating Rink in Montreal, which was vividly described in newspaper reports at the time and from which the organized version of the game can clearly be shown to have spread from city to city and eventually around the world.

Spalding insists the Halifax lithograph, in combination with the 1867 newspaper report describing a "hockey match" on the Dartmouth lakes, undercuts Montreal's claim and trumps all other known images—including the Toole painting, which is held by the prestigious U.S. National Gallery of Art in Washington.

[RANDY BOSWELL, *VANCOUVER SUN*, MARCH 16, 2004, A5. MATERIAL REPRINTED WITH THE EXPRESS PERMISSION OF CANWEST NEWS SERVICE, A CANWEST PARTNERSHIP.]

 EXERCISE 4.5

Investigating to Increase Understanding of Images

1. Find a painting you like in a book on art; then see what the book tells you about who painted it, when, and why. What does this information add to your understanding of the picture?

*2. Choose a magazine advertisement for a luxury product such as jewellery or an expensive car, and one for an everyday product such as cleaning supplies. What can you see in the first image that helps signal "luxury" that contrasts with what is shown in the second image?

3. For either of the images you have just examined in question 1 or 2, consider what is omitted. Where is the viewer positioned in relation to the image? What else might have been visible outside the edges of the picture? What does that indicate to you? Who is not in the target market for these products?

Soundscape

We can ask similar questions of the auditory elements of a scene. Just as with images, sounds can be carefully chosen to create a desired effect. The soundscape, even more than the imagery, is likely to evoke an emotional response, so it needs to be examined thoughtfully. An appeal to emotion, as we'll see when we evaluate information in Chapter 9, must be handled carefully if it is to be legitimate instead of misleading. Again, we can reasonably ask these questions:

■ What are we *not* hearing? Have some natural sounds been omitted to create a particular effect?

■ Are we drawn in or held at a distance? For example, does the music invite us to dance, or is it meant only to be listened to? What does this tell us about how we are meant to relate to the situation?

■ What are we hearing that we would not hear if we were at the scene? For example, is there romantic music accompanying a kiss out in the desert with no musicians present? Is the huge spaceship rumbling as it passes overhead in empty space?

■ Do these sounds have particular significance for the creator or the listeners? For example, is the composer of the music making reference to popular songs or to other composers? Is the music identified with a particular type of event?

Investigating a Soundscape

Choose one scene from a movie or TV show with a musical soundtrack, and one with no music added. Listen to the two scenes in succession. What do you notice about the music? What does it suggest about how you are supposed to engage with the scene? What signals or references might the music be suggesting to its listeners?

Investigating the Importance of Emotions

What are emotions signalling? In Chapter 1, you identified emotions during observation. In this section, we'll see how you investigate these emotional clues to prepare for an evaluation of their role in reasoning.

Emotions are often a signal that something significant is at stake. Emotions can indicate what deserves more investigation. If you are afraid, that is a signal that something in your surroundings may be cause for concern, and until you have investigated, you should not proceed further. (See, for example, Gavin de Becker's book, *The Gift of Fear,* about the importance of recognizing and respecting your own fears as a way to avoid assault or abuse.) The object of an emotion is what the emotion is "about." For example, if you are angry at Henry, then Henry is the object of your anger. The cause of the emotion is what has triggered the emotion. The cause can be investigated from a number of different angles and there can be more than one cause of a single emotion. For example, the cause of your anger at Henry might be his calling you "chubby"; another cause might be the fact that you haven't slept, so you are irritable and you're not in the mood to be teased. Investigating the objects and causes of the emotion gives you information that will allow you to later determine how much weight to give the emotion in your reasoning. For example, if your anger is caused by lack of sleep, you would be wise to discount your anger as a source of information about your relationship with Henry.

Investigating emotions illuminates connections between our emotions and the situations in which they arise. For example, consider a situation in which you feel uneasy about a financial advisor you have just met. Your uneasiness deserves investigation, because you will have to decide whether to accept this person's financial advice. Your observation of your emotions and your surroundings reveals that you do feel uneasy and that your emotion is linked to the advisor and not to anything about your surroundings. But does your uneasiness indicate there's a problem with the financial advisor? Not necessarily. You need to investigate the object and cause of the emotion before you decide what role emotion should play in your reasoning.

Investigating your uneasiness with the financial advisor involves asking yourself what it is exactly that is making you feel uneasy. Could it be that the financial advisor seldom looks directly into your eyes? Could it be the clothes he is wearing? In a multicultural society, you and your financial advisor may be of completely different cultural backgrounds. He, or you, may feel that to look away from the other person is a sign of respect. He, or you, may feel that frequent direct eye contact is the best signal of honesty. And even if you are confident that you and he come from the same background with the same expectations, perhaps one of you is simply shyer than the other. The object of your uneasiness is the financial advisor, and one cause of uneasiness may be that he rarely meets your eyes, but other causes might include cultural and personal differences. It is also possible that your emotion has been caused by behaviour that is genuinely suspicious, but unless you have investigated the causes of your emotion, you cannot be sure exactly what the emotion is signalling.

Investigating your emotions brings to light possible causes you might not have recognized and gives you detailed information that you can use when it is time to evaluate the role of emotion in reasoning.

Reporting Investigations: Keeping Track As You Go

You will usually need a record of the research you did. These records help locate the information again if it's needed, and help confirm that you did check enough reliable sources. You will probably need a backup record or a way to re-discover the information as well.

It is regrettably easy to find that the one piece of information you forgot to record is the one piece you need most when you use the information later. For example, you might have saved information from a website but not copied down the details of the web address. You might think you don't need this, because it will appear when you print it out. You cheerfully promise to send someone else the address for this site you recommended to them. However, when you print from your saved copy, you find the document lists your file name, not the original web address. Time to search your desk in the hope you did make a printout from the website, or go back to your original scribbled notes that led you to the website in the first place!

To report your research,

- list the sources you checked, with complete citations,
- list the results you got from each source, and
- organize your list so you can track what you've done and what you might still need to do.

EXERCISE **Searches**

1. *Strategic search:* For any of the following topics, or for a topic assigned to you, spend a maximum of one hour searching for information. Report your search results using the guidelines above.
   a. Newspaper articles discussing how to help the homeless
   b. Academic journal articles on the mental development of young adults

     c. Local businesses that accept used items on consignment

     d. Internet sources on adventure travel

2. *Serendipity search:*

   ■ Go to a library or bookstore and pick two shelves at random.

   ■ Scan the titles on each shelf until you have found three books or videos that interest you.

   ■ List the titles you chose.

   ■ Now think of a possible connection between two items that you picked from different shelves. How could you use them together?

   ■ Write up your results: where did you start, what did you select, and how were you able to connect the two items?

It can sound a bit alarming to open up your investigation as broadly as we've described. How are you ever going to be able to finish a task if you have to research not only the obvious links but all the non-obvious ones as well? On the other hand, if you have been taught that you must have a solid grounding in the facts before you can question or criticize, then you may find it especially frustrating to stop while you know there is still more information out there.

Again, it becomes a question of balance. How do you balance what you already know against what else might still be out there that you also need?

Three kinds of practical problem might arise:

■ The information we need may not be available at all.

■ We may be able to find only a single source.

■ We may find too much information to sort through easily.

In all these situations, we will need at least one more step before we can complete our search. There will be three corresponding strategies we must be ready to use:

1. Unavailable information means we need to check whether we did look in the right places.

2. If there's only one source, we may have to investigate the source itself for adequacy. Is it the right source for our needs?

3. If there's too much information, we may need to back up and reconsider the questions we asked in our search. Did they really capture what we were looking for?

1. Missing Information

What if our search is not successful? Our research may not always be able to give us "the facts," even when we have permission and there are no ethical obstacles to getting the information. There is a crucial difference between saying, "There isn't any information on this topic" and "I couldn't find any information on this topic." If all you know is that you personally couldn't find information, you don't yet know if there isn't any information or if you simply haven't found it yet. Were you searching in the wrong places or using the wrong search terms? In an unsuccessful search, you need to decide whether there really is no information or you just haven't found it yet.

For example, like the person who actually had to look for a guinea pig to photograph for a magazine cover, you might spend all day on the phone to pet stores and have no luck at all. Some of them don't carry guinea pigs, others laugh at the notion of renting them instead of buying them, and none of the stores have any other useful sources of information they can suggest.

Now what? Did you just phone the wrong places or are there really no guinea pigs to be rented? The records that you kept as you were investigating come to your rescue here. They can be used to show your supervisor or someone else knowledgeable what you have already done that need not be done again. This may be enough to help decide where else to look, or whether there really is no information available. At the very least, your records show you did a responsible and realistic search.

2. Minimum Information

The second scenario is what to do when your search has turned up just what you were looking for. You've been asked to find three articles for a research essay; you've found exactly three. You mentioned your guinea pig search to someone in the office, who says his daughter's kindergarten teacher keeps a guinea pig. You phone the teacher and she'd be delighted to lend you the guinea pig for a day if you take good care of it. Are you done? Reasoning is required to confirm that you really have met the objectives of your search.

You have three articles, but are they all suitable for your essay? Do they overlap so much in content that you still don't really have enough to work with? Is one of them so hard to read that you can't work with it or so old that it is no longer relevant?

You have a live guinea pig, but the object of your search was a guinea pig for a photograph. What do you know about photographing guinea pigs? Are they easy to photograph? Do they just sit there, or do they run around and hide from the lights? Do they sleep so much it will be hard to get one to stay awake long enough to do anything interesting in front of the camera? Your search is probably not quite over yet. You still need information on how this guinea pig behaves, so you have a sense of whether it is likely to perform well in front of a camera, and you may also need information from a photographer who can suggest what will be needed to photograph an animal effectively. Should its owner be there with it? Will it need treats to make it cooperate? In a similar scenario in Japan, a team from Sony was working to develop a camera that could automatically track a white ball moving at random. The team had the idea of using a hamster in an exercise ball as the target ball. The ball had to be painted white for the camera to track it. Each time they started filming, the ball moved for less than two minutes and then stopped completely. They did not realize that hamsters stay active only for short periods of time.

With minimum information, your search is not done as soon as you have the information. Even once you've figured out everything needed to get a guinea pig, or a hamster, to perform well on camera, you may still need more information. The Sony team, planning to take their experimental camera to Los Angeles, faced objections from U.S. animal-rights organizations who monitor the use of animals. Was it acceptable to confine a hamster to a dark ball? You may need not only practical information but legal information about what is permitted.

In a successful search, you need to be able to decide whether you have the right information to meet your goals. The key principle is to be sure you have asked, and answered, at least the obvious additional questions to check whether this information is enough for your purposes. This may require going back and forth between investigating and evaluating. In Chapter 7, we will see how to check the quality of information to be sure it meets our needs. For now, as you investigate, keep your search going until you know whether additional sources are available if you do need them, and make sure you have recorded all the details of what you found and where you found it, so you can examine it later for credibility.

3. More Information Than You Need

An *Adam* cartoon in 2004 showed a little boy searching for "the meaning of life" using a search engine on the Internet and getting "18,200,000 hits" (http://www.ucomics.com). The father is shown saying, "This generation has it too easy." Is he right? Are you really any closer to your goal if you have a million or more sites to check? (If you try typing in "meaning of life" yourself, you'll probably get only 850,000 hits—better, but not much better, to start looking through.)

Too much information is as frustrating as too little. What is worth your time to check? How would you narrow a search for a topic as broad as "the meaning of life"?

Your best bet is probably to rethink what it was you set out to find. If you really were just playing around, seeing what would happen if you typed in "the meaning of life," then you actually do have the answer to your search question—there are an enormous number of sites that say they have something to do with the "meaning of life." You could stop here or take one more small step by sampling just a few of the sites to see what they offer.

However, perhaps you were researching to prepare for an essay in which you will have to explore and compare different answers to the question "What is the meaning of life?" For this, a random sampling of interesting sites may not be sufficient. If you consider that what you will need from your search is some detailed information about particular views, you could switch instead to whichever site is your favourite for checking books and videos, and try "meaning of life" in a subject-term search. This site is much more likely to show where you'll find detailed discussions, and book or video titles often come with enough added information for you to identify more easily which are worth looking into. (A sample search of three sites yielded 2,088 hits, 256 hits, and 472 hits respectively—still a considerable number, but all the lists were sorted so the first few gave a good indication of what might be worth investigating.)

Perhaps all you wanted was to figure out the source of the saying that "42" is the "answer" to the question "What is the meaning of life?" For this, you may be better off abandoning the Internet and trying your friends instead. Does anyone remember whether it was in a Monty Python video, or in a cartoon, or in the TV show that had the man with two heads and the spaceship? Was that *Red Dwarf* or was it *Hitchhiker's Guide to the Galaxy*? Clues about when, where, or by whom it may have been said can send you back to a much more productive search.

Again, the general principle is that keeping an ongoing record as you search will help you. More skilled searchers or people more knowledgeable about the topic may be able to show you how to narrow your search or to find more suitable sources.

When to Stop: Limiting a Search

Now comes the question of balancing the need to keep an open mind and to investigate widely against the need to know when to stop. When can you stop investigating? When can you say you have done enough? The balance we try to strike in reasoning is to meet reasonable, realistic expectations. Have you done enough to meet reasonable expectations? We don't want to stop too soon, and we don't want to keep going so long that we have no time to do anything with the information.

This is something you can check as you go. After each round of research, you will have some new information—either you have additional facts you did not have before, or you have discovered that some information is inaccurate or unconfirmed. The chances are that you will not have answered all the questions you had or found all the sources you hoped to find. Do you keep looking or can you stop?

One of the valuable aspects of the reasoning cycle is that it allows us to make the most of what we've got, however much or however little that happens to be. We can think about the information we do have and use our thinking to decide whether we must have more information or whether we can work with what we have. At some point in your search, you check what you've got against what you're expected to have.

For example, you phoned two pet stores, a school, and an animal photographer. Is it time to go back to the boss and say there's not a guinea pig to be had? Or should you stop looking for guinea pigs and switch to checking into sources of photographs of guinea pigs and artists who can digitally alter photographs to create a desired effect? That way, you can present your boss not just with a failure, but with a possible backup plan that might still get the right image for the magazine cover.

Consider the question of when you have done "enough" research for a paper or "enough" studying for an exam. If you are a student, at any level from high school right through to graduate school, you will probably experience more than once that terrifying stage when there is a project deadline fast approaching and yet every book and article you read points you to some new source you really should check. When can you stop? When have you done enough to be able to stop reading and start writing? Will you study all night before an exam or sleep instead? Which will help you do best in the morning?

The real question here is not whether you have learned everything to be learned about the subject. The question is what is enough to work with, given the task at hand. What counts as "sufficient" will vary from context to context. Most often, "sufficient" means "enough to be safe." We can meet something more than the minimum expectations, even if we can't reach the maximum. We've done enough reading to write intelligently about the topic, even though we know there will be some unanswered questions. We've studied enough to be able to pass the exam comfortably, even if we can't ace it this time.

The key considerations in deciding what is sufficient in any given situation are

- the level of risk involved, and
- the values you wish to uphold.

Managing Risk

If we have sufficient evidence, we can handle all of the most likely outcomes.

For example, consider a situation where you are required to check ID before selling cigarettes or liquor. You can see the person, so you can guess the age from the appearance, but that is definitely not sufficient—you know that people can look much older or younger than they really are. So you ask for one piece of ID, and the person produces a driver's licence. That might be enough, if the picture matches the person. But even then, we know that fake ID is available. (Several newspaper reports in June 2004 indicated that British Columbia drivers' licences were particularly popular on an Internet site offering fake ID.) Perhaps we'd be safer to ask for two pieces of identification. It's harder to fake two pieces of ID, especially major credit cards and drivers' licences. So we settle for two pieces of ID, knowing that most likely the person we are dealing with really is the person with that name and age on the ID.

Occasionally, our presumption of sufficiency won't be correct: the ID will turn out to be fake. If we are selling a product, such false assumptions may not happen often enough to cost us many problems or bad debts. It may be just as reasonable to plan for the cost of covering a few bad debts as to try to set up tougher procedures. If you set up tougher procedures, you run the risk of increasing the time needed for each transaction, which may be unprofitable. Worse yet, you may risk violating privacy or offending the customer if you ask for information they would not normally be expected to reveal.

Sufficiency often varies according to what is at stake or the degree of urgency in the decision: do we have enough evidence for now? If you have a mole on your skin that seems to be getting larger, that's probably enough to send you to the doctor. Skin cancer might be an unlikely cause, but you'd prefer to be sure. If the mole "looks funny" but you don't think it has changed recently, you may prefer to wait and see.

As the stakes increase, so may the price we pay for being safer. We live now in a world where an increased risk of terrorism worldwide pushes us to gather more personal information on travellers to protect our security, yet the computers that collect the information are themselves vulnerable to hackers who can collect the information for their own uses. We are caught between the need to reveal more information and to conceal more. How do we strike a balance between safety and privacy?

Sufficiency, then, is often an open question. In some situations, we can specify exactly what will be enough information. An assignment might specify that you must use five articles from reputable journals. If you have found five suitable articles, you know you have sufficient information, even if you also know there are many more articles out there. In some situations, we will be constantly revising our expectations depending on what happens. The information needed to increase airline security has changed frequently and in many different ways as hijackers found new ways to take over control of a plane.

Upholding Values

Sufficiency may vary in ways that reflect social or personal values rather than personal expectations, in the context. What kind of evidence, and how much, must you have before you are required by law to report a suspicion of child abuse? When do you have sufficient reason to breach a promise of confidentiality? Typically, in these situations, we set priorities: harm to others outweighs individual privacy. If a person threatens to harm someone else, a counsellor can breach confidentiality to alert police to the danger. Yet because we also value a promise of confidentiality, we typically expect that a counsellor will warn the person in advance—"If you tell me you're planning to harm yourself or others, I will have to notify the authorities, but otherwise everything you say will be held in strictest confidence." This creates a sufficient protection of both values, avoiding harm to others and protecting confidentiality.

Expectations, Standards, and Accountability

We've been talking so far as if investigation is just a search for information. There is another major aspect of investigation, and that is the standards of performance you will be expected to meet. Expectations and standards indicate both minimum and maximum levels of acceptable performance. Accountability is being held responsible for meeting acceptable expectations and standards.

Expectations are people's hopes and best guesses about their performance. You will have expectations for your performance—for example, that you'll be able to score at least one goal this game. Your coach may have different expectations for you—for example, that since you're coming off an injury, you should play only a minimum time in the game. Expectations may be more general. For example, we all expect public transportation to be reliable: the bus should arrive on time, follow its scheduled route, and reach its destination on time.

Note here that people may have very different expectations of reasoning itself. Some people enjoy reasoning and do mathematical puzzles for fun. Some people would rather not reason and usually rely on intuition to guide them. Some people will not be open to reason from people outside their age group, their culture, their profession, or their faith. We'll be discussing these differences and how to manage them in Chapter 12. For now it is enough to remember that you cannot expect everybody to engage in reasoning with equal enthusiasm or equal ease.

Standards are rules for what counts as good, satisfactory, or unsatisfactory performance. They indicate the quality of the results. Employers set standards for job performance—for example, punctuality, thoroughness, and teamwork: have you been on time, completed all your assigned duties, and helped your co-workers as needed? For an argument, there will be standards of quality, as we'll see in Chapter 5. There are good arguments and bad arguments, and they are judged as good or bad depending on whether they meet standards of reasoning.

Standards can vary between contexts. All lawyers are responsible for producing the best evidence to support their case, but the standards that must be met will vary with the type of law. The criminal law requires that a charge be proved "beyond a reasonable doubt." Before an accused person can be judged guilty, it must be unreasonable to believe that someone else could have committed the crime. In civil law, however, the standard of proof is only "on a balance of probabilities." It must be more likely that the accused person did do what he or she is charged with than that he or she did not. In administrative law, the standard of proof is lower still; here, it is the "most credible testimony," that is, who sounds most believable. Clearly, it will take more evidence to prove someone guilty in criminal court than to prove someone guilty in civil court, and more in civil court than in an administrative tribunal.

Similarly, the standards of care to which doctors are held will vary tremendously between a well-equipped hospital in Canada and a field hospital in a war zone or a mission station in Africa. It is not that medicine itself sets different standards but that the standards of care will need to vary realistically with what is possible given the equipment and qualifications of the people there. A minimum standard of care, not a maximum, is set by the familiar dictum, "First, do no harm. . . ."

To hold a person—or to hold yourself—**accountable** is to hold the person responsible for meeting a particular level of performance. If people do less than they were accountable for, we expect them to fix anything they didn't do right the first time, or at least to pay any penalties that result. For example, we expect a restaurant to write up a new invoice with the correct charges on it if we've been overcharged for a meal. Conversely, accountability also protects people in situations where something goes wrong or they do make a mistake but it would be unfair to blame them. For example, if a nurse sees a doctor doing something unwise in treating a patient, the nurse is required to speak up and question the treatment. A nurse who sees a mistake and does not speak up is as accountable for a medical mistake as the doctor who made the mistake. If the nurse speaks up and the doctor can justify the treatment as reasonable in the circumstances, neither of them is at fault if the patient does not get better.

Expectations and standards can be realistic or unrealistic, reasonable or unreasonable. Maybe it's unrealistic to expect to be back in goal-scoring form so soon after an injury. Maybe, for once, you really do have a chance to get an A in a subject you usually struggle with. Maybe it's reasonable to expect you to stay after the end of your shift to close up, and maybe it's unreasonable to ask you to do it with only a few minutes' notice.

Before you get too far into a task, good reasoning suggests you should check what the expectations and standards are, and investigate whether they are realistic and reasonable. If there's going to be a problem, you want to know before it's too late to do anything about it. You do not want to be held accountable for something you could not reasonably have been expected to remember or do in the circumstances. This does not mean that a person who has acted responsibly will always be right, or always be safe. You can drive responsibly and still get into an accident—for example, the person behind you might rear-end you. The snow might be deeper and heavier than forecast, and your car might slide off the road in spite of your most skilled driving. You want to avoid extra or unreasonable penalties by knowing in advance what the standards are.

EXERCISE 4.8

Standards at Work

Pick any job with which you are personally familiar. For that job, which of the following would be reasonable to expect from a probationary employee?

   *Punctuality, to the minute
   Patience—never speaking harshly or negatively, or getting frustrated
   Completing all work assigned within a day
   Helping others with their jobs
   Obeying orders without question

Are any of the standards for this job unreasonable, in your considered opinion? If so, explain why.

Accountability is often a combination of what you are responsible for simply as a person and what you are responsible for in your job or profession—your professional responsibility. In the Introduction, we reviewed what counts as personal and professional responsibility. Personal responsibility is what you hold yourself accountable for—in other words, what you consider yourself responsible for just because of the particular person you are, with the particular values you hold. Professional responsibility is what you are accountable for because of the job or profession you are in.

In a number of situations, responsibility is defined for us. It might be defined informally, as a set of expectations that other people hold. It might be defined more formally, in institutional policies—for example, postsecondary institutions typically determine what acceptable conduct is for students and professors, including the standards that shall be used for assigning grades and completing programs. And responsibility might be defined in an explicit set of rules such as a professional **code of ethics**—a formal expression of the moral obligations of members of a profession.

Now we need to see how we can find out what our responsibilities are. Probably the most common reasoning question we forget to ask ourselves is "Do I have a choice here?" We often step into the middle of a situation because we think it's expected of us. Something may need to be done, but not by you. Perhaps you are not qualified or do not have the right authority. Conversely, perhaps you should be the one to take the initiative and step forward when no one else has done so.

For personal responsibility, you investigate your own skills, knowledge, and values. As you consider what role you should play in a particular situation, consider it from two different perspectives:

- What can you contribute? Where do your personal strengths, abilities, and interests fit in?
- How can you benefit by participating? Which values will you be upholding? What can you learn, what might you achieve, and what might you take away from the experience?

These two perspectives are important reminders that it's not always about you—self-interest isn't a good enough reason to join in the game or stay on the sidelines, to show up for your shift at work or call in sick. At the same time, complete unselfishness works no better—it doesn't help the team if you play the position you're least suited for. It doesn't help your co-workers if you take on a job you hate. Your personal responsibilities lie somewhere between being free to do nothing and feeling obliged to take everything on yourself.

For example, think about the scenario from Chapter 1, where you imagined watching a group of teenagers in a park. The focus there was on how you could decide if they were just horsing around, or whether there was trouble. If you do decide there is trouble, it doesn't necessarily follow that you should be the one to intervene—nor does it follow that you are free to walk away and hope someone else will deal with it. You do need to decide whether you have a responsibility to help reduce harm. How can you help, using the skills and knowledge you have? If you have a cellphone, you could call 911. If the teenagers are in the grounds of a school, you could alert the school authorities. If you are afraid for your own safety, you are responsible for getting yourself out of danger first, and then calling for help.

Typically, our responsibilities will vary with our role in the situation. Are you a friend, or a counsellor? As a friend, you cannot be expected to give the best advice or to stay neutral. As a counsellor, you can and will be expected to do both. Are you the owner of the car or just the person who happened to be driving it at the time of the accident? If you're the owner, you'll have to deal with the insurance details, but if you were just the driver, you won't.

 EXERCISE 4.9 ## Choosing Personal Responsibilities

Consider the following situations. What responsibilities would be best for you personally to take on?

1. Two jobs are available at the local community centre. There's an opening for a children's activity program coordinator, and there's an opening for

a groundskeeper. If you were to apply for one of these jobs, which would it be and why?

*2. You've stayed behind to clean up after a big social event. All the following tasks need to be done: taking down decorations, vacuuming, washing the dishes, rearranging heavy furniture, and putting out the garbage. For which of these tasks should you volunteer and why?

3. Two of your friends have been arguing with each other, and relations are very strained. Should you intervene? If so, why and how, and if not, why not?

*4. Your car has broken down yet again. The problem is something you could fix, but only if you had the time. Your car would be back on the road much more quickly if you took the car to a garage. Do you fix the car yourself?

5. You are coaching a sports team, and one of your players is struggling with a weight problem. Do you try to help the player with this problem, or do you refer the player to other people who could help?

To investigate professional responsibility, you often have to look for information specific to the profession or the employer. In many professional fields, such as law and medicine, you'll find reference to "professional responsibility" and "due diligence." You can use these as search terms in a library or on the Internet. You can also look for a "code of ethics" or guidelines for "professional conduct."

Professional responsibility covers the role and duties the professional has—the lawyer must provide the client with complete and competent representation. Due diligence covers the checks and investigations the professional must do to make sure he or she is making the right decision or taking the right action.

For example, a nurse must check that the medication is the right dose for the right patient before administering it. A doctor has to perform certain tests to be sure she is making the right diagnosis, and she has to keep up-to-date on the research to know she is recommending the right treatment. The lawyer has to check files and documents to be sure he has all the facts straight, and he has to be sure he has kept up-to-date on changes in the laws and regulations to be sure he is recommending the right action. A real estate agent has to be sure the buyer is informed of the true condition of the property. A mechanic had better check each piece of the exhaust system before recommending that the whole thing be replaced.

In all these cases, if the professional has failed to carry out necessary checks or has been too lazy to keep up with important developments, he or she can be sued for negligence: failure to carry out his or her duties responsibly.

Again, as noted earlier, this does not mean that a professional who has acted responsibly will always be right. The doctor may not know that allergies can be one trigger for depression. The physiotherapist may not have enough training in specialized orthotics to know that the client's back pain could be helped by better footwear.

The purpose of expecting "professional responsibility" is precisely to protect people in the cases where they do make a mistake but it would be unfair to expect them to do any better. Standards for professional responsibility allow us to say when we have done "enough" and have acted responsibly, even if our clients or customers would have liked more.

Codes of ethics set out precisely the standards to which members of a given profession will be held, and typically a professional body is responsible for enforcing this code. So, for example, if a nurse sees a doctor performing what seems to be the wrong procedure, and the nurse does not protest, the nurse can be held liable for acting irresponsibly. The Nursing Code of Ethics requires nurses always to put the patient's interest first, and that means a nurse must not defer to any other member of any other health profession if there is good reason to believe the treatment is misguided.

If you are a student, you are typically held to the standards of responsibility maintained in academic work: the same standards to which your professors are held. These standards are defined in the institution's policies and code of ethics. The primary responsibility of anyone doing academic work is to achieve rational beliefs, by being able to defend those beliefs as the conclusions of good arguments. Academic responsibility requires proof in the form of sufficient evidence of the type acceptable to the discipline. This typically includes sufficient research using reputable methods and sources, and complete citations for all sources consulted.

EXERCISE 4.10 ## Academic and Personal Responsibility

*1. Are you aware of your own institution's policies on academic responsibility? Provide evidence that you are familiar with the expectations by citing policy numbers and by noting briefly in your own words what each one calls for. (Check websites and other institutional resources such as handbooks, calendars, and course outlines, looking for references to academic standards, academic misconduct, plagiarism, etc.)

2. Pick a profession that interests you. See if it has a professional code of ethics, and if so, find a copy. What does it tell you about this profession's expectations of confidentiality or its need to check information?

*3. *Written Assignment*

Research component: Choose a topic that interests you. Find two articles on the same topic. Make sure both articles were written within the last two years, and that both contain arguments that offer contrasting views on the topic.

Write-up: In a one-page write-up attached to the articles, demonstrate your personal and academic responsibility in carrying out the research by answering the following questions:

Why did you choose this topic? How is it relevant to your personal or professional interests?

How did you carry out the search? What sources did you check? How were you able to tell that the two articles you found were suitable choices? How would you be able to demonstrate that you have met your own institution's standards for academic responsibility?

Key Points in Review

- Gather information step by step, stopping frequently to assess what you've learned and what you need next. Strike a practical balance between doing too little and doing too much.

- There are practical, ethical, and conceptual limits on gathering information. Not all of the information you might want will be available.

- The search for information may take you in directions you did not expect. You may be stopped or restricted in ways you did not expect, or your investigation may open up new avenues you did not anticipate.

- Nonverbal aspects of the context (numbers, images, sounds, and emotions) are additional sources of information about the context. To investigate nonverbal aspects, ask what effects they are intended to achieve. What significance might they have that is not obvious on the surface?

- Emotions are a signal that something significant is at stake. Investigate these emotional clues to develop a deeper understanding of their significance, especially where they indicate beliefs or values.

- Keep a complete record of your research, so you can locate the information again if it's needed and confirm that you did check enough reliable sources.

- Know where your own responsibilities begin and end, so you don't take on too little or too much.

Chapter 5

Making Connections: Investigating Argument Structure

■ Perspective

The principles of investigation covered in the last chapter showed you how to research and gather information about the claims you have observed. In this chapter, we turn to the investigation of arguments. As you've seen, reasoning often requires you to analyze arguments. We introduced the concept of an argument in Chapter 2, where we also took the first steps in observing the structure of an argument.

In this chapter, we investigate the structure of an argument in more detail, to see what will determine the success or failure of its reasoning. All arguments aim to support the conclusion of their argument with premises, but the nature of the support can vary and not every argument is meant to establish the absolute certainty of the conclusion. We will look at different types of reasoning an argument can use to reach its conclusion, and we will look at the different levels of support an argument might need to reach its conclusion. You will see what general principles guide an argument's success.

■ Scenario

You have just picked up your glass from where you left it in the kitchen at a party. As you are about to drink from it, another guest grabs your arm. "You shouldn't drink from a glass you've left unattended!" the guest exclaims. The guest goes on to tell you about a number of recent incidents where Rohypnol, the "date rape" drug, was dropped into drinks at parties or bars. Not only that, the guest says, there was also a case where someone took a drink from an open soft-drink can in the garage, and the can contained antifreeze, not pop. How is the guest's information meant to work to convince you not to drink from this glass?

■ Key Question

How is the argument meant to work?

Investigating Arguments

In the observation stage you learned how to recognize arguments and distinguish them from non-arguments. In the investigation stage, you consider the goals of an argument and examine the way it reaches its goals. In Chapter 2, we looked at what an argument is: a set of premises offered to support a conclusion. We took a first look at the argument structure—the way in which the premises are connected to the conclusion. In this chapter, we'll investigate argument structure in more detail: *how* do the premises work together to support the conclusions? This investigation will show us what the argument can do. Is it a **well-structured argument**—that is, is it well enough designed to be capable of reaching its goals?

By definition, the goal of an argument is to support its conclusion. As we saw in Chapter 2, arguments can be offered in a variety of contexts and for a variety of purposes. Arguments can defend or justify a belief or an action. Arguments can persuade other people to share a belief. Arguments can explore a new belief or uncover a new course of action. Consequently, arguments do not all have the same goals. Some arguments need to make their conclusions certain—to show that it would be unreasonable to deny them. Many arguments need only to establish that their conclusions are probable—that they are the most likely or the most reasonable option to consider. Some arguments only need to show their conclusions are one possibility worth considering. That makes a difference to what it means to "support" a conclusion. All arguments are offered to show that their conclusions are acceptable, but acceptable to what extent? In its context, an argument may be designed to end debate by presenting a final answer. This argument needs to make its conclusion certain. An argument may be designed to offer a practical solution that can be acted on without delay. This argument needs to make its conclusion probable. An argument may be designed just to entertain an interesting possibility. The purpose of the argument makes a difference to the kind of structure it needs to do its job.

As we investigate argument structure, we will see how the goal of the argument affects the level of support the premises need to provide for the conclusion. Think of the many kinds of houses that are built in Canada. There are stone mansions and wooden longhouses built to last for many years, following traditional building methods. There are cabins, hunting lodges, and cottages, built using whatever methods will work for that season and that climate. There are lean-tos and shelters and experimental architectural designs, built to hold up long enough to get through the night or ride out a storm or show what might work for the future. We would not fault the construction of a sod house on the prairie because it lasted only a few winters instead of a few centuries. Similarly, as we investigate argument structure, we will see how the goal of the argument affects the level of support the premises need to provide for the conclusion. If the argument offers good support for its conclusion, we should accept the conclusion. We will judge the structure of an argument by whether it meets the goals set for it, not by whether it can make its conclusion stand for all time.

The Connection between Argument Structure and Argument Success

Our main concern in evaluating arguments will be to determine whether the premises can provide good support for their conclusions or whether they fail. Investigating the **structure of an argument**—seeing how it works—will take us only part way to that goal.

Whether the argument is well-structured or not will be one crucial factor in deciding if the argument succeeds. However, it is not the only factor. The second factor is whether the premises are acceptable. We must investigate these two factors separately, because neither one alone is enough to make a good argument. All good arguments must have good argument structure, but not all arguments with good structure will be good arguments. All good arguments must use accurate information, but not all arguments using good information will be good arguments. We've already seen how to begin investigating whether the premises are true, by using the methods described in Chapter 4. Now we will investigate how arguments must be structured if they are to work.

Argument structure and accurate information are both essential to a good argument. Let's look at some easy examples to make that clear. Both of the following arguments are bad arguments, but they are bad in different ways.

A. All dogs are poodles. Lassie is a dog. So Lassie is a poodle.

B. All dogs are mammals. Lassie is a dog. So Socrates is mortal.

Example A is a bad argument because it has one false premise. Obviously, not all dogs are poodles. Argument B does not have any false premises (we'll accept that Lassie is a dog), but it is still a bad argument because the premises simply do not support the conclusion. The problem is not with the accuracy of the information. There's something wrong with the structure of the argument.

When we examine the structure of an argument to see how it works, we must bear in mind that we may not yet know whether the argument is presenting accurate information. At this stage, we may not yet have had any opportunity to find out if it is using accurate information. Investigating information, as we did in Chapter 4, cannot always come first. Our investigation of the structure of an argument is not enough to show that the argument *does* work, only whether it *could* work. The value of investigating argument structure is that if an argument could work, then it will be worth making the extra effort to investigate the accuracy of the information given in the premises. We also can often see from the structure exactly what we need to investigate further. However, if an examination of the argument structure shows the argument could not work, we are saved the effort of investigating further.

Components of Argument Structure: Level of Support and Type of Reasoning

Investigating argument structure shows whether the argument can work. The first key element involved in determining how the premises support the conclusion, then, is what *level of support* the premises are meant to provide for the conclusion. The goal of the argument might be to make the conclusion certain, probable, or merely possible. We need to know what the argument is intended to achieve in order to be able to tell whether it meets that goal. As we will see shortly in more detail, the more certain the conclusion is meant to be, the stronger the support needed from the premises.

The second key element in argument structure is the *type of reasoning* being used to connect the premises and conclusion. What kind of reasoning links the premises, and how do those links help to show that the conclusion is acceptable? We need to see how an argument is put together in order to understand whether its premises can provide the level of support needed.

These two steps will help us investigate how an argument is supposed to work and whether it could succeed.

Levels of Support: Argument Goals

When we consider the goal of an argument, we investigate how strongly the premises could support their conclusion if we consider only the argument structure. Could the premises show that the conclusion is absolutely certain or only that it is probable? Consider the following short arguments.

"This store always gives refunds without requiring the customer to present a receipt. The customer returned a product to the store without a receipt. So, the store will give the customer a refund."

"Many stores give refunds without requiring the customer to present a receipt. The customer returned a product to the store without a receipt. So, there's a good chance the store will give the customer a refund."

"Stores can give refunds without requiring the customer to present a receipt. The customer returned a product to the store without a receipt. So, the store might give the customer a refund."

All these arguments offer premises to support their conclusions. They all have a similar structure: two premises offered together to support a conclusion. However, they do not offer the same level of support for their conclusions. The first argument intends to make its conclusion certain: the customer is guaranteed a refund. The second argument only concludes that the customer will probably get a refund—a refund can be expected, but is not guaranteed. The third argument offers only the possibility that a price reduction will be given—a refund might happen but shouldn't be expected. There is a difference in the level of support that is needed to make the conclusion acceptable.

If an argument is offered to establish its conclusion as certain, its premises must offer the highest level of support for the conclusion. We will call these **arguments to certainty**. Arguments with this goal occur in criminal law, when the accused must be proved guilty "beyond a reasonable doubt," using legal reasoning and physical evidence. Arguments with this goal also occur in mathematics or theoretical physics, using mathematical proofs. Arguments with this goal will also occur in ethical decision-making, using reasoning from ethical principles—for example, when it must be decided whether a patient has given informed consent to a medical procedure.

Arguers do not always intend or need to construct an argument that makes the conclusion a certainty. They may only want to show that the conclusion is probable: the most likely or the most reasonable of several possibilities. Arguments with this goal only need to accumulate enough evidence to show why the conclusion is most likely or most reasonable. They do not need to rule out every other possibility, because they already acknowledge that there may be some other less likely possibilities. We will call these **arguments to probability**. Arguments with this goal are common in the natural and social sciences—for example, when biologists explain why moss can grow even on a sunny lawn, or when psychologists work to understand why some victims of abuse grow up to become abusive but others do not. They are found in statistics and economics—for example, when a poll is taken to predict the outcome of an election, or when transit officials try to find out how likely it is that more people will take public transit if the price of gas goes up. There are also many everyday contexts where we give arguments with this goal—for example, when we argue that it is not safe to take the car out on icy roads because there's too great a chance of having an accident.

In other contexts, the goal of the argument is just to show that its conclusion is an option worth considering. Arguments with this goal only need to show that their conclusions are possible. The conclusion may be only one option among many, but it is an option that is nevertheless interesting and worth further consideration. These arguments only need to produce enough evidence to show that there is nothing inconsistent or improbable about the conclusion. Because they already acknowledge that there may be other likely possibilities, they do not even need to show that their conclusion is more likely than other plausible alternatives. We will call these **arguments to possibility**: the conclusion is possible, given all the information available. Arguments with this goal occur in history, theatre, literature, anthropology, and many other humanities disciplines. For example, a historian might argue that practices such as "mumming" in Newfoundland or parades by organizations such as the Calathumpians in the Maritimes in the nineteenth century can be seen as an effective way to protest and subvert authority, not merely as lively entertainment. We also use these arguments in many everyday contexts, such as interpreting behaviour—for example, "He might have been so busy and preoccupied that he didn't even notice you, so perhaps he wasn't deliberately ignoring you."

The distinction between different goals enables us to recognize how an argument structure can succeed or fail in providing sufficient support for its conclusion. One common way an argument can fail is for there to be a mismatch between the level of support the conclusion is intended to have and the level of support the premises are capable of providing. It is a mistake in structure to give only enough support to show a conclusion is probable when the aim of the argument is to prove the conclusion is certain. For example, it is a structural mistake to argue, "You've been late the last five times we've met up. Clearly you are incapable of being punctual." The conclusion is intended to be certain—you are incapable of being punctual. But the premise offers only enough information to show that you tend to be late. This information points to a possibility or a probability, not a certainty. Similarly, it is a mistake to give only enough support to show that the conclusion is possible when the aim was to show that the conclusion is probable. For example, it is a mistake of structure to argue, "Look, it is possible for her to get so absorbed in a book that she doesn't notice what's happening around. Probably she's late because she got shut into the library after closing time." The conclusion is intended to be probable—she's most likely in the library. But the premise offers only enough information to show that this is one possibility; we have no idea how likely it is. We can recognize these as mistakes even when we have no information about whether the premises are acceptable—for example, when we don't know the person who was late, so we don't know how often this person has been late, nor do we know whether the person who might be in the library is capable of getting lost in a book. This is why we can call these mistakes "mistakes of argument structure": they are a problem with how the argument has been put together, not a problem with the specific information the argument uses about particular people or events.

Another failure of argument structure is to provide so little support that the argument cannot even make its conclusions possible. This happens when the premises—even if we assume they are all true—still add nothing helpful to increase the chances that the conclusion is true, or when the premises point in the wrong direction entirely and make the conclusion unlikely or even impossible. For example, "It's important to eat breakfast to give you energy for your day. Milk is a good source of protien. So a bowl of delicious Nutzy cereal is the best start to your day." The premises are acceptable, but they don't help support the conclusion that you should have Nutzy cereal for breakfast. Even if you have the cereal with milk, it may be better for you to have the milk by itself, or to have a more nutritious cereal.

Arguments can make even more dramatic mistakes in their level of support. They can inadvertently point in the wrong direction, thereby making the conclusion improbable or even impossible. For example, "He's been so nice to me at work lately. He's helped me rearrange the stock and finish the inventory, and he's even treated me to coffee. I haven't seen him act this nice for months. He must be trying to cover up something he's done wrong." Even if we assume the premises are true, we would be wrong to accept the conclusion based on this argument. What these premises do is point increasingly toward a different conclusion: that the co-worker has had a few tough months but is now back to his normal friendly self. The conclusion is intended to be certain: the co-worker must be covering up. Before we look at any supporting premises, the statement "He must be trying to cover up something he's done" is a possible explanation for a co-worker's behaviour. Background knowledge tells us that co-workers do sometimes cover up mistakes. However, even the first premise starts off in the wrong direction. "He's been so nice to me at work lately." When people are unusually nice, it is possible that's because they are trying to distract you from noticing something that's wrong. However, it is also possible that people are unusually nice when they're in a really good mood. The premise actually opens up this additional possibility for equal consideration with the possibility of a cover-up. The next premises take us farther in this direction. Helping with work that needs to be done and buying coffee are average, fairly low-key ways of being nice to a co-worker. They aren't extravagant enough gestures to be clear evidence of a problem. The final premise indicates he used to be this nice before, so this is common behaviour for him. Even without knowing anything about this employee or what he has actually done, as the premises combine, it seems more and more probable that the co-worker is simply in a good mood and that the suspicious conclusion is unjustified. The mistake in argument structure is that the premises point away from this conclusion, not toward it.

To see that premises can even make the conclusion impossible, consider the following short example. "I know I told the students I would not mark late papers under any circumstances. There's only one late paper here, though, so it's reasonable to go ahead and mark it." The mistake in structure here is that these premises could point only toward the opposite conclusion. It's not possible to be justified in marking even a single paper given a firm principle to accept no late papers at all.

The ways in which the structure of premises can succeed or fail to provide sufficient structural support for a conclusion are set out in Figure 5.1.

FIGURE 5.1

Truth of Conclusion					
Certain	Probable	Possible	Unknown	Improbable	Impossible
Level of Support Provided by Premises					
Guarantee	Make probable	Consistent	Neutral/ irrelevant	Inconsistent, improbable	Contradict
Argument Structure					
Valid	Cogent	Plausible	Faulty		

Identifying Argument Goals

How can you tell whether an argument is an argument to certainty, an argument to probability, or an argument to possibility? Sometimes, the goal of the argument will be revealed in the wording. For example, phrasing in the conclusion such as "obviously," "without a doubt," "it has to be," "surely," and "certainly" are clear indicators that the argument is intended as an argument to certainty. Phrasing such as "most likely," "usually," "we'd expect," and "probably" are equally clear indicators that the argument is intended as an argument to probability. Phrasing such as "it could be," "it makes sense to," "perhaps," and "possibly" indicate an argument to possibility.

Sometimes the goal of the argument can be determined only by an investigation of the context in which it is given. For example, a new member in a club might tactfully say, "I wonder why the club has its executive organized this way. I used to be in a club that was run with two co-chairs, and it was a surprisingly flexible and efficient structure. It's possible this club might also benefit from two co-chairs." On the surface, given the words alone, this looks like an argument to possibility. In the context, it might actually be an argument to probability. The new member cannot imagine why the club has a single chair and thinks that although there might be some extenuating circumstances, the club would probably be better off with two co-chairs. The tact of the newcomer masks the level of certainty that the conclusion is intended to have and also the level of support that the premises should provide. Context can also weaken the apparent level of support for a conclusion. For example, a parent may say to a teenage artist, "Jobs in art pay so little! You're much more likely to find yourself starving than you are to make a living wage. You ought to pick another career." On the surface, this looks like an argument to probability. However, the parent might be intentionally exaggerating the risks just to get through to a teenager who has evidently never considered how much money it takes to live alone. As long as the teenager pays reasonable attention to the possibility of a low salary in art, that will be all the argument needed to achieve. In the context, this is an argument to possibility.

The principle of charity is a guiding principle of interpretation that was discussed in Chapter 3; it should be applied when deciding whether the argument is an argument to certainty, probability, or possibility. When there is more than one possible interpretation of the goal of the argument, you should use the interpretation that makes the best sense in the context—the interpretation that gives the argument its fairest chance of success.

EXERCISE **5.1**

Recognizing Goals: Arguments to Certainty, Probability, and Possibility

*1. For each of the following short arguments, decide whether it has the goal of an argument to certainty, an argument to probability, or an argument to possibility:

a. My rent's due tomorrow. I had to pay my course fees yesterday, and that took almost all the money I had. I have no way to get more money by tomorrow. I certainly won't be able to pay the rent on time.

b. Heraclitus wrote that you can't step into the same river twice. He could have meant that nothing remains the same. But given the fact that he thought there was an underlying unity to the universe, I think he meant that something can be the same and different simultaneously.

c. I've seen Sarah at the mall every Saturday this month. She may have a job there now.

d. The robins are making exactly the same steady chirping noise they did last year when we found a baby robin in our garden. There's probably a baby robin out of the nest again.

e. Experiments have shown there is a high risk of Reye's syndrome in children and young adults who take aspirin for fever or headache. Acetaminophen has not been shown to have the same risk. Therefore it would be better to take acetaminophen rather than aspirin for pain or fever.

2. Look ahead to the arguments at the end of Chapter 8 (pages 253–257). For each one, decide whether it is an argument to certainty, an argument to probability, or an argument to possibility. Explain your decision by describing which elements of the argument indicate the level of support needed for the conclusion.

3. Find your own examples of an argument to certainty, an argument to probability, and an argument to possibility. Investigate the context in which the argument is given. Explain what evidence in the argument itself and what evidence in the context supports your decision.

Well-Structured Arguments

As we have already indicated, an argument can have a good structure even when it is not a good argument. We would like to be able to identify good structure without causing any confusion about whether the argument itself is good as a whole. From now on, we will use the term "well-structured" to refer to an argument that does use the structure required to give the level of support needed by its conclusion. As we look more closely at the structure of arguments to certainty, probability, and possibility, we will investigate what is required for a well-structured argument in each category.

Category 1: Arguments to Certainty

Arguments to certainty are intended to meet the most demanding standards we can set for an argument: the premises must establish that the conclusion is either necessarily true or so highly likely that doubting its truth would be pointless. In all arguments to certainty, the key element is that the premises establish that any competing conclusions have been effectively ruled out. We'll call a well-structured argument to certainty "**structurally valid.**"

Structurally valid arguments are such that, given all the information offered in the premises, either we are *guaranteed* that the conclusion is also true or it's close enough to make no practical difference. We test the structure of arguments to certainty by seeing if there are any plausible loopholes to be found. If there is any competing conclusion that can be shown to be plausible given all the premises, the argument to certainty is not well structured.

Although the word "valid" is commonly used to mean "good" or "well thought out," and in our everyday speech we may talk about a valid point or a valid perspective on an issue, for the purposes of argument analysis, the phrase "structurally valid" has a much narrower meaning. Only arguments

> **DEFINITION**
>
> An argument is **structurally valid** if assuming that the premises are true makes the conclusion either necessarily true or so highly likely that doubting its truth would be pointless. Arguments that are not structurally valid are called "structurally invalid."

can be structurally valid or invalid. Premises and conclusions taken separately can be true or false, but they cannot be structurally valid or invalid.

Here is a more detailed example of an argument to certainty to show how they can work:

1. The rule is that if you want to officially contest a parking ticket, you must submit a Notice of Dispute within thirty days of the date served.

2. You received a ticket, and the date served will be shown on the front of your ticket.

3. On the front of the ticket, the date given is July 1.

4. You have submitted a Notice of Dispute.

5. The date on your Notice of Dispute is August 3.

6. The period of time from July 1 to August 3 is thirty-three days, and that is more than thirty days.

---

7. According to the rule, you cannot officially contest the ticket.

This argument is a well-structured argument to certainty: it is structurally valid. It intends to guarantee its conclusion, and step by step it does exactly that. It states the rule it is applying. It examines the facts of the situation to see if they fit within what is permitted by the rule. The facts do not fit—in this case, according to the rule you cannot challenge the ticket.

Arguments to certainty fail whenever they overlook a contrary conclusion that is consistent with assuming the premises are true. For example, consider an argument where the attempt to play by the rules fails:

1. Paying a ticket in full or in part is considered a guilty plea of the offence described on the front of the ticket.

2. You have appeared in court and pleaded guilty to the offence.

---

3. You must have paid all or part of the ticket.

This attempt at an argument to certainty fails because it misunderstands or misapplies the rules. It leaves a loophole—it overlooks a circumstance in which the premises can be true and the conclusion can still be false. Suppose the premises are both true—we have given the right rule about what it means to pay the ticket, and you did appear in court, and you did plead guilty. Can the conclusion still be false? Yes, it can. You might not have had enough money to pay the ticket, and you might have had to show up in court to say so. In fact, if you investigate, you will find that not only is this possible, but there's a provision for exactly that situation: "The full ticketed amount is due and payable immediately. Non-payment may affect your ability to obtain or renew licences or permits, and collection measures may affect your credit standing." (All the information on disputing tickets is from the ICBC Road Sense brochure, "How to Pay or Dispute a Violation Ticket.")

These two examples show you the key structure of reasoning to certainty: it is well-structured when the conclusion is certain if all the premises are true.

As we'll see when we come to evaluate arguments, this means that our principal method of evaluating whether an argument has a valid structure will be to see if we can find even a single plausible case where the premises would be true but the conclusion would be false—we'll look for "the exception that proves the rule" in exactly the original sense of that saying, an exception that tests whether the rule really is true.

As we've mentioned earlier, arguments are often given when a conclusion is not so obvious that people accept it without question. An argument to certainty is meant not just to move us toward accepting the conclusion, but to remove all reasonable doubts we might have about the conclusion. For example, in arguments in formal logic or mathematics, there is a specific procedure that must be carried out to complete a proof. A set of accepted rules or axioms must be chosen, variables must be defined, and the rules applied accurately and systematically with every step visible, until the conclusion is reached. (We will see examples of this method later in the chapter.) Because these kinds of argument are so systematic and are meant to establish their conclusions to the highest possible degree of certainty, they have often been taken as the model all arguments to certainty ought to follow. These arguments aim to show their conclusions are necessarily true—it is impossible for the conclusion to be false if the premises are true.

Arguments to certainty, as we've defined them, do not all have to meet the standards set in formal logic and mathematics. Some successful arguments to certainty do not establish their conclusions as necessarily true because there is still a very small possibility that the conclusion is false. However, that possibility is so small and so ridiculously unlikely that it is a mistake to take the conclusion as anything other than certain.

For example, picture two hikers standing by a bridge on a trail. One is hesitating in front of the bridge. The other says, "That bridge is safe. It will easily hold your weight. This is a well-maintained park. The wood looks new. We just saw two people cross it together safely, and they both looked bigger than you." The conclusion is that this bridge is safe. This conclusion is not guaranteed, because the hiker who gives the argument could be hallucinating. However, both hikers can see the bridge, and if the condition is exactly as described, there is no reasonable competing conclusion they could believe. The chances that the bridge is not safe in spite of all this evidence are so remote as to have no practical value.

In some cases, certainty is defined neither logically nor practically, but by set standards that indicate how highly probable a conclusion must be before it is accepted as certain. For example, one variety of argument to certainty that establishes high probability rather than necessity occurs in criminal court proceedings. A verdict of "guilty" can be given only when the accused is shown to be guilty "beyond a reasonable doubt"—in other words, the judge is certain the accused committed the crime. The methods of proof used by lawyers in arguing for guilt or innocence, and by the judge in handing down a decision, do not look like mathematical proofs. The tests of certainty used in the courts are a complex sequence of arguments by lawyers, evaluation of those arguments by a judge applying the law and precedents set by previous cases, appeals of the judge's decision if the reasoning seems mistaken, and final judgment by the Supreme Court, a court given the power to make binding decisions about what proof must be accepted. If an accused person has been found guilty even after appeal to the Supreme Court, this verdict is certain: in the eyes of the law, it is no longer reasonable to accept the conclusion that some other person committed the crime of which this person has been accused. Following prescribed court procedures accurately and completely is what is meant by proving a case. Very rarely, someone who was found guilty and imprisoned is later found innocent and released. This only shows that the court proceedings do not aim for necessary truth—conclusions we cannot even imagine to be false. The courts use a method of attaining certainty that is defined by law. A guilty party cannot claim to be innocent in the eyes of the law because the court did not give a mathematical proof of guilt.

Category 2: Arguments to Probability

An argument to probability offers premises to prove its conclusion "on a balance of probabilities." Not all arguers are attempting to establish that their conclusions are certain. When an argument is not even trying to establish that its conclusion is a certainty, it cannot be faulted when its structure could not support such a strong conclusion. When the goal of an argument is to establish that a conclusion is probably true, but competing conclusions are still a live option, we hold the argument to different standards than those for an argument to certainty. There is possibility that the conclusion could be false, but that possibility is low. Consequently, the standard for an argument to probability is that it does show how its conclusion can be true, and it effectively shows that contrary conclusions are less likely to be true.

> **DEFINITION**
>
> An argument to probability is a **cogent argument** if assuming the premises are true makes the conclusion *probably* true and the probability that the conclusion is true is not so high that doubting the truth of the conclusion would be pointless. Competing conclusions are possible, but are less likely or less important.

Well-structured arguments to probability can take many different forms. The argument may offer specific figures to indicate a numerical measure of probability—for example, "Given the weather patterns in the area to the west of us, there is an eighty percent chance of rain tomorrow. So I'd say we probably need an indoor location we can use if it rains." The argument may simply assert an unspecified probability: "I can't see the animal clearly enough to be sure, but given the area we're in, I'd say it's most likely a black bear." In the first case, we're being given an indication of just how much more likely it is to rain than to stay dry. In the second case, we're being given no indication of how likely it is that the animal is a black bear—we may not even know what other animals are in the area.

What is important to keep in mind about the distinction between arguments to certainty and arguments to probability is that with arguments to probability we do recognize ahead of time that the conclusion is not the only possible option, and there might be at least one other competing conclusion we should keep in mind. This makes a considerable difference to what will be needed in the structure of the argument to provide the right level of support for its conclusion. The premises taken together are intended to make the conclusion the most likely or the most important to consider given what we know now. But we don't know everything, and we probably can't know everything before we have to take action. It can be reasonable to act based on arguments to probability. We act on what we can say is a probable—even if not certain—conclusion.

For example, consider the short argument, "Squirrels aren't usually dangerous, so it's safe to walk right up to them." We accept the argument and normally approach squirrels without fear. And then, later, something unlikely actually does happen and the conclusion is wrong. We step outside our front door, near a mother squirrel who cannot reach her baby, which is trapped under our front steps—and the squirrel becomes a raging demon, charging and biting. Have we made a mistake in reasoning, just because information we didn't have at the time—about the baby—turns out to work against us? No. The value of arguments to probability is precisely that they show the conclusion is more probable than any of the known alternatives, given all the information we currently have. If the argument structure shows that when we assume the premises are true then the conclusion is probable, it is well-structured: it is cogent. Many contexts do not require certainty. Often, if we have a cogent argument and we have investigated the accuracy of its premises we can act on the conclusion and show we have acted responsibly. We have picked a rational belief. If it does turn out to be wrong, we can't be accused of being unreasonable—this is the definition of "unforeseeable circumstances." For example, when the Tacoma Narrows Bridge collapsed in high winds in 1940, the engineers who designed it had not foreseen that it could vibrate the way it did. The arguments and mathematical proofs used to justify the design were so good—even if not providing certainty—that the bridge collapse caught everyone by surprise. In fact, there was no consensus on how the collapse could have happened, and it has taken many years and the development of new forms of computer analysis to see what caused it.

To see how a cogent argument to probability can be well-structured but still allow for its conclusion to be wrong, consider the following simple example: Your friend in Australia is very excited because he just got a cat. You decide that for a gag gift you'll knit cat booties for his new cat. You present yourself with the following argument as part of justifying why you need to knit four booties.

1. Most cats have four legs.
2. Fluffy is a cat.
   _____
3. Fluffy has four legs.

This argument is structurally invalid because Premise 1 leaves open the possibility that some cats do not have four legs. The conclusion is probably true—but not so highly probable that doubt is pointless or absurd. Still, the conclusion is probable enough that we can reasonably act on it. Even if Premise 1 is true, Fluffy might be one of the few cats that do not have four legs. It is more likely than not that Fluffy has four legs, but the truth of the premises does not entirely close off the possibility that Fluffy has five or three legs. Still, this argument has a formally cogent structure. Its aim is to show what is most likely to be true. Given how rare it is for cats to have three legs or five legs, the premises do make it rational to believe the conclusion. Consider another example that relies on a representative sample.

1. In the local hospital, 200 babies were born last year. One hundred and two were male and ninety-eight were female.

2. The ratio of male to female babies born in one year is a reliable indication of the ratio of male to female babies that will be born in each future year.

3. We can expect that in any given year, fifty-one percent of babies born in the hospital will be male.

In this argument, the sample that was actually measured in one year is being used to generalize about what will most likely happen in every year. This will typically be well-structured reasoning only if the sample size is large enough and has been accurately measured.

Just as we can have arguments to certainty that are failed attempts to establish the certainty of the conclusion, we can have failed attempts at reasoning to probability. For example,

1. Some cars last over twenty years without rusting or becoming unreliable.

2. My car will last over twenty years without rusting or becoming unreliable.

This argument is not well-structured because if the premise is true, the conclusion offers too low a probability that my car is among those survivors. This argument is not cogent. It does not work because unlike the word "most"—which implies more than fifty percent—the word "some" does not give any indication of percentage. "Some cars" could mean "one car" or it could mean "almost all cars." There is no reason to believe that just because there are some examples of cars that last over twenty years mine is going to be one of them.

Arguments to probability are not well-structured when they aim for a higher probability than their evidence can offer.

Category 3: Arguments to Possibility

Arguments to possibility combine pieces of information to show that their conclusions are possible. An argument to possibility only needs to rule its conclusion in as one that ought to be considered. It does not need to rule other conclusions out. It is often intended to show that a particular interpretation is coherent and illuminating, even if there are other equally interesting and defensible interpretations. For example, an argument of this type may be used to support an interpretation of a text, or of a picture, or of a character in a play, or of a cultural practice. Any theatre director putting on a play relies on an argument to possibility: given everything in the play, and what is known about the intended audience, this particular interpretation of the play is possible and the audience will find it illuminating. The argument needs to justify how this interpretation of the play will resonate for this audience in this context: for example, a director might propose that *Romeo and Juliet* can plausibly be set in 1970s Quebec, with the Capulets as federalists and the Montagues as separatists. This conclusion will need evidence in the form of plausible comparisons of the tensions between the Capulets and Montagues and the federalists and separatists in Quebec. Will the interpretation fit with the dialogue in the play? If it can, the conclusion is possible and the play worth staging. A new interpretation will bring out an audience; an audience that wants to see Romeo and Juliet done only as Shakespeare would have pictured it, and done exactly the same way each time, will probably stay home and watch it on DVD. When used to interpret the choices of words and images, this kind of reasoning may be called critical analysis, critical discourse analysis, or literary analysis, depending on the discipline. Arguments to possibility are common in literature, art, and theatre and also occur in anthropology, history, and sociology.

Arguments to possibility are well-structured when every premise is consistent with the conclusion and when there is no information omitted that would point away from the conclusion—that is, when the argument has not left out anything important. We will call a well-structured argument to possibility **plausible.**

Arguments to possibility typically do not try to establish that the conclusion is the only possibility, even if they seem to have that flavour as you read them. They always allow that further information, or a new perspective, may permit even more interesting and valuable perspectives. Other conclusions remain open. If *Romeo and Juliet* has been staged as a drama of 1970s Quebec, how might it be staged using an interpretation from a feminist or an Indo-Canadian perspective, for example? Arguments in fields like anthropology and history also often interpret information in ways that remain open to revision. For example, an anthropologist may have a coherent and illuminating interpretation of why First Nations songs are "owned" by certain families and may not be performed by or for others. However illuminating the interpretation might be, anthropologists must always remain aware that they are interpreting the culture rather than living it, and any interpretation stands ready to be revised in the light of deeper experience.

The principal requirement of these arguments is coherence and consistency with all existing evidence. Where a well-structured argument to certainty must rule out all other conclusions, and a well-structured argument to probability must make its conclusion more probable than the likely alternatives, an argument to possibility need only make its conclusion worth considering as one alternative.

Consider, for example, the following argument.

My cat is panting and his eyes are dilated.

He ran into the house mewing.

This is not normal behaviour for him.

My cat is sick.

I am interpreting the cat's behaviour and concluding that the cat is sick. I may be well aware there are other possible causes—for example, perhaps the cat has been scared by something outside, or perhaps he's panting because it's an unusually hot day. I am not claiming sickness is the most likely cause of his behaviour. I may be well aware that the cat being scared is at least equally likely to cause all this behaviour. All I am claiming is that "My cat is sick" is possible given the truth of all the premises. This is a plausible argument: a well-structured argument to possibility. Even if the conclusion that my cat is sick is not the most likely possible explanation for his behaviour, it may still be worth considering. It may have important consequences—for example, I should consider taking the cat to the vet right away. We pay attention to well-structured arguments to possibility because the risk of ignoring a possibility may be one we can't afford to take.

Another use of an argument to possibility may be to show that an interpretation has interesting consequences. Here is an example of an argument to possibility that offers an interpretation. Sun Shuyun, a Chinese writer, travelled the Silk Road from China to India in the footsteps of a Buddhist monk, Xuanzang, who took the same route in 625 C.E. Xuanzang is noted as a selfless Buddhist master who underwent considerable hardship to bring an accurate record of Buddhist sutras from India to China. Sun's guide in the Kucha region, Salim, draws a different conclusion about Xuanzang based on a reading of the monk's record of his travels, *Record of the Western Regions*.

> I think Xuanzang was first and foremost a Han Chinese, and then a Buddhist monk. . . . Although he was a great master, he did not treat people as equals. If you read his descriptions carefully, they were not exactly flattering about us nomads, especially those who were not Buddhists. He described them as violent, greedy and vulgar-looking. Anyway his book was as much military information as a pilgrim's account.
>
> Let's take Kucha for example. Xuanzang said the country was very big, in fact the biggest oasis in the Western Region, with mild weather all year round. The soil was good for growing millet and wheat, rice, pears, peaches and apricots. It was rich in gold, copper, iron and lead. Monks did not need this information. It was for the Chinese army. In fact, it says in the preface that the book was written at the request of the emperor. (Sun 118–19)

Salim is not arguing that Xuanzang must be seen as having political interests and cannot be seen as a selfless master of Buddhist teachings, and he is not arguing that Xuanzang's interests were probably military, not spiritual. He is arguing that another interpretation is possible on the basis of the evidence, and that interpretation is that Xuanzang was as strongly influenced by his Han Chinese birth and upbringing as he was by his faith. Salim supports this conclusion with evidence that is consistent with the possibility. First, Xuanzang was not as egalitarian as a Buddhist is supposed to be. Second, he was willing to provide descriptive details of his travels at the request of an emperor who would be likely to use them for military purposes, even though Buddhists are pacifists. If this is a coherent possibility that fits with everything known about Xuanzang, the conclusion of the argument creates an interesting perspective: Xuanzang's importance at the time and to later generations may not only be as an inspiration because of his faith but also as an influence on Chinese policy because he was a source of information on other lands.

Mixed Support

We've assumed so far that all the premises lead in the same direction: all supporting the conclusion, or all pointing away from it. What happens if an argument contains some supporting premises and some non-supporting premises? We have already raised this possibility in Chapter 2, when we looked at counter-considerations (page 73). As you saw there, when we are considering the structure of the argument, we usually set aside the counter-considerations while we look at the premises that do support the conclusion. There are also premises that do not support the conclusion because they are irrelevant or obviously false. For these, we also ask, can we remove the non-supporting premises and still have a good argument?

For example, suppose a gambler says, "This is a trick coin with a head on each side. A tossed coin could conceivably land on its edge. Still, if I bet heads, I'll win." The non-supporting premise, "A tossed coin could conceivably land on its edge," is a counter-consideration. It points away from the conclusion that you'll win if you bet on heads. However, the non-supporting premise names a possibility so unlikely that the probability of the coin showing "heads" is virtually unchanged. In this case, the non-supporting premise can be removed without affecting the conclusion. This remains a structurally valid argument.

However, even though we set aside the non-supporting premises, we do not forget they were there. Even before we do any independent research into the acceptability of the premises, we can and should be aware that the information does not all point the same way. Now that we are investigating, not merely identifying structure, we keep track of the non-supporting premises as a possible source of problems for the argument.

It becomes a question of balance. Arguments in which the non-supporting premises outweigh the supporting premises cast doubt on whether the arguer has correctly interpreted the premises used. For example, consider the following argument. "It's not raining right now, but the forecast is for rain and I can see clouds building up quickly. I'd rather not walk in the rain. The weather is probably good enough for a long walk." The conclusion, "The weather is probably good enough for a long walk," is supported by only one of the premises: "It's not raining right now." The speaker prefers not to walk in the rain, and the remaining premises point to a probability of rain. If this argument is rewritten in standard form, we can see how little support its conclusion has, because the non-supporting premises are omitted.

1. It's not raining right now.

---

2. The weather is probably good enough for a long walk.

It's possible the weather is good enough to take a long walk without being rained on, but that one premise is not enough to make the conclusion probable. Furthermore, since the arguer has offered us additional information in the form of non-supporting premises, we are entitled to use that information. The non-supporting premises undermine the probability of the conclusion by indicating it is less likely to stay dry than it is to begin to rain and spoil the walk. When we consider the combined effect of all the premises, we can see that the reasoning is not as good as it needs to be. This is not a cogent argument: it is not a well-structured argument to probability. When non-supporting premises are left unchallenged by the argument, they also raise doubts about how we are to understand the arguer's use of these premises for this conclusion. Is the speaker unaware how quickly rain clouds can move in? Is the speaker an unreasonable optimist? Examples of mixed support can range all the way from a well-supported argument with only a single problematic premise to an argument with one sub-argument that supports the conclusion and many other sub-arguments that fail. Again, it will be a question of balance. Does the one supporting sub-argument provide enough support for the conclusion? Can we safely disregard the remaining sub-arguments? At the investigation stage, it is enough to be able to recognize that some premises and sub-arguments do provide support for the conclusion and some do not. We may not be able to make a firm decision on whether the argument is well-structured. At the evaluation stage, in Chapter 8, we can apply the principle of charity to deciding whether the non-supporting elements do cast the conclusion into doubt.

As we investigate whether arguments are valid, cogent, or plausible, we need to look more closely at how the premises are connected to provide the support. What types of reasoning do they use?

Types of Reasoning

The second main component of argument structure is the **type of reasoning** used: the way in which premises are linked to provide the level of support needed. Arguments can use different types of reasoning to reach the same level of support. By reasoning "type," we mean the way the connections are drawn between the premises and the conclusion. What makes premises capable of supporting certainty, or probability, or possibility? It's the reasoning: how we see the connection between the statements. Different types of reasoning work in different ways to rule in or rule out conclusions.

For example, if I want to argue that it's time to take your car in for a tune-up, I could say, "Cars generally don't run well unless they get regular tune-ups. I know there are exceptions, but your car definitely seems to run better when it's tuned up. It's been six months since you last took it in; it's due for its next servicing. I think you should take your car in for a tune-up."

Alternatively, I could say, "Look, you wouldn't drive your body all day without eating and expect to perform well, would you? So why would you

DEFINITION

The **type of reasoning** used is the way in which one or more premises are connected to support the conclusion. A **well-structured argument** uses the connections appropriate for its type of reasoning.

expect your car to perform well if you don't take it in regularly for an oil change and tune-up? I think you should take your car in for a tune-up."

Or I could list everything I've noticed about your car: "The last few times I've been with you, I've noticed that the car is running rough. It doesn't seem to start as easily as it used to. You said your gas mileage seems to be dropping. And the car was losing power on that last big hill. It's time to take your car in for a tune-up."

Those three short arguments all support the same conclusion: it's time for a tune-up. These are all arguments to probability: they all attempt to show that your car most likely should be taken in for a tune-up. But each one works in a slightly different way. For an argument to be well-structured, it must make its connections correctly—it must use good reasoning. Some connections work and some don't.

Are they all equally well-structured? That is, do they all provide enough support to show that the conclusion is probable? We may not be able to answer these questions just from what we already know about the arguments' structure. We also need to look at the type of reasoning used. How are the premises connected to the conclusion to indicate a probability? The first argument appeals to experience: it offers generalizations about what usually happens, as a guideline to what you can most likely expect in your own circumstances. The second argument is different. It appeals to a comparison between two different kinds of things: it suggests you should treat the workings of your car with the same awareness of its needs as you treat your own body. The final argument simply lists a number of facts about your car, hoping they will add up to a probability.

All these types of connections between a set of premises and a conclusion can be used effectively, to create a well-structured argument to probability, or ineffectively, to create a bad argument that cannot work. What makes them effective will be different for each type of reasoning. As we did with levels of support, we will need to avoid confusion between "good reasoning" that creates a *well-structured* argument, and "good reasoning" that produces a *good* argument. In the investigation stage, we are still looking only at how the argument is put together and whether it *could* work. Since the type of reasoning used is really just another level of detail in the argument structure, we will continue to use "well-structured" as the term for connections that work.

Different types of reasoning can be used in any of the argument categories. Whether we judge them as structurally valid, cogent, or plausible arguments requires a detailed examination of that type of reasoning. For example, consider another pair of arguments. I could say, "All cars need a tune-up every 20,000 kilometres. It's been 22,000 kilometres since your last tune-up, so it is certainly time you took it in." This argument appeals to a firm rule: all cars need tune-ups at regular intervals. Using the added information that your car fits the conditions described by this rule, the reasoning deduces that there is no doubt that your car should be taken in for a tune-up. That's one type of reasoning that could support the conclusion, but it's not the only type. Another argument to certainty might be "It's irresponsible to own a car you don't take care of. You and everyone else on the road are at risk if your car is not running properly. You should get your car tuned up." Although these premises are offered with as much confidence and certainty as the previous premises, they don't connect in the same way. Unlike the two previous premises, which must work together to lead to the conclusion, these two premises can work independently to support the conclusion. What makes it irresponsible not to take care of your car need not be the risk you pose to others. It may be irresponsible to disregard how much money you spent to get the car, and to let its value deteriorate too quickly because you don't maintain it. Are both arguments equally well-structured? In both cases, we look at the structure by assuming the premises are true and determining whether the conclusion is then certain.

Grouping reasoning into categories by "type" often reveals more clearly how the reasoning works and when we can count the arguments as successful. Exactly how reasoning can be grouped by "type" is open to discussion. The types may not be as different in their workings as they seem, or there may turn out to be important differences between groups of arguments that have all been lumped together in the same category. Nevertheless, the study of different types of reasoning has revealed some very useful patterns. There are recognizable patterns of well-structured arguments in which the premises will provide the right level of support for the conclusion, and patterns of faulty arguments in which the premises cannot support the conclusion. A detailed study of specific patterns of reasoning is beyond the scope of this book. We will take a brief look at four well-researched "types" of reasoning, to illustrate how some of the different types of connections between premises and conclusions create a well-structured argument. The four recognized types of reasoning we will review are analogy, conduction, induction, and deduction.

Analogical Reasoning

Analogical reasoning uses a claim of similarity between one thing and another to draw conclusions about one of the things being compared. The analogy points to close parallels between the items—such as similarity in appearance or function. Typically, the things compared are also different in some important ways. At the beginning of the chapter, we compared arguments to houses. Arguments and houses are very different kinds of things. The purpose of the analogy is not to blur the differences and treat arguments as something we literally build, but to highlight one or more features of the more familiar thing to shed light on the less familiar thing. There is a useful parallel between the way a house is built to suit its environment and its purpose, and the way an argument is constructed to suit its conversational environment and its purpose as a piece of argumentation.

Analogies are an appealing type of reasoning because they follow a pattern that is easily identified and understood: A is like B in one important respect, so we can expect A to be like B in another important respect. For example, the argument for a tune-up that compared a human body to a car relies on an analogy. Your body is like a car in being vulnerable to breakdown if its parts stop working. So we can expect your body to be like a car in needing regular checkups to prevent unexpected breakdown.

Analogies create good connections when they draw a fair comparison between unlike things—the things are comparable, and understanding one of them does help you understand and predict the other. An analogy that provides good connections contributes to a well-structured argument when the comparison is as possible, probable, or certain as the conclusion is intended to be.

Does the comparison between the body and a car work well enough to make it probable that regular bodily checkups are as important as regular mechanical tune-ups? Your body is not made of metal and your car is not self-repairing. When an analogy admits the two things compared are not identical, it builds in a possibility that they might not work quite the same way. Other conclusions may remain unchallenged. Perhaps your body is not as much in need of regular "tune-ups" as your car. Perhaps your body needs even more regular maintenance than your car.

Analogies fail when they do not provide the right level of support for the conclusion—for example, when they do show that a conclusion is possible, but the conclusion was intended to be probable. Suppose a psychologist who has been experimenting on rats argues that the rats' behaviour on the test can be used to predict how humans will behave under similar stress. This is not a well-structured argument until it also includes some evidence about why we can expect humans to respond similarly to rats. How similar are human brains to rat brains? Typically, analogies work best as support in arguments to possibility and work least well in arguments to certainty.

Arguments that rely on reasoning by analogy also fail when the analogy does not work at all because it is not close enough to justify the desired comparison. For example, consider the analogy from a letter you saw first in Chapter 1: "Can you imagine yourself going through your day wearing one of those suits for deep diving? The kind that have airhoses and cables attached to a ship somewhere on the ocean surface. Now imagine having to wear that suit 24/7 and perform your daily tasks. This is how I feel most days." This was used in an argument to support the conclusion that Alzheimer patients should be free to use the drugs that seem to help them. At most, the analogy supports the possibility that living with Alzheimer's disease can be as difficult as wearing a diving suit. Before we criticize it, we should also remember that just like narratives, analogies do not have to be offered as reasoning. The analogy might have been intended only as an image to evoke a sense of difficulty and discomfort: that would be an example of using an analogy as an illustration, not as part of a proof, and we would omit the analogy when deciding whether the argument is well-structured. Reasoning by analogy fails us when it is used as support in a context where analogies can only illustrate. For example, suppose a theoretical physicist argues that we know how the universe can expand because it is just like a balloon with spots painted on it: as the balloon is inflated, the spots get farther apart. Therefore, as the universe expands, the galaxies get farther apart. This common illustration in books on astronomy can work only as an illustration to help readers imagine the expansion. The analogy cannot provide even the minimum level of support needed for a well-structured argument to possibility. The universe is not wrapped around a space of empty air, like the balloon skin, and there is no physical equivalent of air blowing into that space to inflate the balloon. Only scientific evidence of how much the universe is expanding and theoretical proofs of how the expansion might happen can provide well-structured arguments to possibility for the expansion of the universe.

Since analogies depend on at least one of the items compared being familiar to the readers of the argument, an analogy can also fail if neither of the items is sufficiently familiar for the connection to make sense. One difficulty in judging whether an argument is well-structured when it relies on reasoning by analogy is judging how the analogy is supposed to make sense to its intended audience. An analogy can resonate for some people, given their background, but not for others. Consider the following argument about human rights by Michael Ignatieff, which uses reasoning by analogy.

> Citizens of a democratic country must be made equal if the country is to be run fairly. We can only achieve a fair outcome for all if each person can function with the same level of freedom—that is, if they are all on a "level playing field." The citizens of the country are like the atoms making up a solid, and atoms are like identical billiard balls. Picture the country as a pool table, and its citizens as the pool balls. The country's laws are the bumpers limiting the movement of the citizens, and the playing surface is the shared territory they occupy. If the balls cannot roll equally freely and independently across the table, the game will not be fair. So if the balls are not equal, we must make them so. (Adapted from Ignatieff 56–57)

Does this argument intend to show that it is most probable that citizens must be made as equal as possible, and that we must be free and independent individuals to have a fair society? Or does it intend to show only that it's possible we could see ourselves as part of a game, and if so, we should think about what would make the game fair? How we take this argument may depend on the context in which we read it. Ignatieff uses the example to illustrate how liberal thinkers in the late seventeenth century pictured a democracy. They were powerfully influenced by Isaac Newton's physics and his model of the world as made up of atoms interacting like separate rigid billiard balls. For educated seventeenth-century gentlemen, this analogy would likely have the force of an argument to probability. They would have seen balls, atoms, and people as being very much like one another because all have characteristics fixed by nature and all can be understood scientifically. For readers today, this argument more likely has the force of an argument to possibility: it is one interpretation of how people interact, and it may help us understand the "level playing field" concept of equality. Is it how a democratic country is most likely to operate? With the change in the background of the audience, the analogy itself works less well. Today, the analogy is less obvious. Atoms are no longer seen as rigid balls but clouds of energy. Humans are not seen as determined only by their biology. The analogy may seem a little closer to the comparison between a diving suit and mental difficulties—conveying a possible connection, but not a compelling one.

Both the level of support and the success of analogy as a type of reasoning may sometimes be determined by the context, not just by investigating the argument in isolation.

Conductive Reasoning

Conductive reasoning accumulates information as a way of supporting its conclusion. As more information is added, the sheer weight of it taken all together can make a conclusion highly probable, and in some cases certain. Piece by piece, the evidence combines to rule out other conclusions. Think, for example, of a murder case in which the sheer weight of forensic evidence points to a single individual: The murder weapon was found at the scene; DNA was found on the murder weapon; the DNA at the scene matches DNA taken from the suspect; DNA testing makes it virtually impossible that any other individual could have used that weapon at the scene; the inquest showed that the death of the victim was caused by this weapon. As the evidence accumulates, it becomes more and more likely that this suspect should be arrested and charged with murder. When the accumulation of evidence makes it certain that this is the right individual to stand trial for murder, the conductive reasoning has produced a well-reasoned argument to certainty. Notice, though, that this is an argument used in the context of deciding what case to take to court. The same argument might not work as an argument to certainty to prove that this individual committed murder. As we've already discussed, arguments to certainty for deciding guilt and innocence in the court system have their own specific rules. It might be that some of the evidence was obtained illegally and cannot be relied on in court. It might turn out that additional evidence shows that the suspect did kill the victim, but that the action cannot count as murder because it was carried out entirely in self-defence.

One of the reasons we do accumulate as much evidence as we can before presenting a case or defending an academic thesis is that reporting all the information combines the results so we can see whether all the evidence is consistent with the conclusion. The more evidence we accumulate, the more probable the conclusion becomes. Conductive reasoning creates a well-structured argument to probability when the premises are consistent and make it less likely that any other conclusion is true. For example, the conductive reasoning to support the need for a tune-up makes it probable that the car needs a tune-up. "The last few times I've been with you, I've noticed that the car is running rough. It doesn't seem to start as easily as it used to. You said your gas mileage seems to be dropping. And the car was losing power on that last big hill. It's time to take your car in for a tune-up." All the stated symptoms are consistent: they all indicate deterioration in the car's performance. All the symptoms of deterioration point to problems with the engine and fuel efficiency rather than to other car problems such as worn tires or bad brakes. The chances that a tune-up is the right solution are much greater than the chances that the car is running fine or that it needs a different type of repair.

Conductive reasoning fails in an argument to possibility when the evidence points in different directions or is obviously inconsistent or incoherent. That means either some of the pieces of information conflict with other pieces or the information does not form a coherent whole: it provides mixed support, as described earlier. The premises do not point in any clear direction.

Conductive reasoning fails in an argument to probability when its evidence is equally compatible with conclusions other than the intended one. For example, "I've been sick for more than a day, and I can't keep any food down at all. This came on very suddenly—I was fine the day before. I have a high fever, too. I don't remember eating anything that could have made me ill, and nobody else in the house is ill. I've probably got food poisoning." This fails as an argument to probability because the evidence does not all point in the same direction, and because it is equally compatible with a different conclusion. The fever and the absence of similar symptoms in other people point away from food poisoning. The combination of symptoms could also support a different diagnosis: a "stomach flu," one of the viruses that cause digestive problems. One of the challenges of medical diagnosis is precisely the difficulty of weighing symptoms that may point in different directions and may have more than one possible cause. Are these symptoms caused by a common virus or a rare one? Are the symptoms all caused by a single underlying problem, or does this patient have several different problems? Exploring conductive reasoning requires careful piecing together of the premises to see how well they fit together and which conclusions they could support. In deciding whether conductive reasoning produces a well-structured argument, we often return to assessing the overall level of support. Premises offered in conductive reasoning do work when they combine to provide "enough" support. Which conclusions did they need to rule out, and have they ruled out those conclusions? We will be looking more closely at what counts as "enough" support later in the chapter, under the heading of "sufficiency."

Inductive Reasoning

Inductive reasoning also accumulates evidence to support a conclusion, but it adds one important component: it compares different instances that are of the same type. It relies on what we have learned or come to expect about the world, and how similar things work, to conclude that one conclusion is more probable than any other. In other words, it relies on known examples to be good predictors of what is true of other examples of the same type. It may connect examples to each other, or it may construct and apply generalizations about all members of a category. Consider the fact that you need only one spoonful of soup to test whether the whole pot of soup needs salt. This is reasoning by induction. You know that the small spoonful is representative of the whole potful of soup, so if this spoonful needs salt, then the whole potful must need salt. You don't need to test spoonful after spoonful simply to accumulate consistent information that the soup needs salt. The single spoonful is enough proof to make it certain that—to your taste—the soup needs salt, because the rest of the soup could not be sufficiently different to make it reasonable to support the competing conclusion that the soup is already salty enough.

At the same time, the effectiveness of this reasoning in producing a well-structured argument does depend on how well it is established that one spoonful can represent the whole pot. When can we generalize from one example to all examples because they are the same kind of thing? For instance, knowing that we need to test only one spoonful of soup because ingredients in soup mix evenly, we can generalize that taking one spoonful is a good way to test whether a dish needs salt. For soups, gravies, and other liquids where we know ingredients quickly mix to become a uniform broth, this generalization works. For lumpy stews or dry mixes like a rice pilaf, it is no longer immediately obvious that one spoonful is a fair test. These dishes need stirring to mix their ingredients, and perhaps the pot just hasn't been stirred well enough to distribute the salt. When we have no way to be sure the generalization holds, good inductive reasoning would admit this and argue only to probability or possibility, not to certainty. "This spoonful of stew needs salt. I think the stew's been stirred. Probably the stew needs more salt."

Since inductive reasoning works by linking representative examples to each other and to generalizations about a whole category, it must use generalizations that are accurate and examples that really are representative. If it's going to be good reasoning to generalize from one spoonful to the whole pot, the single spoonful really must be exactly like the rest of the pot. If it's going to predict successfully what will happen in one case or all cases based on what's happened in previous cases, then the new case really must be in exactly the same category as the previous cases. For example, consider the reasoning in this argument. "One non-defective car battery was found to last five years. Most car batteries should last five years." This reasoning jumps from a single case to a generalization about all cases. Although that looks risky, it is still good inductive reasoning if this battery really is typical—that is, if the one sample we were able to examine really is representative of most things of its kind.

So far, we've given examples that go from one instance to a conclusion about many or all instances of the same type. Inductive reasoning more usually gathers several instances, or studies many cases, before drawing a conclusion about most or all instances of that type. For example, the company making the car batteries will test many batteries before it offers a warranty that its batteries can be expected to last five years. The key issue in inductive reasoning is not how large a sample has been tested, but whether the sample is a fair representation of the whole category.

Because we recognize that it is risky to jump to conclusions based on very little evidence, we often try to expand our range of samples enough to be able to produce at least a realistic estimate of how probable the conclusion is. Consider the following argument. "Fifty-one percent of babies born are male. Jodi is a baby. Jodi is more likely to be male than female." This inductive reasoning is good enough for a store serving Jodi's parents to decide to stock two percent more infant diapers with the extra absorbency in front—fifty-one percent male diapers and only forty-nine percent female diapers. However, even though it is good inductive reasoning to conclude that it is slightly more likely that Jodi is male, if you're sending a card to congratulate Jodi's parents, you'd probably better check before you write that you hope "he's" doing well.

The search for larger samples, clearer evidence, and stronger support takes us into the realm of statistics and quantitative research methods. So many occupations require the ability to interpret statistical data or to carry out empirical tests that courses in these areas are often required in an undergraduate degree. Without embarking on a more detailed investigation here, we can at least highlight several crucial factors that will be essential to good inductive reasoning from statistical data.

First, the sample used must be properly representative. That is, if we are going to study only some samples of a general category, we must choose enough samples and we must choose samples that share all the relevant characteristics in all the same proportions as the remaining members of the category. We must not pick only the items closest to us, or only the animals we can study in captivity, or rely only on e-mails sent in by people who are willing to take the time to respond to an online survey. If we're surveying the entire human population of a country, for example, we need a random sample, which includes people far and near, people with their phones turned off and people who can't afford phones, and people who are computer illiterate. For a sample to be truly random, that means every item in the category—in this case, the population—has to have exactly the same chance of being chosen. Random samples have to be selected by computer from a complete list, not by a fallible human hoping to cover every possibility.

Second, anything less than a survey of every single member of the category will always have a possibility of error. Suppose we survey 1,068 people to find out whether new drivers have a twenty percent chance of having an accident in their first two years on the road, and the results do indicate a twenty percent accident rate. Even if we know our sample was large enough to give meaningful results and was well enough chosen to represent all ages and backgrounds of new drivers, we still cannot say that the accident rate is exactly twenty percent. Because we have not surveyed every new driver, the sampling method used only gives us a high probability of measuring the right probability. That is, we have a ninety-five percent chance that we are right to within three percent of the right figure: if we repeated the same experiment 100 times, ninety-five of the experiments should result in accident rates between seventeen percent and twenty-three percent. We should expect some variation in our results.

Third, however high the probability of a connection between two things we are interested in, we have to remain aware that we may only be seeing a correlation, not a cause. A correlation happens whenever two events or characteristics typically, or always, occur together. For example, perhaps we find a perfect correlation between pain, such as a headache, and a feeling of stress. Did the headache cause the stress or did the stress cause the headache? The correlation cannot tell us. A classic argument in philosophy even argues that we cannot confidently recognize a cause through experience alone. David Hume argued in Book I of *A Treatise of Human Nature* that all we can ever confirm by experiment is that two things consistently occur together. We infer that one must cause the other, but it takes added reasoning to decide which of the two things is the effect and which is the cause.

The problem with inferring causal connections too quickly is that we don't know what else might account for the correlation. Consider the evidence that new drivers have a twenty percent chance of an accident in their first two years of driving. It's tempting to read the study of the accident rate of new drivers as showing that their inexperience causes the accidents. As an argument to possibility, it is plausible. The inductive reasoning indicates that inexperience is a possible cause. However, as long as other conclusions remain equally possible, the data do not yet permit us to conclude this is the most probable cause of the accident rate. For instance, another possible cause that could produce the same accident rate is teenage physiology. If a majority of new drivers are teenagers, and if the sample did not separate out teenage new drivers from older new drivers, then it is possible that the cause is the age of the driver, not the inexperience.

When inductive reasoning is being used in an argument to probability, we have to check very carefully that there are no other possible conclusions that could be supported equally well by the same data.

Deductive Reasoning

Deductive reasoning works by applying rules that admit no exceptions. To make a successful deductive **inference**—to deduce the truth of one statement from the truth of another statement—to a certain conclusion, the premises must combine to show that the conclusion is the *only* possible option. It must be completely impossible for the conclusion to be false when the reasons are true. All other imaginable claims that contradict the conclusion can be shown to be inconsistent with the set of premises taken as a whole. That is, we start by giving the argument the benefit of the doubt: we imagine (or pretend) that all the premises are true. If they are true, could the conclusion still be false? If it can, the argument will not work as a deductively valid argument to certainty even if the premises are all true. A deductively valid argument is a type of structurally valid argument. A **deductively valid argument** is an argument in which assuming the premises are true means that it is impossible for the conclusion to be false. For example, consider the following short argument. "If you ate the last cookie, there'll be chocolate around your mouth. But there's no chocolate around your mouth. So it was not you who ate the last cookie."

This is good deductive reasoning: a well-structured argument to certainty, structurally valid and deductively valid. *If* it's true that you couldn't possibly eat the cookie without getting chocolate around your mouth, *and* it's true that there is no chocolate around your mouth, then it must also be true that you were not the one who ate the last cookie. When we can confirm that there was no way to eat the cookie without getting chocolate around your mouth—for example, that you couldn't eat the cookie in one bite, and you didn't have time to wipe your mouth—and we haven't overlooked any smudges of chocolate on your lip, then we have a good argument to certainty. We are absolutely sure you didn't eat the cookie. The rule being applied is that if B always follows A, as the chocolate on the mouth always follows the cookie-eating, then when we don't have B, we can't have A either. This rule is a universal claim, like those we examined in Chapter 3. It doesn't say B probably follows A, so if we don't have B we probably don't have A. It says that A cannot possibly happen without B happening too. If B happens, A is certain.

Here's another short example that uses a different rule and is also a structurally valid argument to certainty. "Either he's playing soccer or he has gone out with his friends. I know he is not playing soccer, so he must have gone out with his friends." *If* those are the only two options—playing soccer or being out with friends—*and* if we know one of the options cannot be happening, then we can be sure the other option is the right one. When we can also confirm that these are the only options—he couldn't have gone to a movie or club by himself—and we can confirm the soccer field is empty, then we have a good deductive argument to certainty. He is out with his friends.

There are many different rules that can be used with deductive reasoning to construct structurally valid arguments. Unfortunately, we don't always apply these rules effectively or accurately, so it is easy to make mistakes that produce bad deductive reasoning and cause faulty arguments. These mistakes produce deductively invalid arguments. They do not guarantee the certainty of the conclusion even if all the premises are true. Consider the following example. "If you ate the last cookie, there'll be chocolate around your mouth. There is chocolate around your mouth. You ate the last cookie!" Now, before you assume you can get mad at me for taking the last cookie, stop and look a little more closely at your reasoning. I do have chocolate around my mouth. Is eating the last cookie the only way I could get chocolate around my mouth? No. Perhaps I just haven't wiped my mouth since I had a cookie earlier. Perhaps I've been licking the bowl from some chocolate cake batter, or I have been eating a candy bar I just bought. Maybe I did eat the last cookie, but this argument cannot prove it. The reasoning has left any number of loopholes that prevent the conclusion being certain.

This structural pattern is worth remembering because it is so common and so tempting to see as valid. It involves a misunderstanding of how inferences work. "If you ate the cookie, then you'll have chocolate around your mouth" is a universal claim. "If you ate the cookie" is the *antecedent*—the condition that has to be in place before we can apply the universal rule. "You'll have chocolate around your mouth" is the *consequent*—as the word suggests, it's the consequence of the rule. It is what happens when the antecedent condition is in place. But when we consider situations in which we don't know if the antecedent happened, we can't even reasonably guess what the consequence would be. We no longer know what rule we're supposed to play by. What are the rules that tell us what we can conclude from chocolate around the mouth? We haven't been given any. One option is "If you have chocolate around your mouth, you licked the bowl of batter clean." Another option is "If you have chocolate around your mouth, you just ate a chocolate bar." Another option is "If you have chocolate around your mouth, you ate the last cookie." There will be other options as well. The premise "You have chocolate around your mouth" supports any of these conclusions equally well. As soon as we realize that the premise does not point only toward the desired conclusion, we can see that at best all we have is an argument to possibility. The premise is consistent with the conclusion, but it does not even make it probable, much less certain.

The mistake made here is characteristic of problems in deductive reasoning. We easily misinterpret or overlook possibilities. Why this happens is a puzzle of great interest to researchers in cognitive psychology and to philosophers. How does the human brain make such errors in reasoning?

Might there actually be survival value in some of the mistakes we make, or is it only that our language simply is not clear enough to send our brains down the right paths?

We can see why the mistakes are easy to make and hard to explain by comparing the following two rules.

1. "If you pass Calculus I, then you can register for Calculus II."
2. "If you passed high-school math with a grade of B or better, then you can register for Calculus I."

Both rules are expressed the same way, "If A then B," but they don't work the same way. Anyone who has navigated through the complex processes of postsecondary course registration easily interprets the differences. Rule 1 typically works both ways. Passing Calculus I works to get you into Calculus II, and to get into Calculus II you must have passed Calculus I. There are no other options. Unlike in other disciplines where you might be able to demonstrate that you deserve a chance to enroll in a higher level course without the prerequisite lower level course, mathematics typically won't accept anything other than a pass in the previous course as the prerequisite for letting you into the next course. Rule 2, however, is not as strong. It only works one way. If you've registered for Calculus I, then like many introductory courses, passing high-school math with a grade of B or better is likely to be only one of many ways into the course. You might have dropped math in Grade 10 but recently taken an upgrading course and passed a high-school-equivalency test. You might have been out of school for many years and passed a math admission test. From rule 1, if we know you are registered in Calculus II, we can conclude that you did pass Calculus I. From rule 2, if we know you have registered for Calculus I, we *cannot* conclude that you passed high-school math with a grade of B or better.

These two examples show how the language we use and our familiarity with the context will influence our interpretation of a rule and how to apply it. Because we use the expression "if . . . then . . ." to cover both types of rule, we can slip into assuming the stronger, two-way version is intended. "If . . . then . . ." is ambiguous. It can mean "If A then B *and* if B then A," or it can mean "If A then B, but B may have other causes, too." As discussed in Chapter 3, we need to resolve the ambiguity before we can proceed. As we examine argument structures that use deductive reasoning, the most important check to make is whether there are possibilities that are not ruled out. You'll see this again in Chapter 8 when we evaluate whether reasoning is good or bad by looking for common mistakes that cause reasoning to fail.

EXERCISE 5.2

Recognizing Different Types of Reasoning

1. For each of the following examples, tell which type of reasoning is being used: reasoning by analogy, conduction, induction, deduction, or none of those four.

*a. The speed limit is clearly posted. It says sixty kilometres an hour, and you were doing seventy. There's just no question that you broke the speed limit.

*b. The robins are making exactly the same steady chirping noise they did last year when we found a baby robin in our garden. There's probably a baby robin out of the nest again.

*c. Experiments have shown there is a high risk of Reye's syndrome in children and young adults who take aspirin for fever or headache. Acetaminophen has not been shown to have the same risk. Therefore it would be better to take acetaminophen rather than aspirin for pain or fever.

*d. That old dog at the shelter has not been adopted yet. Most people choose younger dogs. I've always liked having a dog around. We've got enough room for a dog, and I'm home often enough to be able to walk her and play with her regularly. In fact, walking her daily will be good exercise for us. We should adopt her.

*e. If the landlord phones this month because the rent cheque is late again, I'm going to be really annoyed. I get so worried when I don't know if you sent the cheque in on time. You should let me know when you send the cheque.

*f. Heraclitus argues that even things that we consider the same are not really the same over time. He wrote that you can't step into the same river twice. The river might seem the same in appearance, but the water in it is not the same water that was there when you last stepped in. Similarly, humans might seem unchanging on the outside, but the cells inside them are constantly changing and being replaced.

g. You seem to have unusual trouble writing down your ideas, even though you can explain them very clearly when you're talking. You may be one of the people who has a learning difficulty related to memory, one that prevents you holding ideas in your mind long enough to put them down on paper.

h. Near-death experiences can all be explained by what is going on in the room or in the person's brain at the time the heart stops. The similarities between people's stories about going toward a bright light and feeling people waiting to welcome them only show that all humans' brains react the same way once the heart stops pumping blood to the brain. So there is no clear physical evidence for life after death. It is still a matter of faith.

i. I read a story in the newspaper about someone who accidentally glued her eyelid shut because she picked up a little squeeze bottle of glue instead of the eyedrops when she went into the bathroom and didn't put the light on. And I'm sure you've heard of cases where people have used hairspray instead of deodorant. You should put the light on when you go into the bathroom at night.

j. She's been the assistant manager of a sandwich store, and she knows how to do basic bookkeeping. Her volunteer experience shows she's obviously interested in riding and horses in general. She's the best candidate for running the office in our new facility for disabled riders.

    k. My friend in Australia didn't get a cat after all. I've just found out Fluffy is the name of his iguana. Iguanas are reptiles, which means they should be cold-blooded. I'll put ski hand warmers in the booties; then his iguana will probably appreciate the booties even more than a cat would have.

*2. Find four examples, one for each type of reasoning: analogical, conductive, inductive, deductive.

3. Create your own examples of each type of reasoning.

Revealing Patterns of Argument: A Brief Introduction to Symbols

If an argument uses inductive or deductive reasoning, there is a way to recognize whether it does or does not support its conclusion. Inductive and deductive arguments often reveal recognizable patterns. Some of these patterns create well-structured arguments, and some create faulty arguments. Some work as arguments to certainty, and others work only as arguments to probability. Putting arguments into symbols can be a good way of identifying a structural pattern. Identifying a pattern helps check whether an argument is using a type of reasoning that can provide the right level of support for its conclusion. Not all well-structured arguments follow recognizable patterns, but if an argument does use a deductively valid or cogent pattern, then you can be sure the argument is well-structured. We may not yet know whether all the premises are true, but we can at least see whether they could work together to make the conclusion certain or probable.

To convert an argument into symbols, we replace words and sentences with single letters, so we can focus on the patterns of logical connection instead of on the details of a particular argument. Although not all arguments fit neatly into patterns that you can symbolize, you'll find that many arguments have premises that can be reworded and matched to argument schemes. When you come across an argument that seems similar to one of the patterns listed below, try putting it into symbols and seeing if it matches one in our list of structurally valid and formally cogent arguments. Once you can identify an argument as having a valid or cogent pattern, you know that the argument is well structured.

When we turn patterns into symbols, there are two different types of symbolization we can use, depending on the focus of the argument. The two types of logic use symbols in slightly different ways to represent the premises and the conclusion. Patterns in *categorical logic* focus on which individuals belong to which categories and category membership in general. For example, "All cats have four feet. Fluffy is a cat, so Fluffy has four feet." The focus here is on what we can conclude if the individual, Fluffy, belongs to the category "cats." Patterns in *propositional logic* focus on the connections between statements. For example, "If Fluffy is a cat, then Fluffy will only pay attention to you when she needs something. Fluffy doesn't need anything now. So

Fluffy will not pay attention to you." The focus here is on the relationship between one claim—Fluffy is a cat—and another claim—Fluffy will only pay attention to you when she needs something.

The detailed study of these types of logic is a branch of philosophy closely related to mathematics. We have included a brief look at how the two types of logic use symbols differently because it helps to show how inductive and deductive patterns of reasoning can work.

Categorical Logic

Categorical logic is concerned with conclusions that can be drawn when you have information about characteristics of individuals and groups. As you have seen, this is a common type of reasoning by induction, and it can also be used in reasoning by deduction. Symbols in categorical logic use capital letters like A and B to stand for groups, categories, and characteristics of things or properties. Lowercase letters like x, y, or z are used for individuals that may belong to the group or may have the properties or characteristics of that category. For example,

All As are Bs.

x is an A.
_____

x is a B.

This is a pattern in categorical logic. The argument draws a conclusion based on information about the relationship between the category of As, the category of Bs, and the individual, x.

To see how the symbols can represent the basic pattern of an argument, consider the following example.

1. All the cats in my house are female.
2. Fluffy is a cat in my house.
   _____
3. Fluffy is female.

"The cats in my house" is one group of things. Replace "the cats in my house" with "A."

Being female is a property. Replace "female" with "B." Fluffy is an individual. Replace "Fluffy" with "x." In symbol form, the pattern of the argument is exactly the same as the first example:

All As are Bs.

x is an A.
_____

x is a B.

A key feature of a categorical argument is that when we put it into symbols, we break up each sentence into parts and symbolize the parts of the sentence. The subject, "cats" or "Fluffy," is symbolized by letters. The "quantifier words" (like "all," "most," "some") that specify how many of the items have the specified property can also be put into symbols; for example "∃" would represent "Some, or at least one" and "∀" would represent "all." However, for our purposes, we do not need this level of detail, and we can leave the quantifiers and the verbs as words.

Propositional Logic

Propositional logic is concerned with the relationship between entire propositions—entire sentences. Propositional logic focuses on what propositions can be true at the same time, under the same circumstances. Which things must always be true, which things can never be true, and which things might be true in some circumstances but not in others?

An example of a pattern in propositional logic is

If P then Q

P
_____

Q

Again, we are replacing words with letters, but here we use only capital letters and each letter represents a complete sentence or independent clause. For example, "P" could represent anything from "It is raining" to "Fluffy will ignore you" or "The soup needs salt." In propositional logic, the key connections between sentences or independent clauses would also be replaced by symbols. For example, "~" represents "is not," and "⊃" represents "If . . . then . . ." and "≡" stands for "if and only if." Again, for our purposes we will not need this level of detail. To symbolize an argument used in propositional logic, we first break complex sentences into their simple-sentence components. Then we substitute a letter for each complete simple sentence.

For example, let's look at how to put the following argument into symbols.

1. *If* it is raining *then* the streets are wet.
2. It is raining.
   _____
3. The streets are wet.

Sentence 1 is a complex sentence. "It is raining" and "the streets are wet" are complete sentences in themselves. "If . . . then . . ." links the two sentences to express a connection between them. What is highlighted in propositional logic is the connection between propositions—sentences expressing claims. For our purposes, we need only replace the simple sentences with capital letters and leave the words indicating relationships between these sentences in English. Here, for example, we would replace "it is raining" with P, and replace "the streets are wet" with Q. We leave the words "if" and "then" as indicators of the relationship between P and Q.

In symbols, the argument becomes

If P then Q

P
_____

Q

With symbols, it can be much easier to see when two different arguments have the same pattern, and to see whether the pattern is deductively valid or invalid. For example, "If the cat's asleep then the dog is outside. The cat is asleep. So the dog is outside." This short argument is unrelated in subject matter to whether it rains or the streets are wet, so we would use different letters to indicate the new content. Symbolize "the cat's asleep" by A and "the dog's outside" by B. Now we have

If A then B

A
_____

B

Different letters, same pattern. If the first argument is deductively valid, the second must be too. And indeed they are: this pattern has the name *modus ponens,* and it indicates that whenever the "if" part (the *antecedent*) of an "if . . . then" condition is true, the "then" part (the *consequent*) must also be true.

Here is a brief list of some deductively valid argument patterns, some formally cogent patterns, and some poorly structured, faulty argument patterns.

Deductively Valid

All As are Bs.	All As are Bs.
X is an A.	X is not a B.
X is a B.	X is not an A.

If P then Q	If P then Q
P	Not Q
Q	Not P

P or Q	P if and only if Q
Not P	Not Q
Q	Not P

Cogent

Most As are Bs.	If P then usually Q.
X is an A.	P
————————	————————
X is a B.	Q

Poorly Structured (neither deductively valid nor formally cogent)

If P then Q	If P then Q
Not P	Q
————————	————————
Not Q	P

All As are Bs.	All As are Bs.
X is a B.	X is not an A.
————————	————————
X is an A.	X is not a B.

Most As are Bs.	Most As are Bs.
X is a B.	Most Bs are Cs.
————————	————————
X is an A.	Most As are Cs.

EXERCISE **5.3**   # Checking Argument Patterns

1. Put the following short arguments into symbols. Check the arguments for deductive validity.

   *a.

   1. If it is snowing then the roads are slippery.

   2. It is snowing.
   ————————————————
   3. The roads are slippery.

   *b.

   1. If I invite my stepmother to Thanksgiving dinner then my mother will be upset.

   2. I will not invite my stepmother to Thanksgiving dinner.
   ————————————————
   3. My mother will not be upset.

   *c.

   1. If it has just snowed, the roads are slippery.

   2. The roads are slippery.
   ————————————————
   3. It has just snowed.

d.

    1. If fish are mammals, then bagels taste good.

    2. Fish are mammals.

    <u>   </u>

    3. Bagels taste good.

e.

    1. Either he's out with his friends or he has gone to a movie.

    2. He's out with his friends.

    <u>   </u>

    3. He has gone to a movie.

EXERCISE **5.4**

Recognizing Successful Patterns of Reasoning

State whether the following arguments have cogent patterns, deductively valid patterns, or neither.

*1. If there is a party at Sam's house, then Mariko is there. Mariko is at Sam's house. Therefore, there's a party at Sam's house.

*2. She has emus on her farm and an emu is a bird. All farms with birds on it must be quarantined. Her farm must be quarantined.

*3. All people who are in the ski club are great skiers. She is not a great skier. So she must not be in the ski club.

*4. Some elephants are scared of mice. Dumbo is an elephant. Dumbo is scared of mice.

*5. Dumbo is an elephant. I know that's true because most elephants are named Dumbo and that's his name.

6. The finals of the 2004 Olympic men's gymnastics individual all-around was won by an American. Almost all events won by Americans were well covered by NBC. The finals of the 2004 Olympic men's gymnastics individual all-around was well covered by NBC.

7. If it is Monday at noon, then my son is probably at school. So I know he's at school because it's Monday at noon.

8. Your dentist would probably recommend chewing sugarless gum because most dentists do.

9. She has probably expressed the wish to die because many terminally ill patients express a wish to die and she is terminally ill.

10. It's obvious that he hasn't forgiven me for being so rude. I know that because if he gives me a kiss, then he's forgiven me and he hasn't given me a kiss.

Combining Types of Reasoning

The types of reasoning we have described do not always occur in isolation. As you know, a layered argument can have several different lines of reasoning, with each one creating a sub-argument leading toward the main conclusion. Some arguments may use—and may need—reasoning of different types to support steps in the argument. That is, different types of reasoning may be used to construct different sub-arguments on the way to the conclusion.

For example, consider a lawyer acting for a spouse in a relationship that has broken down. Imagine that the couple signed a prenuptial agreement that was supposed to determine how the couple's property would be divided if they divorced. The lawyer is representing the spouse for whom this agreement will be less advantageous, and the spouse wants to claim "hardship" and ask for the property to be divided differently. In this case, the lawyer's argument may need several types of reasoning. Deductive reasoning could be used to say how the law and the provisions of the prenuptial agreement would specify the division of property. That would be a sub-argument to certainty, establishing what division of property is required. Inductive or conductive reasoning could establish what the spouses intended when they signed the agreement, whether they could have predicted that their current situation is one they would find themselves in, and what the financial impact of the property settlement would be. That would be a sub-argument to probability, establishing how likely it is that the settlement provisions were appropriate. Analogical reasoning might be used to illustrate what constitutes "hardship" and make comparisons to previous cases and to how the word is used, in order to conclude whether one spouse will experience hardship to a relevant extent if the prenuptial agreement is enforced.

Where an argument needs several types of reasoning, the complete argument is only well structured if each sub-argument is well structured. To be well structured, each sub-argument must meet the expectations of each type of reasoning. For the lawyer to argue that enforcing a prenuptial agreement would cause undue hardship to one spouse, it will not be nearly enough simply to give a cogent argument that the separation agreement probably contained appropriate provisions. The structurally valid argument that there is a legal justification for not enforcing the contract must also be given.

Relevance and Sufficiency: The Marks of a Well-Structured Argument

So far in this chapter we have been considering argument structure in general—what it takes for arguments to be well structured, to be capable of supporting their conclusions. Our goal, however, is to be able to evaluate particular arguments—to find out if they are good arguments that do provide support for their conclusions. (We'll do this in Chapter 8.) How do we move from "well-structured" arguments to "good" arguments? We do know that if an argument is not well structured, its reasoning has failed and it cannot be a good argument. That means our investigation of argument structure will at least show us which arguments can be dismissed as not worth further consideration. What remains to be done is to see how we can move forward on the arguments that do seem well structured. How can our investigation of structure help point us in the right direction for evaluating well-structured arguments to see if they are good?

We know one thing an examination of argument structure cannot do—it cannot tell us whether the premises are acceptable. Determining the acceptability of the premises themselves has to wait for a separate check. However, structure may be able to help us with relevance and sufficiency.

In describing the levels of support and the types of reasoning, we have been considering how premises connect to create a well-structured argument. We can sum up the expectations for a well-structured argument by saying that we are looking for the "relevance" and "sufficiency" of premises. These two concepts can capture what it is about the level and type of support that will make an argument good, not just well structured. We will describe relevance and sufficiency in general terms. Then we will see how we can use an understanding of argument structure to see whether a particular set of premises could be relevant and sufficient for its conclusion. In Chapter 8, we will see how to apply relevance and sufficiency directly to determining the quality of an argument.

Relevance

Relevance in general simply means that the information presented is connected in some way to the topic under consideration. Relevance in an argument means that its premises are connected in some way to the conclusion. The connection must be clear enough and strong enough that we can see why the premises provide support for the conclusion. This condition ensures that the information does apply to the conclusion. The premises are on the same topic, and we can picture a connection. In general, we have an intuitive sense of what is relevant and what is not.

For example, consider this short argument, set out in standard form for clarity:

1. I've just dropped my key.
2. It fell into the storm sewer.

   _____

3. I'll never find my key.

We can see that 1 and 2 are relevant to the conclusion—a key that falls into a storm sewer is going to be hard to rescue and most likely is gone forever.

A more challenging example would be this:

1. I left my wedding ring on the counter.
2. The parrot's out of her cage.

   _____

3. I'll never find my wedding ring.

Are 1 and 2 relevant to the conclusion? It's a bit of a stretch, but we can imagine that the speaker's parrot is known for taking small objects. She drops or hides them in places her owner can't get to. The connection between 1 and 2 is that the ring is gone and the parrot may have taken it. The connection between 2 and the conclusion is that when the parrot takes small things, her owner almost never finds them. The relevance isn't obvious, and we really would expect the speaker to give more details. However, we would probably err on the side of counting the premises as relevant unless we are absolutely sure they are not.

One final example:

1. I dropped my key.

2. The parrot's out of her cage.

    ---

3. I'll never find my wedding ring.

Even imagination can't produce any obvious connection between 1 and 2, or between either of the premises and the conclusion.

To illustrate how relevance affects whether a set of premises can provide support for a conclusion, consider the following example:

1. Washington, D.C., is the capital of the U.S.A.

2. Ottawa is the capital of Canada.

    ---

3. Therefore Paris must be the capital of France.

This argument has true premises and a true conclusion. But this is not a well-structured argument. The logic of the argument is deductively invalid: the connection does not work. If we put the argument into symbols, you can see why: the form would be

$$P$$

$$\frac{Q}{R}$$

The premises, even though they are true, fail to be relevant. They not only do not guarantee the conclusion, they do not give us any reason to accept that the conclusion might be true. Yes, all three statements are about capitals of countries, and so in that sense they are related. But the premises are not relevant to the conclusion because they show no connection between why these cities are capitals or why these countries are related. Because the truth of the premises is irrelevant to the conclusion, this argument is not well structured.

Here is an example where premises are relevant and the argument is well structured:

1. Countries always choose their largest cities as the capital.

2. Ottawa is the largest city in Canada.

    ---

3. So Ottawa must be the capital of Canada.

Here, we've fixed the problem of relevance—we can now see clearly what the connection is. And the conclusion does happen to be true. This argument is structurally valid. Unfortunately, in spite of being valid and having relevant premises, it is not a good argument—its premises are both false. There are many examples of countries with smaller cities as their capitals—Australia, Brazil, and Canada, for example. This example reminds us why we need to look at not only argument structure and relevance, but also the acceptability of the premises before we can decide that an argument is good.

Sufficiency

Premises are **sufficient** to establish a conclusion when they present enough reasons to make the conclusion rationally acceptable. As we've already seen, how much evidence is sufficient will change depending on whether the argument is designed to show that the conclusion is certain, probable, or possible. When an argument is well structured, the premises, when they are true, will provide sufficient support for the conclusion: that is implicit in the definitions of "structurally valid," "cogent," and "plausible."

For example, in the discussion of arguments to certainty we saw that the following argument does not offer premises that are sufficient to establish that the conclusion is probable: "You've been late the last five times we've met up. Clearly you are incapable of being punctual." At most, the premise supports the possibility that you are incapable of being punctual. The premise is relevant, but it is not sufficient. It does not provide enough support to make the conclusion probable. While this may count as a well-structured argument to possibility—it is plausible—it is not cogent.

As the discussion of levels of support and well-structured arguments has already shown, we can often determine whether an argument meets the standard of sufficiency just by investigating its structure. What level of support did it need to provide for its conclusion, and did its structure provide that level of support? However, we cannot always tell from the structure we are given whether an argument can succeed.

When we investigate sufficiency, we are working out whether the premises, taken as a whole, do make the conclusion more reasonable than competing alternatives—that is, if the premises are true, they do effectively rule out contrary conclusions. The premises can answer any questions we might have had and can resolve any reasonable doubts. In general, to investigate sufficiency, we raise questions and look for alternatives; then we see if the premises we have been given can settle these questions and eliminate the alternatives. You"ll see more on how to generate questions and recognize alternatives in Chapter 6, when we look for assumptions in arguments.

To give us one way to see whether an argument is capable of providing sufficient support for the conclusion, we can use what we know about inductive and deductive reasoning structures. We can review the argument to see if the argument we have been given can be reasonably interpreted as a well-structured argument. To do this, we see if there are any premises that could be added to complete a valid or cogent structure, without distorting the meaning of the argument as it stands. As you will see, if we can add a premise to "complete" the structure, we can confirm that the argument can be considered well structured. If we can, then all that we will still need to check in evaluating the argument is whether its premises—including the ones we added—are acceptable.

Implicit Premises: The Principle of Charity Applied to Arguments

When we examine actual arguments, we often find they don't exhibit clear patterns of deductive reasoning or inductive reasoning, or their premises don't seem to add up to the right level of support for the conclusion. This is not necessarily a fault in the reasoning, and it deserves further investigation before we try to evaluate the reasoning.

Even the best-written argument won't spell out every detail that it would need to make its inference work. In oral and written language, we do take some things for granted. We rely on people's background knowledge, or the context within which we speak and write, to do much of the job of making it clear what we mean. Similarly, in understanding sentences, we may realize that there are unstated things we are expected to understand—if you say, "You can't get more people to take public transit if it's not convenient" you're assuming that there is public transit, that some people do take it and some people do not, and that convenience is an important factor in people's choice of transportation.

However, when it comes to seeing whether an argument meets the expectation of supporting its conclusion with a well-reasoned deductive or inductive argument, it can be very useful to nail down precisely what is needed to complete a well-structured argument. We can put back any missing pieces, fill in any gaps, so that we can see if the argument could possibly work and what exactly would be needed to make it work. When we add a missing piece to the argument, we are not trying to change the meaning of what was written. We aren't taking the attitude of "What she meant to say is . . ." In fact, we must be careful not to do this. We are not expected to do the job of improving on the argument. We are meant to make clear the structure of the existing argument. We compare what we see to known patterns of argument and decide whether the arguer may have intended to use one of those common patterns, or whether the argument can fairly be represented by one of those patterns.

The principle of charity needs to be used when adding implicit premises because it is a way of ensuring that when you come to evaluate an argument, you will be evaluating the argument using its best possible structure. This is important because it allows you to see whether there really are good reasons to believe the conclusion.

The principle of charity assumes that when you are analyzing arguments you are trying to find out what it is rational to believe or do. Giving the argument its fairest chance of success also gives you the best chance of discovering what is reasonable to believe. If you examine only the worst version of an argument, you may be ignoring an interpretation that gives you good reasons to believe the conclusion. Using the principle of charity, we assume that the arguer intended to produce a well-structured argument. We decide what type of reasoning best fits the existing argument, and we add an additional premise—an "**implicit premise**," which is a premise that is not clearly stated, but would need to be included in the argument if the reasoning is intended to have a deductively valid or cogent argument pattern. Once we have added the implicit premise, we now have a complete argument; we can see how the premises are connected to one another and to the conclusion, and we are able to see if the reasoning actually works.

For example,

DEFINITION

An implicit premise is a premise that is not clearly stated but must be part of the argument if the reasoning is to have a deductively valid or cogent argument pattern.

1.   All crows are black.

2.   So, Sparky is black.

Implicit premise: Sparky is a crow.

The implicit premise in this case should be intuitively obvious, but let's look at the steps you could take to uncover the implicit premise. If you think about the intended argument as following a familiar logical scheme or pattern, the argument is clearly meant to have the following valid pattern:

All As are Bs.

x is an A.

x is a B.

But all that is actually stated is

All As are Bs.

x is a B.

The implicit premise is the missing piece of the logical pattern: x is an A.

Here is another example:

1.   If there is thunder there is lightning.

2.   Therefore, there is lightning.

Implicit premise: There is thunder.

Identifying implicit premises is usually straightforward when the author clearly states a general premise and what is implicit is a claim about a particular.

Familiarity with logical patterns helps us see what an arguer intended and what the missing piece must be. Here is an example based on a different logical pattern.

1. Sandra is not a firefighter.

2. So, she must be an RCMP officer.

Implicit premise: Either Sandra is a firefighter or she is an RCMP officer.

In this example, the pattern is the same as in the example you saw earlier, "Either he's playing soccer or he has gone out with his friends. I know he is not playing soccer, so he must have gone out with his friends." The implicit premise is the "either . . . or" piece that would be needed to complete that pattern.

Finding implicit premises can be straightforward, as in the examples above. However, finding an implicit premise that works as a general premise is usually much more difficult than finding an implicit premise that works to express a premise about a particular. Consider the following example:

1. Sandra is an RCMP officer in Chilliwack.

2. So, she must have a university degree.

Although it is clear that the implicit premise in this argument is a general claim that relates Sandra's being an RCMP officer with having a university degree, it is harder to see which claim is being assumed. The pattern of the argument as it stands is:

x is an A.

x is a B.

There are a number of different ways the arguer could be linking the premise to the conclusion. And in this case we have no clue as to what level of support the author intended. What we are looking for is an implicit premise that is neither too narrow nor too broad. "Sandra is an RCMP officer with a university degree" is much too narrow—it says that x is an A and a B, which will certainly show that x is a B. However, it won't show anything at all about whether there is a connection between RCMP qualifications and university degrees. Similarly, "All Canadian police officers have university degrees" is too broad. The argument is making a connection between RCMP officers and their training—we have no obvious justification for stepping outside this scope into making claims about all police forces in the country.

The argument could be missing "All As are Bs" or "Most As are Bs," and there can even be some variation in what A symbolizes. Here are some of the possibilities:

All RCMP officers have university degrees.

Most RCMP officers have university degrees.

Most women RCMP officers have university degrees.

All women RCMP officers have university degrees.

All RCMP officers in Chilliwack have university degrees.

Most RCMP officers in Chilliwack have university degrees.

All women RCMP officers in Chilliwack have university degrees.

Most women RCMP officers in Chilliwack have university degrees.

Part of investigation is being properly cautious and recognizing when you can see two or more equally workable missing premises. On occasion, you will have contextual clues that will help you choose which general premise is being assumed. Sometimes you will be able to ask the arguer what he or she is assuming. Sometimes you will know the arguer well enough to be able to make an educated guess.

The general rule when adding missing premises is to try to avoid attributing a claim to the author that is not warranted by the explicit premises and the context. For example, there is no reason to believe that the author's implicit premise should limit university degrees to women. However, the mention of Chilliwack can be taken as a limitation of the implicit premise to a claim about RCMP officers in Chilliwack.

We are then left with two options: "Most RCMP officers in Chilliwack have university degrees" or "All RCMP officers in Chilliwack have university degrees." In this case, the conclusion is phrased as "She *must* have a university degree" which implies an argument to certainty. If that is the case, we should take the implicit premise as "All RCMP officers in Chilliwack have university degrees."

However, if you have no information that will help you choose among the various options, it is best not to add this implicit premise into your **standardization** (conversion of an argument from its original prose format to the point-form format of a standard form) or report of the argument. You don't try to make the argument follow a deductively valid of cogent pattern. You leave it as it stands and deal with any possible missing pieces as assumptions (see Chapter 6).

Implicit Premises and Standard Form

If the intended reasoning of the argument is clear enough that you can see what implicit premise is needed, you include that implicit premise in your standardization of the argument. You indicate that it is an unstated premise by writing "(implicit premise)" next to it.

For example,

1. Sandra is not a fireman.
2. Either Sandra is a fireman or she is an RCMP officer. (implicit premise)
   _____
3. So, she must be an RCMP officer.

If we cannot insert a suitable implicit premise, then the argument is not deductively valid and does not follow a cogent argument pattern. It may not be a well-structured argument at all. For example:

1. Some people who ski out-of-bounds have to pay the costs of being rescued.

   _____

2. So Andy must have paid the cost of being rescued.

We can tell what the implicit premise would be here: "Andy skied out-of-bounds." Add that implicit premise and you can see how the conclusion was meant to follow from the premises. However, even though this is easily the best choice as the implicit premise, in this case adding it is not enough to make the argument well structured. We still don't have sufficient reason to believe that Andy is among the "some" people who have to pay the costs of their rescue.

 EXERCISE **5.5**

Identifying Implicit Premises

Add the implicit premises in these arguments. Indicate the implicit premise by writing "implicit premise" beside it.

*1. All students must go to class. So you must go to class.

*2. If there is a will, there is a way. Therefore, there is a way.

*3. Mark is a hard-working and intelligent person. So he is sure to succeed.

4. She's sleeping in, which proves that she is on holiday.

5. Voluntary euthanasia is not against the wishes of the person being killed. Therefore, it is not murder.

6. It's time for her to move out because she is not paying her rent.

7. If the clock is correct, then I'm late for my meeting. So the clock is incorrect.

8. You should adopt a baby! There are so many children who have no parents and could use a good home.

9. No one has the right to take another person's life. That's why capital punishment is wrong.

10. No person has a right to take another person's life. That's why capital punishment is justified.

 EXERCISE **5.6**

Completing Standard Form with Implicit Premises

Put the following arguments into standard form. Make sure you add any implicit premises.

*1. Violent video games promote violence as thrilling, enjoyable, and an immediate response to certain stimuli. So, violent video games are creating a generation of violence addicts. There is no doubt in my mind that these games need to be completely eliminated from our society.

*2. All people who have experienced both physical and intellectual pleasures would agree that intellectual pleasures are superior. Therefore, intellectual pleasures are superior.

3. There are so many different forms of healthy entertainment that surely we don't need violent video games to amuse the youth of our society.

4. Children die of starvation every day. Good people get horrible diseases. So bad things clearly exist in the world. We cannot expect life to be fair.

5. What mysterious essence do humans have that gives them the right to life, the right to be free from harm, and the right to happiness? The traditional response is that humans have reason and purpose. But if that were the case, then people who were better at reasoning and had a clearer sense of purpose would have more rights than those who reason badly and are undirected. Infants and the developmentally challenged would have no rights at all.

   Our rights do not come from the fact that we are rational; our rights arise because we are creatures who are capable of suffering pain and feeling pleasure. That suffering is not wrong simply because it is a human being who suffers; that suffering is wrong because it is wrong for an innocent being to suffer—period. Those who can suffer are those who have the right not to suffer unnecessarily. Animals have that right just as much as we do.

Key Points in Review

- The structure of an argument is the way in which the premises are linked together to support the conclusion.
- There are three main types of argument structure.
  - Arguments to certainty, which aim to guarantee that their conclusions are true. Well-structured arguments to certainty are called "structurally valid."
  - Arguments to probability, which aim to establish that their conclusions are more probable than any alternative. Well-structured arguments to probability are called "cogent."
  - Arguments to possibility, which aim to show that their conclusions are possibly true. Well-structured arguments to possibility are called "plausible."
- When we check the structure of an argument, we are not concerned immediately with whether the premises of the argument are actually acceptable. We are checking only the connections made in the reasoning: does the argument hold together well enough to do its job?
- "Patterns" are what argument structures can have in common when the arguments are on different topics and use different information in their premises. There are patterns that succeed as good reasoning and patterns that fail.
- We use the principle of charity to interpret arguments fairly. When an argument cannot work with only its stated premises and it seems that a deductively valid or cogent argument was intended, we see if there is an implicit premise we can add to make the argument work.
- All arguments have one important feature in common: they can only succeed if their premises are relevant and if they are sufficient to establish the conclusion.

Chapter 6

Investigating Background and Context

■ Perspective

So far, we have investigated whether our information is trustworthy, and we have seen what it will take to put an argument together reasonably. In this chapter, we cast our net wider to see where to focus our attention, and we investigate our options: what is possible?

■ Scenario

You're feeling very stressed. (You can imagine the kind of situation that pushes you to the limit.) Maybe you've taken on too much—it all seemed reasonable at the time, but now everything's due at once and you don't see how to manage. Or maybe you've been dealing with a difficult person or a difficult situation, and you keep trying to get things to work better but nothing seems to help. Whatever the situation is, you've reached the point where you can't succeed and you can't give up. You have good reasons for doing what you're doing, and if you just stop you'll let people down or let yourself down. What do you do?

■ Key Questions

What is important here? What might happen besides what I expect?

Investigating the Context

To investigate the overall context or situation, we need to think about what is most important in the situation—what the real issues are—and we also need to recognize what options we have to choose from. In this chapter, we'll look at both aspects in turn.

The scenario for this chapter is intended to remind you of what it feels like to be stuck, thinking you have no choice. When someone helpfully suggests you could simply abandon one of your commitments, you barely hear them out before saying, "Yes, but . . ." and defending everything you are doing. That is often the time you most need to step back and investigate further. What assumptions have you been making? What principles have you accepted without question? In this chapter, we will see how to open up options when all doors seem closed—how to find choices you didn't realize you had. As you think about how you might see the situation differently, you are also in a position to review what is most important. What is the core issue or the central concern? We will look first at how to recognize a core issue, and then how to recognize when an option has been overlooked because an assumption was made.

What Is at Issue?

When we investigate information or arguments, we are investigating in a particular context—for a particular purpose, in a particular situation. Part of the investigation, therefore, must cover the context itself. For each particular context we must ask the following:

- What are the issues?
- What are the options open to us?

When you realize that you need to rethink what has brought you to where you are now, one vital element to consider is what the **issue**—the subject of discussion—is. Engaging in debate with others helps you on a personal level: it clarifies your own thinking, helping you to explore and deal with your own attitudes and reasoning. It also helps you to deal with the agreements and disagreements that underlie our everyday interactions with other people. And it offers the promise that you might be a part of the progress in, or solution to, the issue.

Some issues tug at our emotions, some affect us personally, and some do not affect us very strongly. Whichever ones we care to be involved in, we need good critical thinking to deal with them, and we need to make them manageable. Recognizing the issues is key to being able to participate effectively.

When we consider arguments in more detail in Chapters 8 and 11, we will need to be able to identify the issue. In what context and for what purpose is the argument being given?

DEFINITION

The **issue** is the subject of discussion.

There can be more than one issue in a piece of writing or speech. We can distinguish between the **main issue**—the central, unifying topic of discussion—and **sub-issues**—topics that are raised as relevant to the main issue—to keep track of the subject of discussion. For example, if you say, "I really think you need to lose weight because your BMI score indicates you are not a healthy weight for your height and my friend Jacob said that the best indicator of healthy weight is a person's BMI score," the main issue in what you've said is that you think I need to lose weight. A sub-issue that is also raised is whether or not a person's BMI score is the best indicator of a healthy weight.

For arguments, identifying the main issues and the sub-issues clarifies what the real source of disagreement is. It also establishes what each person or side thinks is at stake, which will help channel the discussion into more productive directions. For problem situations, identifying the issues helps to clarify the goals—what needs are to be met?

To identify the issues, you can ask the following questions:

1. What are people disagreeing about? This identifies the main issue and sub-issues.

2. What would each side like to see happen? This identifies their position on the issues.

3. Why should people be concerned about this issue? What values do the issues address? This identifies why we need to solve the problem or resolve the dispute instead of letting it continue.

It can be a difficult task to identify the central argument in a long piece of writing or a long speech, and when you have to analyze and compare two long pieces of writing or speeches on the same topic, the task can seem overwhelming. The main issue may be clear, but often there are numerous sub-issues. What we need is a focus: we need to pick out the most important theme, idea, or disagreement.

In this section you will learn how to identify the key point of disagreement. First, we can see how to identify the main concern in a single argument. You already know how to pick out a conclusion and see how the premises support that conclusion. The argument's conclusion is the answer to a question about the main issue. For example, consider the statement "Dogs should be kept on a leash any time they are off their owners' property" made as the conclusion of an argument. The supporting premises for this argument show why dogs should be kept on a leash—they're safer, other animals are safer, and neighbours are happier. Now, why are we being given the argument in the first place? Presumably, there is some question about dogs and the need for leashes. "Dogs should be kept on a leash" is one answer to the question "Should dogs be kept on a leash?" The main issue is the issue that gives rise to this question. If there have been problems caused in parks by dogs running off-leash, then there is an issue about what is acceptable conduct for dogs and their owners. It is this issue that will give rise to questions, and then to arguments, about what is and is not acceptable conduct for dogs and their owners, and what will and will not be reasonable solutions to the perceived problems.

When describing an issue, avoid using a single word. For example, the main issue about dogs in parks is not dogs. The main issue is "What is acceptable conduct for dogs and their owners?" Thus, the main issue is a question about dogs. Another way to describe an issue is to state the conclusion or subconclusion in a way that indicates it is the subject up for debate. For example, "The issue is whether dogs should be kept on a leash any time they are off their owners' property."

To find the main issue, work backward from the conclusion of the argument. To what question would the conclusion be an answer? What current events might have made that question come up? What values or concerns lie behind that question?

EXERCISE **Recognizing an Issue**

*For the argument below, pick out the main issue. What is the topic discussed, what is the main problem or concern, and what position is the arguer taking on that issue?

The case for banning pit bulls

Pit bulls are inherently dangerous animals, more bull than pet, and therefore should not be haunting the streets, fields and family rooms of Ontario. A remarkable, silent majority is finally being heard on this issue.

But the debate over banning pit bulls is not exclusive to Ontario. Bans are in place in places like Kitchener-Waterloo, Windsor, Winnipeg, and abroad in Britain and New Zealand, and are being considered in London, Brantford, and Toronto. Why ban these beasts?

There are statistics to back up the thousands of e-mails I have received of unreported pit bull attacks, but nothing makes the case for banning pit bulls better than the experiences of Winnipeg and Kitchener.

Winnipeg was experiencing more than 30 serious, reported pit bull attacks a year. Today? Zero.

Kitchener saw 18 pit bull attacks annually, and in a few short years since the ban was introduced, they now have about one a year.

That means that people in those cities who otherwise would have continued to be attacked by pit bulls were, instead, spared serious injury.

Ten years ago, when I saw the 5-year-old Toronto girl whose face was savagely mauled by a pit bull, many wondered how many more children would be harmed by these incomparably vicious dogs. Ten years from now, maybe there will be no more, if this pit bull ban passes in Queen's Park.

Even more interestingly, attacks in Winnipeg by all breeds of dogs—once numbering 30 to 40 per year—have decreased overall. A decade after their pit bull ban was instituted, dog attacks number about one per year, refuting the claim that

pit bull owners will turn to other dangerous dogs. Similarly, in Kitchener, no other breed has filled the gap left by the banned pit bulls.

The truth is, while other dogs can be dangerous, no other dog is as dangerous as a pit bull.

No other dog can match the severity of the attack, and the unpredictability of the attack. Even a U.S. study from 2000, sometimes cited as evidence by opponents of the pit bull ban, finds that one-third of dog-bite related fatalities—yes, fatalities—were caused by pit bulls.

While it may be difficult to say definitively how many pit bulls there are in North America, it is certain that one-third of dogs are not pit bulls, a breed that is killing and attacking at an alarming rate.

Some say government should punish the deed, not the breed. I say, we should indeed punish the deed. And the government's

(Continued)

The case for banning pit bulls *(Continued)*

proposed bill would, if passed, seriously punish irresponsible dog owners with tougher fines, doubling them to $10,000, and even jail time for extreme cases.

But we also need to face the fact that pit bulls are a breed apart. They don't scare the hell out of people because they're not always pretty; they are frightening because of the injuries they routinely inflict upon people and their pets.

Some say pit bulls aren't a breed at all, they can't be identified.

My experience is that those opposing the pit bull ban are the only ones who believe rules cannot be crafted to permit the identification of what everyone knows to be a pit bull.

In fact, Ontario intends to adopt the definition of pit bull utilized by Winnipeg in its successful pit bull ban. To be sure, if legal regulations can identify harmful emissions, dangerous pesticides and complex narcotics, we can do the same with a dog that can often be spotted (and heard) a block away.

There is an underlying ideology advanced by those opposed to the pit bull bans, arguing that dog bans are wrong. It's a fundamentalist argument that knows no exceptions.

I don't disagree that dog bans are extreme, but I would have thought that those who love animals also agree that there are some animals that do not belong in public.

We don't permit muzzled wolves on leashes in public parks. Why? Because they're just too dangerous.

So it is for pit bulls.

Michael Bryant is Attorney-General of Ontario and MPP for the Toronto riding of St. Pauls.

[*TORONTO STAR*, OCTOBER 21, 2004, A25. REPRINTED WITH PERMISSION OF MICHAEL BRYANT, ATTORNEY GENERAL OF ONTARIO.]

Identifying the Crux of the Debate: The Central Issue

In most debates, even those between people who seem to be very far apart in their views on an issue, there will be areas of agreement. When analyzing the differences between two pieces of writing, we can note the broad areas of agreement and disagreement and then focus on developing a more precise account of where the two disagree.

DEFINITION

The **crux of the debate** is the key point of disagreement.

A good way to discover the **crux of the debate**—the key point of disagreement—is to think about the broad argument presented by one arguer and then figure out which premise the other arguer disagrees with.

For example, here are two speakers disagreeing with each other.

> **Lee:** Giving our government power to censor what it deems inappropriate is essential if we are to keep our country pure and untainted by pornography, violence, and racist slander. By censoring these offensive elements we protect our children and show evil adults what type of behaviour will not be tolerated in our society. Censorship must be allowed.

> **Fee:** Unrestricted government censorship cannot be allowed. Censorship will destroy our country. Although those who support censorship believe that they are helping preserve the virtue of the country, they are attacking its very foundation. Censorship takes away from the freedom of the individual to choose what to read, watch, and believe.

These two short arguments will allow us to practise the steps involved in noting the crux of the debate between Lee and Fee.

Steps in Identifying the Crux of the Debate

1.   Find the main issue that is up for debate.

This step can be accomplished by thinking about the main conclusions of the two arguers. Ask yourself what the overarching issue is. Once you have discovered this main issue, you can reconstruct one of the arguments in a very general way to get a sense of what the arguer's basic position is on this issue. When you do this brief and general reconstruction, you are not trying to present the details of the argument, you are simply trying to jot down the main framework of the argument being pursued. It is a good idea to read the argument carefully once and then write out a general reconstruction based on your understanding of the argument as a whole.

The main issue for debate between Lee and Fee is whether we should give the government the power to censor all material it deems inappropriate.

2.   Find the broad areas of agreement.

Once you have written out a general reconstruction, which can conveniently be set out as a standardization of the first argument, you can review the second argument to see if there are premises that the arguer might agree with.

Lee's very general argument is this:

1.   Giving the government the power to censor all material it deems inappropriate is good for our society.
2.   If giving the government the power to censor all material it deems inappropriate is good for our society, then we should give the government the power to censor all material that it deems inappropriate.

3.   We should give the government the power to censor all material that it deems inappropriate.

Here, it is possible that Fee agrees with premise 2. In any case, there is no indication in what Fee writes that Fee disagrees with premise 2.

3.   Find the premise (or premises) that is the main point of contention.

In this step you are looking for the crux of the debate, a premise that takes a stand on the sub-issue central to establishing the author's arguments. Check to see whether your general reconstruction of the argument contains a premise that the other arguer specifically disagrees with. If the debate centres on a particular premise, then that premise is the crux of the debate. If the debate does *not* seem to centre on one particular premise, check for these possibilities:

a.   The original topic was already a central focus, in which case you continue to deal with each argument as a whole.
b.   There are two or three premises on which the arguers disagree. In this case there is more than one issue that is central to the disagreement. The best strategy will likely be to take each of the areas of disagreement in turn and complete the following steps with each one.

Here, Fee takes issue with premise 1. The main point of disagreement between the two writers is the issue of whether censorship is good for our society. In fact, the main portion of Fee's argument is spent defending the claim that censorship is not good for our society.

4. Set out or standardize just the portions of the arguments that work for and against the premise that best captures the point of contention between the two arguers.

Once you have found the main point of contention (the crux of the debate) you can examine just the portion of the original arguments that deals with the narrower issue. Standardizing the arguments enables you to use your skills without getting bogged down in an overly long standard version of the argument.

The arguments of Lee and Fee can be reconstructed in the following way.

Lee's argument:

1. Giving the government the power to censor all material that it deems inappropriate keeps our country free of pornography, violence, and racist slander.
2. Giving the government the power to censor all material that it deems inappropriate protects our children.
3. Giving the government the power to censor shows evil adults what types of behaviour will not be tolerated.
4. Almost all things that keep our country free of pornography, violence, and racist slander and protect our children and show evil adults what types of behaviour will not be tolerated are things that are good for our society.

5. Giving the government the power to censor material that it deems inappropriate is good for our society.

Fee's argument:

1. Giving the government the power to censor takes away from the freedom of the individual to choose what to read, watch, and believe.
2. All government actions that take away from the freedom of the individual to choose what to read, watch, and believe are not good for our society.

3. Giving the government the power to censor is not good for our society.

The arguments reconstructed in the fourth step are not the complete arguments presented by the authors. The complete arguments draw conclusions about the main issue of whether the government should be given the power to censor. However, the reconstructions are short and manage to capture what is at the heart of the debate between the two authors. The relative brevity of the reconstructions is an advantage, because short reconstructions can be used in essays as a way to clearly present an argument.

As a further example, see how a third person can effectively identify the key concern and focus a debate. First, look at two letters to the editor taking different sides on the same topic:

Ballot box primer wipes out unpleasant memories

We wish to congratulate the managers and editors of *The Vancouver Sun* for recognizing the importance of two major ethnic languages in B.C., Chinese and Punjabi, by publishing vital community information on voting for the benefit of those who really needed to know. It is important for the health of a democratic system that all of its subjects are aware of their rights and duties.

By publishing this information, *The Sun* has not only performed its obligation toward a large segment of households and potential readers, but also has been a pioneer in recognizing the diversity of the multicultural fabric of our Canada.

Coincidentally, in May 1919, conspiratorial efforts were being made by some members of Canadian immigration and politicians to prevent 376 passengers of the *Koma Gata Maru*, a stranded Japanese ship carrying potential immigrants of Indian origin, from coming ashore.

The Sun has made Punjabi Canadians feel at home, thus caressing their injured pride after living with the painful memories of this unpleasant episode for nine decades.

Aman P. S. Sara, Burnaby

[*VANCOUVER SUN*, JUNE 15, 2004, A13]

Multilingual primer perpetuates tyranny by minorities

It was with much disgust that I opened *The Sun* on June 12, noting that it had provided a "ballot box primer" with Chinese and Punjabi translations. People unable to read or understand English or French should not be allowed to vote in this country.

Publishing guides such as this will only allow immigrants to carry out their lives in this country without learning one of the official languages.

Unfortunately, years of Liberal government (and actions such as this by aligned media outlets) have created a tyranny of minorities perpetuated by the Liberal policy of "multiculturalism," which it has force-fed Canadians for decades too long.

Daniel Kosick, Delta

[*VANCOUVER SUN*, JUNE 15, 2004, A13]

Two weeks later, a third writer, Michelle Ng, reported her experiences as a scrutineer at the advance election polls and, as part of her article, identified both the key differences and the key similarity between these two arguers:

More than meets the eyes in cultural mosaic

… As a scrutineer in a riding that has a high percentage of ethnic voters, I saw how a sari-clad South Asian woman was able to find her way through the voting procedures, thanks to her teenage child, who translated the instructions of the voting registry officer. I saw a middle-aged Chinese man giving the voting officer several bows, his

way of thanking them for having so patiently explained, in his language, the voting instructions.

Such are scenes (and there were many more) that would warm the heart of *The Vancouver Sun* reader [Aman Sara] who recently wrote to laud the decision to provide Chinese and Punjabi versions of its voting primer, a move the reader

saw as making *The Sun* "a pioneer in recognizing the … multicultural fabric of our Canada."

The primer, however, aroused "much disgust" from another reader [Daniel Kosick]. "Publishing guides such as this will only allow immigrants to continue to carry out their lives in this country without learning one of

(Continued)

More than meets the eyes in cultural mosaic *(Continued)*

the official languages," he contended, then added that "people unable to read or understand English or French should not be allowed to vote in this country."

The difference between the first and second readers shouldn't conceal what they share in common: Both think allegiance to one's adopted homeland is important.

The first reader thinks occasions such as an election help immigrants express their allegiance to their adopted country and, therefore, measures should be taken to ensure they can sail through voting procedures with ease. The second reader equates the lack of language ability with the lack of allegiance. . . .

Michelle Ng

[*VANCOUVER SUN*, JUNE 29, 2004, A19]

Notice that what Michelle Ng has done is identify the central issue, the core of the debate, as the idea that voters should be fully committed to Canada. She sees this issue as the principal concern of both the previous writers—the value they would likely both share. Everyone who votes in Canada should care about Canada. This identification of a central, shared issue then allows the debate to be focused more clearly on the aspect of that issue on which the two writers disagree: does linguistic competence in English or French make a difference to a person's commitment to Canada? Sara says no; Kosick says yes.

Ng's analysis not only clarifies the debate but moves it forward by showing what is at stake in being able to understand and participate in voting. It provides an essential focus for future discussion.

EXERCISE **6.2** ## Identifying the Crux of the Debate

*1. Pick out the crux of the debate in the following passages, based loosely on a disagreement from February 2005 about whether it was appropriate for the leader of the Conservative Party, Stephen Harper, to require all his party members to submit their speeches on same-sex marriage to his office for approval before delivering their speeches in the House of Commons.

   a. "It makes good sense for the party leader to make sure that all members of the party present a consistent front on this issue. We don't all have to say the same thing, but we do have to make sure we do more good than harm when we speak. If we want public support, we have to be sure we do not alienate the public. In the past, some members of the party who are extremely right-wing have caused enormous controversy and damaged our party's credibility by expressing their extreme views on minority rights."

   b. "The party leader has no business checking members' speeches. It's a violation of our freedom of speech. Yes, we're members of the same party, but that doesn't mean we speak with a single voice. And it definitely doesn't mean we speak with the leader's voice. A party leader doesn't have the authority to dictate what party members may or may not say. We need all views aired, and we need to air our views in whichever words we see fit."

2. Pick out the central issue in these two passages, based on the disagreement about the right age for consensual sex. The age varies from country to country, from as low as twelve to as high as eighteen.
   a. "Canada should raise the age of consensual sex to at least sixteen. Fourteen is absurdly young to understand what's involved in sexual relationships. How many fourteen-year-olds even know how to practise safe sex? If we leave the age of consensual sex at fourteen, then we'll continue to have situations where girls of twelve or thirteen can pass themselves off as fourteen. They couldn't possibly pass themselves off as sixteen, so they'd be much safer."
   b. "It doesn't matter what the age of consent is. The age of fourteen was set in 1987, and it was dropped from eighteen for the perfectly good reason that consensual sex among teens should not be illegal. There's no magic age that makes it right. Fourteen, sixteen, or eighteen doesn't make enough guaranteed difference to how old you look, and it certainly doesn't make any difference to whether you fully understand what's involved in sexual relationships. All we really need is protection against one person exploiting another, whatever their ages. It is illegal to have sex with anyone if you are in a position of power or authority over them. That's what we need: clearer standards for when a relationship is consensual and when it's not."

3. Pick out the central issue in the following two passages. The first is an editorial, the opinion of the *Ottawa Citizen's* editorial board. The second is an article reporting a short argument of advocates for the poor.

Respect law on safe streets

Some city councillors and veteran public protesters want the police to stop enforcing Ontario's Safe Streets Act. This is a bad idea, and city council should swiftly disavow the manoeuvre when it comes up next month.

The relationship between politicians and police is a tricky one. It's good when ward councillors raise policing issues with the force brass: break-ins in a neighbourhood; park vandalism; a gang hanging around a school; or speeding. These are things that citizens will talk to a ward councillor about, and things that politicians rightly bring to the management of a police force for action.

Indeed, the mayors of municipalities have a time-honoured responsibility to work with the local police force to ensure order is maintained within the municipalities' borders.

But for politicians to instruct their police to pick and choose the laws they enforce is another thing altogether. Police are sworn to uphold the law without fear or favour. They have some discretion about whether to lay an individual charge, as they should. But since when are they enforcing the politically popular laws, and not enforcing the politically unpopular ones?

The Safe Streets Act was created by the Mike Harris Conservative government to curb aggressive panhandling, especially "squeegee kids" who descended on motorists stopped at intersections and pressured them to hand over money in exchange for a windshield wash.

Foes of the Tory government, including some homeless protesters in Ottawa, abhor the law as a remnant of the defeated Conservative government. They argue that it's being challenged in the courts and city police should stop enforcing it until the case is decided. But all kinds of laws are challenged in the courts. That doesn't mean we start ignoring them.

As well, the Safe Streets Act isn't quite the demon some have portrayed it as. It prohibits panhandlers from threatening or intimidating citizens, from panhandling around

(Continued)

Respect law on safe streets *(Continued)*

bank-teller machines, from soliciting people who are waiting for taxis or buses, or approaching people for money in their cars. But these are not unreasonable measures.

People should be able to walk or drive through their communities without being harassed by panhandlers, who often have addiction problems. The "squeegee kids" who endangered themselves running into roads, and so upset motorists, are scarcely to be seen because of the Safe Streets Act.

We don't want a city where people are afraid to visit shops or restaurants because of aggressive panhandling. That would be particularly unfair to the people who live and run businesses downtown. It would also be the beginning of the demise of the city's retail and entertainment districts.

The Safe Streets Act does not, in fact, prohibit panhandling. There are many panhandlers in central Ottawa, even though Ottawa's police enforce the act.

The fact that city police are legally equipped with a provincial law to curb the activities of panhandlers is simply not a problem.

[EDITORIAL, *OTTAWA CITIZEN*, SEPTEMBER 27, 2004, D4. REPRINTED WITH PERMISSION OF THE OTTAWA CITIZEN.]

Let us panhandle, say protesters: Group demands repeal of "mean-spirited" law

If Chris Keats had a dollar for every time someone told him to "Get a job" he might not be living in a tent outside city hall.

"I've been arrested 45 times," says the slender 31-year-old panhandler.

His crime?

"Being poor. Being homeless.

"It's all fine and good to say: 'Go get a job,' but give a person an address so they can get one."

Keats, his fingernails black with grit, stands amid seven tents pitched near a monument to human rights outside Ottawa's handsome stone municipal buildings.

On a steamy summer day he's sporting the jersey of his beloved Vancouver Canucks of the NHL, beat-up jeans and dreadlocks styled in a Mohawk gone awry.

The lack of affordable housing creates a vicious circle, Keats said.

He's one of about 10 protesters who've taken up residence in the tent village under the windows of city hall, to highlight what they see as an unfair countrywide crackdown on society's outcasts.

Tourists and government workers stroll past along the busy street lined with popular bars and bistros. Most ignore the polite requests for change; some think the campers are just there to pocket cash.

Water bottles are strewn about and two good-natured dogs lounge in the heat, tied to a concrete block.

The tenters use washrooms at nearby fast-food restaurants and shower across the street at a drop-in centre.

The protest hasn't always gone smoothly, Keats says. Some rowdy drug users were finally pressured to leave the area after causing fights and late-night chaos, he said.

But those who stayed are serious about the rights of homeless. Since Canada Day, they've been collecting signatures on a petition demanding that the Ontario Safe Streets Act be repealed.

The 1999 legislation, passed by the province's former Conservative government under Mike Harris, was aimed at clearing the streets of aggressive beggars.

But it's routinely used against even the most peaceful street people, say advocates for the poor.

They call it one of the most disturbing examples of how governments across Canada have moved to criminalize begging, "illegal camping" and other mainstays of the very poor.

"The Safe Streets Act is really unnecessary," says Robert Arnold, president of the National Anti-Poverty Organization.

[*SUDBURY STAR*, AUGUST 2, 2004, A6. THE CANADIAN PRESS.]

4. Pick out the central issue in the following two letters. The topic is the same as the previous pair of articles, but the crux of the debate may not be the same. Both letters are responding to an editorial that argued that "squeegee kids" washing windshields at intersections may be irritating motorists, but it is not necessary to pass a law to restrict them.

Squeegee kids: Does a nuisance require new laws?

I am writing in response to your editorial "Squeegee kids may be irritating ..." (May 14) which compared the nuisance of squeegee kids to the inconvenience of spam e-mails and telemarketers and concluded new laws are unnecessary.

It is hard for me to see the parallel between these activities. While you can easily screen phone calls and e-mails, there is no escape from aggressive behaviour encountered while walking or driving in one's own city. The Safe Streets Act proposed by MLA Lorne Mayencourt is not just about "squeegee kids," it is about providing the police with sufficient tools to address aggressive behaviour on our streets. It is about protecting our public spaces for all citizens, including the poor, addicted and mentally ill.

Contrary to your editorial, the members of our Safe Streets Coalition believe that new provincial legislation is necessary. Provincial laws would allow police to attend to a complaint and choose from a number of different options—warn, ticket, or arrest. The arrest option under a provincial statute is critical. Used as a last resort for repeat or non-compliant offenders, it attaches a real and immediate consequence to unwanted and aggressive behaviour. The coalition is particularly supportive of provincial legislation to ensure that all communities have the same laws and penalties.

Kathi E. Thompson
Chair, Safe Streets Coalition, Vancouver

[*VANCOUVER SUN,* MAY 18, 2004, A13. REPRINTED WITH PERMISSION OF KATHI E. THOMPSON, SAFE STREETS COALITION, VANCOUVER.]

I couldn't agree more that larger public nuisances merit legal restraining, rather than a few kids at traffic lights.

Having been accosted at knife-point on the meaner streets of both Los Angeles and New York, I can say local squeegee kids are at least performing a service in an entrepreneurial business pursuit.

It could be a lot worse, and is a reflection of the more kind society in which we live.

As a motorist, when I see a squeegee kid approaching I consider if he or she is one of the mentally challenged our government has cast into "community care" instead of a now-closed institution, or is the kid from a good home and simply hitch-hiking through the world for now?

Either way, the gamble I take as I reach into my wallet for a looney or toony is about the same as a purchased cup of coffee being good or stale.

Considering those meaner streets which produce meaner kids, I decide the gamble is worth it. I smile and speak politely to the kid, my windshield gets washed, and in almost every case, the kid is extremely polite to me.

For those who still get their noses twisted at this being allowed to occur, how much would it cost the city to post those little "maximum fine" signs related to aggressive panhandling at busy intersections?

Not much, considering those meaner streets elsewhere. We have much to be thankful for.

Al Hawirko, North Vancouver

[*VANCOUVER SUN,* MAY 18, 2004, A13. REPRINTED WITH PERMISSION OF AL HAWIRKO.]

Reporting the Issues

Once we have identified the most important issues, we need to set them out as a focus for future debate. In oral discussions, you can pause to ask if you've correctly understood each person or each side's main points. This check helps to focus the discussion and helps everyone involved to confirm that the main concerns have been identified; it prevents people from arguing at cross-purposes. (A good chairperson will do this when people seem to be repeating themselves or when the discussion becomes heated.)

In written work, if you report each argument and then indicate what you take to be the central issue (or issues) on which the arguers disagree, you'll keep the main concerns clear by giving an overview of the disagreement. This will put the issue in context for yourself and others.

In oral or written work, it is best to speak neutrally at this point. If you stay neutral in tone and do not mention which view you favour, you are more likely to get the cooperation of supporters of both sides because you are more likely to be seen as open-minded and really willing to listen.

Identifying Options by Recognizing Assumptions

The next question we ask in exploring what is important in the context is what options do we have. Whatever the issue is, whatever has been said, whatever has been proposed, we ought to be aware of the options open to us before we make a decision. Here is where investigation of the context takes us beyond what we have observed or even what we've researched and requires us to imagine what else is possible.

What Options Are Open to Us?

In Chapter 4, we considered the possibility that research might turn up conflicting facts. Research usually reveals whether there are plausible—that is, realistic or potentially true—alternatives to these facts, and you now know that you must suspend judgment as to which alternative is correct. Similarly, there will be opinions that conflict, and once you become aware of them, you must also suspend judgment as to which is correct.

These alternative opinions are assumptions. You probably have a good intuitive understanding of what an **assumption** is. For example, if you give your friend a hilariously funny birthday card, but your friend doesn't find it funny at all, you quickly realize that you shouldn't have assumed that you have the same sense of humour just because the two of you get on so well.

Perhaps your friend does have the same sense of humour as you do—or perhaps not. When you take something for granted, you are making an assumption. When you choose to investigate only one option, even though you do know there are others, you are making an assumption. The important thing about assumptions is not that you shouldn't make them—you can't possibly avoid them—but that you should remember *when* there may be alternatives to your views and you should be aware of *what* those alternatives are. This is what the investigation seeks to establish: are there alternatives of which we should be aware?

You have already seen one form of assumption in Chapter 5: implicit premises. When you add an implicit premise to an argument, using the principle of charity, you are recognizing that the argument has made an assumption. For example, consider the short argument

DEFINITION

An **assumption** is a claim for which there are plausible alternatives that have not yet been ruled out by evidence or argument.

Most car batteries typically last five years.

My car battery will last five years.

This argument works only if we add the implicit premise "My car battery is like most car batteries." When we add this implicit premise, we can see that there are alternatives of which we should be aware. The obvious one is that my car battery is not a typical battery. Perhaps I bought a less expensive battery and that brand averages only three years of life. Perhaps my battery has a design flaw and it's going to fail completely the first time I accidentally leave my lights on. These are alternatives. Are they plausible? That will depend on our background knowledge and on the further fact-checking we will do. If I have absolutely no reason to assume my battery is in any way unusual, I have made a reasonable assumption and the principle of charity helps by filling it in for me. If I find the receipt for the battery and realize I did pay an unusually low price, I have cause to think my assumption may not be the only reasonable one in the circumstances. It may be equally likely that my battery is not typical, but is a cheap brand that won't last as long.

As the principle of charity helps to reveal, we aren't always aware when we are making assumptions. A person may indicate an assumption by saying, "Let's assume . . ." or "For argument's sake, let's say . . ." or some other expression indicating that he or she is well aware of other possibilities. The person may then be able to easily discuss these possibilities and show why the assumption was a good one to make—and therefore why this information or this line of reasoning and this conclusion are more plausible than the alternatives. For example, someone might say, "Let's assume we do get the bank loan. Then we can shop for a more reliable car." This person clearly realizes that the bank loan might not come through. If you point this out, the person is likely to be able to recognize and deal with alternatives. Perhaps the person has some additional evidence that the bank loan is likely to come through: "We'd have heard by now if there was a problem." Perhaps the person already has another source of money in mind: "If the bank loan doesn't come through, I'm pretty sure my parents can give us enough to help with a car." Perhaps the person recognizes the assumption was risky: "If the loan doesn't come through, we're going to have to try to keep this car on the road, but I'm not sure how we'll manage that."

Alternatively, the person may believe the statement to be obviously true and may be entirely unaware that there are alternatives. In that case, he or she may be surprised that there is any other way to see the issue and may be reluctant or even unable to give more support or to explore alternatives. "What do you mean, we might not get the bank loan? How could they possibly turn us down?"

The alternatives are there, whether the person making the assumption recognizes them or not. If these alternatives are plausible, they may make a difference to the conclusion we can reach. Is a more reliable car in our future or not? Once we know that the bank might turn down the loan, we can't risk shopping for another car until we can check how likely it is that the loan will come through.

In a diverse society, it is particularly important to recognize assumptions and be able to see the alternatives to them. It is better by far to be prepared in advance to realize the harm that can be done by assuming something that you cannot expect to be true. You don't want to risk losing a friendship just because it never occurred to you that your friend might not find the same things funny as you do.

This is often a key step in reasoning: freeing ourselves from the limits set by what we observed. If we're lucky, some additional options will have turned up during research—we will have found conflicting evidence that points to other conclusions.

Each piece of conflicting evidence is a potential option we may need to explore. When two pieces of information clash, and neither one is obviously wrong, then we must continue to keep both options alive as possibilities.

Even without conflicting evidence in hand, we still need to do a mental check to see if we can imagine options that we ought to consider. If we don't do this, we can find ourselves limited to the unsatisfactory options already presented. Yet there may be a better alternative that is even more realistic.

To imagine additional options, we have to brainstorm possibilities. Brainstorming is an activity often best done in groups because each person will make different connections and increase the range of possibilities. You're probably familiar with brainstorming. Whether you do it by yourself or with others, the procedure is simply to come up with any ideas that seem in any way connected to the topic. Brainstorming in general asks you simply to think of what might be—how could things be different from the way they actually are? What could have happened instead of what did happen? What might happen next? What could have been there instead of what you have actually observed?

It is essential to record all the ideas when brainstorming, not ruling any out too quickly as impossible. Stopping to consider the ideas only inhibits you from being sufficiently creative. Don't be overwhelmed by the number of options. At the investigation stage it is important to remember that no action is called for yet. It is safe simply to list as many options as you come up with, and leave them recorded so you can come back later to pick out just the one or two most realistic.

The Value of Recognizing Assumptions

The value of investigation often is not that it answers questions but that it raises them. As in the scenario of a stressful situation presented at the beginning of the chapter, investigation shows where more thinking will be needed, and where we should open our minds a little wider instead of starting to close them. How did we get ourselves into this situation? How might someone else handle the same situation differently? What might we have done instead of what we did? What might happen instead of what we currently expect?

Even if our assumptions turn out to be good ones, it can be very helpful simply to have looked for, and become aware of, the alternatives. Checking for assumptions reveals other perspectives that we might have taken and gives us a better sense of where we stand. It does the useful job of showing us that there are other options, and it prevents us from assuming that something is true just because the arguer asserts it so positively and confidently. For instance, it is common for people to resist change in major industries by saying jobs will be lost. This assumes the lost jobs cannot be replaced. However, rejecting the assumption that jobs in the auto industry, or forestry, or fishing can't be replaced allows us to explore other possible ways to make sure that people can earn a living in a changing economy. It doesn't guarantee that there are other options, but it does prevent us from getting trapped into only one set of options.

Dealing with Competing Assumptions

When we investigate and evaluate an argument, we will want to know whether its conclusion is more probable than the opposite. For example, does moderate drinking increase your life span or decrease it? Would toughening the Young Offenders Act reduce violent crime, increase it, or make no difference at all?

Notice that all we have done so far is identify competing assumptions, or **contraries**. We have no idea yet which of the assumptions is correct, so we have no idea which of the conclusions is correct. What we do know is that we need further information before we can decide what is true.

Three main possibilities arise when contrary assumptions are explored.

1. First, the original assumption may seem *more plausible* than the alternatives. The effect is that we accept the assumption.

2. Second, the contrary assumptions may seem *equally plausible* or acceptable. The effect of equally plausible alternatives is that we must suspend judgment until we have a chance to investigate further. For instance, it may not be immediately obvious that jobs lost in the forestry, mining, or fishing industries can be replaced by jobs in other industries such as tourism. Nor is it obvious that the jobs couldn't be replaced; Canada has considerable tourist appeal. Tourism is offered along with environmental concerns as one of the reasons to stop logging in British Columbia; it is also offered as one way that people can continue to live in isolated fishing villages in Newfoundland. As a result, we must suspend judgment on what is the best approach to the risk of job losses in a resource industry.

3. Third, the original assumption may seem *less plausible* than the alternatives. The effect is that anything derived from that assumption becomes less credible. Although we still suspend judgment pending confirmation, we tentatively discredit this line of thought or action.

The crucial point is to reserve judgment until you can investigate further. In the scenario at the beginning of the chapter, for example, you were asked to imagine that you felt you could not handle everything expected of you. It is likely that you are making an assumption that you know what others expect. Perhaps their priorities have changed. (Have you ever rushed to return something on time, only to have the recipient say, "Oh, I'd forgotten all about that"?) Perhaps their priorities never were quite what you thought—you believed they wanted a carefully planned event, when all they wanted was someone to book the room and line up some food. Or perhaps you are trying to improve a relationship at work, on the assumption that it can improve and that you can be the agent of change. Both these assumptions might be mistaken. Perhaps, for factors completely outside your control, the person you are working with is unable to change in ways that would improve your working relationship. Recognizing these alternatives may open the possibility that you can do less than you'd planned, or to a lower quality, or abandon the task altogether because it's not a good use of your time and energy.

A cautionary note: for these kinds of situations, where you did not feel you had any alternatives, it can be hard to accept the options even when they are pointed out to you. How can you possibly give up on a task that was

DEFINITION

Contraries are competing statements that cannot both be true at the same time.

worth doing in the first place? If it's worth doing, it's worth doing well. How can you possibly delegate a task that was your responsibility in the first place? If you started it, you should finish it.

Whenever you find yourself, or other people, resisting alternatives that are not obviously impractical, that is one signal to look for a particular kind of assumption—assumptions about what we *should* do, not just what we *could* do. These are assumptions of principle.

Assumptions of Principle: Choices Not Lightly Challenged

Assumptions of principle are assumptions about the way our world works or should work: assumptions about beliefs or values that are not universally held. For example, do you believe all human beings are equal or not? Can we control our own future or are we at the mercy of unpredictable forces? These assumptions are the most challenging type of assumption to uncover and to deal with.

In any situation in which you are dealing with people from diverse backgrounds, or when you are investigating an argument on a controversial topic, you will need to recognize an important source of disagreement: the matters of principle on which people of integrity can reasonably disagree.

Arguments often confront us with perspectives other than our own. We often find it difficult to recognize that another perspective could be legitimate, let alone to realize that there are several perspectives. One value of the study of arguments is that we begin to understand perspectives very different from our own.

Our beliefs often derive from our backgrounds. If we were raised with certain values, we might adopt those values without question. For example, if you were raised by same-sex parents, you might find it hard even to imagine why people could oppose same-sex marriage. Equally, if you were raised within a church tradition that maintains that homosexuality is wrong, you may find it hard to imagine how same-sex marriage could possibly be supported. From either perspective, you are likely to find it difficult to picture additional perspectives. For instance, there is the perspective that same-sex relationships are not wrong in themselves, but it is wrong to have or raise children in such a household. There is also the perspective that there is no problem whatsoever with same-sex relationships, but that the notion of marriage itself is outmoded and a very bad structure on which to base legal rights of couples.

At the same time, values such as these are not simply a matter of our personal history or our psychology. There may be cultural or family causes that explain how we have come to hold certain beliefs, and there may be psychological reasons why we still find these beliefs comfortable. But the causes of the beliefs do not prevent us considering why these beliefs make sense. We can reason about our beliefs. We can still discuss our beliefs with others, and we can examine them for ourselves to see if they are rational beliefs. The difficulty in doing so is that it is often hard to identify and express our beliefs.

Identifying Beliefs and Values

What we need to be able to do is to unpack and recognize the beliefs and values that lie hidden inside the views we do express. This is very like identifying the key issues, the crux of the debate, as we did earlier in the chapter. In fact, the crux of the debate often is a value or belief on which people can legitimately hold widely different perspectives. This search for assumptions gives you another way to recognize key issues in debate—you can ask, for example, "What does this person think is fair?" or "Who does this person think should be treated with the most respect, and why?" or "Who does this person think should be entitled to make decisions?"

You can construct parallel sets of competing perspectives for any controversial topic. The main point of recognizing these alternatives is to stay aware that there are many perspectives on an issue.

Consider once again the scenario from the start of the chapter. Suppose someone has heard you out as you talked about your problem and told you that you could just "drop it"—abandon the project, give up on the relationship. You are horrified. "I can't just give up!" Hard as it may be to recognize, this is an assumption. Not everybody believes it. There are people who don't find it hard to quit, even for important jobs or long-term relationships. If you disagree, that doesn't make you wrong, but it does mean you can recognize that your view must come from a particular perspective, a particular belief system in which this, for you, is a key element. Perhaps you believe that "when the going gets tough, the tough get going." This suggests that you believe it is important to be tough, and to be able to prove yourself by handling challenges. Perhaps you believe that "my word is my bond": if you said you'd do it, that's a commitment you must honour. You cannot let anyone else down.

Notice that these two principles, "When the going gets tough, the tough get going" and "My word is my bond," each serve as a guiding principle to back up the conclusion "I can't give up." However, they express different priorities. One promotes personal strength and competence in the face of adversity. The other promotes the value of other people and the importance of recognizing and meeting their needs.

Once you realize which principles are at issue for you, you are in a position to think about whether these principles are indeed your highest priority in the difficult situation or whether there are other priorities you need to balance.

Reasoning about Beliefs and Values

When we begin to consider or discuss our own beliefs or the beliefs of others, we re-enter the realm of argument. Beliefs are not something we change on a whim. Here, perhaps more than anywhere else, we want to see reasons and arguments. A successful argument has the obligation of showing either why its perspective makes better sense than others or why it can legitimately ignore some of the others. For example, an argument in favour of same-sex marriage within a church that opposes it may be expected to show why this position is more compatible with the church's teachings than perspectives that oppose same-sex marriages. Alternatively, an argument against same-sex marriages might choose to ignore arguments related to legalizing such relationships and argue only that the members of one particular faith should neither engage in nor endorse such relationships.

Within academic subjects, you will also encounter deeply held convictions that support one or another of several competing academic theories. Are teenage brains, as reported in *Time* magazine in 2004, physiologically incapable of rational decision-making (Wallis and Dell)? If you are studying psychology, you will probably be aware that there are psychological theories that could not even entertain the possibility that brain chemistry is relevant to behaviour. Whenever you make or evaluate an argument in a psychology assignment, you usually need to proceed with a full awareness that not everyone accepts that brain development is a factor in personality development, let alone that it is the crucial factor.

We may not settle difficult issues such as these in the course of evaluating any particular arguments, but we need to be aware that the disagreement is out there.

Recognizing Assumptions in Arguments

The art in reasoning is to remember to keep an eye on the world beyond the words of the argument. You need to be able to step outside what you are hearing and reading and ask what *isn't* there, what *isn't* being covered, what possibilities are being overlooked. Especially for arguments, it is invaluable to be able to realize what the arguer isn't mentioning. What has he or she not thought to discuss or rule out?

As soon as you can think of plausible alternatives, you know that the argument will need more evidence and other conclusions are possible. So understanding an argument often requires you to look between and behind the lines for what *isn't* said. Doing so gives you the power to see which alternatives haven't been explored and what other conclusions might be possible.

Whenever you read an argument and

- you cannot understand why the arguer says what he or she does; or
- you see no faults in the reasoning because the argument seems to provide good, logical support for its conclusion, but you still disagree with the conclusion; or
- you can figure out which person or position the arguer is opposing (and so can see the arguer's purpose),

then you should check to see what assumptions the arguer might be making. You can identify assumptions by asking these questions:

1. What does the arguer's attitude seem to be? What different attitudes could there be on this topic?
2. What noun phrases are used as subjects or objects of the sentences? Anything used as a noun may indicate that the arguer believes that the entity exists.
3. What else can you imagine this arguer agreeing to or going on to say? You may discover the arguer's overall perspective.
4. What situations can you imagine in which the arguer's claims would seem implausible or untrue? What general principles might fit those situations better?

This procedure is very similar to that for checking and revising a claim as we did in Chapter 3. When you identify assumptions, check to see whether any of their alternatives would make a difference to the conclusion of the argument. Can the assumptions be challenged? Do they indicate that the discussion must shift to a different level before there can possibly be agreement? Detecting these alternatives, seeing how plausible they are, and seeing what difference they make to the conclusion may be the first steps in seeing where the weaknesses are in the argument and where we might look for more acceptable alternatives.

What is crucial to note about assumptions is that they are not mistakes. They are simply claims that have not yet been sufficiently investigated. Until we investigate which of the alternatives is most likely to be correct, we must suspend judgment. The impact of assumptions on an argument is that they leave open the possibility that conclusions other than the intended one may still be reasonable.

Assumptions as Paths to Different Conclusions

When we make an assumption, we make a claim that is not obviously or necessarily true. We are following only one of several possible lines of argument or adopting only one of several plausible competing hypotheses about a situation.

For example, someone who says, "I never let myself get depressed" is making the assumption that depression can be controlled by willpower. This is one view of depression; there are others. For example, depression may be a biochemical response to stress or illness that cannot be prevented by conscious effort. It might also be a combination of the two. It is important to notice here that none of the views is obviously correct, and none is obviously wrong. But they cannot all be true—eventually, we will have to make a decision between them before we can choose the right treatment.

Worries about the safety of antidepressants for children have led to increased calls for therapy instead of medication. That is premature: we do not yet know that therapy can resolve all depressions. Equally, we cannot conclude that drugs are safe enough. At the very least, we'll need to know whether the risk of suicide for children and youths taking antidepressants is higher or lower than the suicide rate for unmedicated children.

When we encounter conflicting assumptions—contraries, as defined earlier—we must be ready to investigate further, because any conclusion or action we take based on one assumption might prove to be completely misguided.

When we check the other choices, we may find that they point us in very different directions. If we assume that depression can be controlled by willpower, then we would support the conclusion that people can make themselves recover from depression, and we will encourage them to get counselling. If we make the contrary assumption, that depression cannot be controlled by conscious effort, then we would support the opposing conclusion that people cannot make themselves recover from depression, and we will encourage medication or other non-psychological treatments.

Generating alternatives in this way will help you see what facts you should check, and where the information you have been given or have found might be incorrect. It will help you target another round of background checking if needed.

Recognizing Alternatives

1. Can you give three to five alternative responses for each of the following?
   *a. What behaviour might be a good indicator that an immigrant is committed to Canada?
   b. What courses of action can be considered responsible with respect to "squeegee kids"?

*2. Look at the argument given by Daniel Kosick on page 197. Find an assumption made by Kosick. Give a plausible alternative and explain why it is plausible.

3. Look back at the actual arguments given in Exercise 6.2. Can you pick out some assumptions made in each one? For each assumption you find, list a plausible alternative and explain why it is plausible.

4. Choose an argument on a topic that interests you. (You might use one of the articles you found for the application exercises at the end of Part 1.) Identify three assumptions made in this argument. For each of the assumptions you found, list one alternative assumption that is as plausible as the assumption made in the argument. Explain why the alternative assumption is plausible. If we accepted the alternative assumption, how would that affect the conclusion of the argument?

Preparing for Evaluation

Now that you know there are alternative conclusions and perspectives that will need to be examined, you are in a position to move on to evaluating. In evaluation in general, we will be checking which available option is best in the circumstances. In evaluating arguments, we will be checking whether the conclusion is the one best supported by its premises. Have other possible conclusions been sufficiently ruled out by the premises of the argument? If not, we must continue to suspend judgment and investigate further.

Key Points in Review

- When we investigate information or arguments, we are investigating in a particular context—for a particular purpose, in a particular situation.

- The value of investigation often is not that it answers questions but that it raises them—it shows where more thinking will be needed, and where we should open our minds a little wider instead of starting to close them.

- Identifying the key issues finds a focus for our further investigation and helps to clarify the goals—what needs are to be met?

- Before we move on to adopting a belief or making a decision, we should be aware of all the reasonable options open to us. To identify options, look for assumptions—any beliefs that might not necessarily be correct.

Part 2
Summary

Getting the Best out of Investigation

Nothing has such power to broaden the mind as the ability to investigate system-atically and truly all that comes under thy observation in life.
— *Marcus Aurelius*

Attempt the end and never stand in doubt; Nothing's so hard, but search will find it out.
— *Robert Herrick*

Investigation Overview

Observation seldom tells us all we need to know. Thorough investigation almost always requires us to search for information that we could not find through obser-vation alone. In particular, we need more information about claims that have been made so that we can ultimately evaluate those claims. Investigation through research has been the focus of this section. After your observations are complete, you explore in more detail what you observed. You compare what you observed with what you expected. You discover what was missing or not yet discussed. However, during the investigation stage we still refrain from judgment. Investigation is similar to observation in that it is non-judgmental and still an open-minded search for information related to the situation or argument being considered. Our task is only to gather as much information as we can about the claim or the situation. We need to understand what kind of evidence would indicate that a claim is true or false and also gather evidence pertaining to the truth or falsity of the claim. We need to understand what information might change our interpretation of a situation and also gather as much of that information as we can. When we are trying to create our own reasoned opinions, investigation encourages us to explore more than one approach and consider more than one source of information.

One part of investigation is interpreting arguments. Because we use the principle of charity when interpreting arguments, we assume that the speaker or author means to present a rational argument. So knowing how to interpret an argument involves understanding the standards of rational argument. We have drawn a distinction between types of rational connections between claims. Some connections guarantee the truth of a conclusion. Other connections demonstrate that a conclusion is highly probable. A third type of connection shows only that the conclusion is possible. One way to recognize the difference between these types is through recognizing argument patterns, which allows us to fill in the missing pieces of an argument.

In the final chapter of this section, we broadened our focus to look beyond the immediate situation or arguments. We looked for the deeper concerns that might be at stake in a disagreement, and for the additional options that might be available to deal with a situation.

A good critical investigation will also ensure that you understand the central issue—the crux of the debate. When you understand the central issue, you are able to direct your efforts more effectively toward the most important concerns. As you explore issues in more detail, it becomes necessary to recognize when there are additional options and alternative beliefs that should be considered.

Lastly, we are reminded that it is not only arguments that need to be investigated, but also other elements of situations we think about. We make sure we have fully investigated any relevant images, sounds, numbers, and emotions before continuing to the next stage in the critical thinking cycle: evaluation.

Part-Ending Exercises

Comprehension Questions: Review

1. What is the difference between strategic search and purposeful observation?
2. Why are expectations and standards often good things to investigate?
3. What is the purpose of the investigation stage?
4. What is an argument to certainty?
5. What is an argument to probability?
6. What is an argument to possibility?
7. Define "structurally valid" argument. Give one example.
8. Define "cogent" argument. Give one example.
9. What two standards must be met to ensure that an argument is well structured?
10. What is an implicit premise? Give one example of an argument with an implicit premise.
11. Describe some strategies for recognizing assumptions. Give one example of an assumption.

Application Exercises

1. Take one of the arguments from your collection and describe what type of argument has been presented. Explain your reasoning.
2. Describe methods of research you have used to check information for personal needs, or for assignments.
3. Find a piece of writing that offers an argument. What types of arguments does it contain? What further information would you need to gather before evaluating the argument? Are there any assumptions being made in the article? If so, give alternatives.

We might hope to establish a system or set of opinions, which if not true (for that perhaps is too much to be hop'd for) might at least be satisfactory to the human mind, and might stand the test of the most critical examination.

David Hume, *A Treatise of Human Nature*, ed. L. A. Selby-Bigge, Book I, Oxford: Oxford University Press, 1973.

Until this stage, you have been encouraged to be as open and as flexible as possible. Open-mindedness is essential to making sure nothing important is overlooked.

But the purpose of critical thinking is to choose rational beliefs and to act responsibly. We must now exercise judgment to choose between the options we have uncovered. We must select which arguments lead us to rational beliefs and which options constitute responsible actions. And in exercising that judgment, we must be fair-minded—not looking for what we might intuitively prefer, but for what really does best meet the agreed-upon goals and expectations.

What we are doing here is like what a building inspector might do when looking over an old house or what a mechanic might do when checking a used car you're thinking of buying. Is the building design sound, so the building won't crack or leak? Is the car mechanically sound, so it will run without requiring expensive repairs? The building might have been designed by a good architect, but the good design might still not have held up well in Quebec cold or B.C. rain. The used car's owner might never even have known the car's head gasket was starting to leak, so the owner could not have told you that the engine would need an expensive repair.

All your efforts so far in observing and investigating will now enable you to effectively evaluate the situation or argument you are faced with. You have objectively observed and noted what is immediately obvious and

you have investigated claims, assumptions, roles, and responsibilities. You have been creative and open-minded and non-judgmental in your approach. Observing has allowed you to slow down and take stock of what you are dealing with. Investigation has given you further insight into what you have observed and allowed you to explore assumptions, issues, and possibilities. These two stages have now put you in the position of being able to critically assess the situations and arguments you have been examining. You are now in the position of having a lot of information but you still need to ask what it is rational to believe. How do you sort the rational beliefs and reliable information from the trash? How do you give yourself a dependable basis for action?

In the previous section you learned about expectations in reasoning and research. In this section these expectations are applied as standards against which we judge claims, arguments, and reasoning in general, including the use of imagery, sounds, and emotions. We also judge the practicality of proposed courses of action. There are two principal checking steps. First, you need to check the accuracy of the information you are being asked to rely on. In Chapter 7 we begin by assessing the quality of our information. Next, you need to check how well the reasoning fits together to support a particular conclusion or solution. In Chapter 8 we judge the accuracy of reasoning. In Chapter 9 we take context into account to separate practical options from impractical options.

Chapter 7

Evaluating Information

■ Perspective

This is the first of two principal checking steps—checking the accuracy of the information you are being asked to rely on. You know from the observation stage what you are dealing with. You know from the investigation stage what is expected. Now you have to put the two together—does the information you have meet the expected standards for accuracy and credibility?

■ Scenario

Scholarships, grants, and bursaries often require you to fill out a budget that indicates financial need. Before you are approved for any award or loan that is based on financial need, your budget will be checked (usually by your institution's financial aid office) for credibility. The same will be true when you apply for a bank loan. Suppose that you have already been able to estimate how much you really think it will cost for your rent, food, fees, books, clothing, transportation, and entertainment. Can you tell in advance whether your application has a good chance of being approved? Do you know what the standards are for credible expenses in the areas of rent, transportation, and clothing?

■ Key Question

Is this information acceptable?

Evaluating Information: The Standards

We'd like to know that our information is acceptable: in other words, it is reliable—all the facts are correct and the opinions well justified. To evaluate information we determine its credibility by objective standards. How likely is it that the information is correct?

Credibility

Credibility is a measure of how reasonable it is to believe the information. Credibility can be used as a preliminary check on information. Can we take it seriously before we investigate further? Is it trustworthy? Is it likely to be true? In other words, we are *estimating* probable truth. When we decide that something or someone is credible, we have decided that it or the person is *provisionally* acceptable. For example, we may not be sure the information is accurate, but if the source is one that we can normally count on for reliable information, then we have good reason to believe that the information is credible. Credibility can also be used as an ongoing check as new information is found: does the new information seem as credible as what we already have? When we combine new information with what we already have, does the overall credibility increase?

As we investigate, we check for credibility as a minimum level of acceptability for the information we have. If information is not credible, we do not want to waste any time recording it or trying to use it. A large part of critical thinking is realizing that we must suspend judgment much more often than we are inclined to.

Here is where reasoning helps you start from where you are and work your way up to the level of checking you need:

1. Start with just what you are already given and your existing background knowledge.

2. Discover what you are not sure about, and investigate it further.

3. Check the acceptability again, given your new information.

4. Repeat as needed until you can confirm that the information meets the standards of acceptability for the context in which it is being used.

As a preliminary step, collect all the information you found during the investigation stage. (See Chapters 4 and 6.) Be sure that you have correctly listed the bibliographical information for every argument and every source you used in checking the information. The date indicates how current the information is, and facts in reputable sources have usually been checked. Providing this information also allows other people to carry out independent checks of the information for themselves.

Credibility typically means that the information must be

- consistent with information in other sources, and/or
- from an authority that we have reason to believe.

> **DEFINITION**
>
> Information is **credible** when it is reasonable to rely on the source of the information. When sources conflict or we are in doubt about the reliability of a source, a credibility check is used to estimate the probability that the information is correct.

Notice that credibility does not guarantee acceptability. We may find consistent information from a reputable authority. The information is credible and so we are justified in using it. However, the information may be inaccurate and the authority might be wrong. The errors may show up only in a later investigation. We realize then that the information was unacceptable, but we also are reassured that it was reasonable at the time for us to use the information—it did meet the standards for credibility. When we decide that something or someone is credible, we have decided that it, or the person, is provisionally acceptable. We may not yet be sure the information is acceptable or the person is trustworthy, but we are confident that our information is at least consistent with our background knowledge and does not seem implausible. If you can be absolutely sure that the information is correct, then and only then is the information acceptable.

Provisional acceptability at least lets us get started. We may not yet be sure if the information is accurate, but if the source is one that we can normally count on for reliable information, then we have good reason to believe that the information is acceptable.

To see how provisional acceptability can be based on your general understanding of the subject matter and does not have to be based on firsthand experience or studies you have done, consider the following example: "All plumbers in Halifax are bald."

Is that claim provisionally acceptable? People who have firsthand knowledge of a plumber in Halifax who is not bald can immediately reject this premise as unacceptable. But even those who have never seen a plumber in Halifax can provisionally reject this claim. The claim that all plumbers in Halifax are bald is not consistent with most people's background knowledge. Halifax is a large city and so it is reasonable to believe that there are quite a few plumbers in Halifax. If there are quite a few plumbers, chances are very good that not all of them are bald. Some plumbers will be young men, who are less likely to be bald than older men. Some plumbers are women, who are seldom bald.

So even when you do not have direct knowledge you can often reasonably accept or reject information as credible based on background knowledge. Usually, however, determining credibility requires that you do at least some additional checking.

Checking for Consistency with Information in Other Sources

The most basic check of credibility and acceptability is **consistency**. Is the information the same all the way through the source, and is it the same in different sources? There are two basic checks that you can carry out as a preliminary assessment of credibility:

1. *Internal consistency:* Check whether the argument is internally consistent in the information that it uses. If the speaker changes his opinion halfway through his speech or from one speech to the next, we won't find him credible—if his opinion is inconsistent, we aren't even sure which opinion he holds. If a name is spelled one way in an article and a different way in the caption under a picture, we will not know which is the correct spelling.

2. *External consistency:* First, check that none of the information conflicts with your background knowledge—don't assume that you are wrong and an arguer is right, especially if you have personal experience in the area. If an article claims that farms are safer places to work than they were ten years ago, and you personally know of two people who have had accidents on farms in the last year, you are entitled to question whether the article is correct. Your evidence is anecdotal—it is not enough to make an accurate judgment about what is generally true. However, it does give you reason to investigate other sources before you accept what was said. Next, check whether it is consistent with other information that you have collected during investigation. If one article says that deaths in farm work have dropped by five percent in the last decade and another says that deaths have dropped by seven percent, there is an inconsistency here and we can question whether either figure is accurate.

If the information fails either of these checks, point out where the problem is: explain where there is an inconsistency or apparent inconsistency. At this stage, it is not necessary to resolve the inconsistency, unless you can easily track down a source sufficiently reputable to resolve it.

Now the research you did in Chapter 4 can be used to do fact-checking. Do the details that turned up in other sources match the details you started with?

Fact-checking is the activity of confirming information you already have by consulting an authoritative source or by comparing several reliable sources to see if the information is consistent. For example, how do you pronounce the word "Halkomelem" or the name "Hnatyshyn"? Are both names correctly spelled? Can a tourist see the Rockies and the Pacific Ocean from Vancouver, as advertisements and travel guides like to claim? Is it true that sixteen-year-old drivers are more likely to have accidents when they have passengers in the car? How frequently do children under thirteen suffer from clinical depression or from strokes? In all these examples, it is important to use accurate information to answer the question. To determine whether the information is accurate, we need to be able to check it by dependable methods in reliable sources. As you will see later in the chapter, this in turn means that we must determine which checks to make, and which sources will be considered sufficiently reliable. When we check, we may find that information is not readily available or is not easy to confirm.

EXERCISE **Checking Sources**

1. For one of the following questions, look for at least two different sources that give numbers you can compare. If you are unable to find two different sources that can be compared, detail what you achieved in your search: where did you look, why did you expect these sources would be useful, and why do you think you were unable to find two sources? If you do find two comparable sources, describe the results of your search and make the comparison between them. Make sure each source indicates clearly where its numbers came from. Are the sources consistent in their information?

     a. What is the accident rate for people who talk on cellphones while driving?

     b. What winter sport has the highest accident rate?

    *c. Is it true that washing dishes by hand uses more water and energy than using an automatic dishwasher?

2. For one of the following items, check as many of the facts as you can in one hour. List the sources you were able to find and state whether they confirm the stated facts.

     a. An average cruise ship with 3,000 passengers and crew on board discharges the following into the ocean every day: 11.5 tons of garbage, including plastic and Styrofoam; 23 gallons of hazardous waste, such as cleaning solvents and chemicals from on-board photo labs; 270,000 gallons of "grey water" (water from bathing, laundry, cooking, and swimming pools); 7,000 gallons of bilge water (containing oil); and 30,000 gallons of "black water" (human sewage waste).

    *b. "Walking along the beach of Normandy for the first time in 60 years, Second World War veteran Henry Geunter of Abbotsford broke his gait, removed his shoe, and dipped his foot into the Pacific ocean, submerging himself in the memories of his fallen comrades. . . . He returned to Normandy the chosen delegate of the Royal Canadian Army Medical Core. . . . Geunter was a member of the fourth armored division and arrived as the second wave of invading troops. His primary duties made him responsible for ensuring safe drinking water from the Orne River for some 18,000 troops. The waters were checked daily for enemy poisons." (Spalding 17)

3. Canada has had a significant problem with counterfeit money and has recently been replacing the older bills with new bills that are harder to fake.

     a. Do you know how to spot a fake $5, $10, or $20 bill? If so, what are the key features to look for? If you don't know, how could you find out?

     b. Can you find information on how big a problem counterfeit bills were before the new bills were introduced?

Information from a Credible Authority

If we have conflicting information, this is a clear indicator of a credibility problem. However, even when we have consistent information, we are still not guaranteed it is accurate. This is why we also need to know which sources carry more weight than others—where are we most likely to find correct information?

So far, we have been talking about weighing the credibility of information directly: can we tell whether the information is accurate? However, we often cannot weigh the credibility directly. We don't have enough knowledge or enough time to test everything. Instead, we rely on a **credible authority**—such as people or books that are reliable sources of information. We may have no independent way to be confident that what this person says is true, but we do know this person well enough to believe that he or she is as honest and well informed as we could hope. We trust this person's information because we trust the source as a "credible person."

One credible authority is you—for information you have directly experienced. If you have direct knowledge, you may be able to establish the truth or falsity of a claim. For example, if you have travelled to Vancouver, you will know that you can't see the Rocky Mountains and the Pacific Ocean from there. (The Rockies are on the B.C.-Alberta border, and the Pacific Ocean is on the western side of Vancouver Island.) If you've travelled in that area, you may also have heard that Halkomelem, the language of the Sto-Lo people, is pronounced Hal-co-MAY-lem. If you are a student who has repeated a course with a different instructor, you may know that not all professors teaching the same course use the same criteria when marking papers. If you've lived in Saskatchewan or taken a course in recent Canadian history, you may know that Ray Hnatyshyn was Canada's governor general from 1990 to 1995, and his name is pronounced Na-tish-in.

Testimonial Evidence

A second credible authority is testimonial evidence. Most of the time, we do not have direct personal experience and we must rely on the testimony of an expert or a source. **Testimony** is information presented to confirm information or to support a conclusion, provided by a person or written source that can reasonably be assumed to have direct knowledge or to have appropriate expertise.

For example, we might ask for the testimony of a witness to confirm that this really is Uncle Joe's signature on the will. We might ask for the testimony of a qualified engineer to tell us if this dam is safe enough to withstand the levels of water it may have to contain when the river's in flood.

Whenever we accept that a claim is true simply because someone tells us it is true, we are relying on the testimony of the speaker or writer. Once you start thinking about how many claims we accept on testimony, the importance of the role of testimony in argument becomes startlingly clear. We rely on the newspapers to report studies and quote accurately; we rely on the TV guide to give us truthful information about what's on TV; we rely on labels on cans, instruction manuals and maps, teachers and doctors all to provide us with information that it is reasonable.

Of course, we don't accept these various sources of testimony as equally reliable. Sometimes we have our doubts about the expertise and truthfulness of the sources. Sometimes sources conflict and we cannot decide right away.

It may be reasonable to accept an expert's words—*if* we can be sure that she is an expert in the right area. It may be reasonable to accept the results of a study—*if* we can be sure that the study was unbiased and correctly carried out. But it may be hard for us to check the expert's credentials or the accuracy of the study. So, for example, we can ask which studies are more recent, which have more data, which were done by the most reliable researchers, which researchers have the most experience, which publisher is the most reputable, and so on—all the checks of credibility that we can manage.

The adequacy of these checks themselves is based on probabilities—the person with the most experience usually has the best chance of being right; the most up-to-date information is usually the most accurate, so the information from the most experienced person with the most up-to-date information is most likely to be correct. Of course, the experienced person might not have kept up with the research, and the up-to-date information might not have been checked carefully enough, so our assessment of credibility can be in error.

Anecdotal Evidence

One type of personal evidence must be weighed with care. Any person speaking only from personal experience is limited by that experience. What happened to me is one thing; I cannot assume that my experience is shared by others. Perhaps I had a bad experience trying to sort out a problem with a credit card. I can't assume the credit card company always deals badly with its customers. Perhaps I had a long wait in the emergency room and the staff seemed rushed and impatient with me. I can't assume that the standard of patient care at this hospital is always poor. I must be even more careful about assuming that something is wrong if the story about the bad credit card experience or the emergency room wait happened to someone else and was just told to me.

"Anecdotal evidence" is called that because it comes in the form of anecdotes, the little stories we tell to package our experiences for others. It tends to be vivid and memorable—the listener can practically see me groaning and bleeding in the emergency room as I bring the experience to life in my telling. Anecdotes have the power of narrative: a story told with sufficient drama and cohesiveness to make it memorable. And since narratives often are used to make a point or offer a lesson, we are predisposed to give them weight as evidence.

The problem with anecdotal evidence is that one case is almost never enough to establish the facts of the situation—not even the facts in your particular case. Was the wait as long as you felt it to be, or was it under an hour by the clock? Was the credit card company representative as rude as you thought, or did you take offence at what was said because you were upset to begin with? As we will see in Chapter 8, even when we can confirm the facts in one specific case or a few cases, that is only enough to support the conclusion of an argument to possibility. It is seldom enough to support any conclusion to probability.

Anecdotal evidence can work well to challenge a generalization. As noted earlier, if you know personally of some accidents on farms, you are in a position to challenge whether farms are safer workplaces than they used to be. Your anecdotal evidence doesn't show the claim is wrong, but it does help you see there may be other possibilities.

Information from Internet Sources

One major problem is the credibility of Internet sources. Information available on the Internet ranges from the best possible to the worst possible, and the sources themselves don't always give you an indication of where they found their information or who they really are. Are you getting a reviewed scholarly article or a student paper? Are you getting up-to-date information on grant applications or information that was posted months ago and is no longer accurate? Are you chatting online with a cute kid or an undercover cop? Our suspicions extend not just to the source itself but to the uses made of it. There have always been ways to buy essays, but the Internet made it far easier and quicker to get a paper customized for your course. And the Internet has also made it easier for instructors who are suspicious about the originality of student papers to check, through services such as turnitin.com. Consequently, because we cannot easily take the information at face value, we tend to want more checking of sites, dates, and sources before we decide that something that may be from an Internet source is credible.

EXERCISE **Credibility of Internet Sources**

Find three Internet sites on one of the following topics:

*Life span of moose

Canadian policy on international affairs

Hotel accommodations in St. Boniface, Manitoba

Which of the sites is the most credible, and which is the least credible? Explain your judgment.

Checklist for Credibility

To estimate credibility in general, you can consider the following criteria:

Information:

✔ Is the information supported by knowledgeable people or other credible sources?

✔ Are facts or studies included to help back up claims?

✔ Does your own personal experience or knowledge agree or disagree with the arguer?

Sources:

✔ Who is the speaker or author? Does he or she have the right credentials to talk about this issue?

✔ Does he or she have experience in the right area? Does he or she sound knowledgeable and objective?

✔ Who is the reporter (if different from the speaker)? What are the reporter's credentials? Do you know if this reporter generally does careful reporting?

✔ Where did this information appear? Is it in a current source? Is it in a source that usually checks facts and presents issues responsibly? Is it peer reviewed?

If information is not credible, we stop. If it is credible, we ask if it confirms or conflicts with other information available to us. Exercise 1.5 (page 41) asked you to prepare a checklist of your own to assess credibility. You may find it interesting to compare your checklist with this one. How much do the checklists overlap?

EXERCISE **7.3**   ## Credibility Check

*For the sources you used in Exercise 4.3 (rates of violence compared to percentages of left-handers in a society), list the consistencies and conflicts: which sources did you compare, and what discrepancies, if any, did you find? Evaluate the credibility of the information you found. Which sources did you check, and did you find them credible? Explain your answer. On the basis of your answer, which information do you think is most likely correct?

Acceptability of Information

Acceptability is a stronger condition than credibility: it requires not just that we can take the information seriously but that the information is most likely accurate. Accurate information is correct information: the facts must be as stated, the words quoted must be what the person really said, the opinions must be those the person does hold, the photograph must show what was really there, and so on. We want our reasoning not just to seem good but to be good: to rely on good information. We don't want to rely on or accept misinformation.

However, as soon as we want to move beyond credibility and provisional acceptability to the higher standard of accuracy, we face a problem. Information may be accurate, but we may not be able to prove it given the time and resources we have available to us. For example, perhaps a new drug tested in the laboratory is able to halt the progress of Alzheimer's disease. Before we can confirm that this drug does halt Alzheimer's disease, there will need to be extensive testing on people. Even though it is already true that this drug works, we can't prove it until after the testing.

Given this problem, we acknowledge that there may be a difference between what *is* accurate information and what we can *prove* to be accurate information. When we ask, "Is that accurate?" we often mean only "What reason do you have to believe that it is accurate?" What we really want to know is whether you have done some reasonable checking to find out if the information is likely to be accurate. We are concerned to find out whether your belief is reasonable, and whether the evidence for your belief can help us decide what is reasonable. In other words, we want to know if we can reasonably *accept* your information even when your evidence is not conclusive—when it does not establish the accuracy beyond doubt.

Consequently, the standard we use for evaluating information within practical time limits is more than credibility but less than accuracy: acceptability. Information is **acceptable** if there is good evidence to support its accuracy. For example, information is acceptable if it is found in reliable sources or confirmed by any reasonable checking that can be done in the time available. What we are looking for is some assurance that it makes good sense to rely on the information even when we cannot guarantee its accuracy. Acceptability is this assurance that the information is well supported.

When we judge acceptability, we are looking for assurance that more than the minimum checks for credibility have been done: we have gone on to find enough evidence to make the information highly probable. We can produce an argument to probability showing that the information is probably accurate, using premises about what checks we did and what results we found.

Since our principal interest is in the support for the accuracy of information, our checks for acceptability often ask not about the information itself, but about how good the evidence that supports it is. Suppose, for example, Sam quits work on Friday, saying, "I don't need the job. I'm going to win the lottery on Saturday," and Sam does indeed win the lottery on Saturday. Sam's statement "I'm going to win the lottery on Saturday" is accurate. If accuracy is all that concerns us, we should be happy to accept Sam's statement on Friday even if we don't know until Saturday that it is accurate. However, we'll find it hard to believe, and Sam will find it hard to prove, that it is acceptable to say on Friday, "I'm going to win the lottery on Saturday." By comparison, if Sam quits work on Monday and says, "I don't need the job. I won the lottery on Saturday," the statement "I won the lottery on Saturday" is accurate and is much more clearly acceptable. On Monday, Sam can produce the ticket and the published winning numbers that match. Sam may already have the cheque and a newspaper photo of the smiling merchant who sold the winning ticket. On Friday, Sam has no such evidence. Unless Sam has rigged the lottery draw and is willing to admit it and explain how it was done, there is no supporting evidence that makes it reasonable on Friday for Sam or anyone else to rely on the information that Sam will win the lottery.

Acceptability is the standard we apply to judging any information that is not already considered too obvious to question. To determine how this standard works in practice means that we must determine which checks a responsible person should make and which sources will be considered sufficiently reliable. The amount and type of evidence we require for acceptability may reasonably vary from context to context. We have a commonsense notion of what's acceptable and what's not. This was illustrated in the example of the difference between Sam's claim on Monday to have accurate information about winning the lottery on Saturday, compared to the same claim made on Friday. We can expand and vary our notion of acceptability to meet different concerns or different levels of risk in accepting information.

The standards used to judge acceptability may be a matter of personal choice. If you're deciding on a used car, you may decide that you're going to accept the word of friends who've driven various makes and models, or you may decide that you want to check a source such as *Consumer Reports* or *Car & Driver* for details on which makes and models have the best repair records. Where it is your decision to make, you can also decide the standards of proof you will rely on. You can use whatever standard of proof makes you confident you can reasonably compare the cars you are considering.

The standards for evidence of acceptability may also be decided by discussion. For example, organizations often have to discuss how they will do their hiring. They need to decide what will be acceptable information for making hiring decisions in different contexts. Will they go by résumé alone, or will they check references as well? Will they go by the results of an interview, or will they also want the candidates to take a typing test or a physical fitness test?

Issues of acceptability may not be ours to decide: for example, different disciplines may have guidelines that we must follow in preparing work in that discipline. Which sources? How recent? How much supporting documentation? Of what type? What each discipline insists on is a measure of what it takes to indicate acceptable information. History may prefer primary sources. Mathematics may want to see a proof worked out with all the steps in complete equations and with complete sentences explaining key steps. Correct citation format is often stressed because it is an indicator of the acceptability of the information taken from the sources. Different professions will also have different standards. Law will refuse to accept hearsay evidence except in certain specified situations. Medicine wants exact quantitative measurements, not subjective impressions.

Given this variation, we need to understand and agree on the standards of acceptability that are right for the context before we can check information to see if it is acceptable.

EXERCISE ## Recognizing Different Standards for Acceptability

Use your knowledge of assignments in different courses to compare the standards of acceptability in two or three different subject areas, such as English, computer science, geography, human kinetics, criminal justice, or biology. (You may want to check with professors to confirm your impressions.) Check the following:

- What sources do they require you to use? What citation format do they require?
- How recent must information be?
- Are there authorities in the field you must be able to quote?
- What kind of investigation or research are you required to do to complete an assignment?
- Do you have to be an expert in the field before your opinions are welcomed in an argument?
- What evidence does this field not accept that other fields do (for example, personal opinion)?

EXERCISE ## Checking Acceptability of Information

Follow up on the scenario presented at the beginning of the chapter. Choose whichever is more helpful for you to check out: *either* imagine you are applying for financial aid (scholarships, grants, or bursaries) *or* imagine you are applying for a bank loan.

1. Prepare a draft budget for yourself for twelve months—give monthly totals and an annual total in all the following categories:

    Housing (including utilities)
    Transportation
    Food
    Clothing
    Entertainment

*2. Check with your institution's financial aid office or a local bank (depending on which type of application you have chosen). What are their standards for credible expenses in three of the categories you have estimated (e.g., housing, transportation, and clothing)? Do they calculate the categories the same way you did? Explain any differences you have found. For example, do they include utilities in housing? Do they lump entertainment into some more general category? When you calculate your expenses using their categories and methods, would you qualify for financial aid or for a loan?

Written Assignment: Hand in a written answer to question 2 only. The personal financial information you used in question 1 is confidential and should not be mentioned in your written answer.

Relevance of Information

It is not enough to check just the accuracy of information you already have. As you weigh possibilities against one another, you need to be sure you are including all **relevant evidence**—information connected in a causal or explanatory way to the topic under investigation. You might find you have overlooked information that would be relevant to your needs and would make a difference to how you judge the information you already have. It's also possible that you have more information than you need, and it would not be a good use of your time to check everything. Some of the information you collected while investigating an issue may be exactly what you need, and some may be unnecessary. How do you decide what information must be included and what can be ignored?

For example, suppose Sam is going to spend those lottery winnings on a wonderful house, car, and vacation. Accurate information on the costs of the car, house, and vacation aren't enough to ensure Sam can go ahead with the purchases. Sam quit work after winning the lottery, so Sam also needs accurate information on how much money to set aside to cover living expenses without a job. If Sam doesn't want to have to go back to work the minute the lottery winnings are spent, Sam needs to weigh the costs of the car, house, and vacation against the costs of living without a job.

At the opposite extreme, suppose you have decided it would be a good idea to take a first-aid course. You have found one course close to home that you can afford. You've checked that the course will be run, and that the days and times will fit your schedule. Someone happens to mention another course, farther away, that might be even better for your schedule. You begin to look into that option, and you discover many courses are available. Should you start checking all the courses in your area to find out which is best? On the surface, this seems like relevant information to weigh when making your decision. Yet you already had a reasonable decision before you had this extra information: you had found a course that would meet your needs. The extra time it would take to find a better option is not likely to produce an option that is so much better it would be well worth the time to look for it.

Relevance can be a very difficult judgment to make, especially with regard to principles, feelings, and opinions. Until recently, for example, the medical profession seemed reluctant to consider women's emotional reactions to breast removal relevant when deciding whether to do mastectomies to remove breast cancer. If a doctor acknowledged a woman's horror at the prospect of losing a breast, but explained that there was really no lesser operation that would work, the doctor would be treating the woman's distress as relevant but as a non-supporting premise. Saving her life outweighs her distress. But if the doctor ignored her concern, saying that emotions are a matter for psychologists to deal with through counselling, not for oncologists to deal with through selecting different medical procedures, the doctor would be treating her concern as effectively irrelevant to the medical decision. Similar conflicts about relevance occur with treatment for prostate cancer.

Doctor and patient may disagree on what is relevant to the selection of a medical procedure. At this level of disagreement, we often want to stop the discussion to ask whether the other people have really heard and understood our concern and to point out why we consider it relevant. The discussion may shift to considerations about what will be accepted as relevant and why.

In other contexts, what is relevant is open to discussion at some stages, but once a decision is made, it is strictly applied. For example, law devotes considerable argument to what will count as relevant in court cases. Evidence obtained by illegal wiretaps is inadmissible—officially irrelevant—even though it provides accurate information and is certainly relevant to the case. Evidence of a victim's previous sexual conduct was at first admissible in rape trials, then completely inadmissible, and is now inadmissible except in special circumstances. What will count as relevant information to determining the accused's guilt or innocence is sharply constrained by what information is currently considered legally fair to rely on.

Sufficient Information

As you can see from the discussion of acceptability and relevance, it can be challenging to tell when you have sufficient information. As noted in Chapter 4, your investigation may turn up less information than you hoped for, exactly what you hoped for, or more than you could easily deal with. One factor we considered was the point at which you can reasonably stop your search because you believe you have enough information to meet your goals. That is a matter of evaluation, and we will consider it here.

In Chapter 6, you saw that assumptions may have plausible alternatives. One requirement of sufficient information is that it should ensure you can do at least a minimum check on whether the assumption is plausible. Consider, for example, the scenario from Chapter 4 of searching for a guinea pig to photograph for a magazine cover. Suppose you have investigated, and your friend Kari has a guinea pig she's willing to let you borrow. You've asked, and this guinea pig is lively and friendly and should perform well for the camera. Happy that your search is over, you can already picture its bright little black eyes on your magazine cover next month. You go to pick up the guinea pig—and find that you can't even see any bright eyes on this guinea pig at all. This particular guinea pig may indeed be lively and friendly, but it happens to be a Peruvian guinea pig with long silky hair that covers its whole body including its face. Only when it moves can you figure out which way it's facing. Frustrated, you exclaim, "Kari, why didn't you tell me this guinea pig doesn't have a face?" Kari, quite reasonably, can say, "You didn't ask!" You had assumed that all guinea pigs look alike. One basic check would have been to realize that this was an assumption, and that guinea pigs might not all look alike. You could have asked what this particular pet looked like before you made the wasted trip. You were overlooking some relevant information, and as a result the information you did have was insufficient for your needs.

It's very risky to assume you'll be told all the relevant information—that is, **sufficient information** to ensure you can complete your task to a satisfactory standard. Checking for sufficiency can help you make sure you have answers to all the questions that could affect your decision. Does the hardware store stock light bulbs for recessed spotlights? Yes. Do they stock the bulbs with the large bases that you need, or just the ones with the small bases that won't do the job?

This is one reason investigation and evaluation are intertwined—often, it is only experience that leads you to realize the questions you should ask next time that you forgot to ask this time.

As with relevance, sufficiency may be a matter of discussion or there may be explicit rules as to what will be sufficient. When you have gathered enough information about a movie, you can decide for yourself whether to pay to see it. An organization may change its hiring practices and decide that from now on it will require more information—it will ask every applicant to take a test related to the type of job applied for. A profession may have standards for "due diligence"—what counts as enough effort by the professional to gather required information before taking action. For example, a lawyer must check that the seller of a house does own the house and is entitled to sell it before drawing up a contract for sale.

When we need to confirm that we have seen sufficient information, we can appeal directly to the standards for that context. For instance, when scholarship and award applications are reviewed to determine a winner, there are usually a set of specific requirements, such as two letters of reference, a statement of goals, a transcript indicating credits completed and grade point average (GPA), and an application on the correct form. If any of that information is missing, such as one letter of reference or the transcript, the application is simply rejected. Similarly, if the information is not provided on the correct form, the application is typically rejected—the information might be there, but it is not in recognizable form. If all the information is there, and the award must go to the person with the highest GPA, then the selectors search the pile of accepted applications for the highest GPA—no matter what other information might be there, the GPA is sufficient to determine the award.

Another problem with sufficiency comes from people wanting more than is reasonable—for instance, when endless studies and reports are commissioned because the decision-makers are reluctant to act. (Think, for example, of the many studies on the risks of secondhand smoke before there were any moves to ban smoking in public places.) Or the problem may occur when the issue raises difficult moral questions—for example, what is sufficient evidence to report suspected child abuse? Knowing the harm that will continue to be done to the victim if the abuse goes unreported, and the harm that can be done to a person falsely accused, we may deliberate indefinitely—to our later sorrow—about what is enough evidence to be sure that we should report the abuse.

EXERCISE 7.6

Considering Relevance and Sufficiency

*1. What would be enough information to show you what counts as a good health practice (such as eating more protein or less protein, eliminating caffeine or sugar, or not smoking)?

*2. What information do you think ought to convince a friend to make a change in his or her health practices?

3. What information would be enough to persuade you to change your spending practices, to spend more freely or to be more frugal?

4. What information do you think ought to convince your partner, or your parent, to change his or her spending patterns?

What Happens When You Find No Information?

So far, we have spoken as if you will always find at least some helpful sources when you are investigating. However, as noted in Chapter 4, it is always possible that your investigation may not turn up any useful information, even after you reconsider your search strategy or try new sources. Each time you learn a new search tactic, you decrease the chances that you'll get stuck without information. But sometimes even the best of searches doesn't turn up the kind of information you are looking for. What do you do when you have found nothing useful?

Depending on what's at stake, you will have several ways to proceed. If an informed guess will do, you can extrapolate from the information you did find. For example, if all you could find about left-handers was that they typically make up 10 to 15 percent of the population, you can at least say you have sufficient information to confirm that a rate of 3.4 percent among the Dioula people is unusually low, and a rate of 20 percent among the Eipo is unusually high. In turn, this is sufficient to suggest that a difference in homicide rates between the two groups is at least a possible indicator of a connection between handedness and homicide rates. If an informed guess is not enough—and it would not be if you were yourself a researcher—you may find that you have opened up questions that need research. More information must be collected in the field or by experiment, not just by uncovering it in existing sources.

New research, in turn, leads us back into the realm of argument, since it would take argument to show why a particular hypothesis was worth testing, and what information would be relevant and sufficient. As you will see in Chapter 8, when we evaluate arguments we do move back and forth between evaluating their reasoning and investigating further in case there is any additional information we may need to reach a conclusion.

Completing Your Assessment of Information

Based on your assessment of credibility, relevance, and sufficiency, you are now in a position to evaluate the information, either piece by piece or as a whole. There are three possible verdicts you can reach:

- *Reliable* information: acceptable, or at least credible
- *Uncertain* information: too little supporting evidence to determine acceptability or even credibility
- *Incorrect* information: credible sources contradict or conflict with the original information

If the information is reliable, you use it as needed. If the information is incorrect, you replace it with the correct information. If the information is uncertain, you proceed with caution, making sure you keep alternatives in mind. However, as you will see in Chapter 8, you will be able to proceed usefully by checking the accuracy of any reasoning that has been used.

Key Points in Review

- Credibility is a measure of how reasonable it is to believe the information. It is an estimate of probable truth.
- Acceptability is a stronger condition than credibility: it requires not just that we can take the information seriously but that we have some reasonable assurance that the information is accurate. We must understand and agree to the standards of acceptability before we can check information to see if it is acceptable.
- Information must also be relevant—related in some useful way to the topic we are investigating. Like acceptability, relevance may be a matter for discussion.
- Before we stop investigating, we must have sufficient information to meet our needs. The information must be enough to satisfy expectations for reliability and safety. Sufficiency also may be a matter for discussion.
- If no information is available, then depending on what's at stake, you will have several ways to proceed. If an informed guess will do, you can extrapolate from the information you did find. If an informed guess is not enough, you may be committed to carrying out research to collect information.

Chapter 8

Quality Control for Reasoning: Evaluating Arguments

■ Perspective

In this chapter, we evaluate arguments: that is, we explain whether an argument has provided adequate support for its conclusion. First, does it rely on accurate information? Second, does it connect its information using good reasoning? We can do these evaluations as separate steps, but whichever order we do them in, an argument must pass both tests before it can be considered good. To evaluate the accuracy of the information presented in the premises we can use the same techniques we used in Chapter 7. In this chapter, we check the accuracy of the reasoning as a whole. You'll see how to evaluate arguments by applying what you have learned about types of reasoning and accuracy of premises. You'll review the reasoning for its strengths and weaknesses—the connections that hold and the connections that fail. You'll also see how to report your findings by preparing a short written evaluation of an argument.

■ Scenario

Consider again the scenario from Chapter 5. You have just picked up your glass from where you left it in the kitchen at a party. As you are about to drink from it, another guest grabs your arm. "You shouldn't drink from a glass you've left unattended!" the guest exclaims. The guest goes on to tell you about a number of recent incidents where Rohypnol, the "date rape" drug, was dropped into drinks at parties or bars. Not only that, the guest says, there was also a case where someone took a drink from an open soft-drink can in the garage, and the can contained antifreeze, not pop.

Now take the scenario a step further. Have you been given sufficient reason to believe you shouldn't drink from this glass?

■ Key Question

Do we have enough good evidence to confirm that this belief or claim is reasonable?

Evaluating Arguments: Assessing Accuracy of Reasoning

Once we have understood an argument, we want to know if it works: should we accept it? Does the argument make it reasonable for us to believe the conclusion? What is at stake here is our response to the argument. If it works, we can go on to act in accordance with it. We can believe its conclusion; we can take actions based on that conclusion. If the argument does not work, we cannot justify using that conclusion. Either the conclusion is wrong, so we must reject it, or we don't yet know whether the conclusion is true. In both cases, we need to be able to show where and how the argument has fallen short of confirming its conclusion. This usually puts us in a position to recognize what else we need to know and how to find it.

We have to evaluate the argument as a whole, not simply judge its conclusion. We need to confirm that the premises really do provide enough of the right kind of support to make the conclusion as possible, probable, or certain as it is claimed to be. When we come to evaluate an argument, we draw together everything we have investigated and checked so far. We confirm that each premise really is acceptable, using the investigation methods described in Chapter 4 and the measures of acceptability described in Chapter 7. We identify how certain the conclusion is intended to be, what level of support is needed, and the type of reasoning used, as outlined in Chapter 5. We identify assumptions and options as outlined in Chapter 6 to recognize what other conclusions might need to be ruled out before this one can be accepted.

Argument evaluation is an objective process. It is essential to distinguish evaluation from reaction. When we evaluate something, we are not judging simply whether we like or dislike it, or whether we can use it ourselves. We are judging whether the argument has done what it set out to do: has it made its case? What are its strengths, and where are its weaknesses? When you evaluate, you are standing outside an argument, looking on, not caught inside it wrestling for a definite outcome. You are *judging the support already provided*—the premises already put forward by the arguer and those premises that you can reasonably assume given the logic of the argument. Do the premises of the argument provide the right level of support for the conclusion?

This method of evaluating an argument shows whether its reasoning is objectively acceptable. If it is objectively acceptable, we can be confident the conclusion is a rational belief. Should you take that job? Should we take action about pollution in the Arctic? Should Canada support legislation to permit euthanasia? On any of these issues, we should look for good arguments to persuade us. When an argument has given us reasons that really are acceptable, relevant, and sufficient for the standards it must meet, then it is reasonable for us to accept its conclusion.

Dealing with Obstacles to Evaluation

To do a good job of evaluation, we need to work past some of our own tendencies to make mistakes in reasoning. Arguments often seem better than they really are because the very act of understanding tends to make us see only how the arguments might succeed. For example, consider the scenario at the beginning of the chapter. As we listen to the anxious guest, we begin to picture something being dropped into a drink. We are reminded of cases where people have been harmed by food or drink. Even if we don't feel that it's likely we'd be the target for someone putting drugs into drinks, we do understand why the guest would be concerned. We tend to weigh the conclusion just by our own standards—a cautious person might decide it's safer to throw out the drink, while a bolder person might go ahead and drink anyway, willing to take the chance. We use the guest's argument as a springboard for our own adventures in thinking, and we don't check carefully enough whether we are being reasonable. It's just as foolish to be swayed into unreasonable apprehension as it is to jump into unreasonable risks. We are often much less accurate in judging reasoning than we would like to be. Skills that help us in other areas, such as good reading skills and an appreciation for the beauty of a well-turned phrase, can prevent us noticing an inaccurate connection in the reasoning. If you have good reading skills, you are surprisingly likely to judge an argument as better than it really is. It might seem strange that good reading skills could be a disadvantage in reasoning. However, some of the skills of good reading do pull us away from critical thinking. Good readers are good because they can make sense out of the prose they read. They pull it together in ways that make sense because they assume that the author intended to make sense. This is why we emphasized in Chapter 1 the importance of reading carefully, using a technique that reminds you to check what problems might occur as a result of what has been said.

For example, one very common mistake is to think that an argument is good because it is well written and unbiased—it presents both sides of an issue clearly. We can follow it easily, and we find it persuasive in its presentation. We couldn't have said it better. Unfortunately, good writing by itself is no guarantee of good content. Part of the reason we have stressed the importance of putting arguments into standard form, checking the acceptability of premises, and examining the types of reasoning used is to make sure that we are seeing beyond the surface of the writing and into the substance of the reasoning.

An equally common mistake is to think an argument must work because we personally like its conclusion. Thinking, perhaps, of the good support that we would provide, we scan the reasoning and presume that it must be good. After all, if the point of judging an argument is to see if we would be justified in accepting its conclusion—and we know the conclusion is acceptable—then haven't we done what we set out to do? But don't jump too quickly to acceptance: it is both unreasonable and unsafe to agree with a good conclusion for bad reasons. For example, suppose that you are a committed environmentalist, dedicated to protecting species and habitats. When someone concludes that we must restore all natural habitats, this conclusion may sound good to you. But suppose that the arguer's premises are that we humans are the sole cause of the damage and that we have no right whatsoever to use the earth's resources for our own ends. If you accept the conclusion that we must restore natural habitats on the basis of this person's argument, you may be seen as accepting those premises—and committing yourself to denying humans any use of the planet's resources. Unless you accept those premises, you ought not to accept the argument. Its premise that humans are the sole cause of the problem is an assumption. If you can provide good support for the conclusion yourself, or have heard other good arguments for the same conclusion, that support and those arguments are good—but not the argument that tempted you. You can go on to replace the bad reasoning with good support, but that is a second step and does not redeem the bad argument.

A further obstacle is presented by general patterns of error in human thinking, common errors that people seem to make regardless of intelligence or training. None of us is as rational as we might like to think. Any number of everyday situations make it hard for us to think clearly—if we're tired, hungry, stressed, or excited, we'll find it extremely hard to concentrate. We'll lose track of details and misunderstand information. What's worse is that even when we are at our very best, our most clear-headed and wide awake, we are prone to make mistakes in inductive and deductive reasoning. Study after study in the field of cognitive psychology has shown that some types of reasoning mistakes are very common, even among well-educated people and even among people educated in reasoning. (See the supplementary reading list in Appendix B.) This is why we emphasized in Chapter 5 and Chapter 6 the importance of being able to identify assumptions in arguments—they represent hidden possibilities that we might otherwise overlook.

Knowing that there are common difficulties in reasoning, we have to be particularly careful in evaluation: we have to be systematic, because we cannot rely on our habitual reasoning by itself to do the whole job every time. In this chapter, you'll see how to check reasoning more systematically and reliably.

To reason well, we need a clear idea of what we are to look for and a way to shift our perspective from understanding to judging. Here's where the observation and investigation stages prove their value. If you have read carefully, as described in Chapter 1, you have already reviewed what you read with an eye to potential problems. If you have done some independent checking and research, as described in Chapter 4, you have at least some additional information, so you are in a much better position to see if the original material is confirmed by or conflicts with the independent information.

In the evaluation stage, you may need to use some additional strategies to give yourself the best possible chance to judge more accurately. One helpful strategy is to take time between reading and responding. If you can wait at least overnight before responding to what you've read, you have a better chance of thinking, "Wait a minute . . ." or "But what about . . . ?"

If you have to respond even before you have a chance to investigate, another useful strategy is to imagine a person who completely disagrees with what you've just read. What might such a person say? We are quite good at imaginatively putting ourselves into other people's shoes. This conscious step into a different viewpoint can raise points you would not otherwise have noticed.

To evaluate arguments, then, we typically cannot rely on our initial judgment of whether it made sense. Instead, we rely on taking the time for a systematic examination of the premises of each argument. We remind ourselves to judge by all the standards that arguments are supposed to meet.

You can begin evaluating an argument by asking the following questions:

- Is any key premise irrelevant or unacceptable in this context?
- Can I think of any situation in which the premises would all be acceptable but in which some other conclusion would be better supported than the intended conclusion?
- Are there situations in which the conclusion simply doesn't fit or apply, even though it is supposed to?

To answer these questions, we need to review what is needed to make premises acceptable, relevant, and sufficient: the standards for good reasoning.

Applying Standards for Good Reasoning

For all types of argument, we have the same expectations for the quality of the reasoning. The premises must support the conclusion to the extent required. We want to be sure not only that it makes sense to accept the premises but also that they give the right kind of information, and enough of it. Arguments to probability have to pass an extra test. Not only must premises be acceptable, relevant, and sufficient, there must be no way to defeat the argument through background information that is more convincing than the argument under consideration.

These general expectations lead to the following three conditions for a good argument using any type of reasoning. The premises, taken together, must be

1. acceptable (must be established well enough to be reliable given the context in which they are being used),
2. relevant (must have the right type of connection to the conclusion), and
3. sufficient (must present enough reasons to make it rational to accept the conclusion).

Good arguments to probability must also be

4. indefeasible (there must be no disconfirming evidence).

If an argument fails on any of these conditions, it cannot be counted as good. However, it is important for you to remember that if an argument fails, that doesn't automatically make its conclusion wrong. All it means is that we haven't yet been given any reason to believe the conclusion. It might be true; it might be false. We know this argument can't prove it. We have already introduced acceptability, relevance, and sufficiency. The fourth condition, indefeasibility, simply brings in explicitly what we have been considering in the investigation stage—is there any information that would cause us to doubt or disbelieve the conclusion even if the premises do support the conclusion? The word "indefeasible" simply means "cannot be defeated," and that is exactly what we want from a good argument. It must not merely look good, it must *be* good. It must not merely pass one inspection, it must pass repeated inspection. If that contract to buy a used car is safe to sign, it must be safe not just when you read the fine print, excited at the prospect of owning the car, but when your mother, a lawyer, reads it through later before she offers you the money to cover the car insurance. We can evaluate how an argument works by looking just at what is placed in front of us—the kind of examination of argument structure we did in Chapter 5. The added condition, indefeasibility, reminds us of the need to look not just at the argument itself, but outside it as well, to check how well it holds up in the real world.

Acceptability of Premises

Acceptable premises are premises that it is reasonable to believe because they are supported by the available evidence. When we look specifically at the acceptability of statements as premises in an argument, we also need to determine whether they can be relied on as part of the reasoning. If you have already had a chance to do some investigation to judge the credibility and acceptability of the information, then you have three preliminary choices for each premise in the argument:

1. You can decide that the premise is reasonable to believe, and accept it.
2. You can decide that you truly don't know whether the premise is reasonable, and therefore you suspend judgment.
3. You can decide the premise is not reasonable to believe, and reject it.

If you must evaluate an argument before you have a chance to investigate its premises independently, you can still do a preliminary check that will at least rule out some obvious mistakes.

Mistakes of Acceptability

Mistakes of acceptability occur when an argument uses premises that we have no good reason to believe. For example:

> Full-time workers work harder than part-timers, and they are more dedicated to their jobs. If more work is available, we should give full-timers overtime before we hire more part-timers.

These premises are unacceptable. The conclusion might still be justified—it might make sense to offer overtime to the full-time employees before hiring more part-timers—but dedication to the job is unlikely to be the reason. Background knowledge will probably be enough to remind you of full-time employees who were bored with their jobs and not at all loyal to the company; you can also recall some part-time employees who cared a great deal about their jobs and would gladly have worked more if more hours were available. This background knowledge isn't enough by itself to show the premises are not acceptable—further investigation would be needed. But it is certainly enough to show why we have reason to doubt the premises.

For the most part, errors of acceptability turn up when we investigate, as we discover confirming or conflicting evidence. Sometimes, as in the example above, we can recognize a potential error just on the basis of our existing knowledge. There are also errors that are made often enough to have been given names that describe what has gone wrong. Here are examples of specific, named mistakes of acceptability.

Improper Appeal to Authority

This is the mistake of relying on an authority without any evidence that the authority can be trusted in this particular case. Here are some samples:

> "Three out of four doctors recommend product X. It's the right choice for your family."
>
> "Joe Sports Great recommends insurance company Y. You'll appreciate its services."
>
> "Backpacks designed by women to fit women: the right backpack to wear for your next trip."

These could count as mistakes of relevance because we don't know if the "experts" have relevant experience. They might also count as mistakes of sufficiency because what is missing here is enough evidence within the premise to assure us that these recommendations are credible. The premises are believable, so they are acceptable to that limited extent. But the purpose of appealing to an advisor or an expert is to show that the premise is acceptable without further support. Credibility has not been established here. It's assumed that, just because these "experts" have credibility in some areas, they must have credibility in everything they recommend. If the alleged expert hasn't studied the product, used the insurance service and compared it to others, or had credible experience in designing backpacks, then he or she is no better able than we are to say what's a good choice. This is particularly so if the expert is not trained in the field in which his or her opinion is being sought. If we are responsible for making a decision based on what an expert says, then we can't stop our check of credibility at this point: we have to find out if what the expert says deserves to be heard.

False Dilemma

This fallacy claims that there are only two choices—and, almost invariably, one is so bad that you clearly ought to choose the other. It is an attempt to coerce you. For example,

> "Eat your vegetables, or you'll get no dessert."
>
> "Stop clearcut logging completely, or the environment will be ruined."
>
> "If we don't allow clearcut logging, our economy will be ruined."

These are mistakes because they try to narrow you to one choice when there are other reasonable choices still open. There are two ways out of this type of argument by coercion. One is that there may be a third option—for instance, partial clearcutting with proper replanting may save both the economy and the environment. The other is that the allegedly bad choice may not be as bad as it's said to be—perhaps you don't mind going without dessert. It is even possible that the allegedly good option won't help: maybe we stop logging, but the environment still gets ruined—by pollution from tourists' cars. As soon as you recognize that other options are open to you, the false dilemma loses its coercive power.

However, passing the test for acceptability is only a first step. Even if all the premises are reasonable to believe, that by itself is not enough to make the argument good. As you saw in Chapter 5, acceptable premises can be used in bad reasoning. Any given premise may be reasonable to believe in its own right—but that does not show it is doing the job it is expected to do in the context in which it is offered. When we consider whether an argument works, we are concerned not just with whether its premises are individually acceptable as statements, but with whether the premises, taken together, work as acceptable support for the types of reasoning being used. Now we are finally in a position to check whether the premises are not only acceptable, but work together to support the conclusion.

This takes us back to considering relevance and sufficiency: how do the premises work together to support the conclusion?

Relevance and Sufficiency

The concepts of relevance and sufficiency in relation to reasoning were first introduced in Chapter 5. Now we apply them to deciding whether a set of premises works to support its conclusion.

For the premises of an argument to be relevant to the conclusion there must be a clear connection between them and the conclusion to be drawn from them.

For premises to be sufficient for the conclusion, the premises *taken as a whole* must provide enough evidence to give the level of support for the conclusion required for that type of argument.

That means, as we've seen in Chapter 5, the premises must

- guarantee the truth of the conclusion or make it highly probable, for an argument to certainty;

- make the conclusion more probable than any alternative, for an argument to probability;

- make the conclusion clearly plausible and consistent with all the available information, for an argument to possibility.

These two conditions, relevance and sufficiency, guarantee that the structure of the argument is good. As we saw in Chapter 5, if an argument uses inductive or deductive reasoning, one good way to test for its ability to provide relevance and sufficiency is to see whether the argument has a deductively valid or inductively cogent pattern. If an argument has a well-structured pattern, then the premises must be relevant, and if the premises are acceptable, they will be sufficient to support the conclusion.

More generally, in a simple argument—an argument where the premises are all meant to work together to directly support the conclusion—each premise must be acceptable, each must be relevant, and the premises taken together must be sufficient for the argument to be a good one.

In a complex argument—an argument that contains sub-arguments or many different strands of argument that could each stand alone—the argument as a whole can still be good even if some of its parts are rejected as bad reasoning. There may be enough acceptable and consistent premises left to support the conclusion. For example, look again at the scenario at the beginning of this chapter. The guest argues, "You shouldn't drink from a glass you've left unattended! There were a number of recent incidents where Rohypnol, the 'date rape' drug, was dropped into drinks at parties or bars. There was also a case where someone took a drink from an open soft-drink can in the garage, and the can contained antifreeze, not pop."

As part of evaluating the argument, you might point out you are drinking from a glass, so it is not relevant what might happen to a soft-drink can. Here is the value of standard-form representation of arguments, because that premise will not be included in the standard form:

1. There have been cases where drugs have been added to unattended drinks at parties or bars.

2. If drugs have been added to unattended drinks at parties then you should not drink from a glass you left unattended. (implicit premise).

3. You should not drink from this glass that you left unattended.

In this example, the statement about pop cans being used to store poisons is not relevant to the conclusion. However, dismissing this one premise does not show that the conclusion is not properly supported. The remaining premises are relevant, and they might be enough to support the conclusion. The argument appears to be an argument to probability, so the premises must make it probable that it is unsafe to take the drink. Your own background knowledge and any checking you can do should confirm that premises 1 and 2 are acceptable. Whether the premises are sufficient is a matter of context. If you are at a large party in an urban area where you do not know all the guests, then the probability of your drink being tampered with is most likely high enough to support the conclusion. The risk is probably not worth running. If you are at a small party where you know most of the people and your drink was left unattended for a very short time, there is only a possibility that your drink could have been tampered with. The probability of tampering is too low to support the conclusion that you should not drink from this glass.

In this example, the reasoning works at least as reasoning to possibility, and perhaps as reasoning to probability, even when we can see that one premise is irrelevant.

Relevance can be challenging to establish and can drive us back to questions of interpretation, as considered in Chapter 3, and forward to questions of procedure, as considered in Chapter 12. For example, the legal system in Canada has considered whether it is relevant to discuss how much harm an offender did to a victim before sentencing an offender. To the Canadian legal system, yes: it helps to establish the truth of what actually happened and the degree of severity of the crime. To many traditional Cree, Ojibway, or Inuit, no: what's past is past, and all that is relevant is working to restore the offender and the community to health and to prevent future crime. The Canadian legal emphasis on arguing through the precise details of what happened, when, and to whom seems irrelevant and counterproductive to those traditional belief systems.

Before we agree on what is relevant in a particular argument, we may need to discuss what seems relevant. We may need to check whether something has usually been accepted as relevant, or we may have to engage in complex negotiations such as how to accommodate very different principles of justice.

Similarly, sufficiency may be a matter for discussion or negotiation. There may be accepted standards we must go by, such as what ID is sufficient to establish credit or to cross a border. There may be complex discussions about what should be sufficient evidence of the safety of prescription drugs.

EXERCISE 8.1

Evaluating Relevance and Sufficiency

There are some common situations in which we can reasonably disagree on what is relevant or sufficient. Decide on your own answer to the following situations. For question 1, compare your answer with an answer given by someone who has experience in hiring. For question 2, compare your answer to the answer of any other voter. Do you have the same standards for what is relevant? If not, how might you resolve the differences?

*1. Are your hobbies and interests relevant information for a job application? Are they different from volunteer experience? In what circumstances, if any, should you include them on your résumé as part of your evidence that you are a good candidate for the position?

2. What factors do you consider relevant when you vote for a particular candidate in a federal or provincial election? Why are these factors relevant to your decision on how to vote? Are they different from the factors you consider when you vote for a chairperson or president of an organization in which you are personally involved, such as a community group or a club?

3. You have a pet in need of a new home. You put up an advertisement that says "free to a good home." What will be sufficient evidence to convince you that your pet is going to a good home?

4. What should be sufficient evidence to question or detain a person as a suspect in a terrorist activity?

Mistakes of Relevance or Sufficiency

Many errors in reasoning related to relevance or sufficiency fall into recognizable patterns. The errors typically come from misunderstanding or misrepresenting the connections between premises. Some errors are mistakes; some are deliberate attempts to mislead. Regardless of the cause, we cannot accept even a good conclusion on the basis of bad reasoning.

You have seen some patterns of error in Chapter 5, contrasted with patterns of good deductive and inductive argument. These patterns of error have been given names under the general category of fallacies. A fallacy is a type of common mistake in reasoning. It is a piece of reasoning that fails to make a good connection between the premises and conclusion. However, people tend not to recognize the reasoning failure. As a result, fallacies are unreasonably persuasive: we accept the reasoning even though we ought not to. The study of fallacies is interesting because it has yielded many insights into how reasoning works and where we are most likely to make serious mistakes. Here are some examples of arguments that fail on relevance and sufficiency.

Mistakes of Relevance

Mistakes of relevance happen when the arguer sees a connection between the premises and the conclusion but does not show what the connection is. For example:

> We must give more money to food banks. They provide an invaluable service for people who cannot manage on present welfare rates. They offer responsible ways to use up extra produce from hotels and farms. Donating food reminds us that others are less fortunate than we are and do need our help.

The premises are irrelevant—even though they provide information on the value of food banks—because the conclusion is not that food banks are good but that we should give more money to them. We could put in an implicit premise: "We should give money to all good causes." The premises will make the argument work, but it will be a stretch even for the principle of charity to assume this is what's intended. We're missing too much on why the food banks need more money—how much money is currently being given, why it is not enough, and why we should increase financial support to food banks instead of campaigning to increase welfare rates so that more food banks are not needed. None of this information is given—so the argument gives no relevant support for its conclusion.

Here are examples of some specific, named mistakes of relevance.

Two Wrongs Don't Make a Right

This fallacy tries to excuse one bad situation by redirecting our attention to a worse one. Here are some examples:

> "It's not fair to ban marijuana for recreational use while we still allow people to smoke and drink—smoking and drinking are far more harmful to your health than marijuana!"

> "Don't complain about losing your job. At least we've got a welfare system in Canada. Think about all the people who are starving in Africa or dying in war zones—they are much worse off than you are."

No matter how hypocritical the situation may seem, if an action or policy is wrong, then it's reasonable to criticize it. It may seem absurd to ban marijuana based on alleged health risks while other known health risks are still legal. But if the arguer admits marijuana is unhealthy too, then making it legal for recreational use should stand or fall on its own health merits. No matter how much worse other problems are, if a problem deserves fixing, it should be fixed. If losing your job was unfair, or is causing you real hardship, you need help even if there are also people worse off than you. These other bad situations are not relevant to your situation. The fault in this reasoning is to assume that, unless everything bad is stopped at once, it should all be allowed to continue—or at least that problems should be fixed in order of priority, starting with the worst. This is a common and reasonable principle—"Let's get our priorities straight"—gone wrong. It has overlooked the possibility that we could and should work on several problems simultaneously.

Ad Hominem

Ad hominem means "to the man" in Latin—i.e., criticizing the person or the appearance instead of the reasoning. This fallacy points to faults in the person as reasons to doubt the person's arguments. For example,

> "We can't trust him as a cabinet minister. He's been divorced three times."

> "This report is full of spelling mistakes. We can't possibly accept its conclusion that students deserve more financial aid."

The mistake here is that divorces do not indicate anything about skills in cabinet, and spelling mistakes don't show that there is no need for money. This mistake probably has its roots in our nonverbal standards of judgment. Often enough, the warning signs that make us suspicious of a person—for example, unkempt appearance, impatience, or overeagerness—are good indications that something is wrong. But when our nonverbal standards for judgment conflict with our standards for verbal reasoning, we cannot automatically reject the verbal reasoning. We may be entitled to reserve judgment on the argument until we can find independent confirmation from sources that we trust, precisely because we do not trust the person who offered it or the presentation that we saw. Nevertheless, thinking critically means that we should not reject reasons just because they come from an unwelcome source.

Mistakes of Sufficiency

Mistakes of sufficiency occur when there is too little evidence to support a conclusion. As we saw in Chapter 5, the premises can even point away from the truth of the conclusion—they provide evidence that is inconsistent with the conclusion, makes it unlikely, or even contradicts it. For example,

> "I know the children of homosexuals don't grow up to be homosexuals, and I know homosexual parents can be loving parents, and I know that it's far better for children to grow up with their biological parents, but I still think children should not be allowed to grow up in households with same-sex parents."

The arguer acknowledges that homosexuality isn't learned and that homosexuals can love. The premises are relevant but they are all counter-premises. They make it unreasonable to accept the conclusion because they contradict it. They point toward the opposite conclusion—that homosexuals are as likely to be good parents as heterosexuals. You can see the mistake most clearly if you rewrite the argument in standard form, where counter-premises are not included: the only piece of the argument that survives is the conclusion. There are no supporting premises mentioned!

> but I still think children should not be allowed to grow up in households with same-sex parents.

Here are examples of some specific, named mistakes of sufficiency.

Affirming the Consequent

When we make an inference, we draw a connection between two things or events, saying that one leads to the other. "If it's a bear, then it's faster than I am." One particularly common mistake presumes that the connection is so strong that only these two things are connected to one another. "If it's faster than I am, it's a bear." We discussed this mistake in Chapter 5 as a problem caused by misinterpreting how "if . . . then . . ." works. We tend to assume the connection works both ways when it only works in one direction. This mistake overlooks other connections that are equally likely: the creature that is faster than I am could be a moose or a deer. Here is another example:

> "People who are discriminated against don't get the jobs they apply for. He didn't get that job he wanted, so he must have been discriminated against."

Even if the first connection is accurate, the second is not the only possible one to make. People can fail to get jobs because they are unqualified or were rude in an interview.

The fault in this reasoning is to assume that the connection holds both ways: that people who are discriminated against don't get jobs (true), and that the only reason not to get a job is discrimination (false).

Post Hoc Ergo Propter Hoc ("After this, therefore because of this")

This mistake happens when a set of premises undermines its conclusion by overlooking a possibility that is the exact opposite of the one supported.

> "I took Product A, and my headache went away. Product A sure got rid of my headache!"

Noticing a common feature or a particular sequence of events isn't nearly enough to identify a cause. The observed phenomenon could be a coincidence—perhaps that headache would have gone away just as quickly without the medication. In fact, perhaps the headache would have gone away more quickly without the medication and not returned. There is a competing possibility, based on evidence that pain relievers can trigger new headaches, creating an endless cycle of headaches alternating with temporary relief. Consequently, the evidence given in this argument—that the headache went away after taking Product A—is compatible with the opposite conclusion, that it did not "work" on the headache, just relieved it temporarily. When an argument doesn't support its conclusion any better than it supports the opposite conclusion, it effectively provides zero support—it is completely insufficient.

Slippery Slope

This fallacy sees one type of action as the start of an unstoppable descent into a very bad state of affairs. It claims that we must stop the first action in order to prevent this disastrous slide. For example,

> Concerned about a possible loss of access to health-care funded treatments for autism, lawyer Fiona Sampson, representing two women's groups, said: "For us particularly, young girls with autism will become women with a disability, and as women with a disability such as autism, their destiny is pretty much social isolation and institutionalization, and once women with disabilities are institutionalized, they're at huge risk of experiencing sexual assault and physical violence."
>
> [Maurice Bridge, "A-G's comments on autism case 'unseemly,'" *Vancouver Sun,* June 8, 2004, B7]

One cause of this mistake is failing to recognize important differences in nature, quality, or likelihood between actions at the "top" and the "bottom" of the slide. It is a mistake of sufficiency because it does not give enough support to show that the threatened result will happen. Is lack of funded access to autism treatment in childhood sufficient to ensure a significant risk of sexual assault and physical violence in adulthood? This is reasoning to probability gone wrong: the links might be there, but we are not given the level of probability of each step in the chain. Typically, the effect of increasing the number of links is to decrease the overall probability of the final result, not to increase it.

Whenever we can show that the progress from beginning to end is not inevitable, but can be halted at one (or more) of the stages, we have shown that the evidence points away from the conclusion. For instance, if we find ways for autistic men and women to be well cared for outside hospitals, then they will not be at risk of institutionalization.

EXERCISE **8.2** ## Testing Relevance and Sufficiency

*A selection of arguments is given at the end of this chapter. Choose one, and examine it for relevance and sufficiency. (You may find it helpful to set it out in standard form as described in Chapter 2.)

1. First, which level of support would be needed for that conclusion?

2. Second, is all the information provided consistent with your background knowledge?

3. Third, when you pick out the premises and consider them as a set, do they provide the required level of support? To test this, can you identify any other conclusions that could be supported by the same premises set? Can you detect any assumptions for which you can imagine plausible alternatives that would point away from this conclusion?

4. Based on your answers to all these questions, can you see whether further investigation would be needed to check the relevance or sufficiency of the premises?

Indefeasibility

Indefeasibility is the final test that an argument must pass. An argument is indefeasible when the premises of the argument have met the criteria of acceptability, relevance, and sufficiency and there is no other background information that would show the argument fails. In other words, the argument can stand up to attempts to knock it down, even when those attempts bring in information not mentioned in the argument.

Some arguments can pass this test just by their structure. If an argument to certainty uses deductively valid reasoning and premises that are relevant and sufficient, and the premises are acceptable, then there is no room for doubt about the truth of the conclusion. No check for indefeasibility is necessary because deductively valid reasoning builds that requirement into the very structure of the argument. For example,

1. All mothers are women.
2. Queen Elizabeth II is a mother.
<hr>
3. Queen Elizabeth II is a woman.

The argument structure is deductively valid, and the premises are acceptable, therefore the conclusion is certain. If the premises are acceptable, background information that would defeat this argument simply cannot exist.

Arguments to possibility generally do not need to face a check for indefeasibility because the conclusions of these arguments are not meant to be certain or even probable. These arguments can still be good, even if a further check on evidence suggests that other possibilities exist. For example, a literary or critical analysis designed only to show that its conclusion is coherent and illuminating must withstand scrutiny by others at the time it is developed, but has very little worry about standing the test of time. All that is really expected of it is that it should be consistent with all the evidence available at the time it was developed. If an interpretation of Margaret Atwood's writing doesn't work well once she publishes her next book, the interpretation may still be a valuable insight into her earlier works. If a more illuminating interpretation is constructed, the original interpretation may still be considered a valuable insight into the mind of the interpreter or the time period in which the interpretation was popular. However, arguments to possibility may be vulnerable to information that challenges their consistency and coherence. For example, suppose the interpretation of Atwood's writing is based only on her novels and has completely overlooked her poetry. An examination of the poetry might reveal an inconsistency in the interpretation. If the argument cannot resolve the inconsistency by explaining why the novels would be different from the poetry, the new information from the poetry does defeat the argument as a possible interpretation.

Arguments to probability typically need to undergo the sort of background check provided by the indefeasibility condition. In an argument to probability, premises can be acceptable, relevant, and sufficient to prove that a conclusion is probable, yet other information can come along and establish that the conclusion is in fact false. We can't say that an argument to probability is good if there is some information that will prove the conclusion is not probable at all no matter what the statistics say.

Consider this example you saw in Chapter 5. Your friend in Australia acquired a cat and you decided to knit little cat booties as a gag gift. You knit four booties, justifying your decision with the following argument.

1. Most cats have four legs.
2. Fluffy is a cat.
   _____
3. Fluffy has four legs.

In this example, the premises are acceptable, relevant, and sufficient to show that the conclusion is probably true. Now you phone your friend to tell him that you've knit four booties for Fluffy. Your friend tells you that Fluffy had been caught in a trap and now has only three legs. The argument has not changed. It still has premises that are acceptable, relevant, and sufficient to show that the conclusion is probably true. If you confine yourself to looking at just the premises presented, you still have good evidence that Fluffy probably has four legs. But you've now got further information that establishes that the conclusion is not probable at all! The new evidence shows that this argument is not good enough to establish that the conclusion is probable. The argument does not pass the test of indefeasibility.

If an argument is indefeasible, then not just the information already given but information not mentioned in the argument will support it. An argument shouldn't collapse immediately some new evidence comes along.

Consider another example. You are pacing the floor late at night. Your roommate should have been home hours ago. You call the home of a mutual friend, but your roommate is not there. "You shouldn't worry," says your friend. "Chris often stops at Sam's on the way home from a late shift at work and loses track of time. Chris is probably just at Sam's." Very often, an argument like this is a good argument. The premises are true, they support the conclusion, and if you do an indefeasibility check—you phone Sam—then sure enough, Chris is just on the way out the door. Nevertheless, the same argument can fail if it is offered on an occasion when it cannot pass an indefeasibility check. Chris is later than usual once again, your friend reassures you just as before—but this time, although neither you nor your friend knows it, Sam is out of town. This time, when you do the indefeasibility check, it fails. There's no answer at Sam's. On this occasion, the premises support the conclusion, but the added information significantly changes the probability of the conclusion. Chris is not accounted for and perhaps you are right to be concerned.

Sometimes we already have the information we need to defeat the argument at the time we hear the argument. For example, perhaps we already know Sam is on vacation—then, as our friend offers the argument that Chris is probably at Sam's, we can already say that the argument fails because it is not probable that Chris stopped at Sam's today. More typically, the information turns up after we evaluate. You've just relaxed and gone to bed when the phone rings: Chris has been in an accident and needs your help.

Indefeasibility is the condition that allows us to strike a balance between being too confident and not confident enough about our evaluations of arguments. It reminds us that often all we can say in evaluation is "To the best of our knowledge, this is good reasoning." It is a way to testify that we have done a responsible amount of checking, but that we acknowledge there might still be more to do. There is no point suspending judgment if every piece of evidence we have points us in the direction of accepting the conclusion. At the same time, we don't want to close our eyes and minds and presume everything is settled from then on. As we'll see in more detail in the Postscript (beginning on page 341), we should always remain open to revising even the firmest of conclusions in the face of new evidence against it.

During the evaluation stage, therefore, we should take the time to do at least the most obvious indefeasibility checks. We should at least check any obviously shaky assumptions or any less probable but still likely outcomes. Is Kari's pet a common guinea pig or a rarer longhaired Peruvian? Is Sam at home? Could your drink have been tampered with while you were not looking? Once reminded of the possibility, you may think it wise to check whether there are any strangers at the party before you assume there couldn't possibly be a problem with your drink.

EXERCISE 8.3

Checking Indefeasibility

*1. Consider this argument that you should probably not drink from a glass that has been left unattended:

>   1. If a drink is left unattended, harmful substances can be added to it.
>   2. There have been cases where drugs like Rohypnol, the "date rape drug," have been added to unattended drinks at parties or bars.
>   3. You should not risk drinking harmful substances.
>   _____
>   4. You should not drink from the glass you left unattended.

Which of the following pieces of information would defeat this argument?
a. You are male and therefore unlikely to be a target for date rape.
b. None of the reported cases have happened in your area.
c. Your drink was unattended, but you put it in the fridge and nobody has touched the fridge.

*2. You are a supervisor at a store. One employee called in sick a few minutes before the store opened. You find out later in the day that this employee was seen shopping in a drugstore only an hour after calling in sick. Can any of the following arguments be defeated by this information?
a. "There's a bad flu going around, so the employee probably is sick."
b. "People who are sick always stay home, so the employee isn't sick."
c. "People who are sick usually don't go shopping, so the employee probably isn't sick."

Results of an Evaluation: Assessment of Argument Quality

When we have completed an evaluation of the reasoning in an argument, we can make a judgment on the argument's success or failure. If we can demonstrate that there are mistakes in the reasoning, we know the argument has failed. We don't need any investigation of the accuracy of the premises. This is why a check of reasoning is often done first in evaluating an argument—it saves us research that can be time-consuming. However, if we see no mistakes in the reasoning, we may still not be able to confirm that the argument succeeds until after we have done an investigation and evaluation of the information used as premises. Consequently, we may sometimes be unable to tell whether an argument succeeds or fails until we have a chance to do further research.

We have three options for judging an argument based on an examination of its reasoning alone: it may succeed, it may fail, or we may be unable to tell without more investigation. If its reasoning succeeds, it's a good argument. If its reasoning fails, it's a bad argument. If we cannot tell just from the reasoning whether it is good or bad, it must count as "unproven"—we can't yet judge its quality.

Argument Quality: Good, Bad, and Unproven

We can classify arguments into good, bad, and unproven depending on how close they come to satisfying the four conditions of acceptability, relevance, sufficiency, and indefeasibility. The closer they come, the more reasonable it is to accept them and to act on their conclusions.

A **good argument** meets all four conditions satisfactorily, and we are likely to do well if we rely on it. However, good reasoning does not necessarily mean getting it right for all time on the first try. As already discussed, indefeasibility can be hard to check, especially within tight time limits. This is why we ought to see reasoning as a cyclical process. Good reasoning does the best that can be done at the time: the arguer may learn from, and build on, discussions and experiences that follow. How you proceed when you cannot be sure that an argument is good will be discussed in Chapter 11.

An **unproven argument** is one that has met the conditions for relevance and sufficiency, but not acceptability or indefeasibility. However, it cannot quite count as a bad argument. A bad argument has one or more premises that are clearly unacceptable. An unproven argument is one for which you have had to suspend judgment for lack of time or lack of available evidence. It has one or more premises that you are unsure of—an assumption or a premise explicitly stated by the arguer—because you simply do not have enough information to confirm or disconfirm them. If we had only two options, good or bad, these arguments could not count as good. However, the reason we won't call them bad arguments is that we also don't have enough evidence to call the argument bad. Instead, the argument is one that we have to put on hold while we run a more thorough check on the acceptability of the premises.

When an argument has not given us good enough support, we would be unwise to accept its conclusion without checking further or making contingency plans for what we will do if the conclusion turns out to be incorrect. We suspend judgment pending further investigation.

A **bad argument** is an unacceptable argument, one in which the intended support clearly does not work. It is important to remember that the *conclusion could be right*. Failing to prove that the conclusion is true isn't the same as proving the conclusion is wrong. The fault may be entirely in the premises, not in the conclusion. The truth of the conclusion is unknown, because we have absolutely no reason to accept it on the basis of the evidence given. In a poor argument, the premises are unacceptable, irrelevant, or so far from sufficient that they actively work against the conclusion and indicate that a contrary conclusion is more likely to be right. In the worst cases, the premises make it impossible for the conclusion to be accepted.

Bad arguments may fail on any of the four conditions: they may be inadequate because they use obviously unacceptable claims, provide irrelevant evidence, or are so far from sufficient that they actually support opposing conclusions much better than their intended conclusions, or we quickly turn up disconfirming evidence that alters the probability of the conclusion.

Because bad arguments offer no effective support for their conclusions, we don't even know if any of their reasons are worth using. We would need a new argument with acceptable reasons before we could believe the conclusion.

It may seem surprising that bad arguments are as common as they are. Arguers do not generally set out to make mistakes or to provide poor reasoning. However, when we argue, we may be biased or too emotional to think straight. We may see a connection between the issue being argued and a principle that we value strongly, and we may make every effort—even unreasonable ones—to defend that principle against the perceived threat. And we make characteristic reasoning errors even when no strong feelings are pulling us. As you will see in Chapter 11, this will make a difference to how we can best respond to a bad argument.

Preparing an Evaluation of an Argument

When you evaluate an argument you explain why its reasoning works or does not work. To carry out the evaluation, you need to test it by each of the three standards, acceptability, relevance, and sufficiency. Indefeasibility, as noted earlier, is the one condition you cannot check in advance. We always evaluate arguments as a whole, not reason by reason, sentence by sentence. Some premises might be unacceptable or irrelevant but might not, on balance, make any difference to the conclusion. The argument may still support its conclusion because one part of it is strong enough to make the conclusion highly probable.

Your evaluation shows where the strengths and weaknesses of the argument are, so you know how acceptable its conclusion should be. You give credit for what it has said accurately and what good points it has made. You also explain why it is good or where it falls short of providing adequate support for its conclusion: where it has given unacceptable premises, where it has overlooked alternatives or been misleading, and where it has failed to give enough information.

This approach generally means that you identify only the faults that make the most difference to the acceptability of the conclusion. Only rarely is it worth pointing out and discussing minor faults. Your evaluation is intended to be not only objective but also constructive, and it is hard for an arguer to accept an evaluation that gleefully reveals faults in exhausting detail.

Objective Report of an Argument

An objective report at the start of your evaluation enables your readers to make independent assessments of the argument. This report is a neutral presentation of the structure of an argument, including all key details of its reasoning. This makes it possible for them to see everything that you have seen and ensures that they can see why you evaluate the argument the way you do. (You prepared a report of this type in Chapter 2: see Chapter 2 to review the procedure.)

Oral Evaluation

In an oral discussion, you may be able to do some evaluation as you go, or you may need time to think over what you've heard. If you are evaluating as you listen, it is generally unwise to offer evaluative comments before everyone involved has had a chance to speak or before you have indicated your appreciation of the contribution. Direct, immediate evaluation, however objective, can be as confrontational and unwelcome as negative reaction.

As the discussion takes place, you may make notes, offer comments, or ask questions when you are unsure that you can accept some statement, uncertain that it is relevant, or doubtful that you have heard enough to persuade you. You can check if others agree on what counts as acceptable, relevant, and sufficient.

In oral discussion, the conversation may flow in a new direction with each new question and comment. If you are responsible for confirming whether a good argument has been given, you may need to stop and summarize at several stages. You may find that new issues emerge, and you will want to stay focused on the main concerns expressed so that the discussion does not get lost in unhelpful detail.

You may also need to take time afterward to evaluate what you've heard and said. Many people find it very hard to evaluate as they listen: there is too much to absorb. If this is true for you, you need to check in advance that you will not be pressured for a decision during the discussion: make sure that you will have time later to think. You'll also need notes on the discussion. When you evaluate your notes and recollections afterward, use the same techniques that you would for evaluating written arguments.

Written Evaluation

Your evaluation should be understood and agreed to by your readers (regardless of your position or theirs on the topic being discussed), so it is wise to first report or summarize the argument clearly enough for them to see what reasoning the arguer actually used. Then your evaluation should explain any problems that you have identified.

Discuss the argument with other people. Each person is likely to focus on slightly different aspects of the argument, and the result of the discussion should help to identify problems where the argument does not work yet.

Picture yourself talking to someone who disagrees entirely with the position taken in the argument. What might this person say? When you have the opposing view clear in your mind, you may be able to see where the argument does not say enough to convince its opponent or where it makes some assumptions or choices that its opponent does not accept. This will show you where the argument may be insufficient.

If you make yourself reconstruct the argument in your mind, you'll be more likely to realize where it was not explained well. This reconstruction points you toward places where the premises might not have been relevant or sufficient. If you can, wait before you react. After several hours or days, you'll have forgotten some of what was said. You'll also think of other aspects or questions that didn't occur to you at the time. Re-creating the argument makes it more likely that you'll spot where it did not give sufficient evidence.

In Part 4, we will look at guidelines on how to proceed once you have a sense of whether an argument is good, bad, or somewhere in between.

Checklist for Written Evaluation of Argument

✔ Have you included the title, source, and date?

✔ Have you made it clear which person holds which views?

✔ Have you clearly indicated the conclusion?

✔ Have you reported all the main reasons?

✔ Does your evaluation start with a separate paragraph to make it clear which views are yours?

✔ Have you explained the main strengths and weaknesses of the argument? (And have you explained your criteria for evaluation if you think that there may be some disagreement?)

The following sample shows what an evaluation might look like. Here is the original argument.

Cruise Clampdown Critical

Re: *Westworld's* Smooth Sailing column

Perhaps this is an issue that BCAA Travel has overlooked in the past. But B.C.'s marine resources are at risk from continued unregulated pollution from cruise ships plying our fragile coastal waters to and from Alaska six months of the year.

Every day, one cruise ship produces on average (based on 3,000 passengers and crew) 11.5 tons of garbage, much of it plastic and Styrofoam, most of which is incinerated and often discarded as highly toxic trash into the ocean. Also dumped at sea: 23 gallons of hazardous waste (including solvents used in cleaning, photo labs and dry-cleaning); 270,000 gallons of gray water (sink, shower, heavily

(Continued)

Cruise Clampdown Critical *(Continued)*

chlorinated laundry, swimming pool and galley water); 7,000 gallons of oily bilge water; 30,000 gallons of black water (human sewage waste); and more. In addition, many cruise ships operate without advanced wastewater treatment equipment.

In response, both California and Alaska have enacted laws to protect marine resources. But B.C. also needs such strong legislation to prevent degradation of our already compromised marine resources.

Len Walker, Qualicum Beach

[*WESTWORLD* (BCAA PUBLICATION), SUMMER 2004, 6]

Report:

In "Cruise Clampdown Critical" (*Westworld*, BCAA, Summer 2004, p. 6), Len Walker argues that B.C. needs strong legislation to protect its marine resources from pollution by cruise ships. The coastal waters are "fragile." Cruise ships sail these waters to and from Alaska for six months of the year. Every day, each cruise ship discharges large quantities of harmful wastes into the ocean. The average, based on 3,000 passengers and crew, is 11.5 tons of garbage, much of it plastic and Styrofoam, which is incinerated and often discarded as highly toxic trash; 270,000 gallons of grey water, including sink, shower, swimming pool, galley, and heavily chlorinated laundry water; 30,000 gallons of black water (human sewage waste); 7,000 gallons of oily bilge water; and 23 gallons of hazardous waste such as solvents used in cleaning, photo development, and dry-cleaning. Many cruise ships do not have advanced wastewater treatment equipment. California and Alaska have already enacted laws to protect marine resources. B.C. should follow their lead.

Evaluation:

Walker might be right that cruise ships present a significant hazard to marine environments in B.C. However, the information provided in this letter is not yet sufficient to support the conclusion that B.C. needs strong legislation like California and Alaska. The most crucial missing information is what harmful impact this waste has on the ocean. Do all the waste products have the same impact on marine resources? Are the ocean and shoreline worse than or the same as they were before cruise ships? The information provided is not yet enough to show that the ocean cannot absorb even these large quantities of waste and dilute them to harmless amounts. A second missing element is how the present B.C. legislation differs from legislation in California and Alaska, and how all three compare to legislation in other jurisdictions affected by cruise ship passage, such as Washington state, Mexico, or Panama. Is stronger legislation enforceable? Perhaps California and Alaska do have better legislation, but their legislation has not yet had any positive effect on cruise ship waste management.

While the conclusion is possible, Walker apparently intended to make the conclusion probable or certain and he has not provided sufficient evidence to do so. We should suspend judgment until we have information to confirm the extent of the hazards and the effectiveness of legislation.

EXERCISE 8.4 **Report and Evaluate an Argument**

Written Assignment: Report one of the following arguments. Evaluate its reasoning using what you have learned in Chapter 5 and Chapter 8. Explain any problems you find. If you see no problems, explain why you think the reasoning succeeds. Make sure you indicate clearly where your report ends and your evaluation begins.

Arguments for Use in Exercises 8.2 and 8.4

1. Berry falls into regulatory crack

When the Europeans put the squeeze on our farmers by ratcheting up their farm subsidies, we stood there and took it, like sheep.

When they banned our genetically modified canola, we sighed and said, "We'll just have to find markets elsewhere."

But they've gone too far this time.

Now the British and the European Union are talking about banning the poor little saskatoon berry, the tasty little treat unique to the prairies. They're calling it a food safety issue, but that's really just shorthand for obstructionism.

The Europeans intend to put saskatoon imports on hold because the berry is described by their regulators as a "novel food."

God forbid the Europeans should embrace anything from the New World without putting it through a series of regulatory hoops. Heavens, no. The saskatoon has only been growing wild along prairie riverbanks and coulees since time immemorial. Our First Nations people have only been making pemmican from bison and saskatoons for thousands of years. Goodness knows the bureaucrats in Britain would hate to rush to judgment.

According to Britain's Food Standards Agency, the saskatoon has to be reviewed under legislation which applies to any food "not substantially consumed" in the United Kingdom before 1997. Unless and until the nabobs within the EU can be satisfied that the saskatoon is what it appears to be, it will be kept out.

What's happening is that the Europeans' paranoia over GMOs has reached such a fever pitch that it is sideswiping natural products. As it happens, there is no such thing as a genetically modified saskatoon. There are about eight varieties of the berry, but they've all come from bushes growing in the wild and cultivated domestically.

The ruling stands natural justice on its head. Rather than being seen to be innocent until proven guilty, the EU policy essentially condemns saskatoon berries to exile until proven innocent.

As the Saskatoon Berry Barn's Garnet Erlandson puts it, "it sounds like cutting off the chicken's head before you know what's wrong with it."

As we know, there's not a thing wrong with the chicken. Plenty of European consumers and food processors know it, too. Over the past few years, they have come to know the saskatoon berry to be a versatile product that can be used in many ways.

"They're looking for new flavours, new products, they're very innovative in using fruit in lots of different ways, much more so than we are here and there's some neat possibilities, even in the pharmaceutical end of it," says Grace Whittington, co-owner of Riverbend Plantations, based in Saskatoon.

For example, saskatoons contain anti-oxidants that can be extracted and used in capsules in the health food market. You can sprinkle the stuff on your cereal in powdered form, if you like.

The nub of the regulatory issue is this. In order to get around the ruling that saskatoons are a "novel food," Canada has argued the saskatoon is like a blueberry—something that is already well established in European markets.

The Europeans didn't buy it. They think the saskatoon is more like an apple. Now we have to demonstrate that the saskatoon has been used safely for a long period of time. That is patently obvious to anyone from Saskatchewan, but it's a long and costly process in the regulatory world.

(Continued)

Berry falls into regulatory crack *(Continued)*

At the moment, Saskatchewan producers are not exporting berries to Europe; Manitoba is ahead of us on that. However, the European market represents a part of the industry's future. Anytime a diversification opportunity for Saskatchewan farmers opens up, it's good for everyone. In this case, the window is slamming shut before we can get our products through.

I'm sure Princess Anne would be appalled at this turn of events, if only she knew. I'm sure she'll understand that for Britain to ban the saskatoon would be akin to Canada declaring Yorkshire pudding unfit for human consumption, simply unthinkable in the Commonwealth.

Indeed, what do you suppose the Princess Royal will be served when she sits down to dine with Lieutenant-Governor Lynda Haverstock Sunday night in Regina?

You guessed it. Roast bison with saskatoon berry sauce. Will Princess Anne refuse to eat her dinner because of obscure regulations back home in jolly old England? I think not. I expect she'll enjoy every morsel of it.

Of course, the Royal Family is above politics, so it would be too much to expect her to put in a word for Canadian berries when she gets back home.

However, Prime Minister Paul Martin is going to visit with the world's leaders at a G-8 economic summit next week, where he intends to raise the issue of international export subsidies on grain.

Why stop there?

Perhaps he could exercise a little natural diplomacy and pass around a few jars of saskatoon berry jam.

[RANDY BURTON, *STARPHOENIX* (SASKATOON), JUNE 5, 2004, A2. REPRINTED WITH PERMISSION OF THE STAR-PHOENIX, SASKATOON.]

2. Alzheimer's drug eases the daily strain

Re: Major study pans Alzheimer's drug, June 26

Can you imagine yourself going through your day wearing one of those suits for deep diving? The kind that have airhoses and cables attached to a ship somewhere on the ocean surface. Now imagine having to wear that suit 24/7 and perform your daily tasks. This is how I feel most days.

Some days are easier than others, but only because I take a drug called Aricept. A recent British study said that Aricept doesn't work. I'm here to tell you that it does. And I think if you ask anyone else in the early stages of Alzheimer's, they would agree with me.

I admit it might not work for some people: Not all medications work for all people. Just ask anyone with a life-threatening illness if the first medication prescribed was the one that allowed them to function normally.

So shame on the British researchers and double shame on B.C. Health Services Minister Colin Hansen because he would sooner believe a study involving 565 people and not take the word of thousands of people who might say something different.

Robin Kilburn, Abbotsford

[*VANCOUVER SUN*, JULY 2, 2004, A11. REPRINTED WITH PERMISSION OF ROBIN KILBURN.]

In the following article, pick out and evaluate the arguments given on behalf of the University of New Brunswick by Ms. Mesheau.

3. University expels blind man for unilingual dog: Black Lab responds only to French

When it comes to teaching English as a second language, the University of New Brunswick does not mess around. Slip into your mother tongue back in the dorm and you can be expelled. A T-shirt with a non-English slogan is enough to get you kicked out. And as Yvan Tessier, a blind man from Trois-Rivieres, Que., learned this week, don't even think about telling your guide dog "Assis!" instead of "Sit!"

After being accepted into the five-week summer immersion program last spring and offered a federal bursary, Mr. Tessier was denied entry on Sunday when he was unable to sign "the Pledge" required of all applicants. In Mr. Tessier's case, it was not enough that he agree to speak to the professors and other students in English; the university insisted that he sign a contract promising that "all communication with your guide dog will be exclusively in English."

The problem for the 39-year-old master's student at Ottawa's Saint Paul University is that Pavot, the black Labrador that has helped him get around for the past two years, was trained to respond to 17 concise French commands. Tell him "Stay!" and he would be lost.

For the administrators of UNB's English language program, allowing French commands to a dog would be a dangerous step on the road to Babel.

Susan Mesheau, the university's director of public relations, said that permitting Mr. Tessier to speak French to Pavot during the immersion program would be like admitting someone with substandard marks into the engineering faculty.

"We cannot lower a standard," she said in an interview from Fredericton. "'OK, you're a nice guy, I'll lower it for you. You might not be as good an engineer. You might build bridges that people can fall off of, but that's OK.' That's silliness. Academic standards are academic standards."

Mr. Tessier, who arrived in Fredericton on Sunday, has remained in the New Brunswick capital in the hopes the university will reverse its decision. If not, he is considering a human rights complaint. He said he was looking forward to the program as a chance to perfect his English, which he has been practising for three years.

"I think it is marginalizing me, excluding me, discriminating against me," he said by phone. "I knew other people experienced this, but to experience it myself is very frustrating. I have been to two other universities, and I never suffered discrimination."

He said his dog cannot understand English commands. He was told by the group that trained him, the Mira Foundation in Quebec, that it would take months of training to familiarize Pavot with English instructions. He had told the university that apart from the commands, he would speak only English, even when he was just talking affectionately with Pavot.

The university initially accepted Mr. Tessier into the program in March. Later, after he had made inquiries about services available to the blind, his application was transferred to Dalhousie University in Halifax.

Ms. Mesheau said this transfer was done at the request of a Quebec government representative, but Brian Monast, a Saint Paul University official who helped Mr. Tessier with the application, said it was done because UNB was reluctant to accommodate Mr. Tessier.

Mr. Tessier rejected the transfer and by June, UNB had agreed to enroll him in its program. Then on June 28, the university asked him to sign its "Understanding of Course Academic Standards," in which he had to promise to speak to Pavot in English.

Mr. Monast and Josee Lajoie, co-ordinator of student services at Saint Paul, decided to intervene, writing on June 30 to the president of UNB, John McLaughlin, asking that allowance be made "for Mr. Tessier's unique circumstances as a visually impaired unilingual francophone." They noted that forcing him to speak in English to his dog "could jeopardize the safety of both himself and his guide dog."

The response from Debbie Pepin, administrative co-ordinator of the English Language Programme, was unbending.

"Regardless of his disability, Mr. Tessier must meet the demands and requirements of the course like any other student," she wrote in an e-mail.

"All students who take the course must sign and abide by the Pledge."

Ms. Mesheau said it was not just the language issue that made Pavot's presence problematic.

"We have students here who are allergic to dogs. We have students here who have religious affiliations that they cannot associate in the same room with a dog. *(Continued)*

University expels blind man for unilingual dog:
Black Lab responds only to French *(Continued)*

Those kinds of things we have to take into account," she said.

And it would be irresponsible of the university to let Mr. Tessier loose on the streets of Fredericton without proper guidance, she added.

"The class went out today downtown, to City Hall, to restaurants, interviewing people on the streets," Ms. Mesheau said. "This man has not been in Fredericton, he doesn't know. Would you not be concerned about his safety? We certainly are."

The university is not excluding Mr. Tessier, she said.

But first, Pavot will have to undergo an English immersion of his own, and necessary support structures have to be put in place, a process that would take two months.

By then, though, Mr. Tessier will be back in school in Ottawa.

Mr. Monast said Mr. Tessier, who is studying religion, and Pavot have never caused a problem at Saint Paul. "He is welcomed here," he said.

"There are no impediments to him coming here or to any other university. When he wants to go to class, he walks up the steps, opens the door and sits at his desk."

[GRAEME HAMILTON, *NATIONAL POST*, JULY 7, 2004, A1. MATERIAL REPRINTED WITH THE EXPRESS PERMISSION OF NATIONAL POST COMPANY, A CANWEST PARTNERSHIP.]

In the following article, pick out and evaluate the argument by Premier Williams.

4. Premier banishes Maple Leaf

Premier Danny Williams ordered Canadian flags removed from provincial buildings Thursday in protest of a breakdown in Atlantic Accord talks, as he lashed Ottawa for attempting to "humiliate" Newfoundland and Labrador.

But the feds accused Williams of using angry rhetoric to try to earn political capital, while privately taking on a different tone.

Williams told reporters in St. John's that federal Finance Minister Ralph Goodale is a "Grinch," and vowed never to sit down with Ottawa on the offshore oil issue again.

"It's also quite apparent to me that we were dragged to Manitoba in order to punish us, quite frankly, to try and embarrass us," Williams said.

"To bring us out there to get no deal and send us back with our tail between our legs ...

"My best guess is that Ralph and (Natural Resources Minister) John (Efford) decided that the government of Newfoundland and Labrador was going to be brought out, was going to be put through this process, and then humiliated and sent back to Newfoundland and Labrador without a deal."

He suggested that Wednesday's meeting in Winnipeg—which was also attended by Nova Scotia Premier John Hamm—was little more than an ambush.

"They were trying to set us up. It was a jam.

"They were trying to give us less than what we were promised by the prime minister of the country, and we said no."

But Goodale told *The Telegram* Thursday the premier's angry comments contrast with his private ones about Ottawa's latest written offer.

"I took the premier through that piece of paper point by point by point by point—both premiers," Goodale said. "Premier Williams said it's an excellent piece of work, it's a great place to start, and I'm comfortable with it. That's what he said to me in the room."

Goodale said Ottawa will continue to work towards a solution despite the subsequent "very harsh" comments by Williams.

"To say that I am somehow a Grinch, I think, is an attempt to reap political capital, but it's simply not true," the finance minister said.

He pointed at Ottawa's continued "constructive dialogue" with Nova Scotia as a sign that the feds are working in good faith.

Nova Scotia's premier agreed to further meetings on the offshore issue in January.

John Hamm has been more restrained in his criticism of the pace of talks.

But Williams suggested Hamm's reaction was more muted because Nova Scotia has fewer chips in the offshore pot.

"His stake is minuscule compared to our stake," Williams said. "(On Wednesday), the government of Canada was prepared to buy John off. John Hamm is an honourable man. He stood his ground, he wanted to get a commitment in writing, he will go back (for further talks)."

As for Ottawa keeping its word at those talks, Williams said: "Good luck, John."

The premier said Ottawa's latest written offer shortchanged the province by $1 billion over eight years.

"Now they're going to spin across the country that we're double-dipping, that we're trying to get equalization when we're off equalization. Nothing is further from the truth."

In fact, he said, the latest offer could result in the province retaining less than 100 per cent of its share of oil revenues by Year 3 of the deal.

That's when Newfoundland could eke out of so-called "have-not" status, by no longer qualifying for support from the federal equalization program.

Ottawa wants new offshore oil payments to end when equalization does, save for the declining offsets currently available under the Accord.

The feds have also placed a series of conditions on the deal being extended for a further eight years—such as continued balanced budgets on an accrual basis.

Newfoundland's projected accrual deficit for 2004–05 is $707.5 million. The cash component of that is $118 million.

Entirely erasing the accrual deficit too quickly could devastate the province, Williams said.

"That means taking that money—$700 million to $1 billion—on gross revenues of $4 billion to $5 billion. That's a fortune. That means less hospitals, less schools, less services, less economic development."

Asked what he hoped to accomplish by his harsh words and decision to lower Canadian flags at provincial government buildings, Williams pointed at several maple leaf banners behind him.

"I'm not lowering the flags, I'm removing the flags. After this is over, that flag will be gone, that flag will be gone, and that flag will be gone . . .

"We're partners in this country. We're in this together. It's a federation. We expect to be treated fairly like other provinces. We have not been treated fairly. And as a result, down goes the flag."

Newfoundland and Ottawa have been at loggerheads for months on the Accord issue.

The province wants to retain 100 per cent of its share of offshore revenues, with no effects on the equalization program, and no strings attached.

Williams thought Martin pledged to do just that on June 5, when he said during a campaign stop in St. John's that "I had a discussion . . . with the premier this morning, and I have made it very clear that the proposal that he has put forth is a proposal that we accept."

But trouble cropped up soon after, when the feds and province clashed on exactly what Martin meant.

Williams said top federal officials pledged to have the issue resolved by Christmas.

When Wednesday's meeting in Winnipeg came and went without a deal, he decided all talks were off.

[ROB ANTLE, *TELEGRAM* (ST. JOHN'S), DECEMBER 24, 2004, A1. REPRINTED WITH PERMISSION.]

Key Points in Review

- Evaluation of an argument means checking the structure to see if all the pieces are in place and properly connected, regardless of the eye-appeal or the arguer's goodwill.

- To be accurate, your evaluation must be *objective:* the faults that you see should be those that people using the same standards would recognize in the same context, faults that are violations of shared standards of reasoning.

- To see if the premises support the conclusion of an argument, we want to be sure not only that it makes sense to accept the premises but also that the premises taken together meet the standards for good reasoning. These standards are acceptability, relevance, sufficiency, and indefeasibility.

- When we evaluate arguments, we consider not just whether the premises are individually acceptable as statements, but whether the premises, taken together, work as acceptable support for the types of reasoning being used. Is the argument well structured? Do its premises give the right kind of information, and enough of it? Is there no way to defeat the argument through background information that is more convincing than the argument under consideration?

- A report of an evaluation shows where the strengths and weaknesses of the argument are, so we know how acceptable its conclusion should be. In your report, give credit for what the argument has said accurately and what good points it has made. Explain why it is good or where it falls short of providing adequate support for its conclusion: where it has given unacceptable premises, where it has overlooked alternatives or been misleading, and where it has failed to give enough information.

Chapter 9

Evaluating in Context

■ Perspective

Evaluating arguments is only part of deciding whether we have good reason to adopt a belief or take an action. An argument, by itself, shows only whether it is rational to believe the conclusion of the argument. This is seldom the end of the discussion. Why were we paying attention to the argument in the first place? Which of our interests or concerns did it speak to? By what additional standards do we need to judge its value to us or its value in general?

■ Scenario

You belong to a group that needs to do some fundraising. One member of the group is proposing a new approach and has brought in colour brochures and a sample of a fascinating new product that the group could sell door to door to raise money. Your group hasn't done door-to-door sales before, but this person argues that door-to-door sales will help your group members gain confidence in dealing with strangers and will bring in at least as much money as your usual methods. The reasoning seems to support door-to-door sales as a good fundraiser. What would it take to make this a practical proposal for your group?

■ Key Question

Does this proposal work for its intended purpose?

Evaluating in Context

For an argument, **evaluating in context** means checking the impact the argument has in the context in which it is presented. We use specific expectations, standards, needs, or goals to judge whether an existing or proposed item is suitable for its purpose. For example, what are we meant to do as a result of evaluating the argument? How does it compare with other arguments offered to support competing conclusions? What have we learned that should influence what we do next?

More generally, we also evaluate in context when we match actions to purposes. Again, we check the impact of the information or the action in the context in which it is used. For example, we may evaluate whether the imagery and music we use in a video create the effect we intended, and if not, how we might improve them. We evaluate which details of our casual summer employment to include in a résumé. We evaluate whether it would be better to stay on in a shared apartment or move out when a roommate leaves.

Evaluating in context calls for the same reasoning skills that you have used in the rest of the book. As you think through why you might choose each option, you are giving (or getting) reasons to support each possible choice. From your work in the previous chapters, you know how to collect information as you need it, and how to recognize all the options that are open to you. Now you need to separate the valuable information from the unhelpful information, and the practical options from the impractical ones.

The first example of evaluating in context we will consider is what to do when you have more than one argument on the same topic. Following that, we will look at how you evaluate nonverbal elements in their context: numbers, images, sounds, and emotions. Finally, we will consider how you can evaluate proposed solutions to problems and courses of action.

Comparing Arguments

Arguments seldom occur in isolation. Throughout the book, you have been encouraged to think about the issues and the wider context in which arguments are found. Arguments are often created in response to other arguments, precisely to show where they went wrong, or where it is possible to defend an alternative. (See Chapter 2.) For the last few chapters, we have focused on examining individual arguments in detail. Now we need to see how this careful examination helps us compare one argument to another. Where do we stand on the issue that was the crux of the debate?

The first step in evaluating progress on an issue is to compare the arguments you have found so far, after evaluating each argument individually. The second step is to offer suggestions that will help us to make progress, which we will postpone to Chapter 10 because it involves choosing actions. As you compare arguments, you focus on how they deal with the main concern—the crux of the debate, which you identified during the investigation stage. (See Chapter 6.) When we put arguments in context, we are primarily looking at what they teach us about the issue they address. To evaluate arguments in context often means comparing different arguments on the same topic so that we can see the most reasonable direction in which to proceed. What we are looking for is the common ground and the crux of the debate, so that we can isolate the remaining areas of disagreement and discuss what to do next. Your aim will be to isolate the main areas of disagreement so you can start to see how to move forward.

The goal of comparing arguments is to see how we can move forward on the issue or solve the problem we are dealing with. The issues on which we disagree are seldom those on which we can disagree indefinitely without causing hardship or unfairness. Think of euthanasia, refugees, or the Atlantic cod and Pacific salmon fisheries. People's livelihoods and lives are at stake in some of our disagreements; we do not want to argue endlessly so that unnecessary hardships continue. Yet we also have to recognize that few issues are settled definitively. Even if the issue is settled in favour of one side, fresh controversy may arise.

When you evaluate in context, you still keep the fair, objective stance you took in evaluating arguments individually. You compare competing arguments without initially favouring one over another. Then you decide what you can conclude from the comparison. Finally, you identify the areas that need to be worked on and see what you can suggest that might help.

We don't simply pick the side we prefer unless that really is all that is at stake. For example, which movie should you go to when two that interest you are on at the same time? You can hear arguments for each one but still simply pick the one you prefer. On the other hand, which political party should you support in the next election? As a responsible voter, you should not simply pick a candidate with an appealing name—you should consider the candidates' and their parties' stand on the issues that matter to you.

It's tempting, but not very responsible, to react to competing arguments just by saying, "Well, you've heard the competing views, and now you can make up your own mind" or "The two sides are so far apart it doesn't seem likely they'll ever agree." Have you ever been tempted to end a critical essay this way? If you have, your reader has almost certainly growled with frustration! Similarly, if you have been in a dispute, heard both sides, and then said, "Well, we'll just have to compromise," probably the speakers on both sides have wanted to throw eggs at you. Responses like "It's up to you to decide" or "Just compromise" are unhelpful because they don't move us any further forward than we were before the debate began. You could have said the same thing right at the start and saved everyone the trouble of trying to organize their arguments.

Conversely, on difficult issues, don't worry at this stage about trying to reach a firm conclusion yourself on the issue. Partly because controversial issues are so seldom settled conclusively, you may still be undecided after you complete your analysis. You do not have to presume that one side is right or that there must be some merit on both sides. Your analysis is a step in the critical thinking cycle: it becomes part of what you and the other people involved will consider when you continue your investigation.

Checklist for Comparing Arguments

To compare arguments to see how far they have brought you, check the following:

✔ Where do we now stand on the issue? Do we agree what the real issue is—the crux of the debate?

✔ What can we agree on that need not be discussed further?

✔ What are the remaining areas of disagreement and what do they indicate? What alternatives are still open to consideration?

✔ What further information do we need and why?

A comparison of arguments answers these questions. If we are lucky enough to find a good argument among the ones we have compared, that may mean we can simply support its conclusion and explain why the other arguments should be rejected. If there is more than one good argument for competing conclusions (and this can happen if two arguers reason equally correctly from competing assumptions) or if there are a number of unproven arguments, we need to show where we could best put our future effort.

When you compare the arguments you have already evaluated, you can answer all four questions. To report your comparison, you need to make sure that you link the arguments together rather than simply report first one and then the other.

1. From your understanding of the arguments and their assumptions, you know what is important to each side and whether they agree on what the real issue is.

2. By checking whether they are consistent with one another in both their information and the points that they do not dispute, you know what they do agree on. By checking for poor arguments, you know if there is any reasoning we can agree to reject.

3. By checking which arguments are unproven and which arguments rely on competing assumptions of principle, you know what is not yet settled and must still be discussed. The same check shows you what alternatives have not been ruled out, and whether the arguments have overlooked anything. By recognizing the assumptions in the arguments, you know where it may be necessary to open a discussion on why these assumptions should be accepted.

4. By evaluating where the arguments have not provided sufficient support for their conclusions, you know what alternatives must still be investigated and what further evidence will be needed to test them.

For example, in Chapter 6 you saw a disagreement about whether it was a good idea to produce multilingual primers on voting. In that example, Michelle Ng examined both arguments and identified the key issue.

1. The key issue is whether immigrant voters who speak neither English nor French are fully committed to Canada.

2. The two arguers, Sara and Kosick, do seem to agree that everyone who votes in Canada should care about Canada. As Ng puts it, "Allegiance to one's adopted homeland is important."

3. They disagree strongly on whether it is necessary to speak one of Canada's official languages in order to be committed to Canada. Again, as Ng puts it, Sara thinks an election "helps immigrants express their allegiance to their adopted country and, therefore, measures should be taken to ensure they can sail through voting procedures with ease." Kosick, on the other hand, in Ng's words, "equates the lack of language ability with the lack of allegiance." Neither Sara nor Kosick has yet produced enough evidence to show that competence in an official language is or is not important to feeling allegiance to Canada. Sara did not establish that the multilingual primers did increase the likelihood that new immigrants would vote responsibly. Kosick did not establish that giving immigrants information in their own language would allow them to manage without either official language, or that if they did, they would also fail to understand and respect Canada.

4. What we would need in order to see if there is a connection between immigrants' allegiance to Canada and their fluency in either official language would be information connecting their voting habits with their fluency. Ng herself provides some additional information that helps. As an election scrutineer, she did observe non-English-speaking voters voting successfully, with the help of translators, and she noticed that they seemed to appreciate the opportunity to vote. Ng's information adds some anecdotal evidence to support Sara's belief that feeling respected and accommodated in turn produces respect. However, even a careful study of voters' fluency in English or French compared to their understanding of the issues and their desire to vote would not settle the debate. The key assumption being made in Kosick's letter is that fluency in English or French is itself a crucial indicator of respect for Canada. Without that fluency, there is no clear indicator of allegiance to Canada. Discussion needs to move directly to the key issue itself. How does fluency in one of Canada's official languages fit into our obligations as citizens of the country?

EXERCISE **9.1** ## Comparison of Arguments

Written Assignment: The following pair of arguments was presented as an exercise in Chapter 6. If you did that exercise, you have already identified the key area of dispute. Now prepare a full comparison of the two arguments, answering all four questions (see Checklist for Comparing Arguments, above).

Squeegee kids: Does a nuisance require new laws?

I am writing in response to your editorial "Squeegee kids may be irritating ..." (May 14) which compared the nuisance of squeegee kids to the inconvenience of spam e-mails and telemarketers and concluded new laws are unnecessary.

It is hard for me to see the parallel between these activities. While you can easily screen phone calls and e-mails, there is no escape from aggressive behaviour encountered while walking or driving in one's own city. The Safe Streets Act proposed by MLA Lorne Mayencourt is not just about "squeegee kids," it is about providing the police with sufficient tools to address aggressive behaviour on our streets. It is about protecting our public spaces for all citizens, including the poor, addicted and mentally ill.

Contrary to your editorial, the members of our Safe Streets Coalition believe that new provincial legislation is necessary. Provincial laws would allow police to attend to a complaint and choose from a number of different options—warn, ticket, or arrest. The arrest option under a provincial statute is critical. Used as a last resort for repeat or non-compliant offenders, it attaches a real and immediate consequence to unwanted and aggressive behaviour. The coalition is particularly supportive of provincial legislation to ensure that all communities have the same laws and penalties.

Kathi E. Thompson
Chair, Safe Streets Coalition,
Vancouver

[*VANCOUVER SUN*, MAY 18, 2004, A13. REPRINTED WITH PERMISSION OF KATHI E. THOMPSON, SAFE STREETS COALITION, VANCOUVER.]

I couldn't agree more that larger public nuisances merit legal restraining, rather than a few kids at traffic lights.

Having been accosted at knife-point on the meaner streets of both Los Angeles and New York, I can say local squeegee kids are at least performing a service in an entrepreneurial business pursuit.

It could be a lot worse, and is a reflection of the more kind society in which we live.

As a motorist, when I see a squeegee kid approaching I consider if he or she is one of the mentally challenged our government has cast into "community care" instead of a now-closed institution, or is the kid from a good home and simply hitch-hiking through the world for now?

Either way, the gamble I take as I reach into my wallet for a looney or toony is about the same as a purchased cup of coffee being good or stale.

Considering those meaner streets which produce meaner kids, I decide the gamble is worth it. I smile and speak politely to the kid, my windshield gets washed, and in almost every case, the kid is extremely polite to me.

For those who still get their noses twisted at this being allowed to occur, how much would it cost the city to post those little "maximum fine" signs related to aggressive panhandling at busy intersections?

Not much, considering those meaner streets elsewhere. We have much to be thankful for.

Al Hawirko, North Vancouver

[*VANCOUVER SUN*, MAY 18, 2004, A13. REPRINTED WITH PERMISSION OF AL HAWIRKO.]

Alternative: If you completed Exercise 4.10 in Chapter 4, you have already collected a pair of arguments with contrasting views on your own choice of topic. Compare your two arguments to identify their key points of disagreement.

Evaluating Nonverbal Elements: Images, Sounds, and Numbers

In Chapter 8 you examined arguments to see if they met the standards expected of them. In particular, arguments need to use acceptable and relevant premises and provide sufficient support for their conclusions. The reasoning must show a correct logical connection.

There is an analogous approach we can use to analyze visual, auditory, numerical, and emotional information elements. All these are often used to support or enhance an intended effect. The intended effect is the purpose for presenting the information—it is the destination you are intended to arrive at after being appropriately influenced by all that is presented to you. The images and sounds are intended to influence you by creating that desired effect, not unlike the way in which premises are intended to build toward a conclusion. Images and sounds can succeed or fail in their intended impact. They may be legitimate or illegitimate attempts to influence you. They may be acceptable or unacceptable, relevant or irrelevant, and sufficient or insufficient for their purpose.

In the case of numbers, we can often treat them as premises in an argument, but we cannot evaluate them in exactly the same way we evaluate words, because numerical reasoning requires different skills. Images and sounds also require different interpretive and evaluative skills.

Consider the following real-life problem. A theatre professional is designing a stage set for a play. The play is set on a beach, and the director wants the stage to look like a real beach. It's important to see the actors walking as they would walk on loose sand. The designer's first inclination is to use real sand. It's cheap enough, and the stage is not that big—three metres by nine metres. Covering the stage to a depth of five centimetres should do the job. However, the designer discovers that this amount of sand will weigh almost fifteen tonnes. That's a lot of weight for the stage floor to handle. It's also going to take a long time to shovel the sand onto the stage at load-in (the beginning of the play's run) and clear it off at strike (the end of the run). What seemed like an easy and practical solution no longer seems to meet the director's goals. Can the designer get the same sandy effect the director needs with much less real sand? Further investigation, and the necessary calculations, show that carpeting draped over humps to simulate sand dunes and covered to a depth of one centimetre with sand will use only three tonnes of real sand. The designer tries out the sand on the carpet, and discovers that the rough surface of the carpeting will hold the sand well enough that it won't all slip off. The "dunes" will still look realistic, and the one centimetre of sand is enough to make the actors' movements natural. By going back and forth between investigating and evaluation, the designer has balanced visual appearance against weight, cost, and time constraints. The designer has successfully achieved the desired effect (Kovalick). This is good critical evaluation of nonverbal elements.

Numbers: Quantitative Information

The first form of nonverbal analysis we will consider is the interpretation of quantitative information. Numbers presented in tables or incorporated into text are pieces of factual information that can be judged for acceptability and relevance just like any other. Estimates are like opinions; they can be judged as reasonable or unreasonable. Graphs use numbers and add a visual component, since a graph is a visual indicator of how numbers are related to one another.

Numbers need particular care in evaluation. Reasoning with numbers calls for different skills than those we use with words. Many of us are not as adept at examining numbers as we are at examining words, images, or sounds. Some people have a flair for understanding numbers, calculations, and mathematical reasoning. Some people read numbers less easily than they read sentences: they cannot quickly check the accuracy or follow the implications of the numbers. This common problem makes many of us more vulnerable than we should be to arguments using numbers.

Exact numbers seem impressive—detailed and objective. Yet the numbers need to be checked like any other facts. While you were investigating, you should have checked numbers as part of the information. Typographical errors are harder to spot in numbers than in words. Check that the numbers are in the same order, and that no zeros have been left out. (If it is important that the numbers be absolutely exact, the only safe way to check is to have one person read aloud from the original and a second person read silently from the copy.) Just as with premises, numbers must be acceptable, relevant, and sufficient.

- *Acceptable numbers* are taken from an accurate, objective, and reliable source.

For example: Statistics Canada is likely to be a more reliable source than the Tobacco Growers' Association of Canada for a report that claims, "Deaths among male smokers are decreasing by twenty percent."

- *Relevant numbers* give information that is connected to the point being made.

For example: "Sixty-five percent of first marriages fail" is relevant to the conclusion "You should think very carefully about deciding whom to marry." The statistic is not relevant to the conclusion "Second marriages are unlikely to succeed." We'd have to stretch a long way to claim that, because more than half of first marriages fail, second marriages will also fail.

- *Sufficient numbers* are correctly compared and rule out other hypotheses.

For example: "Thirty-five percent of drivers aged sixteen to nineteen have accidents, compared to an average of only fifteen percent of drivers in any other age group. Therefore, teenagers are less safe drivers than adults." The numbers are correctly compared. Contrast that with "Thirty-five percent of teenage drivers have accidents, compared to only fifteen percent of twenty- to twenty-five-year-olds. Therefore, teenagers are much worse drivers than adults." This is not a correct comparison because twenty- to twenty-five-year-olds are not the only adults who drive. There may also be a high accident rate among seventy-five- to eighty-year-olds; perhaps they are worse drivers. As a second example, suppose that reliable statistics do show that lung cancer rates are much higher than average in towns with pulp mills. Does this evidence help to prove the conclusion that living near a pulp mill is a cancer risk? Not necessarily. It's relevant, and we assume that it's reliable. But it could equally well support a very different conclusion. Perhaps pulp mill towns have a higher than average percentage of smokers, and it's the smoking, not the pulp mill emissions, that causes the cancer. We'd have to check the smoking rates as well, and perhaps other factors, before we decide if the numbers rule out any other causes.

EXERCISE **9.2**

Assessing Numerical Information

*1. Look back at the argument used for a sample evaluation in Chapter 8, "Cruise Clampdown Critical," or the article in the exercise set at the end of Chapter 8, "Premier banishes Maple Leaf." Both these arguments made use of numbers to support their claims. Assess the numbers using the criteria above: are they acceptable, relevant, and sufficient?

2. What numerical information from which sources would be appropriate to support one of the following claims:
    a. Students with the highest GPAs entering veterinary school make the best vets.
    b. Lack of exercise is more important than poor diet in producing childhood obesity.
    c. Violent-offender treatment programs are effective in reducing violent behaviour for offenders once they are released into the community.

Evaluating Images

Thinking critically about images or scenes can cover a very wide range of tasks, from deciding if anything is out of place in a room to designing a stage set, from evaluating a painting aesthetically to considering the subliminal effects of television imagery. When we think critically about what we see, we are concerned with how well the visual components serve their purpose. If we're having company over, does the room look welcoming? If children are coming, is everything dangerous safely put away? Does the stage set for the third act of this play convey the impression of a hot city night? Is the artist's use of colour or sense of geometry the most important aspect of this painting? Does this television show present women as interesting only when they are attractive?

Reasoning about what we see is a natural extension of what we have done with words. We have criteria for what we will consider appropriate. Those criteria may change from context to context and may be a matter for discussion, or they may be fixed by convention. We examine what we see, comparing it against those criteria. We decide how well it measures up. If it is acceptable, we go on to use it or to appreciate it as it is. If what we see is not satisfactory, we decide what would improve it or what should be changed. We may have to justify our decision to others and take their reactions into account in deciding what to do.

Our aims and techniques in thinking critically about images are roughly parallel to what we do with words. We focus on the visual information available to us—on the overall impression the image creates as well as the details from which it is built. What is challenging is that although most of us can do this, we are not often aware that we are doing it and cannot always put it into words. The added skill we need is the ability to explain our impressions in words so that we can share and discuss our judgment.

The strength—and limitation—of imagery used to help convey a message is that its vividness is far greater and far more persuasive than words alone, but it is not usually confined to a single, narrow interpretation. As well as presenting information, imagery suggests indirect and unexpected associations.

However, images can still be judged on whether they are acceptable, relevant, or sufficient. To illustrate this, consider one application of powerful images: using photographs of animals in research laboratories to add power to an argument that we should not do research on animals.

You may have a good argument for the benefits of animal research, but when your opponents produce a pamphlet that has vivid photographs of animals being experimented on, your good argument may be unable to persuade its audience. Pictures of animals undergoing medical experiments have an impact more powerful than even the most vivid word picture. Yet these vivid photographs may not necessarily support the argument that they are used with. Their impact may be unreasonably strong.

For instance, if the pictures turn out to be fake, or to have been taken years ago, they are as unacceptable as any inaccurate premise. The pictures may not be relevant: they may be of animals used in *cosmetic* research to support an argument against the use of animals in *medical* research. And the same pictures of animals with exposed skin or wires in their heads could have a very different effect if they were used with captions explaining how the animals themselves are being cured of ailments that they once would have died from. The photographs that evoked shock and revulsion could equally well evoke fascination and hope. So these vivid pictures of animals could support equally well an argument for animal research and an argument against it.

Emotionally powerful though the pictures may be, they are not sufficient by themselves to show that there is a problem with animal experimentation. We need to judge the pictures in context. Does everything else in the context also support the claim that what is happening is painful and unnecessary? Then we could reasonably agree that animal experiments ought not to happen.

As an example of evaluating imagery for its suitability in context, we will look at one particular application of visual critical thinking: deciding how well the imagery in advertising achieves its purpose.

Advertising always has an intended effect: to make the product or service look desirable to its target market. What will be "desirable" varies from market to market and from time to time, so advertisers must constantly test and update their imagery to have the intended effect. Yet even though advertisements are typically produced by professionals and tested for effectiveness, they are not all equally effective. Sometimes the imagery simply does not create the intended effect—it is not as humorous or as up-to-the-minute as it intends to be.

Sometimes the imagery does create the intended effect, but does not use legitimate methods. For example, think of the many advertisements that use glamorous people to draw your attention to unrelated products—a blond model in a bikini stretched out beside a car engine, or a cute puppy sitting beside a printer/copier. The images evoke feelings that attract you to the picture and may even make the product seem desirable—but the images don't evoke anything directly relevant to the product's characteristics or quality, not even metaphorically.

When we assess visual imagery in advertising, we do not usually focus simply on whether the graphic design "catches your eye." Many visual images—advertisements and movies especially—are the products of sophisticated design studios. The use of colour, the vividness of the image, and the layout or camera angles have been carefully chosen to ensure that your attention is caught, held, and directed to exactly the intended features of the image. This is analogous to well-written prose, which directs your attention and thought exactly where the writer intended. Good prose may successfully influence you, but that does not mean it is acceptable reasoning. A well-designed image may hold your attention, but that does not make it an image that delivers a justified message about the product.

Consequently, we cannot say an image is successful in creating its intended effect just because it makes you see and think of what you are intended to see and think of—just as a verbal argument can't be called "good" simply because it is beautifully written.

Assessing the Choice of Image

To assess an image, we examine our immediate reaction to it and take the time to look at it more carefully to see what may be causing this reaction. In Chapter 1 and 4, you observed and investigated key features of imagery, such as the content of the image, the colours used, the mood, and the viewpoint.

To assess visual support for a message, make sure that you understand the intended effect (which may derive from the images or a combination of the images and words) and then assess the support the images provide for it.

Checklist for Assessing Visual Imagery

✔ What is the intended effect?

✔ Is the imagery acceptable? That is, can you see any evidence of fakery, distortion, or omissions that would make the image misleading?

✔ Is the imagery relevant to the intended effect? That is, does the image appropriately illustrate any text beside it, and does the image connect in some plausible way to the intended effect?

✔ How does the imagery contribute to the intended effect? Look for the overall impression that you get from the picture. What details help give that impression? What do you appreciate in the image? Is there anything about the image that works against the intended effect, or seems inappropriate?

✔ Overall assessment: do the images succeed in supporting the intended effect? Explain your reasoning. How do the details of the image contribute to the intended effect? How well do you think the image as a whole succeeds in creating the desired effect?

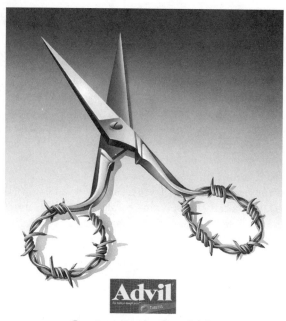

One tough pain. One Advil.
Arthritis can turn everyday activities into everyday pain.
That's why doctors recommend Advil for relief of arthritic pain.
It's easy on the stomach and so effective, one is often enough.
www.advil.ca

Consider the advertisement for the pain reliever Advil. The advertisement pictures a pair of scissors. The handles are made of barbed wire. The handles point toward the viewer, inviting you to imagine yourself grasping them. Below the scissors is a picture of a box of Advil tablets, and the caption, "One tough pain. One Advil." Below the caption is a short paragraph: "Arthritis can turn everyday activities into everyday pain. That's why doctors recommend Advil for relief of arthritic pain. It's easy on the stomach, and so effective, one is often enough."

What is the intended effect? Overall, the intended effect of the advertisement as a whole—the picture with its caption—is to suggest that a single Advil tablet can relieve the pain arthritis sufferers experience when they attempt everyday activities.

Is the imagery relevant to the intended effect? Cutting with scissors is an everyday activity that ought to be simple. The unusual feature, barbed wire handles, turns these otherwise ordinary scissors into something that looks strikingly uncomfortable to pick up. An ordinary object, transformed into something we would rather not touch, is an effective image to convey the concept of everyday tasks becoming unexpectedly painful.

Is the imagery acceptable? Clearly, the image of the scissors has been distorted: this is not a photograph of a real pair of scissors, but an altered image. Yet this distortion does not create an unacceptable image, because it is working the same way as a metaphor. The handles would not literally be prickly, but they might feel that way to the hands of an arthritis sufferer. We are not misled by it.

Is the imagery sufficient to create the intended effect? Here is where there will be some disagreement. Some people find non-literal images unpersuasive—if the advertisement as a whole is intended to persuade arthritis sufferers that Advil can relieve their pain, shouldn't the ad show an arthritis sufferer first wincing in pain while holding scissors, and then smiling after taking a pain reliever? Television commercials can show such extended action, and often do. But a print ad does not have the same flexibility. It must make its point more concisely and dramatically. While some readers might prefer a more literal image of arthritic hands, this non-literal image is still successful as long as it conveys discomfort to enough people. A fair comparison for this image is not a literal image of arthritic hands, but comparable images used in similar advertisements. For example, another version of this same advertisement replaces the scissors with a small saucepan. The handle of the saucepan, pointing toward the viewer, is

Don't let your *child* go to sleep in the *dark.*

Read together and help make your child's future a much brighter one.

a green cactus. The cactus-handled saucepan is an equally non-literal image, and it may even be slightly better in giving the viewer an immediate impression of pain in an everyday task.

One additional feature of the image must also be mentioned. The handles of the scissors point toward the viewer, and the tips of the blades point away into a darker space. Light at the front and dark at the back, the picture creates the perspective that these handles are just where you could pick them up. The immediacy that this creates is also important to the effect of the image—you are the potential user. Some people may say that the image will resonate only for people who are arthritis sufferers—non-sufferers may not even understand the image. Again, however, this is not a deficit of the image. As long as arthritis sufferers do understand it, the image achieves its purpose. So the image can be counted as successful in conveying its part of the message: everyday tasks can hurt. What the image does not do is convey the second part of the intended message: Advil can help. Only the text conveys that part of the message. And at that level, this advertisement is one among many that show only that their product is one possible solution to a problem, but not that their solution is the only one or the best one.

Perhaps Advil does work well. If you are an arthritis sufferer, and a responsible consumer, you will realize that it might be reasonable to look into Advil as a possible medication, but you will need much more information than this before you can conclude that Advil will meet your needs better than any comparable medication now on the market.

As an extension of this type of evaluation, you can evaluate personal appearance or the ambience of a room. Again, you ask similar questions:

- What impression does this person or room want to create? Is that impression appropriate for the circumstances?
- Does the clothing or decor create an accurate impression?
- Is the clothing or decor connected appropriately to the intended impression?
- Is there anything missing or out of place that detracts from the impression?

EXERCISE 9.3 ## Assessing Imagery

Discussion: Consider the advertisements for literacy and milk in this section, or find a pair of illustrations, ads, posters, or brochures in which the images are used to create a particular effect. Work with two or three other people to compare the

imagery in the items. Is there consensus within the group about the intended effect? Can you agree on whether the images succeed in creating the intended effect? Can you explain your decisions? (You should generally find very good consensus. We tend to be quite consistent in our interpretation of images; only a few images evoke very different responses from different people.)

Written Assignment: Look back at the advertisement for Rogers cellphones (Chapter 4, page 125), or find an advertisement in which the imagery is a key component of the intended effect. (That is, if you blocked out the picture and relied only on the words, you would have trouble understanding what the advertisement was about.) Use the checklist to assess the imagery: Identify all its relevant features and explain what the intended effect is. Then explain how the imagery succeeds—or fails—in creating that effect. Which elements of the imagery succeed, and why? Which elements of the imagery are problematic, and why? Based on your explanation, decide whether the images are or are not appropriately chosen.

EXERCISE **9.4**

Choosing Imagery

What imagery would you choose, and why, for the following:

1. An advertisement promoting public transit
2. A campaign to limit cellphone use by drivers
3. A poster for a choral festival
4. A picture to brighten a cancer treatment room
5. A workplace safety poster reminding people to use safety glasses

Soundscape

We can ask the same questions of auditory elements as we have done of visual elements. Just as with images, a soundtrack can be well suited or poorly suited to its purpose. Listen to TV shows or advertisements without facing the screen, and you will hear what has been added to enhance the impact of the words.

For example, a hairstylist who was recording a makeover show for television found that the interviews after the makeover sounded too solemn because they had been taped in a very quiet location. Adding soft music in the background brought the interviews back to life, making the people sound as happy as they really had been. Music can also change a message by clashing with what you see: eerie music to create tension in a calm scene, or calm music to accompany scenes of disaster. Music can suggest that all is not as it seems, or it can suggest that our reaction ought not to be the obvious one. The Soviet film director Sergei Eisenstein helped to write a manifesto declaring that soundtracks ought to create sharp discord with the film imagery in order to cultivate critical thinking in the audience (Ross 102).

The soundscape, even more than the imagery, is likely to evoke an emotional response, so it needs to be examined as carefully as you examine any appeal to emotion. First, you need to review the details that you identified and investigated earlier: the sounds you hear, what they evoke, and what the intended effect seems to be. Listen for the overall impression you get. What details help give that impression?

Checklist for Assessing Auditory Information

✔ To what extent do the sounds support the intended effect?

✔ Is that effect a fair and reasonable one to create in the context?

✔ Can you explain your reasoning? Why do the sounds support (or fail to support) the overall message? How well do you think the sounds support the message?

EXERCISE **Evaluating Choice of Sound and Choosing Appropriate Music**

*1. Pick an advertisement or a short (one- to two-minute) passage from a movie or TV show. Evaluate the soundscape using the criteria above.

2. What music would you choose, if any, and why, for the following:
   a. An advertisement promoting public transit
   b. A campaign to reduce tuition fees
   c. A TV spot for your local MP running for reelection
   d. A movie scene featuring lovers reuniting after years apart
   e. A ballet or modern dance piece mocking materialism

Evaluating Emotions as Reasons

What are emotions signalling and how do we evaluate our emotional insight? In this section, you'll develop a deeper understanding of how these emotional clues can work in context to contribute to good reasoning.

Emotions can be a signal that something significant is at stake. Like intuition, emotions can often be reasonable guides to how you should approach a problem and how you should act. This is because emotions can be clues to your own values and the values of others. Such clues can reveal influential elements of a situation that have not been verbally expressed.

If you feel really upset at the thought of moving, this can indicate there is something important to you about the place you live now and the people there. If you can figure out what is important to you, you'll be able to tell what you will need in a new home to feel equally happy, or whether you ought not to move at all. The recognition of the feeling can also reasonably lead you to check that you are not ignoring certain relevant aspects of the situation simply because of the feeling. If you are afraid, that can be a good reason not to proceed further. (See Gavin de Becker's book *The Gift of Fear,* about the importance of recognizing and respecting your own fears as a way to avoid assault or abuse.)

Most emotions are responses to some triggering belief or perception. An emotion therefore can give us information about the trigger as well as giving us information about ourselves. In some situations, our emotions are responses to details of a situation we are not even consciously aware of. For example, you may feel an instant liking for a new acquaintance and feel very at ease in her company and only later realize that she has some of the same mannerisms as your favourite cousin. Subliminal stimuli can trigger emotions and therefore the emotion can give us information about the trigger that we have not had a chance to notice in a non-emotional way. Sometimes that information will be about ourselves (e.g., "this situation is frightening to me"), but other times the information will be about the situation (e.g., "this situation is very dangerous and I need to find a way out.")

When discussing emotions as reasons for beliefs and actions, we must nevertheless be cautious in the role we allow emotions to play in reasoning. While emotions can be relevant and reliable guides, emotions can also be highly unreliable guides to action: constant fear, whether you're on a busy street or in a deserted parking garage, is not a good indicator that you are constantly under threat. The depth of your emotional attachment to a person or place is not by itself a good indicator that you should never let go and move on. The evaluation stage requires us to focus on determining when emotions are part of good reasoning.

When are emotions good reasons to believe or do something?

Emotions as Sources of Information

We have claimed that emotions are often indicators of deeply held values and commitments. They can give you clues to your own hidden attitudes and clues to the attitudes of the people you are interacting with. In short, one reason we should not ignore emotions when reasoning is because emotions can be a source of information. You've been encouraged to take note of other people's emotions. It is not only your own feelings that should play a role in your decision-making. What you can gather about other people's feelings can also give you good reason to act one way rather than another.

Imagine your eight-year-old daughter approaches you with a school friend and asks if she can go over to the friend's house to play. She is verbally asking to go, but she appears to be sad or worried and you know she usually prefers to have her friends over to her house for the first play date. So you decide to suggest that your daughter's friend play at your house instead.

In this scenario, it is reasonable to make this suggestion based on your understanding of your daughter's emotions. It is reasonable because you know your daughter very well and can be fairly certain that you've accurately recognized her emotion and the object and causes of it. Moreover, your daughter is not an adult, and the risk is very small when your action is simply to suggest alternative plans.

How much you rely on your apprehension of an emotion should depend on the accuracy of that apprehension. Are you quite sure that your daughter is worried? Could it be a mixture of excitement and shyness? If you have accurately pinpointed her emotion, are you sure that she is worried about going to the friend's house? Could she be worried about the piano lesson that will take place at home after dinner?

When assessing our observation of our own emotions or the emotions of others as a source of information, we need to consider the accuracy and the relevance of that emotional information. The guiding questions you need to ask are these:

Checklist for Using Emotions as Sources of Information

✔ How certain am I that I've correctly identified the emotion?

We've seen that in identifying emotions in others we look at body language, facial expression, and past experience. But we also need to rely on what other people tell us about their emotions. Our own emotions can lead us to make mistaken assumptions about what others are feeling. We each have privileged access to what we are feeling, so it is easier to recognize our own emotions, but there is also room for error in the recognition of our own emotions. For example, is your feeling best described as anger or jealousy?

✔ Can I accurately identify the object and causes of the emotion?

If you're angry or anxious right now, is that because you've just been having a bad day, or is it because there really is something here now that's upsetting you? Is it "just you" or is it the situation? In other words, are these emotions genuinely relevant to the situation, or are they a delayed or inappropriate reaction caused by something unrelated to the situation?

✔ Is the information I can gather from the emotion relevant to the situation at hand?

In a particular situation, you may have strong emotions that provide you with information about your own values and even the world around you, but that information might not be relevant to the task before you. Because of its motivating power, emotional information, more than any other information, needs to be assessed for relevance. As a lawyer you might feel disgust at the actions of a client; that disgust might be a good indication of your own values and commitments, but that emotion is rarely, if ever, relevant to what legal advice you should give the client.

(Continued)

✔   How much risk do I take if my assessment of the emotion is incorrect?

You are usually on safe ground in allowing your observations of emotions to affect how you broach an issue or what suggestions you make. However, you must carefully consider whether your understanding of the emotion gives you sufficient reason to act or form beliefs in the given situation.

A clear case of it being unreasonable to act based on how you think someone feels is the excuse given in many date rape cases: "She said no, but I could tell that she really loved me and felt desire for me—she really meant yes." This situation is in clear contrast to the situation where your daughter says yes to going to a friend's house but you believe she really means no. The date rape scenario passes none of the suggested assessment tests. The aggressor could not be sure that what he perceived as the victim's emotion was really what she was feeling. Even if he had been trying to accurately observe his victim's emotions, he has been given conflicting evidence in the form of her saying no. He should have given greater weight to her words than any other indication of how she is feeling and considered other possible reasons for the body language he thought he saw. He has not considered how his own emotions may be blinding him to important and relevant aspects of the situation. Clearly, there is also a problem of relevance. The aggressor's understanding of the victim's emotion has nothing to do with whether he is entitled to act without her permission. Finally, the risk he took if his assessment was wrong was too great. Being wrong meant committing assault and ignoring the rights and dignity of another human being. He also broke the law. These two examples illustrate extremes in the impact of emotional information. Most situations will fall somewhere between the extremes.

When trying to assess the accuracy and relevance of information presented to us by emotions, we must recognize that emotions are very powerful forces in our lives. Our emotional reactions are not always caused by, or in proportion to, what we are actually experiencing in a particular situation. We should try to notice when arguments or statements are presented to us in emotional terms and be careful not to accept them just because of the emotions that they arouse. Just because a claim makes you feel good, that does not mean it is true. Just because a claim makes you feel angry or unhappy, that does not mean it must be false.

We have to be wary of emotional reactions because emotional reactions are hard to change. They can be like habits forged in childhood and hard to break. Suppose that as you grew up you believed the old house on the corner was haunted. Whenever it was dark, you ran past the house in fear. Now you are grown and you don't believe in ghosts, but you may still have an emotional reaction when you walk by the house. The emotion is a hangover from a previous belief.

Perhaps you were raised in a family of racists and despite rejecting their beliefs you still find yourself distrusting people of a certain ethnic heritage. If you have a negative emotional reaction to a person from an ethnic group that you were raised to mistrust, you cannot be sure your emotion is an unconscious awareness of good reasons to mistrust the person. Sometimes emotions are responses to cues that we learned as children and later reject. An immediate, emotional response to a person is not always a good reason to believe that the person has flaws. There are too many other possible reasons for the emotion.

Another reason to look carefully at emotional reactions when reasoning is that emotions are closely linked with physiology. Your physical state affects your emotions. Whether you have had too much coffee, have not had enough sleep, are fighting off a cold, have a hangover, or suffer from depression, your body affects your emotional reactions. For example, one effect of depression can be to distort your emotions until nothing seems to matter much any more. Feeling too little emotion is as much a warning sign as feeling too much. You may be able to make logical connections just as well as when you were not depressed, but you may give too little weight to them. You may be able to work out all the risks and benefits of dropping out of school, but not be able to care whether you can still graduate or whether you are going to find yourself unemployed with no chance of a job.

So far, we have suggested that emotions can be part of good reasoning because they can provide us with information. When considering the information gathered through observing and investigating our emotions, we need to treat it like other information and test it for accuracy, relevance, and sufficiency. In the next section, we'll consider when emotions count as good reasons not because they give us information, but just because we are feeling them. Are there cases in which it is reasonable to do something just because you are scared or in love or feel pity for someone? Is a feeling itself ever a sufficient reason to act or form a belief? You may worry that if you allow emotions to play a role in critical thinking, then anyone can justify any belief or action just by saying they felt like doing or believing a certain thing. A thief could say, "I stole the car because it made me happy," yet the happiness is not a good reason for the theft. We certainly don't want to say that an emotion is always a sufficient reason to do or believe something. However, there are some situations in which emotions themselves are good reasons because they add further support to other good reasons or are by themselves sufficient to make a belief or action reasonable. The next three sections illustrate how emotions can be good reasons.

Emotions as Motivators

Sometimes an emotion can be a good reason to do something or even to maintain a belief because the emotion itself is due to good reasoning about a situation. When an emotion is based on a reasonable apprehension of a situation, it can work as a motivating factor and count as a good reason to do something. It can be the case that an emotion will stay with you long after the reasoning has become hazy. For example, you may have decided that by going back to university you will be able to achieve your goal of being the first person in your family with a university degree. You believe that this is a good goal because it will give you a better education and better job opportunities, allow you to serve as a role model for your younger siblings, and help other family members. There may be times when what keeps you going to class and working in the library is that feeling of pride associated with your thoughts of attaining your goal. Is that a bad reason to keep going? No—not if the emotion is part and parcel of motivating you to achieve a goal that you've reasonably established as good.

Emotions as Tiebreakers

Emotions may also be weighed as sufficient reasons for action in situations where adding up non-emotional reasons does not give you an answer. If you need to choose between two different options and there are equally good reasons to do both, then emotions can reasonably tip the balance. Emotions can be legitimate tiebreakers.

For example, suppose a doctor has offered two different options for a coma patient, and you, as the loving relative, must decide between them. The doctor believes both options make good medical sense, and it really is a question of what the coma patient would have wanted. You feel worried about one option, and sad but relieved to know about the other. You really aren't sure what the coma patient would have wanted. The second option makes you feel more comfortable, and when you consent to the second option, you feel you've done the right thing. You are more at ease. In this case, the emotions have provided tiebreaking reasons for the decision and affirmation that you made the right choice.

Emotions as Goals

We need to remember that emotions are not just part of the process of reaching a decision but often part of the goal as well. Another case in which an emotion may count as a sufficient reason to believe that you should or should not do something occurs when part of the desired outcome of the decision is an emotional state. For example, you're considering going on a new roller coaster but the very thought of it terrifies you. In this case, the fear is good enough reason not to go on the roller coaster because the point of the roller coaster is to have fun and you're unlikely to have fun if you are terrified just at the thought of buying a ticket. A certain emotional state of enjoyment is the goal, and your current emotion is a good indication that goal won't be met on the roller coaster.

The financial advisor scenario introduced in Chapter 4 (page 130) presents a tougher case. It sets up a situation in which your gut feelings trigger emotions that are at odds with your intellectual knowledge. You feel suspicious of the financial advisor, but he has excellent recommendations from people you trust. The scenario prompts you to think about whether emotions or intellect should be trusted when they are at odds with each other. Here, the emotions probably will not be the deciding factor. Your desired goal is not an emotional state—it is a healthy financial situation. Other factors are probably not equal: there will be more objective ways to tell whether this advisor's qualifications are best for your needs. And although your emotions may be indicating an unconscious aspect of the situation that makes you uneasy, the emotion by itself is not enough to conclude that you ought to be uneasy.

> ### Checklist for Assessing Emotions in Reasoning
> When can emotions be weighed as good reasons?
>
> ✔ when they provide relevant information and have been confirmed as useful sources of information
>
> ✔ when they legitimately tip the balance in favour of a particular course of action because all other factors are even
>
> ✔ when they are relevant to the desired outcome of the decision because the desired outcome is to be in a particular emotional state
>
> ✔ when they are based on a reasonable apprehension of a situation and help motivate you to follow through on a well-reasoned decision

Appeals to Emotion in Arguments

An appeal to emotion occurs in an argument when someone tries to persuade you to believe or do something by using one or more premises meant to evoke an emotion in you. The emotion as well as the explicitly stated premise is intended to motivate you to accept the conclusion. Arguments that appeal to emotion can be powerfully persuasive, and if your goal is to persuade, you'll find that adding an appeal to emotion to your argument can help you meet that goal. For example, you think your roommate should help clean up the apartment. You argue, "There's far too much for one person to do alone. The vacuuming needs to be done, the fridge needs cleaning, and we both need to be out in an hour." So far, your premises are simply listing the amount of work and the time to do it. Your roommate seems unmoved: the vacuuming and the fridge could easily wait until tomorrow. You quickly add, "And I've had such a rough week. I really want to come back later to a clean apartment." These added premises evoke sympathy in your roommate, who agrees to vacuum if you clean the fridge.

There are appeals to emotion that are not in arguments. Images can also appeal to your emotions: the beautiful ski trail that fills you with joy, or the scratch on your car that makes you angry just to see it. Sometimes you can appeal to emotions with facial expressions and the way you word a request: you smile and call the person by name, evoking pleasure.

When should you accept an appeal to emotion as providing support for a conclusion—in effect, strengthening the argument as opposed to weakening it?

We appeal to the conditions we have already set for judging whether premises provide the right level and type of support for their conclusion. If the premises that evoke the emotion are part of a good argument and the emotion they are meant to evoke adds another good reason on top of the premises to accept the conclusion, then the appeal to emotion is acceptable. If the premises that evoke the emotion are part of a bad argument or if the emotion evoked is a bad reason to accept the conclusion, then the argument contains a mistaken appeal to emotion. An appeal to emotion fails under any of the following conditions:

- the emotion is evoked by false premises
- the emotion is evoked by premises irrelevant to the conclusion

- the emotion is evoked by premises insufficient for you to make the conclusion reasonable

- the argument is otherwise good but the emotion the arguer attempts to evoke is a bad reason to accept the conclusion

- the appeal to emotion changes the context of the interaction and shifts the focus of the argument

We'll look at each of these considerations in turn.

Emotion Evoked by False Premises

When an emotion is evoked due to a premise that is unreasonable, acting or forming a belief based on that emotion would be unreasonable.

For example, a young man approaches you with tears in his eyes and says, "Please help me! I don't know where to turn. My wallet has been stolen and it had my bus ticket in it. I have to catch the next bus to Calgary because my father's funeral is tomorrow and I promised my poor mother that I'd be there to support her. I don't have any friends here who can lend me money. If you could just lend me $50 I swear to you that I'll send you the money as soon as I get home."

This is an attempt to persuade you to do something that does not just rely on the reasons presented. It relies on evoking pity and sympathy in you. Whether the emotion strengthens the argument by being extra support for the claim that you should give money to this man will depend on if his story is credible. The problem with this argument is not that the man is appealing to your emotions. The real problem with the argument is that he might be lying. In other words, the premises that are triggering your emotion could very well be false. It would be unreasonable for you to do what is asked based on what the man has said if you do some fact or credibility checking and discover that his story is false and he is untrustworthy.

If you discover that the man's story is credible and you don't have any information that might defeat the argument (for example, you don't have $50), then it is reasonable to lend the money. The emotion evoked is a good motivation, added to the stated premises, to act and believe that you are doing the right thing. The emotion can be a good reason in this scenario, because it can supplement the argument by indicating the value you place on the happiness of others and the importance you place on helping others.

Emotion Evoked by Irrelevant Premises

Often arguers attempt to persuade you to believe something by evoking emotions that are not relevant to the issue at hand. This is usually done through the use of irrelevant premises. Believing or acting based on an emotion evoked by irrelevant premises would be a failure to notice a weakness in the reasoning of the argument.

For example: "You should sign up for our fitness program, and I'll tell you why. We have excellent equipment and facilities. We charge a bit more than the other fitness clubs in this area—we're worth it. You wouldn't want to miss out on our special deal you can get by signing up right now. Join us today." This sale pitch intends to evoke fear in you, enticing you to sign up for this program as the route to your fitness goals. Take out the appeal to emotion, and you are left only with the information that the equipment and facilities are excellent, and the prices higher than other clubs. That information does not provide nearly enough support to make it probable that you will sign up. Do the equipment and programs meet your needs? Do the hours and location suit your schedule? Are you the kind of person to stay with a fitness program if you've committed yourself to paying for it, which leads to another question: can you afford it? The premises have not answered any of these important questions. Fear may rush you into a deal that is not right for you. The premise that evokes the fear is irrelevant to any of the criteria by which you would decide if this facility is right for you.

In the example in the previous section, the pity you might feel for the young man who really needs bus fare is based on relevant premises: the predicament of not being able to get home for a funeral evokes pity that is relevant to whether you will choose to spend your $50 for bus fare.

Emotion Evoked by Insufficient Premises

Sometimes the premises evoking the emotion will be relevant to the conclusion and acceptable but will be insufficient to establish the conclusion. For example: "The poor little bear cub is all alone and looks so sweet and cuddly. We should go and feed him some of our food and play with him to cheer him up."

The premise attempting to evoke emotion is relevant to the conclusion that we should feed the bear cub. The emotion of affectionate concern, too, is relevant, since it can be a good reason to try to help. However, the fact that the bear cub is alone and cute coupled with the fact that we feel sorry for it is not sufficient reason to play with it. A bear cub may appear to be alone when its mother is nearby, hidden in the bush because she is more wary of people. Given the danger of playing with and feeding wild animals, even if the bear cub is alone you would be unwise to approach it to feed or play with it. The premises do not give enough support for the conclusion. The emotions of affection and concern are not sufficient to reasonably override considerations of the safety of yourself and the cub.

We've already considered some examples in the previous section where emotion can be judged as a good reason to take action. Similarly, if the premises of an argument provide enough support for their conclusion, and they evoke an emotion that supplements the argument by providing another good reason to accept the conclusion, then the appeal to emotion is acceptable. After you have evaluated the argument as good, the emotion evoked by the premises can serve as an additional reason to accept the conclusion. For example, if you know the young man is telling the truth about needing bus fare, and his story has evoked your pity, that may well be sufficient reason for you to help him. The happy feeling you get from helping someone in a pitiable situation may be a goal you want to achieve.

Appeals to Irrelevant Emotions

So far we've looked at cases where the problem with the appeal to emotion can be clearly located in the premises. The problem in these arguments is not the appeal to emotion but the way emotion is used to mask flawed reasoning.

There are cases where the error in appealing to emotion is not located within the argument, because the argument is good. However, the appeal to emotion evokes an emotion irrelevant to the argument.

For example, an argument can make the mistake of appealing to an emotion that is a bad reason to accept the conclusion. Sometimes this mistake occurs when an irrelevant premise meant to evoke an emotion is thrown in for good measure. For example, "She owes me money for the rent because she signed an agreement when she became my roommate saying that she'd pay half the rent and she hasn't paid her share for two whole months. Plus she ruined my life by sleeping with my boyfriend!" The speaker is trying to create an emotional response in order to motivate the listener to agree with the argument. But allowing the appeal to emotion to be persuasive would be a mistake in this case because feeling sorry for the speaker is not a good reason to believe she is owed rent. This type of emotional appeal might be a successful ploy on the part of the speaker, but when evaluating the argument, it should be seen as a mistaken appeal to an irrelevant emotion. This argument, however, is easily fixed by removing the irrelevant premise that appeals to emotion.

An otherwise good argument can also contain an unreasonable appeal to emotion when it attempts to evoke an irrelevant emotion through premises that are in fact relevant to establishing the stated conclusion. This can be done through loaded and descriptive language. Let's take the same example, but leave out the explicitly irrelevant premise. Now the argument is "That manipulative and greedy woman owes me rent money because she freely signed an agreement when I welcomed her into my home as my roommate. That agreement said she would pay her fair share of the rent. Despite that signed agreement of trust, she has taken advantage of me and hasn't lived up to her commitment for two whole months." In this case, the attempts to evoke emotion are piled onto relevant premises. But the emotion of pity is a bad reason to believe the speaker is owed rent money because it is irrelevant. Your pity for this woman is not a good reason to believe she is owed rent. In this case, the matter of who owes what should be decided based on the agreement that was signed. In this case, an otherwise good argument contains a mistaken appeal to emotion.

Problems with unreasonable appeals to emotion may be the reason why so many formal dispute resolution and decision-making procedures try to suppress or contain emotions. A witness who cries in court may be handed a tissue to wipe away tears, but the sadness cannot be used by the judge or jury in justifying a verdict. The formal processes may go too far in ignoring the information revealed by emotion. As we have shown, emotion can be an important source of relevant information.

Emotions That Shift the Focus of the Argument

The final example we will consider is one in which the appeal to emotion is used as a transition to move from one argument to another argument. In these cases, the value of the appeal to emotion depends on which argument it is really being linked to. The fault does not lie in the premises or their connection to the conclusion, but in the way in which two completely separate arguments have been linked. Appeals to emotion are mistakes if they switch the context of the argument so that the effect is the unexpected abandonment of one argument and the picking up of another without clearly indicating that change is occurring. The issue is not changing, but the ground rules are shifting unexpectedly, and you can make a mistake in your reasoning if you do not recognize this shift.

For example, consider the following short dialogue:

Mia: I am sure I will be able to convince you that our group should do assignment topic 1. This topic is interesting, we've already done some initial research, and my friend worked on this topic last year and got a very good grade.

Sandra: I don't see how your friend's grade last year is really relevant in making our decision.

Mia: Well, let me put it this way. If we don't do topic 1, then I'm not doing any of the work and if you think you can tell the instructor . . . I can make your lives very miserable.

In this example, Mia's last comments are relevant to the main issue of whether the group should work on topic 1. Also, the fact that she won't work and can harm other group members may even (in some situations) be sufficient reason to choose topic 1. But notice how Mia switched tactics. If Sandra now accepts the initial argument based on the final threat, she will be making a mistake in reasoning. The worry that the threat creates does not help the initial argument. Sandra needs to recognize that the first argument has been abandoned and the threat actually belongs in a new argument, one in which it is the only premise: If you don't choose topic 1, I will make your lives miserable. So you should choose topic 1.

In this last kind of example, it is important to recognize that it is no longer the original argument that needs to be evaluated. The arguer herself has already abandoned it and moved to a different set of premises that create a different argument for the same conclusion. If Sandra recognizes the shift to a new argument, she can evaluate the appeal to emotion by considering the criteria for evaluating arguments already introduced, including evaluating emotions as reasons.

EXERCISE **9.6**

Evaluating Emotions as Reasons

1. Describe two situations in which an emotion is a good reason and two situations in which an emotion is a poor reason to act or form a belief. Explain your views for each situation.

2. State whether the arguments below involve reasonable or unreasonable appeals to emotion. Explain your answers.
   a. I have worked all day, I'm wiped right out, and company is coming. I'm feeling really lousy and I could use some help in straightening up the house. Since you aren't doing anything else, could you please, please take pity on me and help?
   *b. I have worked for this company for twenty years. I have helped boost sales, and I have contributed ideas that have helped increase the

company's productivity. I deserve a raise, and if I do not get one, I will have to find a job elsewhere.

*c. Small children are living in terrible poverty through no fault of their own. They live in hovels, have polluted drinking water, and must try to survive on very little food. Some of these innocent and helpless children are dying of starvation as we speak. Can't you find it in your heart to help? All of us should give generously to the Children's Fund.

d. I think this is the perfect job for you because it is in your field, it pays well, and the hours are pretty good. I am just so exhausted from helping you with your job search. I'm doing all the mailing and answering phones for you. I need a break and you should think about me now and then.

e. Francis is an awful guy. He never spends time with his children and I think he's forgotten his wife's name. He spends half his day working out at the gym and the other half drinking at the pub. You simply should not accept that argument he presented in class today about evolution. How could you agree with him?

f. You should see Jasminder's new baby! She's so tiny and sweet. She has that wonderful new-baby smell. Your kids are getting so big. It's definitely time for you to have another baby.

g. We have asked for a three percent wage increase and we are firm on that number. If you do not meet our demands, the union has no choice but to hold a strike vote.

3. Whom would you personally want to make decisions on your health care if you were in a coma, and why? Think about specific people in your life and why you might choose one over another. Explain your choice.

4. What would your best course of action be if you felt uneasy about a financial advisor who was objectively very well qualified to advise you? Would you immediately seek another advisor, would you investigate further before making a decision, or would you set your doubts aside and give this advisor a chance? Think about a specific financial situation for which you can imagine yourself needing to seek advice. Explain your choice.

Evaluating Options: What Suggestions Are Practical?

What do you need in order to move from rational belief to responsible action? You have already decided whether you can accept an argument, whether you can reject an argument, or whether you must suspend judgment. You also know what the key issues and crucial points of disagreement are. You have assessed reasons that are not part of an argument. How can you translate that into action? You look for possible actions that are consistent with the rational belief—actions you might reasonably suggest as ways to make progress. Then you evaluate the suggestions to see if they are practical.

Reasonable options for action must be practical. To identify practical options, you may need to generate a number of suggestions. Some suggestions will not be obvious. There will be situations where it is not obvious what to suggest, but it is important not to stop because you are stuck. If you have an issue in which the same points are repeated without any apparent progress, or a problem situation in which the same events occur over and over, only a new suggestion might get you out of the repeating cycle. You may have to step back to the investigation stage and see what options may have been overlooked, or what further options can be generated by brainstorming. In difficult and controversial situations, it is an asset to be able to brainstorm some unusual possibilities. The more unusual your suggestion, the less likely it is that other people will have already thought of objections to it. You have a better chance of slowing them down to consider the chances of making progress. For this kind of brainstorming, it helps to make yourself come up with ideas that rule out the obvious. For example, when we think of ways to encourage more people to use public transit, the most common suggestion is to increase the price of gasoline. To brainstorm new ideas, we need to ask how we could get more people to use public transportation *without* raising the price of gasoline.

You can brainstorm options for action just as you brainstormed alternatives in Chapter 6—think of as many ideas as you can without ruling anything out. For example, when a group considers fundraising activities, it might list everything from bingo nights and fashion shows to door-to-door chocolate bar sales and raffles. Seeing the full range of options helps the group realize the suggestion to sell a new product may not be the best possible option. Comparing door-to-door sales with other fundraising methods helps ensure the group is choosing the best method for its purpose, not just the best door-to-door product.

The next step is to check the alternatives for practicality. Some suggestions will seem unlikely to work at all. Some will take too long to arrange, or will cost too much, or will require resources or skills you don't have. It is again a brainstorming step to see which factors you must check to ensure a suggestion is practical.

Checklist for Assessing Practicality

For practical options in any situation, you may need to check any or all of the following:

✔ Cost
✔ Time involved
✔ Lead time or preparation time—bookings, shipping, assembling
✔ Number of people required, scheduling, availability, coordination, supervision
✔ Skills needed
✔ Resources needed—transportation, hall rental
✔ Supplies
✔ Risk management—insurance or procedures to cover loss, injury, defective products
✔ Values—is the method compatible with the group's objectives?

Identifying Practical Options

Generate a list of ten possible options, then narrow them down to three practical suggestions you could personally support on each of these topics:

*a. Reducing water consumption in areas of the country that face water shortages

b. Encouraging people to drink more water every day

c. Reducing the risks of childhood obesity

d. Handling situations of bullying in schools

e. Reducing the chances that students can cheat on essay questions

Evaluating Options

Depending on the stage an issue or situation has reached, you may need to tailor your options to that specific stage or they will not seem helpful.

If the debate is far advanced or a deadline is rapidly closing in, it may be necessary to emphasize solutions and actions. For example, if there has already been extensive debate about the unemployment and related problems caused by closing a mine, people will probably want to hear possible solutions, not more argument.

If there are any aspects of the issue or the information that are unproven, you know from your evaluation that the best plan will be to suggest a study or test that can pick out which of the alternatives is most probably correct.

If the dispute is deadlocked and people are far apart on the main issues, you may want to suggest new questions about principles, to encourage people to reexamine their assumptions and view the problem from new perspectives.

When you are making a suggestion for progress on an issue, you must make sure that your suggestions are consistent with what has been agreed on, and that you yourself could live with any of the suggestions. It makes no sense to recommend a course of action that you personally could not support, even if you think one side would be very happy with it.

You will also need to be able to justify your suggestions with good reasoning as needed. If you have just said no to someone, or if you're taking action quickly without waiting for further information, the people affected by your action may be entitled to know your reasoning. For example, if the government doesn't accept a court decision that single parents shouldn't have to pay tax on the child support they receive, why not? If the doctor wants to send you straight from her office to the hospital, why?

Suppose you want to be able to help victims of a natural disaster. Often, the impulse to help translates into immediate action to send money or supplies, but this may not be the best response. After the attack on the World Trade Center on September 11, 2001, people around the world sent money—more money, it turned out, than was needed to support relief efforts and compensate individuals. After the tsunami in the Indian Ocean on December 26, 2004, people around the world sent supplies, including winter coats, high-heeled shoes, and other items of no use in tropical seaside villages. Even some apparently useful supplies won't help as much as you might expect. For example, baby bottles that need to be sterilized cannot safely be used where there is no boiling water to sterilize them. Experienced aid societies will survey the needs of the population or will have policies in place as to what they will accept. Asking, "What can I give that is needed?" will be a more practical first step than simply dropping money into a collection box or gathering up supplies to send. Should you, for example, start an initiative in your town to sponsor a specific village that needs help?

Similarly, if you are preparing for an emergency that might hit your own home, such as a prolonged power outage in a winter storm, or a spring flood, or an earthquake, you have several options to increase your chances of survival. You might buy a recommended "emergency kit" with food, water, flashlights, blankets, a first-aid kit, and other supplies. If you can afford the emergency kit, that is one practical solution. If you hike or camp, you probably have many supplies you'd be able to draw on in an emergency, and pulling together what you already have may be a more practical option. You might take a course on emergency preparedness to give you the knowledge you need to act safely in an emergency, or you might take a first-aid course. If courses like this are offered at work or near your home, this may be a practical solution. If no courses are nearby and you live with someone who already has extensive training, a more practical solution may be to ask this person to help you practise some emergency drills, such as turning off the water or gas in your home. (If you are interested in preparing for emergencies, several websites offer help; see Natural Resources Canada at **www.pgc.nrcan.gc.ca/seismo/eqinfo/prep.htm** and B.C.'s Provincial Emergency Program at **www.pep.bc.ca.**)

EXERCISE 9.8

Planning Ahead

1. You have just agreed to take on a big project. It is going to require you to keep track of more details than you are used to, including people's names, contacts' phone numbers and e-mail addresses, deadlines, whether other people in the project are on schedule and what they are doing, and so on. It is likely that during the project you will experience some periods of stress that will impair your concentration and energy. What practical options could help you keep track of everything so that you don't lose any important information, miss any deadlines, or let anybody down?

2. The best training for the kind of job you want is at an institution in another province. You will need to be away for a minimum of nine months if you take the training. You have recently begun a relationship with someone, and the two of you have just moved in together. It is not realistic for this person to leave his or her job or schooling to come with you. What practical options might help you find a way to deal with this dilemma?

3. You discover that your current grades are not high enough to get you into the program you want. What practical options are open to you?

Key Points in Review

- Evaluating *in context* means checking the impact that an argument or some information ought to have on the context in which it is presented. This is the stage at which you separate the valuable information from the unhelpful information, and the practical options from the impractical ones.

- To evaluate arguments in context means comparing different arguments on the same topic so that we can see what they teach us about the issue they address and what will be the most reasonable direction in which to proceed.

- Visual, auditory, numerical, and emotional information is often used to enhance or support an intended effect. We can evaluate all these elements according to whether they succeed or fail in their intended impact. They may be legitimate or illegitimate attempts to influence you. They may be acceptable or unacceptable, relevant or irrelevant, and sufficient or insufficient for their purpose.

- To evaluate solutions or plans of action, we determine their practicality in the given context. Are we ready for that type of action, or is further study needed? Do the solutions fit within our budget, and do they use the resources and skills we actually have available?

Part 3
Summary

Getting the Best out of Evaluation

One cool judgment is worth a thousand hasty counsels. The thing to do is to supply light and not heat.
— *Woodrow Wilson*

Evaluation Overview

In critical observation and investigation, we emphasized objectivity and open-mindedness. Now, the emphasis has turned to fair evaluation and sound judgment. Evaluation is an essential part of the critical thinking cycle. Observation and investigation will have led you to be well prepared to evaluate the claims, arguments, and other elements of any situation you have been thinking about. All the research you have done must be sifted through and evaluated for relevance, sufficiency, and credibility. Consider which sources you can discount and which sources you must accept as authoritative. Part of evaluating your own investigation is determining whether it has been sufficient. Has the information you have uncovered proved relevant to judging the truth or falsity of claims or relevant to constructing your own considered opinion on an issue?

The investigation stage has already made you familiar with the standards of good reasoning, but in the evaluation stage you must apply those standards in order to evaluate arguments. Has the argument met the criteria of premise acceptability, relevance, sufficiency, and indefeasibility? Nonverbal aspects of the situation you are considering must also be taken into account. Now is the time to evaluate the role of images, numbers, sounds, and emotions. Complete and reasonable evaluation of the problem or argument is the best way to prepare for the next stage in the critical thinking cycle: response.

Part-Ending Exercises

Comprehension Questions: Review

1. How can you distinguish between credible information and information we should not take seriously?

2. Is it ever reasonable to believe something just because someone has said it is true? Explain.

3. List statements that you believe are acceptable. Explain why you find them acceptable.

4. What is a good argument?

5. What is an unproven argument?

6. What is a poor argument?

7. Give an example of an argument that does not pass the test of relevance.

8. Give an example of an argument that does not pass the test of indefeasibility.

9. Give examples of three different types of fallacies. Explain why they are mistakes in reasoning.

10. If an argument is poor, does that mean the conclusion is false? Explain.

11. If an argument is good, does that mean the conclusion is true? Explain.

12. How can imagery create an effect in a viewer?

13. In what ways can emotions count as good reasons?

14. Why do we need to be careful when weighing emotions in reasoning?

15. Are all appeals to emotions mistaken? Explain.

Application Exercises

1. Take one argument from your collection and fully evaluate the argument.

2. Consider situations in which you've allowed emotions to motivate you. In retrospect, were the emotions good reasons or not? Explain.

Where do you go from here? Now that you have analyzed and evaluated the information available to you, you know you have rational beliefs. Now that you have evaluated possible solutions, you know you have practical options open to you. How do you move from rational beliefs to responsible actions? That last step is challenging, because rational beliefs and practical options don't by themselves guarantee that you can carry out your plans. Nor can you stop short of taking action. Very little critical thinking is done purely for our own insight, in contexts where all we have to do is decide what we will believe. Class assignments, work projects, and family disputes are all instances of situations in which other people expect your input or leadership. To respond to their needs and to your own, you need to be able to set reasonable priorities and suggest the best next steps.

In addition, the moment you present your evaluation of an argument or a situation to other people, you must make choices about how you are going to interact with them. At this stage, we are faced with one of the difficulties of reasoning: not everybody values reasoning in the same way. This means that not everyone will be equally open to relying on reason in choosing their actions, and not everybody will welcome you presenting your own reasoning.

There are two key components to responding effectively. You will need to work out

■ what actions you might take or suggest to others (Chapters 10 and 11)

■ how you will present your proposals so you can respect other people's needs and beliefs as well as your own (Chapter 12)

Chapter 10

Moving Forward: Principles of Constructive Response

■ Perspective

The final step in thinking critically is acting responsibly. Have you completed everything that is expected of you, to the standard expected? Are there suggestions to be made or actions to be taken? In this chapter, you will see how to use the results of evaluation to plan an appropriate response.

■ Scenario

Your computer crashed at the worst possible time. You have an important project due, and nowhere near enough time to redo your work or even get to another computer easily. What is it most important to do, and in what order?

■ Key Question

What's the best next step?

Setting Realistic Priorities

As you move from evaluating to acting, you need to set realistic priorities. It is important to be neither overcritical—trying to do too much and being unable to manage it all—nor undercritical—simply doing nothing and hoping everything will somehow sort itself out without you. In the sample scenario above, it would be overcritical to try to fix the computer and somehow restore the project so quickly that nobody else is inconvenienced by your problems. It would be undercritical just to throw up your hands and do nothing more than tell the person expecting the project that there's nothing you can do because your computer crashed. What you actually would do first in such a situation will not be the same for everyone. Some people might dive straight in to try to fix the computer itself, because they love the challenge and they're good at it. Others will abandon the computer immediately and go to work on finding a way to meet the needs of the person who wanted the project in some other way that will work around the delay. No matter how different their abilities or reactions, each critical thinker should still be asking, "What's the best next step for me in this situation?" That is, good reasoners need to set realistic priorities.

Remember that reasoning is a cycle. You collect information, assess options, propose actions, and re-define the problems and issues as you go. So far, you have asked and answered all the following questions.

1. What exactly am I dealing with, and what do I already know and have that can help me? (observation: Chapter 1)

2. Why is this (situation, event, etc.) the way it is? What additional information do I need to help me? (investigation: Chapter 4) What options could we consider? (investigation: Chapter 6)

3. Which options are practical in this context? (evaluation: Chapter 9)

Now is the time to review your answers to the questions above and add a final question:

4. What's the best next step?

This final question requires you to set priorities. Of all the things you could suggest or do next, where should you start? Which option addresses the most practical starting point or the highest priority?

Evaluating Solutions and Priorities

Evaluation at this level requires a reexamination of what was at stake (Chapter 4). Are we most concerned about safety? Then we will risk missing a deadline in order to be sure the necessary safety checks have been done. Are we more concerned about timeliness? Then we may sacrifice quality to get the project in on time. Are we more concerned about protection of privacy than we are about making a process completely open and transparent? Then we will make sure that we report the results of a complaint only in the most general terms and we will not name the complainant, or any details of the situation, or the reasoning that led to the settlement.

For example, if you are preparing for an emergency that might hit your own home, such as a prolonged power outage in a winter storm, or a spring flood, or an earthquake, you have several options open to you. As noted in Chapter 9, you might buy a recommended "emergency kit" with food, water, flashlights, blankets, a first-aid kit, and other supplies. You might take a course on emergency preparedness, to give you the knowledge you need to act safely in an emergency. Both alternatives are practical. However, as you examine your current situation, you should be able to set priorities that help you choose between the two. For example, if you hike or camp, you probably have many supplies you'd be able to draw on in an emergency. However, you may not know what you can and cannot do safely when the power is off or after an earthquake. In that case, your priority will most likely be the course that helps you gain more knowledge.

EXERCISE

Personal Emergency Preparedness

This exercise reviews all the critical thinking steps from observation to constructive response.

*1. How well prepared are you for emergencies?

Observation stage: What do you normally carry with you, or have in your car, that would help you deal with an emergency away from home? List the possessions that could help you.

Investigation stage:
a. Add to your list any knowledge you already have that could help you (e.g., first-aid training)
b. Examine your own list and compare it to others. Look up recommended safety precautions, if necessary.

Evaluation stage: Would you say you are over-prepared, under-prepared, or exactly as prepared as you should be? If you are over-prepared, what might you be able to let go of? If you are under-prepared, what options do you have to increase your preparation? If you are as well prepared as you should be, explain how you have achieved this.

Action/response stage: If you are over-prepared, what would be your lowest priority and why could you afford to let it go? If you are under-prepared, what would be the best next step for you to take to improve your preparations, and why is it the best step? Map out a plan. If you are as well prepared as you should be, draw up a set of guidelines based on your experience that you can offer to others who are less well prepared.

Follow-up: As you'll see in the Postscript, even the best action plan isn't much help unless it's carried out. Can you, in the next week, actually follow through on your priority item? What happens when you try?

2. Carry out the same exercise for your own home or workplace. How well is it protected against fire, theft, accidents, safety hazards, or a prolonged power outage? Which of these concerns would be your priority? Take a walk around your home or workplace, checking for *one* of these hazards—it is distracting to try to check two or three at the same time. List what you observe and set priorities for what you will improve. Make the priorities realistic given the time, money, and skills that you have.

Follow through a week or a month later: did you do what you intended to do? Does it still seem worth doing? Explain your reasoning.

Consulting on Priorities

You may also need to consult others before you set priorities. Often, other people will have the deciding voice—for example, to find out whether meeting the deadline is more important than the quality of the finished product, you may have to check with your boss.

This is where good reasoning comes in again—to recognize the appropriate time to check and the right people to check with. If you have been acting responsibly from the start, you did check when you were assigned the task. Still, circumstances may have changed, and you may find now that you can't do everything you were expected to do in the time available. Do you wait until the last minute, hoping against hope that you can do it all? Or do you go to the boss as soon as you can see yourself falling behind schedule, and ask for further instructions? Do you do a rush job on the assignment, or do you go to the professor ahead of time to ask for an extension on the deadline?

This pushes the evaluation back to the next level—not what to do, but when and how to ask about it. Is your boss (or your professor) approachable and likely to understand? Or is this person busy, distracted, and expecting you to take some initiative to overcome problems? Are you likely to get into more trouble for asking than for going ahead and doing your best? We have a tendency to approach these dilemmas psychologically, trying to predict the other person's temperament or mood and adapting our behaviour accordingly. Good reasoning will go one vital step beyond this and ask also what is ethical here: is the person entitled to be consulted? Will the person feel that you have not been fair or that you have not shown enough respect if you take the decision entirely into your own hands? You will see more on how you might plan an effective consultation in Chapter 12.

EXERCISE **10.2**

Setting Priorities

Use these situations either for discussion or for a written response. For a written response, explain how you would handle the situation and why, using concrete examples wherever possible to illustrate your concerns. For each one, devise a "Plan A," your preferred choice for action, and a "Plan B," a backup plan.

*1. Share your results on your check of your own home or workplace with other family members (or co-workers). Enlist them to try the same exercise and see what each of you notices that the others don't, and how your priorities and plans for action differ. Can you agree on whether you are over-prepared, under-prepared, or adequately prepared? If you agree, can you also agree on what would be the highest priority for change, either to let go of something or to increase preparation?

2. You are a receptionist at a busy front desk. The phone rings while you are talking to a customer. You pick up the phone long enough to ask the caller to hold, but the caller says it's urgent. What do you do next?

3. You've won the lottery—no, not one of the big jackpots, but a very welcome $5,000. You can't afford to waste it. You have a partner who will expect some say in how the money is spent. How will you make sure you are using the money wisely?

4. You are partway through a major project when you realize you won't be able to get one of the resources you need before the deadline. (Perhaps it's a book ordered by inter-library loan; perhaps it's a purchase request that's back-ordered.) How will you handle the problem?

5. You are preparing to make the case for why you should take your vacation this year several months before you were scheduled to go. How will you organize your reasoning so your boss will be able to see that all your concerns are relevant and have merit?

When the Best Suggestion to Make Is None at All

Is there still no consensus on the matter? For some situations, the most helpful step may be no suggestion at all. For heated and bitter debates, such as those on abortion or the legal rights of same-sex couples, no move will be made until people have thought hard about their values—a slow process at best. It may be appropriate not to suggest anything, but to emphasize that there are still puzzles and unanswered questions. Asking further questions, such as why it might be important to have only one type of "marriage," instead of jumping to suggestions, such as having "civil unions" instead of marriages, indicates a willingness to explore and work together.

Accountability: Managing Risk

As noted in the Introduction (pages 14–15), what we must do in any situation depends on what our responsibilities are. Have we done everything for which we were accountable? Again, our aim in taking responsible action is to be neither undercritical—doing too little and assuming that the situation will take care of itself—nor overcritical—aiming for a far higher standard than we can fairly and realistically achieve.

In academic work, our primary responsibilities are to achieve rational beliefs and to discover new truths. This means being able to investigate ideas and theories and to defend our beliefs as the conclusions of good arguments. Academic responsibility requires proof in the form of *sufficient evidence* of the *type acceptable* to the discipline. If the context in which you have been working is an academic context—completing an assignment, preparing an essay or major project—then you meet your responsibilities if you research sufficiently, analyze correctly, and present your information in the format required.

For other contexts, such as dealing with issues in professions such as nursing, teaching, or real estate, "professional responsibility" and "due diligence" will be spelled out explicitly. The checks and investigations to be sure you are making the right decision will be specified, and you must be able to show that you have done the necessary checking.

A trickier context is when you are a consumer or client—you are buying a product or service. Here, there is no specific code of ethics or expectations. Yet if things go wrong, and you want to take the seller or service-provider to court, the law will support you only if you have acted like a "reasonable person." You will have to show that you did not blindly trust the other person or sign a contract without reading it.

EXERCISE 10.3

Risk Management

*1. You are about to rent an apartment. What checks should you do before you sign any rental agreement? What provisions should be in place so that you have sufficient protection if the place does not turn out to be as advertised? What would you look for after you move in to be sure that the contract is being honoured and the place is as advertised?

2. You are responsible for planning a large indoor event with live entertainment. What should you check in advance to make it most likely that the event will go smoothly? What plans should you have in place to deal with anything that might go wrong?

Responses to Nonverbal Aspects of the Context

Numbers

The chances are that to respond to numbers will simply be to report your evaluation, showing where the numbers did or did not meet their purpose—for example, where calculations were done inaccurately, or where the drops or rises in quantities indicated an interesting hypothesis to investigate.

The one additional step you might need to take is to offer guidance on how to make the calculations more accurate, or what to investigate further. Since many people are not confident with numbers, if you are competent and can see how to help another person avoid mistakes or develop greater competence, you can at least offer the help if it will be welcomed. For example, if a friend is trying to choose between two cellphone service plans, you might be able to look at your friend's typical phone use over three months and calculate which of the plans is actually cheaper for that pattern of use.

Imagery

You know from evaluating imagery whether it creates the effect it was intended to achieve. Your response will depend on whether any response is needed and on whether it is your responsibility to make any changes needed. Consider the classic situation: your friend asks, "How do I look in this?" You know—or you'll quickly learn—whether your friend wants any genuine response at all or simply a reassuring "You look wonderful." Often, even though you could make suggestions on what colour or style might look better, you'll simply keep the evaluation to yourself.

However, suppose what's at issue is whether your car or house looks attractive enough to potential buyers. Then, if your evaluation concludes that the house or car looks too unappealing, you might decide on an economical but visually effective improvement—wax the car until it shines, or clear every bit of clutter from the house.

If you're making a suggestion for improvement to someone else—perhaps your friend really does want to know what you think of the outfit—then your response will typically be in the same fair, objective style with which you respond to arguments. You explain not what your own preference would be, but what the objective difference is between the way this outfit looks and the way other outfits look. For example, you might say, "That doesn't flatter you as much as the green one did—the colour makes you look pale" or "That fits you just right in the waist but not the shoulders."

Just as in observing imagery, the skill in responding to images comes in being able to articulate what you notice in terms that your listener will be able to understand and act on.

Soundscape

As with images, you know from evaluating the soundscape whether it creates the effect it was intended to achieve. And again, the appropriate response might vary from none at all to direct action. For example, suppose you are driving and your passenger switches the radio to a different station, saying, "This okay with you?" Maybe it's not your preference but it doesn't matter enough to speak up. On the other hand, maybe you're getting a bit tired and this music is so familiar or so annoying it will just make it harder for you to concentrate on the road. You might say, "I need something with a good strong beat to keep me awake. This just doesn't have enough rhythm for me." Again, you are articulating what the objective differences are between what you've been offered and what would work best.

Emotions

When you have to respond to an argument or situation that evokes strong emotions, you have an added level of complexity to deal with: you need to handle your own and other people's emotions respectfully and compassionately.

As you deal with situations, you need to bear in mind the effect of the situation and the possible solutions on the emotions and dignity of the people involved. For example, if your friend in a wheelchair is struggling to do something, will an offer of help be welcome, or will your friend be upset? Will the offer of help insult your friend's independence? If you want to be sure that a client is still entitled to social assistance, can you go through the person's home and check the closets to see if there are any expensive possessions that suggest the client has another source of income? The client is likely to be feeling embarrassed and humiliated at needing financial assistance. Checking instead of taking the person's word not only invades privacy but adds further embarrassment. Good reasoning will strike a balance, so that enough help or information is obtained without jeopardizing the rights or the self-esteem of the people who receive the help or provide the information.

Emotions are also stirred in discussions where people's principles are at stake. If a person has become upset or angry, the chances are good that the person's moral principles seem to be challenged by the issue under discussion. One very common example would be a discussion about abortion. People are easily upset by discussions of this issue, because whichever side of the issue they are on, they believe that the sanctity of human life and proper respect for individuals is threatened.

Consequently, in an emotional discussion, we may be able to help everyone involved if we move away from reasoning and instead return to investigation—not of facts, but of assumptions of principle (see Chapter 6, page 206). What are the principles being challenged, and why are they important to the people who are becoming emotional about them?

If we move in the direction of exploring principles, we achieve several important goals:

1. We give people a chance to articulate their deepest concerns and fears.
2. By showing interest in these concerns and fears, we show respect for people and their beliefs.
3. We help people understand one another's beliefs.
4. We have a chance of finding common ground—for example, both sides of the abortion debate do agree that human life is valued and that individuals should be respected. What they disagree about is what counts as a human life and what constitutes proper respect.

Handling Emotions: Procedures
Oral Discussion
Your primary objective will be to be sure that people can keep their emotions within comfortable bounds. The best way by far is to ensure that each person is heard fully, and heard in turn. This requires the active listening skills you learned in Chapter 1, so if you have listened actively to a person expressing their concerns emotionally, you have already responded appropriately. Now, though, you also need to express your own ideas, and this may mean you have to deal with your own emotions as well. Writing out what you want to say or rehearsing it in advance are two ways to make sure you will find it easier to stay comfortable.

Written Response

Neutral language is by far your best choice for reporting on a difficult issue. Neutral phrasing is the written equivalent of a calm tone. You have already learned when an appeal to emotion is not legitimate—now you need to be sure you are not making the same mistake yourself. If you slip into sarcasm, or even into strongly positive or negative terms, your reader will see you as trying to evoke corresponding emotions in them.

One way to be sufficiently neutral in phrasing is to replace any problematic terms with objective terms—terms that identify just what anyone could see, hear, or sense. For instance, if we are talking about making buildings more accessible to everyone, and we know the term "handicapped" is offensive, we might replace "handicapped" with "in a wheelchair" or "legally blind," a term that describes more neutrally the person's actual condition. (See Chapter 1, page 32, and Chapter 3, pages 95–97, for a review of helpful strategies.) If we still agree with the reasoning when it is expressed in neutral terms, then we can take it seriously.

Action

Perhaps the response you need is an action: you must give the patient an injection, get your physiotherapy client moving, pack up the belongings left behind after a relationship has ended. Here, where words will not do the whole job, you need to find ways to suit your actions to the emotions: to allow extra time, to provide comfort or encouragement. For example, you might place a reassuring hand on the shoulder of the person who needs an injection. You might get up yourself and invite the physiotherapy client to join you. You might group all the belongings to be packed in one place, so they are ready to be packed more easily when you can face the task.

EXERCISE **Responding Appropriately**

Written Assignment: For each of the following situations, first describe three ways you could respond constructively. Then choose the one you think is best, and explain why you would choose that over the other two options. Finally, explain what would be the second-best option and why.

*1. "I thought the interview went so well! I can't understand why I didn't get the job." You know that your friend is capable and enthusiastic but tends to talk at great length, especially when nervous. You suspect that your friend simply talked too much in the interview, giving the interviewers a poor impression. How might you respond to your friend?

2. You're listening to a lecture on Canada's foreign policy and the reasons for Canada's refusal to send troops to Iraq in 2003. You have very strong feelings on this issue. As you listen, you become more and more angry at what seems to you to be biased or ignorant remarks by the lecturer. What can you do?

3. Looking over your expenses from last month, you see that you've spent an unusually large amount on groceries. Checking back over the previous months, you find that although your spending on groceries does vary considerably, last month was over $50 higher than any other month this year. What might you reasonably do next month?

Key Points in Review

- The fourth step in reasoning is acting responsibly. Have you completed everything that is expected of you, to the standard expected? Are there suggestions to be made or actions to be taken?

- Our aim in taking responsible action is to be neither undercritical—doing too little and assuming that the situation will take care of itself—nor overcritical—aiming for a far higher standard than we can fairly and realistically achieve.

- When you are making a suggestion for progress on an issue, make sure that your suggestions are consistent with what has been agreed on, and that you yourself could live with any of the suggestions.

- Reasoning about situations is a cycle, just like verbal reasoning. You collect information, assess options, propose actions, and re-define the problems and issues as you go. To make sure you complete the cycle, you anticipate what might happen, and you decide what will count as an improvement and what will demonstrate that the improvement has happened.

- Emotions—your own and other people's—need to be handled respectfully and compassionately. Good critical thinking will strike a balance in handling emotions, so that help or information is obtained without jeopardizing the rights or the self-esteem of the people who receive the help or provide the information.

Chapter 11

Making Progress: Responding to Arguments

■ Perspective

In this chapter, we pull together what we've learned in Chapters 2 to 10 to meet one of the goals that we set in Chapter 1: that is, to be able to make a useful contribution to the discussion on an issue. So far, you've collected, understood, and analyzed arguments. For each argument you have examined, you now have a written evaluation of its reasoning. You know whether the argument is good or not. You know which premises are acceptable, which are unacceptable, and where you must still suspend judgment. Now you decide how best to respond.

■ Scenario

You were called for jury duty, and you are now serving on the jury in an assault case. All the evidence has been presented, and the jury has been sent to decide on its verdict. As you listened to the evidence and to the judge's instructions to the jury, it seemed to you that the defence presented the best argument. You are convinced the accused person is innocent. Once the jury has gathered, the foreperson of the jury does a quick poll of everyone's initial impression. To your surprise, you are the only juror who thinks the accused person is innocent of assault. How can you make use of your evaluation to help you in the jury deliberations?

■ Key Question

What is needed from my evaluation?

Responding to Arguments in General

The scenario presented above was one of the examples in the Introduction. It sounds like the script from a movie or play, but it does happen in real life. One person to whom it happened found it very challenging to know how to respond. It's hard to be confident you have reasoned correctly when eleven people just as capable as you have reached a different conclusion. It's tempting to concede instead of standing up for your reasoning. However, the jury process expects you to consider the verdict carefully. It makes no difference if there are six people, two people, or only one person who has reached a different conclusion from the others. The arguments you heard in court have been evaluated. Now the evaluations must be shared and discussed, to see if it is possible to reach consensus.

What is needed from your evaluation in this case is an explanation of why you thought the defence argument was good, and why you believe your evaluation of it is accurate. In turn, you want the same from the other jurors. You heard the same arguments for guilt and innocence as they did, so you don't simply want the arguments repeated. You want to understand exactly what problems they saw with the defence reasoning, and what strengths they saw on the other side. More than that, though, you want to know how you can all make progress. What will it take to move forward and reach consensus? Might you all need more information from the judge on how to weigh one particular piece of evidence? Might you need to clarify a concept, such as "intention"? Might you need to isolate the key areas of disagreement so your discussions don't waste time reviewing everything? Each of these additional steps beyond evaluation is a form of response. Each one offers some promise that you can move toward agreement on the most defensible verdict.

In general, evaluating an argument is seldom an end in itself. Your evaluation helps you reach a decision on whether the argument is good, is unproven, or is bad. Your next step is to decide how best to respond. This next step takes you from argument to argumentation. An evaluation is a judgment about an argument considered in isolation. A response is a reasoned choice about how to make use of argument: argumentation, as we defined it in the Introduction. Arguments are given in different contexts and for different purposes. What is the most constructive response for each argument? In this chapter, we'll look at some general types of response to good arguments, unproven arguments, and bad arguments, in that order, and we will look at how you might respond to several arguments on the same topic.

Responding to Good Arguments

When an argument is good, it offers us a rational belief. We should at least accept its conclusion, since the conclusion has been shown to be rational to believe. We ought also to be able to use it in deciding on actions or in building new arguments. How can we best do that? In analysis, we have shown that the argument presents a valid inference and its premises are all acceptable. Isn't that enough?

Not quite. The catch, as indicated in evaluating arguments in Chapter 8, is that we are as vulnerable to errors and oversights as anyone who makes an argument. The indefeasibility condition, introduced in Chapter 8, means that for an argument to be good, it must stand some degree of test by time. It must withstand repeated scrutiny by other people and by ourselves as we gather new information. What looks valid and acceptable to us now might turn out to have mistakes we haven't managed to recognize.

We can't guarantee that we are perfect reasoners. Given everything that has been said in the previous chapters about the difficulties of recognizing errors and the disputes that are possible in deciding how to apply the standards for arguments in specific contexts, we must proceed cautiously before deciding that an argument is good.

The main concern in identifying good arguments is to be able to distinguish between those that merely look good to us personally at the time we consider them and those that really are good. We must look very carefully for faults in an argument before we conclude that it is good. Even after we have decided that there are no apparent faults, we may have some lingering doubts about whether we have judged the argument's support correctly. Dealing effectively with a good argument means dealing effectively with the two possibilities that we must face: either the argument really is good, and we have recognized this, or it is not good, and we have not spotted its weaknesses.

It helps to keep in mind why we are looking for good arguments: we want results we can live with. A believable conclusion and a well-written argument are not enough to show we are on safe ground. We need to keep the argument in context: what is at stake for us if we accept or reject the conclusion? Why does this issue matter to us? We can look again at the reasoning in the argument. What directions does it point us in? What consequences does it have? We also need to bear in mind that we may see several good arguments for different conclusions (such as arguments that argue equally well from competing principles), so we may need to compare arguments before we decide what we will accept. Once we have made these checks, we will be in a better position to decide if the reasoning still looks good.

Preparing a Response to a Good Argument

Since a good argument has no obvious weaknesses, your response needs to indicate this without it seeming that you have simply failed to notice weaknesses.

Once you have reported the argument, presumably your reader will also be able to see that it looks good. To reassure yourself and your reader that you have not simply missed the faults that a more astute reader might see, you can give some *independent* evidence for believing that the argument is good. This confirms that you did carry out an investigation step—you did check to see if the information provided was accurate and consistent with other sources. If you can give a few new reasons or fresh examples not mentioned in the argument to confirm the evidence that is already given, you demonstrate that the argument has at least been measured against your own background knowledge and independent judgment. Providing *additional* information shows that you have understood the argument and makes the argument a bit stronger than it was.

For example, consider the following argument. It is the closing argument in a book that has presented a series of arguments supporting the conclusion that force may be necessary as a response to terrorism, but that force must be carefully controlled and limited. Michael Ignatieff, a Canadian-born writer and historian currently working at a centre for human rights policy in the United States, has written a number of books dealing with issues of rights, power, and warfare. In this book, *The Lesser Evil*, he compares a number of different terrorist groups and individuals from al-Qaeda to the "loner" Timothy McVeigh who carried out the Oklahoma City bombing, and discusses the responses to them by different countries, from Israel and Ireland to Canada and the United States. This passage sums up his overall argument.

> In an age in which individuals are monstrously empowered, by technology and freedom, to bring Armageddon down upon their fellow human beings, it is suddenly no longer a minor matter that some of our fellow citizens and some of the noncitizens who live among us, happen not to believe in liberal democracy but instead profess a variety of paranoias pretending to be politics. The existence of wild, vengeful, and deluded political opinions, if married to lethal technology in the possession of a single individual, suddenly becomes a threat to us all. I am haunted, as I think we all might be, by the spectre of the superempowered loner as the cruel nemesis of the very moral care our society lavishes on the idea of the individual.
>
> It is a condition of our freedom that we cannot compel anyone to believe in the premises of a liberal democracy. Either those premises freely convince others or they are useless. They cannot be imposed, and we violate everything we stand for if we coerce those who do not believe what we do. In any event, we cannot preemptively detain all the discontent in our midst.
>
> So we are stuck, as we should be, with persuasion, with the duty, now more urgent than at any time in our history, to persuade each and every person who lives among us, whether as citizen or visitor, of two perfectly plain propositions: that we are committed to respect their dignity, and if they fail to respect ours, we will defend ourselves. The threat of terror, the possibility of a terrorist outcome if we fail to convince one of these superempowered loners, makes the burden of justification that falls upon every citizen as a condition of membership in a liberal society heavier than it has ever been. We must be able to defend ourselves—with force of arms, but even more with force of argument. For arms without argument are used in vain. Since I believe in the arguments, since I believe that human beings are unique in their capacity to be persuaded, changed, even redeemed by good ones, I do not doubt that we will prevail.

[Michael Ignatieff, *The Lesser Evil: Political Ethics in An Age of Terror*, Toronto: Penguin Canada, 2004, pp. 169–170]

How might we deal with this argument if we have to respond to it—for example, to write a critical evaluation of it for a political science course, or just to explain to someone else what we thought of the book? It's a challenging argument to follow, especially if you are seeing it by itself without having read any of the rest of the book. If you have to explain your views to anyone who has not read this argument already, then it's going to be very helpful if you can at least get across what you understand as Ignatieff's argument. Your report is going to have to be quite detailed so you do not lose any of his reasoning, because it's his reasoning you want to respond to. Your report might look something like this:

> At the end of his book *The Lesser Evil*, Michael Ignatieff concludes that liberal democracies must rely on arguments, not just on force, to defend themselves against terrorists. He is concerned that even a single individual could possess a dangerous enough weapon to threaten all of society. Liberal democracies value individuals and individual freedom, so it seems particularly frightening to have what we value most turn into our biggest danger. Yet it is incompatible with our values to force people to agree with us, and it is impractical to try to put in custody everyone who might pose a threat to us.
>
> Ignatieff argues that the only route open to us is to persuade others reasonably of our values, so that they can freely choose whether to accept them.
>
> He says there are two crucial principles that we must be able to get across. The first principle is that we are committed to respecting the dignity of every citizen and every visitor. The second principle is that if any person fails to respect the dignity of any other citizen or visitor, we will defend ourselves with force. Every single one of us living in a liberal democracy bears this responsibility to be able to transmit these principles. The democracy must be able to defend itself with force if needed, but each citizen within it must be able to argue for our values. "For arms without argument are used in vain." Ignatieff believes that we can give good arguments, and human beings can be persuaded by good arguments, so he believes we can win the fight against terrorism.

Now that you think your report has captured the sense of the argument, if not its full flavour, what more can you add? First, you can offer your evaluation. Ignatieff hasn't said anything obviously false or irrelevant, so his argument will pass at least those two tests. For sufficiency, he is not arguing that we will win against terrorism but that we might, and he is not arguing that we will definitely succeed if we can reason effectively, but that we could win. This is an argument to probability. Before you can conclude that an argument is good, you also need to show that you have carried out at least a minimum indefeasibility check—have you examined the world outside his words to see if there is any information that might count against it? This argument does not rely on factual information you can check, so you check for assumptions. He does seem to assume that human beings are inherently reasonable, so that our efforts to persuade one another can succeed. You could take a very cynical view of human nature and propose the alternative that humans are seldom reasonable, so arguments only succeed by chance. However, that alternative isn't obviously any more plausible than his, and you probably don't want to defend it. If you have to respond to this argument, your best option is to tentatively accept this as a good argument. To show why you think it's good, you can add something from outside the argument to show you have done some checking, and you can add a constructive suggestion to show how we might apply the conclusion.

> Ignatieff's argument appears to balance the need to be willing to use force if necessary with the need to uphold individual rights and freedoms. Earlier in his book (p. 108) he described an example that fits with his claims: Canada did evoke the War Measures Act and did use force in Quebec in 1970, but Canada never acted to suppress the movement for separatism itself while it was carried out by democratic means. He does not mention it in the book, but I remember that before one of the referendums asking the Quebec people if they would support separatism, Canadians from other provinces made a considerable attempt to reach out individually to people in Quebec and to assure them they were valued and respected. Reasoning with one another, as Ignatieff suggests, may be one way to bridge tensions and create understanding; the simple act of reaching out to connect with other people on a personal level may also be a helpful part of protecting what we value about democracy.

Now you have a response that shows you have read and understood the argument, you have checked not just the words here but other parts of the book and your own memory as a test of acceptability and indefeasibility, and you have looked forward a little toward how we might act if we accept his conclusion. You have begun to take part in a debate of his ideas; you are ready to listen to or take part in further discussion. If someone disagrees with you and finds weaknesses you didn't spot—for example, an assumption you didn't recognize—you are ready to reexamine your evaluation and investigate further if needed.

The type of response modelled here is often a good beginning for a critical essay where you can't find anything to "criticize." "Critical evaluation" of a good argument encompasses supporting its strengths by adding independent evidence and showing what should be protected or endorsed.

Checklist: Response to Good Arguments

A response to a good argument includes the following:

✔ an objective report of the argument

✔ a few independent reasons confirming the premises (from personal experience, background knowledge, or another reputable source)

✔ constructive suggestions (if action is needed) consistent with the argument

Finding and Considering Good Arguments

You can find good arguments in textbooks and professional journals. These arguments are reviewed before publication to catch most or all of the obvious faults. Close examination, however, may still reveal weaknesses in reasoning, perhaps even fatal flaws (especially in assumptions).

Find a short argument from a current textbook or professional journal. Decide the evidence you would want to see and the evidence the discipline expects. (If you are working in a group, then decide as a group.) Examine the argument's reasoning. What flaws do you see? Would you consider the argument good? If so, provide independent reasons or examples to confirm its premises. If not, briefly list the weaknesses that you see.

Responding to Unproven Arguments

For many arguments, a careful analysis will show that we must suspend judgment. At least some of the premises will be open to question. There may be facts we can't check, or assumptions for which we have identified reasonable alternatives.

These arguments are not good, nor are they bad. Their conclusions are "not proven." We count them as "unproven" arguments because more investigation is essential. As we continue to investigate, the most important thing to bear in mind is that there are other alternatives to the conclusion or assumptions that must be checked. The most constructive step, then, will be to show where and how we might look for evidence to test these alternatives.

Preparing a Response to an Unproven Argument

If an argument is unproven, that means there is at least one plausible alternative conclusion that has not been firmly ruled out. In your evaluation of the argument, you should have been able to show that the argument makes good connections between its premises and its conclusion, and that none of its premises are obviously unacceptable. From your investigation step, you should have been able to identify other possible conclusions on the same topic and plausible alternatives to one or more of the premises. Now we need to bring those alternatives forward for further consideration. Our aim will be to show that other conclusions have not yet been properly ruled out.

If we can identify the competing conclusions, we can suggest what might be done—what further information might be gathered, and how it will help—in order to decide between them. Ultimately, investigation will be directed at showing which of the remaining possible conclusions is the most likely. At this stage, we may not be able to achieve certainty, but we should at least be able to reduce the risk of acting on an unlikely conclusion. In an evaluation, you need to indicate only where and how we can look for information that will show which conclusion is the most plausible. Collecting that information and making a decision between the competing conclusions is a second step, which can come later.

Your basic strategy will be to show that the conclusion is plausible, then point out which other conclusions are also still plausible and suggest how we might move on to rule out other possibilities. These steps work for both oral and written evaluation.

Step 1: *Check that the argument is plausible.*

This is best done by reporting and evaluating it in the way that we have done in previous chapters. (See Chapters 2, 5, and 8 for a review of strategies for oral and written summaries.)

Step 2: *Point out other possibilities.*

Explain what other conclusions you think are equally plausible. The burden of proof is on you: the arguer is content with the conclusion already offered, so you need to explain why you think the alternatives are plausible.

Step 3: *Offer constructive ways to choose between the plausible alternatives.*

Suggest sources of information or tests that we could carry out, and explain how they will help us to decide between the plausible alternatives. What is the information or further argument that we need, and what could it tell us? How could we collect that evidence? Think through how to set up a test so that the results will signal clearly which conclusion is most likely to be correct. The design of tests and experiments takes us beyond the scope of this book, but you will find help in other sources. Some references are provided in Appendix B.

Checklist: Response to an Unproven Argument

A response to an unproven argument should include the following:

✔ an objective summary of the argument

✔ other possible conclusions that have not yet been eliminated, and an explanation of why they are plausible and should be considered

✔ a description of further information that would have to be gathered in order to rule out other possibilities

---

As a sample, consider this article by Roger Highfield. You saw it in Chapter 4 as an example of an argument using numbers to support its case.

Study reveals lefties thrive in violent societies

French scientists believe they may have discovered why left-handers are so common despite suffering disadvantages when it comes to handling tools, disease risk and historical prejudice in predominantly right-handed societies against the "cackhanded."

Since this trait is substantially inherited, and because it can be a disadvantage, scientists have puzzled for years over what it is about being left-handed that helps survival or the ability to reproduce.

Now it seems that left-handers are more likely to thrive in a violent society. A French team reported yesterday that because they are in the minority, left-handers have a strategic advantage in fights.

The reason isn't that they are innately superior but that their opponent is likely to be more used to combat with right-handers, according to Dr. Charlotte Faurie and Dr. Michel Raymond of Université Montpellier II, France.

The team was inspired to carry out the study by the observation that, in a right-handed society, left-handers have an advantage in sports such as fencing, tennis, cricket and baseball.

They reasoned that "interactive sports in western societies are special cases of fights, with strict rules, including in particular the prohibition of killing or intentionally wounding the opponent."

Thus it could be that being left-handed in a right-handed society may have offered an advantage in fights.

"If this is true, then the advantage of being left-handed should be greater in a more violent context, which should result in a higher frequency of left-handers."

They decided to test their idea. Earlier studies have shown the number of left-handers in the Kreyol people of Dominica, the Ntumu people of Cameroon, the Dioula-speaking people of Burkina Faso, Baka people of Gabon, Inuit people and the Eipo people in Irian Jaya, New Guinea.

When the team studied the rate of murder in each society, they found "a significant positive correlation between homicide rates and left-handedness frequencies."

The Dioula had a homicide rate equivalent to one-hundredth of a death per 1,000 people per year, while the Eipo had around three deaths per 1,000 people. And the percentage of left-handers was 3.4 per cent and more than 20 per cent, showing how left-handedness thrived along with aggression.

In societies, being able to win fights meant more than killing opponents, enabling warriors to gain status and impress women. A study by the same team of 600 students found that the same forces are at work today in sports, which they describe as "ritualized fights."

Competitive athletes, particularly men, have more sexual partners than their couch-potato peers. Because left-handers often have a competitive advantage in sports, they're more likely to enjoy this benefit, said Faurie.

However, left-handers face disadvantages. Statistics suggest reduced life expectancy, smaller body size and immune system disorders, she said.

"But it seems to be true that they are more frequent among some professional categories as musicians and mathematicians," said Faurie.

"Our team showed that they have some socioeconomic advantages [like a slightly higher income]."

[ROGER HIGHFIELD, *KINGSTON WHIG-STANDARD*, DECEMBER 10, 2004, 31. © TELEGRAPH GROUP LIMITED 2004. REPRINTED WITH PERMISSION OF TELEGRAPH GROUP LIMITED.]

How can we best respond to an argument like this? An evaluation shows that while Faurie's team might be right that left-handers thrive in more violent societies, there are other possible explanations that have not been sufficiently ruled out. First, it is not entirely clear whether the left-handers are more likely to make attacks or just have a better chance of surviving deadly attacks by others. Is it perhaps that they are not among the violent perpetrators, but only among the more successful survivors? Second, a correlation is not a cause. What triggers the violence in these societies? In many societies, use of the left hand is considered unclean and is not permitted. In other societies left-handers are laughed at or pointed out as odd, or they find it very difficult to do routine tasks safely because the equipment is not designed for them. Have the right-handers among the Eipo simply tormented the left-handers until some of them lash out? Do the Eipo use tools that frustrate the left-handers beyond sanity? More seriously, do we even have evidence that the murders are committed or are survived disproportionately by the left-handers in the society? The reports of the study do not make it clear that a social tendency to violence either causes or is caused by left-handedness.

In responding to this argument, we acknowledge that perhaps the weaknesses are in the reporting rather than the study itself, and perhaps the study itself does answer some of the questions we are left with. However, until our questions are answered, our most constructive option is to raise these alternatives and suggest what information would be needed to help answer them.

For example, are there any other societies with a higher-than-normal rate of left-handedness? Is their homicide rate also above normal? If so, it makes it less likely the homicide rate for the Eipo could be explained away by factors unique to them. What are the homicide methods? It's always a very useful murder mystery plot device to show that only a left-hander could have struck the fatal blow. However, which kinds of fatal attack give left-handers their claimed advantage? Left-handers might have the advantage of an "unexpected" direction in striking a blow directly from the front, but they have no obvious advantage in attacking a person by a blow to the back of the head, or causing a fall, or strangling. The homicide method might make it less likely that there is something about the handedness of the killer that makes a difference. How hard is it for right-handed fighters or athletes to learn to compete against left-handers? Left-handers don't always win tennis tournaments or baseball games. Perhaps the left-handers' initial advantage wears off too quickly to matter in any serious struggle. We would need more accurate tests of how left-handers have an advantage in combat or sports.

At this point, notice that we are staying open, not trying to prove that the conclusion is wrong. It's premature to move into further arguments supporting the conclusion or arguing against it. It is possible that the person giving the argument could answer all our questions quickly, and may even have thought we knew enough to make the missing pieces obvious. However, whether the problem is in the argument, in the reporting of it, or simply in our own background knowledge, we are not entitled to support or oppose the conclusion. Until we have more information than we have now, we still have to withhold judgment. Our response at least shows a direction to follow: we need to look for answers to the questions we raised.

EXERCISE **11.2**

Evaluating Unproven Arguments

Many arguments will fall into the "unproven" category at first, before we can do more research on the information. Choose an argument from Chapter 8 that you evaluated as "unproven." Extend your evaluation of this argument to include a response: what other conclusions are still possible, and how might we carry out a test to investigate further?

Responding to Bad Arguments: Mistakes in Judgment

Our objective in evaluating a bad argument was to show exactly where it went wrong, and to explain its mistake in a way that shows how it has failed to provide any useful support for its conclusion. Pointing out that an argument is bad, however, is not always as helpful as we might like it to be. Now we need to decide the most constructive way to respond.

Sometimes, it is enough to be able to explain the faults. For example, if the task is to write a critical essay or report for an academic subject, then often you may be asked simply to point out the errors in an argument you've been asked to evaluate. It is a legitimate and valuable step in academic disciplines to rule out one conclusion, even when you don't offer a better one. Many papers in philosophy, for example, consist only of a clear demonstration of the mistakes in someone else's reasoning.

However, there are many settings, both academic and non-academic, where it is essential to go beyond criticism and be constructive as well. As you know, it can be very frustrating to be told "That's wrong" without also being told what would be right, or what would be needed to fix the problem.

A bad argument really can't be fixed—we would need to start over and construct better reasons to see if the conclusion is true or not. If we look only at the argument, there is nothing helpful we can do. But if we look beyond the argument to its context and to the concerns of the arguer, we can be constructive. If we recognize that strong emotion is likely to be involved, we can identify the concerns that might trigger those emotions. If we identify underlying principles, we can open discussion on the principles.

We can take several different directions after recognizing that an argument is bad. We might reject not only the reasoning but also the conclusion, and look for or create arguments for a different conclusion. We might try to revive the conclusion by providing a new argument for it. We might shift the discussion to an investigation of why the bad argument was produced (what does it reveal about what the arguer considered important?).

Our responsibility with a bad argument, then, will be to find at least one promising step forward. Possibilities include the following:

- demonstrating empathy for the underlying concerns
- redirecting the discussion back to the central issues
- pointing out more useful directions to pursue

Preparing a Response to a Bad Argument

When we respond to bad arguments, we have to remember that mistakes aren't evidence of stupidity. Even the best reasoners can make serious mistakes. As noted in Chapter 10, mistakes can be caused by inaccurate information, overwhelming emotion, or stress, for example. We must look beyond the mistake to what might have caused it and what this might show us about the issue or the needs of the arguer.

An interesting category of mistakes occurs in academic work when some lines of thought have become so well established that it never occurs to even the most independent thinkers to question them. Think, for example, of the many centuries of Western thought in which it never occurred to anyone to challenge whether what was true for men was equally true for women. What we don't say can be as revealing as what we do say. (The field of critical discourse analysis, using interpretive reasoning, looks at this.)

Outside academic work, mistakes often happen when people care so much about an issue that they will say whatever feels right to them at the time. In the heat of the moment they will jump to conclusions or over-generalize and make other mistakes. For example, think of arguments on abortion, euthanasia, or same-sex marriage. These topics disturb people so much that they literally cannot think straight—their reasoning goes astray. Yet they have legitimate concerns that cannot be dismissed just because their arguments do not work. If someone argues that abortion "shows no respect for human life" and we can see that the argument relies on shaky reasoning, we know that the argument is bad, but the concern that we should respect human life is still legitimate and we cannot dismiss that.

Because a bad argument can be an indication that the arguer is concerned that some important principle is being threatened, you may need to tread carefully in expressing your criticism, especially when you are face to face with the person. Most of all, you need to recognize and respect underlying moral principles and create a framework in which disagreements about principles can safely be discussed. Generally, this means asking questions rather than disagreeing or criticizing, unless you know the person prefers heated debate, and it means allowing each person to speak in turn and speak uninterrupted, so the flavour of the conversation moves from debate to open-minded exploration.

Similarly, since stress is a very common cause of bad reasoning, the person who is stressed is also likely not to be able to follow or to care about the details of where the argument went wrong. In these cases, responsible reactions include good timing: figuring out not just what to say but when to say it. (We'll see more on this in Chapter 12.) Some basic strategies are suggested below.

Oral Discussion

In oral discussion, your aim is usually to keep the discussion going until you solve a problem or reach a consensus of opinion. Direct explanation of faults is risky unless you know that the person enjoys a challenge or will not listen to anything less than a head-on assault. Bluntly pointing out faults creates a further threat to a person who already feels threatened; he or she may simply struggle harder to maintain his or her position.

If the person who has given the bad argument is stressed, it will generally be wiser not to continue the discussion at all, but to wait until a better time.

If the person is not too stressed to engage in discussion, it will generally be wise to explore rather than debate. That means you may be far more successful in getting your point across when you turn your insight into a question or a suggestion. For example, here are some questions that you might ask in response to examples of bad arguments:

- "That information doesn't fit with what I've heard so far. Where did you hear that full-time employees work harder than part-timers?"
- "How much money are food banks getting now? What if we campaigned for higher welfare rates instead?"
- "It seems to be very important to you that we take no chances in raising children. Can you explain why?"

These questions give the arguer a chance to produce additional evidence for the conclusion. The arguer has a chance to develop his or her own insights. The search for more evidence may help the arguer to produce a more acceptable line of reasoning to support the conclusion, or the arguer may come to realize that there were serious weaknesses in the reasoning. Having arrived at insights into his or her reasoning, the arguer is much more likely to accept the faults and move on.

Written Discussion

When you are dealing with written material, you do not usually have the arguer there in person. Since you cannot ask questions and wait for answers before proceeding, you must explain why you do not accept the reasoning as it stands. You can explain directly what is wrong with the argument: readers can choose when, or whether, they want to read your response and therefore be comfortable dealing with it.

Your aim is to demonstrate why the support provided is unacceptable—why it is inaccurate, irrelevant, or insufficient. You will show other people why they should not accept the conclusion based on this evidence, and you will offer the arguer a chance to rethink. If there is a legitimate concern that you can see—if you have identified the crux of the debate clearly—then you may suggest this as the topic on which to re-focus the discussion.

Checklist: Response to Bad Arguments

A response to a bad argument includes the following:

✔ an objective summary of the argument

✔ an explanation of how the argument has made a mistake: if there is more than one mistake, treat only those that make the most difference to the acceptability of the conclusion

✔ if needed or appropriate, suggestions on how to proceed: whether to look for a new argument, support a different conclusion, or redefine the issue

---

As a sample, consider how we might respond to Robin Kilburn's argument, which you have seen before.

Alzheimer's drug eases the daily strain

Re: Major study pans Alzheimer's drug, June 26

Can you imagine yourself going through your day wearing one of those suits for deep diving? The kind that have airhoses and cables attached to a ship somewhere on the ocean surface. Now imagine having to wear that suit 24/7 and perform your daily tasks. This is how I feel most days.

Some days are easier than others, but only because I take a drug called Aricept. A recent

(Continued)

Alzheimer's drug eases the daily strain *(Continued)*

British study said that Aricept doesn't work. I'm here to tell you that it does. And I think if you ask anyone else in the early stages of Alzheimer's, they would agree with me.

I admit it might not work for some people: Not all medications work for all people. Just ask anyone with a life-threatening illness if the first medication prescribed was the one that allowed them to function normally.

So shame on the British researchers and double shame on B.C. Health Services Minister Colin Hansen because he would sooner believe a study involving 565 people and not take the word of thousands of people who might say something different.

Robin Kilburn, Abbotsford

[*VANCOUVER SUN*, JULY 2, 2004, A11. REPRINTED WITH PERMISSION OF ROBIN KILBURN.]

This letter involved two types of reasoning. First, there was the analogy to deep-sea diving, which did not work well because it was not easy to see how that type of discomfort compared to living with Alzheimer's disease or how a drug could change those symptoms. Next, there was the reasoning to show the probability that Aricept does work. This reasoning provided insufficient support to show that in comparison to the study of only 565 people for whom Aricept was not shown to work, there really are thousands of people for whom Aricept does work. An overall evaluation of the argument shows that it offers too little support to show that its conclusion is probable, and only Kilburn's own anecdotal evidence to suggest the conclusion is possible.

However, it will not be very constructive to respond to this argument simply by reporting our evaluation. It is unlikely we will make much progress simply by investigating in more detail whether Aricept does or does not work in some small percentage of cases. We can already see that the key issue is not whether it works well, but whether its costs should be covered by public health care for those people, however few, who do feel they benefit from it. Nor will it be constructive just to empathize and agree that it must be hard to live with this disease. Kilburn and people in her situation deserve better than that. They face a very difficult future, with almost no chance of effective medication being developed quickly enough to help them.

A more constructive response will be to identify the underlying issues or concerns raised by the argument, and to bring those forward for discussion. Which imperfect or risky drugs should be offered to people who have no better medication available to them? When should our health care system acknowledge that a patient and his or her doctor are the best judge of which medication is right for this particular person? How is a person diagnosed with Alzheimer's or any other irreversible disease to find the best way to cope with deteriorating mental health?

If we take the discussion to new ground, addressing the deeper concerns, we open up the possibility of moving beyond a failed argument or a disagreement into new perspectives and shared priorities.

EXERCISE **11.3** ## Responding to a Bad Argument

Written Assignment: Look back at the arguments you evaluated in Chapter 8. For any argument in which you identified an error in reasoning, report the argument, report your evaluation, and add a suitable response. Be able to explain why you have chosen this response.

Responding to Several Arguments on the Same Topic

When you are dealing with several arguments on the same topic, your response needs to take all the arguments into account. You may find you have more than one unproven argument, or more than one bad argument. In Chapter 9, you compared arguments on the same topic. The comparison of arguments is a first step toward a constructive response. The next step is to offer suggestions that will help us to make progress. These suggestions should make sense in light of the results of your comparison: they should build on just the elements that you have shown to be the crux of the debate and to warrant further exploration.

As with individual arguments, you may need to generate constructive suggestions for action, as described in Chapter 10. When you are making a suggestion for progress on an issue, you must make sure that your suggestions are consistent with what has been agreed on, and that you yourself could live with any of the suggestions. It makes no sense to recommend a course of action that you personally could not support, even if you think one side would be very happy with it. If the issue is controversial, offer two or more choices suitable to the stage that the issue has reached. Remember to include specific examples to illustrate your suggestions, and make sure that your suggestions are consistent with what has been accepted in the arguments.

For example, suppose you have read and evaluated two arguments that disagree on how Canada should help countries affected by famine and other catastrophes. One argument concludes that Canada should continue to offer money and Canadian expertise to the governments of these countries to use as they see fit. Another argues that the foreign governments often are a large part of the problem and will distribute aid only to the people they favour. It would be better for Canada to assist Canadian groups such as charities and municipalities to sponsor specific groups or villages and to build personal relationships overseas that let the aid flow directly from the givers to the receivers. In your evaluation, you decided that both arguments were unproven at this point. Both agreed that Canada should increase its foreign aid. The argument for government aid continuing as it is seemed slightly better to you, but neither argument had enough evidence to show that the people in need really did benefit from the aid. What might you offer as constructive suggestions?

The first, obvious suggestion, would be to gather more evidence about how well direct government aid works compared to how private group aid or sponsorship works. This is trickier than it looks, though, because it would mean figuring out how to measure how much aid reaches the intended recipients and how they benefit from it. You would need to take your suggestion a bit further, and perhaps do a brief initial investigation yourself, to see whether progress might be measured by per capita income or improved health. (International development work does devote a great deal of effort to deciding how best to measure progress.) You might want to suggest that rather than delay offering aid, Canada could go ahead and try some more sponsorships and monitor what happens. Even given more information, though, we are still looking at only two suggestions for forms of aid. Are there other forms of aid that might be more effective than either government aid or group sponsorship? Again, some preliminary investigation may help: you might, for example, discover the "micro-loan" program that allows individuals to start small businesses by helping them buy, for instance, a sewing machine to make clothing or a large bag of rice to re-sell in smaller portions. If you think this idea is an equally good way to offer aid, you can suggest this as something else to look into, and give a reference where people can find more information on it. Finally, your evaluation might have revealed that both arguments have assumed that it is up to the donor to decide what kind of aid is needed, and that one alternative is that the receivers should decide what kind of aid is needed and leave donors to decide whether they want to give it. You might therefore also want to suggest that we do also need to discuss how we view "aid" in general. Perhaps you'd like to see a conference within Canada where different aid groups and government clarify their goals and expectations. Perhaps you think an international conference or a debate at the United Nations would be better. A suggestion along these lines would be a helpful third idea.

If you make two or three suggestions for possible actions, or for more information, or for new discussion from a different perspective, you have now made a constructive contribution to the debate even if you have not recommended which side to take. When you offer two or three suggestions, you do open the way to practical actions that will help. You also draw other people in to become part of the solution—whichever side they favoured, they have a choice as to how they might move forward.

EXERCISE ## Making Recommendations

*For any one of the pairs of arguments in Chapter 6, or for a pair from your own collection, give your recommendations for making progress in resolving the issue: offer two or more choices suitable to the stage that the issue has reached. Remember to include specific examples to illustrate your suggestions, and make sure that your suggestions are consistent with what has been accepted in the arguments.

Choosing an Appropriate Response Format

When you present your response, you also need to think critically about what will work for this issue in this context. We'll look here just at written responses. In Chapter 12 we'll develop some strategies for responding when you must deal in person with the people involved.

For a written response, think ahead: what do you want to happen when people read what you have written? Do you want to see the discussion broaden, or become sharper in focus? Do you want people to turn their attention to action? How busy are the readers? Will they follow a long report, or must you highlight only the most crucial details? Your answers to these questions will indicate which points you want to emphasize and where you want to begin and end.

Here is one format for a written response that can be adapted to several contexts.

1. Prepare a brief, general, objective overview of the common or interesting lines of argument on that issue: outline the key facts needed to put readers in the picture and give a brief indication of the competing arguments.

2. Organize the arguments into an order that will help the reader follow you through the issue. For example, you might report a particularly informative argument first; or you might arrange the arguments from weakest to strongest, so that the reader naturally follows your reasoning.

3. Sum up what we should realize after reading the argument evaluations. What stage has the disagreement reached? What are the areas of agreement and disagreement? What still needs to be worked on?

4. Give your recommendations for making progress in resolving the issue: offer two or more choices suitable to the stage that the issue has reached. Remember to include specific examples to illustrate your suggestions, and make sure that your suggestions are consistent with what has been accepted in the arguments.

The report format outlined above can be adapted quite easily to other standard written formats. For example, a letter to the editor might use a few sentences from the introduction, some highlights from your evaluation, and then your conclusion. In contrast, a business report might start with the recommendations, followed by the reports and evaluations, with most of the supporting information relegated to an appendix.

EXERCISE **11.5**

Responding to Contrasting Arguments on the Same Topic

Written Assignment: This pair of arguments offers different views on euthanasia. Report and evaluate each argument, then compare the arguments and respond by offering constructive suggestions.

Life and death issues take centre stage

After thousands of years, why are we talking about it now?

The criminal charges against Montrealer Marielle Houle for allegedly assisting her son Charles Fariala to commit suicide, and the arraignment of Evelyn Martens of Victoria, B.C., on two counts of assisting suicide, have catapulted euthanasia (a word I use to include assisted suicide) back into the media spotlight and public debate.

Almost all of the debate is intensely personal and argued on the basis of the rights of individuals and the risks and harms to them of allowing or prohibiting assisted suicide. The case made for legalizing euthanasia is that terminally ill people suffer and want to die and we ought to assist them in killing themselves, or kill them.

But not one of the factual conditions proposed as justifying euthanasia is new—they have been part of the human condition for as long as humans have existed. Why, then, after we have prohibited euthanasia for thousands of years, are we now considering such a radically different response to human dying and death?

The principal cause is not the circumstances in which terminally ill people—and, even less so, non-terminally ill ones such as Charles Fariala—find themselves, but profound cultural changes in post-modern, secular, Western, democratic societies such as Canada. Let me identify some of these and explain how each relates to calls for legalizing euthanasia:

Intense individualism: The question "Whose life is it anyway?" and the response "Mine, and it's no one else's business and especially not the state's to tell me what I may and must not do with it," sums up intense individualism in the context of euthanasia. This approach is implemented by giving absolute priority to rights to personal autonomy and self-determination.

It can result, however, in the exclusion of any real sense of community, and that lack is experienced very powerfully in connection with death and bereavement.

Euthanasia might function as a way out of unbearable isolation or to provide a sense of community with those who advocate its legalization. Moreover, having one's death promote a common cause can be experienced as giving that death meaning.

Intense individualism also reflects a stance about the nature of our relationship with life, that we each own our life, it is our property to do with as we choose. That favours euthanasia. The contrasting view is we hold life on trust and, therefore, what we do with our life affects not only us but also others. Fulfilling that trust requires rejecting euthanasia.

Mass media: We find personal and societal values and meaning in life through creating and buying into a collective story. This has always focused on the two major events in each human life—birth and death. Today, we create and share that story through the media. That can affect its content. We can be most attracted to that which we most fear, and the media provide an almost infinite number of opportunities to indulge our fear of, and attraction to, death. Consequently, we might engage in too much "death talk" and too little "life talk," so the shared story becomes unbalanced.

Then, individual cases of people, such as Sue Rodriguez, pleading for euthanasia make dramatic and emotionally gripping television.

The arguments against euthanasia, based on the harm it would do to individuals and society in both the present and the future, are much more difficult to present visually. Moreover, the vast exposure to death we are subjected to in both current-affairs and entertainment programs might have overwhelmed our sensitivity to the awesomeness of death and, likewise, of inflicting it.

Denial and control of death and death talk: We humans must deal with the knowledge we will die and accommodate that reality into the living of our lives if we are to live fully and well. We do that by engaging in "death talk." Religion used to be the locus of communal death talk, which meant for most of us that talk was confined to an identifiable location and an hour or so a week. In the absence of religion, death talk has spilled out into our lives in general and the media are our forum for engaging in it. This makes it more difficult to maintain the denial of death because it makes the fear of death more present and real. One way to deal with this fear is to believe we have death under control. The availability of euthanasia could support that belief.

Fear: Fear is a source of suffering because it causes intense anxiety. Taking control reduces anxiety and, thereby, suffering and fear. If euthanasia were experienced as a way of converting death by chance to death by choice, it would offer a feeling of increased control over death and, therefore, decreased fear. Although we cannot make death optional, we can create an illusion it is by making its timing and the conditions and ways in which it occurs a matter of choice.

Legalism: Matters such as euthanasia (and, likewise, marriage) that would once have been the topic of moral or religious discourse, are now explored in courts and legislatures—especially through concepts of individual human rights, civil rights and constitutional rights. In this way, we establish the values and symbols of a secular society. One way to view court cases and legislative proposals related to euthanasia is as our engaging in societal level "death talk" in "secular cathedrals"—our courts and legislatures.

Materialism and consumerism: The loss of any sense of the sacred, even just of the "secular sacred," fosters the idea that worn-out people can be equated with worn-out products; both can then be seen primarily as "disposal" problems. As one Australian politician, in advocating legalizing euthanasia, said: "When you are past your best-before date, you should be checked out as quickly, cheaply and efficiently as possible." Euthanasia best fulfills those criteria.

Mystery: Our society is very intolerant of mystery—perhaps for two reasons. It is associated with religion—although it need not be. And it raises uncertainty and lack of control and, therefore, fear. Our response is to convert mysteries into problems. If we convert the

mystery of death into the problem of death, euthanasia—a lethal injection—can be seen as a solution.

Moreover, loss of a sense of mystery might be linked to euthanasia in another way. That sense might be required to preserve room for hope. Research has shown the dominant characteristic associated with a desire for euthanasia by people with serious illness was not depression, but a different state the psychiatrists called "hopelessness"—these people had nothing to look forward to.

The loss of mystery has also been accompanied by a loss of wonder and awe and the sense we, as humans, are sacred within any meaning of this word—that we are, at least, "secular sacred." That also favours euthanasia.

Impact of scientific advances: Among the most important causes of our loss of the sacred is extraordinary scientific progress, especially because science and religion are viewed—although wrongly—as antithetical. New genetic discoveries and new reproductive technologies have given us a sense that we understand the origin and nature of human life and that, because we can, we may manipulate—or even create—life. Transferring these sentiments to the other end of life would support the view that euthanasia is acceptable.

Competing worldviews: Though immensely important in itself, the debate over euthanasia might be a surrogate for yet another, even deeper, one: Which of two irreconcilable worldviews will form the basis of our emerging

"shared story," our new societal-cultural paradigm?

According to one worldview—the "gene machine" or "pure science" position—we are highly complex, biological machines, whose most valuable features are our rational, logical, cognitive functions. This worldview reflects a mechanistic approach to human life. Its proponents support euthanasia, as being, in appropriate circumstances, a logical and rational response to problems at the end of life.

The other worldview, the "science-spirit" position—which does not depend on religion, but is not incompatible with major world religions—is that human life consists of more than its biological component, wondrous as that is. It involves a mystery—at least the "mystery of the unknown"—of which we have a sense through intuitions, especially moral ones.

This worldview includes a sense of a "space for (human) spirit" and of the "secular sacred." It sees death as part of the mystery of life, which means that to respect life, we must respect death. According to this view although we might be under no obligation to prolong the lives of dying people, we do have an obligation not to kill them. And that rules out euthanasia.

Margaret Somerville is the Samuel Gale professor of law and a professor of medicine in McGill University's Centre for Medicine, Ethics and Law.

[MARGARET SOMERVILLE, *GAZETTE* (MONTREAL), OCTOBER 17, 2004, D8. REPRINTED WITH PERMISSION OF DR. MARGARET SOMERVILLE, McGILL UNIVERSITY.]

Matter of personal choice: We should let the terminally ill choose how and when to die—The case for assisted suicide

The most difficult decision we ever make in life might well be about death—our own death, the death of someone close to us, or the death of someone we don't know.

Montreal playwright Charles Fariala, who was suffering from multiple sclerosis, and his mother, Marielle Houle, a nursing assistant, faced just such decisions. Late last month, Fariala reportedly took his own life, and Houle has been charged with aiding his suicide.

Fariala's death has reignited the debate about assisted suicide, about whether we should ever countenance the practice of aiding people in taking their own lives. Such mortal decisions are intensely difficult, and they should be.

The community is split on the issue, although most polls suggest a majority of Canadians favour legalizing some form of assisted suicide. However, despite the advocacy of right-to-die groups, most of those closest to the issue have taken a stand against it.

The Canadian Medical Association opposes assisted suicide, and in 1995 a Senate committee recommended against decriminalizing the practice (although the 1991 B.C. Royal Commission on Health Care endorsed decriminalization). Most groups for people with disabilities argue vociferously against any change to the law, and their voices are worth listening to since their lives are at stake in this.

I have been wrestling with this issue for the better part of two decades, first as a bioethicist and now as an interested layman. While I have had my doubts about the wisdom of permitting the practice, I have, recently and reluctantly, come to support physician-assisted suicide in limited circumstances.

There are many cogent and compelling arguments against physician-assisted suicide, but all tend to fall in two broad (and intertwined) categories: philosophical and practical.

The philosophical argument is made most forcefully by Margaret Somerville, the founding director of the Centre for Medicine, Ethics and Law at McGill University. Although Somerville's argument is complex, she essentially advances the position that permitting euthanasia (the direct taking of a life) or assisted suicide (the provision of knowledge or means to allow people to take their own lives) could fundamentally reduce the respect we have for human life.

Somerville also notes that suicide is not, as is commonly argued, a self-regarding act. It is, rather, profoundly "other-regarding"— when a person commits suicide, the person's family members are deeply affected and so, too, is the community, particularly if the community sanctions the practice.

Somerville therefore worries that assisted suicide could do irreparable harm to the community, and to law and medicine, the very institutions that uphold respect for life.

This is a powerful argument, and the importance of respecting human life is undeniable. Although Parliament decriminalized suicide and attempted suicide 30 years ago, society continues to do everything possible to prevent suicide because we recognize that there are few things more important than life.

I say "few things," because we also recognize that the value of life doesn't always trump all other values, that there are fates worse than death. Both the common law and most ethical systems respect the right of people to refuse life-saving treatment (the right of Jehovah's Witnesses to refuse blood transfusions being the most conspicuous example).

Most people, and most physicians, are also comfortable with the practice of giving large doses of morphine to terminally ill patients, even when it will almost certainly hasten death.

By listing these examples, I don't mean to suggest, as some people have, that there's no moral difference between these practices and assisting suicide. There is a profound difference: By honouring treatment refusals or providing treatment that hastens death, physicians aren't intentionally bringing about death as they are in assisting suicide. And intention is of fundamental importance to both ethics and criminal law.

I do mean to suggest that our sanctioning of practices that lead to death shows that we recognize that respect for life is not an absolute value, that other values sometimes trump the value of life. Specifically, we recognize the value of personhood, a value that encompasses life but also involves autonomy—the right of people to determine how they will live, and how they will die.

And it is out of respect for personhood that I have come to support limited assisted suicide.

One could argue that on the basis of personhood, all people have a right to assisted suicide. But that would be elevating autonomy to an absolute value and could have a devastating effect on the value of respect for life.

Instead, we can maintain an uneasy balance between respect for personhood and respect for life by permitting assisted suicide in only the most dire circumstances. This would involve mentally competent, terminally ill people whose suffering is irremediable—that is, where all efforts at pain-management have failed.

Of course, once we consider legalizing assisted suicide, a host of practical problems intrude. Opponents argue that suicides will greatly increase and it will be just a matter of time before we extend physician-assisted suicide from the terminally ill to other groups. Worse, opponents argue that in light of economic pressures on the health-care system, many people, particularly those with disabilities, will be coerced into accepting suicide.

Yet there's little evidence that suicides rise when assisted suicide is permitted. Oregon enacted its Death with Dignity Act (which allows for physician-assisted suicide) in 1997, yet through 2002, only 129 patients availed themselves of assisted deaths.

In fact, physician-assisted suicide could actually reduce the incidence of suicide. Many terminally ill people never avail themselves of assisted suicide, but feel reassured knowing that the option will be available to them should they need it. In contrast, when assisted suicide is not available, some terminally ill people take their lives before they reach a stage where they would need assistance.

Opponents of physician-assisted suicide also often fail to acknowledge that assisted suicide is currently occurring in Canada. Several people, including physicians, have been charged, and while numbers are hard to come by, former Simon Fraser University graduate student Russel Ogden discovered 34 B.C. cases of assisted suicide or euthanasia among AIDS patients between 1980 and 1993.

Further, many people involved in assisted suicide aren't charged (B.C. has specific guidelines for prosecutors considering laying charges in cases of assisted suicide), and most who are convicted receive light sentences. In fact, in 1983 the Law Reform Commission of Canada recommended no changes to the law precisely because it was so rarely used.

Assisted suicide therefore currently occurs in a legal and ethical vacuum. By legalizing it under certain conditions, we would at least bring this clandestine practice into the open and could subject it to strict legal and ethical regulations.

Regulations are particularly important in addressing the legitimate concerns of people with disabilities. In defence of their argument that disabled and elderly people might be coerced into accepting suicide, opponents point to the "irregularities," and perhaps abuse, in the practice of assisted suicide in the Netherlands.

Yet even though some Dutch physicians have engaged in questionable practices, there's reason to believe that regulations can be designed to protect the rights of both those who wish an assisted suicide and those who don't.

Indeed, Oregon has experienced no evident abuses in the more than six years since it enacted the Death with Dignity Act. The act permits a terminally ill patient to request a physician-assisted suicide provided two physicians confirm the diagnosis and two other people (one of whom must be unrelated to the patient) witness the request.

Further, the patient must be aware of all medical options available, and must not be suffering from any condition that impairs judgment (standard requirements for informed consent).

Once the request is authorized, the patient must wait 15 days and then repeat the request. Patients can change their minds at any time, and no physician is required to participate in an assisted suicide.

While the Oregon experience has been positive, patients might still be influenced by their physicians, given the imbalance of knowledge and power in the doctor-patient relationship. As such, I would suggest some judicial oversight—patients could apply to a superior court and the court could decide if the criteria have been met.

(Former Supreme Court of Canada chief justice Antonio Lamer suggested this condition in his dissenting judgment in R v. Rodriguez, where the court, in a 5–4 judgment, upheld the constitutionality of the assisted-suicide law).

Some opponents of physician-assisted suicide argue that meeting such conditions is a daunting task because of the difficulty in assessing the competence of terminally ill patients, whose autonomy is usually compromised. But that's

(Continued)

Matter of personal choice: We should let the terminally ill choose how and when to die—The case for assisted suicide *(Continued)*

a problem palliative-care workers face daily when deciding whether to honour requests to refuse or withdraw treatment.

Speaking of palliative care, some opponents of physician-assisted suicide worry that our commitment to such care would be undermined if we permitted assisted suicide. That, however, has not been the case in Oregon, where evidence suggests that some aspects of palliative care have actually improved.

In fact, the introduction of physician-assisted suicide might also improve palliative care by illuminating the need for clearer guidelines concerning treatment refusal and withdrawal requests. Given the vociferous opposition to physician-assisted suicide, it's surprising that such practices remain largely unregulated.

Jocelyn Downie, director of Dalhousie University's health-law institute, makes precisely this point in her superb new book, *Dying*

Justice: A Case for Decriminalizing Euthanasia and Assisted Suicide in Canada.

In essence then, assisted suicide can be seen as a proper part of palliative care, as the endpoint in the continuum of care. And in its respect for both life and personhood, a limited regime of assisted suicide can be a welcome part of any system of comprehensive and compassionate care for the living, and the dying.

[PETER MCKNIGHT, *OTTAWA CITIZEN*, OCTOBER 5, 2004, A15. REPRINTED WITH PERMISSION OF THE PACIFIC NEWSPAPER GROUP.]

EXERCISE 11.6

Report on Contrasting Arguments

Written Assignment: Choose a topic that interests you and find two substantial arguments with different positions on this issue. (If you did Exercise 4.10 in Chapter 4, you will already have two arguments you can use here.) Write up a complete report of your analysis as a coherent short essay—introduce the topic, report and evaluate both arguments, compare them, and make constructive suggestions.

Key Points in Review

- Once you have evaluated an argument, your next step is to decide how best to respond.

- To respond to a good argument, it is important to demonstrate that you have not simply missed faults in the argument. You can respond by adding some *independent* evidence for believing that the argument is good.

- To respond to an unproven argument, you can show where and how we might look for evidence that would have to be gathered in order to rule out the remaining areas of uncertainty.

- To respond to a bad argument, it will be most helpful to find at least one promising step forward. Possibilities include pointing out more useful directions to pursue, demonstrating empathy for the underlying concerns, and redirecting the discussion back to the central issues.
- To compare arguments on the same topic effectively, attempt to find the common ground, isolate the remaining areas of disagreement, and discuss what to do next.

Chapter 12

Responding in Context

■ Perspective

The moment you present your evaluation of an argument or a situation to other people, you must make choices about how you are going to interact with them. You know the information you wish to convey. Now you need to decide how, and to whom, you will convey it. Who needs the information, why do they need it, and what will it take for them to accept it and use it? In this chapter, you will explore the challenges of dealing with different people's expectations.

■ Scenario

Imagine you have been given the task of researching and reviewing the use of crisis counsellors by an organization whose employees frequently deal with stressful incidents such as death or violence. The counsellors come in immediately after the event to talk with groups and individuals, to help them deal with their reactions. In the course of your research, you examined a number of articles, some recommending the use of crisis counsellors and some claiming that such counselling either makes no difference or is actually harmful. As a result of your evaluation of this information, you have decided it would be most reasonable to stop using crisis counsellors. You know this recommendation will not be popular. The supervisor of the group was the one who introduced the counselling program and feels very strongly that it does work. How will you present the results of your research?

■ Key Question

How can I respectfully address others' needs as well as my own?

Developing Procedure: Meeting Needs and Respecting Beliefs

You'll need to give as much attention to procedure—the format and sequence of your communication—as you have done to content. Whenever you need other people's involvement and cooperation, you must be able to speak to them in terms they will understand. Mutual respect is important. How do you achieve it?

Think of the difference between getting out a rough draft of a paper and revising it for a final draft. When you write out a rough draft, you need only think about whether you are getting down everything you want to say and connecting it in ways that make sense to you. When you revise a paper for someone else to read, you have to think about what will make sense to another person. You have to look at your own draft as if through another person's eyes and change the wording and the organization so it will make sense to someone who does not think like you do or make the same connections you would. Similarly, in presenting an evaluation, you need to turn your "rough draft" thinking into a "final draft" that is audience-friendly.

How do you present your analysis so that it will fulfill your responsibilities? Good presentation skills, as taught in many courses, are an important part of procedure. But they are not the complete picture. It's only a first step to be able to articulate your reasoning clearly and correctly. That gives you the content of what you want to say. To shape the format of your presentation, you also need to know how to suit your presentation to the reasoning needs and expectations of the people who must hear it.

Often, you must first decide whether to reply at all. Whether you are writing or speaking, you need to consider the value that is placed on argument or open discussion in that specific context. At work, for example, you may find it best simply to ask questions rather than to confront your supervisors or boss with the faults in their arguments. You might, for example, ask questions—"Have you considered . . . ?" or "Can you give me more detail on why you think . . . ?" or "Why did you rule out . . . ?" Your questions may work as well as any evaluation to advance the discussion. At home, you may have listened to one of the ongoing disputes that many families have. Knowing your family, you know whom you can challenge and to what extent. You may even decide that silence is the best response, because family harmony is more important to you than being sure that the dispute reaches a reasonable conclusion.

When the situation is even more complex—for example, if you are dealing with people of very different backgrounds and you don't know how they feel about reasoning or open disagreement—the decision becomes correspondingly more complex.

When People Place Different Values on Reason

What happens when two people disagree but do not share their attitudes to reasoning or their standards for good arguments? For example, some people will not permit any questioning of their conclusions or orders, however tactful and reasonable the questions are. Some people will not argue at all; others will argue every detail and have fun doing it. Some people do not accept reasoning that others consider blindingly obvious. Can we resolve our differences without assuming that some people just aren't reasonable?

Consider, for example, the following passage describing Scottish practices:

> The invitation to "participate," especially to offer critical comment in public, touches a nerve of anxiety. This derives partly from the instinct that to disagree with another person before witnesses is to open a serious personal confrontation; the English or American assumption that "free, open discussion" is non-lethal and even healthy is not widespread in Scotland. The Presbyterian tradition contributes to this reluctance, with its binary right-or-wrong approach which leaves little room for compromise or "agreement to differ."

> One consequence of this attitude towards reasoning in public is that in newspaper editorial conferences, "the English meeting [is] long, argumentative, but aiming for consensus; the Scottish one brief, ritualistic and consisting of little more than the recital of the day's news and features schedule as the desk chiefs gravely nod their heads."

[Neal Ascherson, *Stone Voices: The Search for Scotland*, London: Granta Books, 2002, p. 85]

These apparent differences in willingness to reason publicly occur within a nation that from the outside is treated as a unit: the "British." Just as we would be unwise to assume that the English, Irish, Welsh, and Scots will all behave alike, similarly, we will be unwise to assume that individual people of any of these groups will behave according to the norms for their society. Belief systems vary by background and by personal development.

Another example illustrates differences between Americans. A black male professor had angrily challenged a white female professor in a meeting, pointing a finger at her and speaking forcefully. Seeing that she looked frightened, he said, "You don't need to worry, I'm still talking. When I *stop* talking, then you might need to worry." In spite of his words, the white professor was not reassured, and after the meeting, accused the black professor of threatening her. The author describing this interaction says:

> He was astonished by her accusation. His comment to me afterwards was, "All I did was *talk* to her. Now how can that be threatening?"

> These conflicting interpretations of the black professor's behavior are not unique to this encounter. Whites *invariably* interpret black anger and aggressiveness as more provocative and threatening than do blacks.

[Thomas Kochman, *Black and White Styles in Conflict*, Chicago: University of Chicago Press, 1981, pp. 43–44; italics in the original]

What is interesting in this example is that both participants were professors. They would have a great deal in common in their education and experience and in their expectations of encounters in academic meetings. Although the incident took place many years ago now, it nicely reflects the astonishment people still feel when their reasoning practices are not met with the responses they expect. We may have become more sensitized to the possibility of differences, but we still often don't expect them within what we count as our "community"—the people with whom we share a similar way of life.

When we engage in discussion with people whose backgrounds are significantly different than our own, we're faced with difficult questions about our reasoning practices. Canada, as a multicultural society, is officially bilingual and supports a "cultural mosaic." Differences in language and culture are to be honoured rather than eliminated. How does this affect the way in which we go about reasoning, and the type or amount of evidence that we seek before we accept a conclusion?

Responses in a Multicultural Context

When we deal with people whose backgrounds are significantly different than our own, we're faced with difficult questions about our reasoning procedures. A **multicultural context** is any setting in which people have different cultural traditions and expectations, and may have significant differences in beliefs and values. Culture, background, and temperament produce major differences in the value that people place on reasoning itself. These differences in value produce significant differences in behaviour. For instance, employees encounter bosses who will not let them ask questions. Teachers encounter students who will only repeat what they are told and do not seem to want to think independently. Students encounter teachers who will not allow any difference of opinion. Bosses encounter employees who will not question decisions or take any initiative. We must deal with a full spectrum of **reasoning behaviour**—how reasoning is indicated in practice—in others, from those who refuse to reason at all to those who question every detail.

If you live in a fairly homogeneous community, you may even find it hard to imagine just how dramatic those differences can be. Yet they can show up in the most unexpected places. For example, a teacher used to write "Why?" in the margins of rough drafts of essays to show students where more explanation was needed. One student would hand back the revised essay not with more explanation but with completely different points—not better, just radically different. After this had happened several times, both the teacher and the student were understandably frustrated. Eventually, they talked it over carefully enough to realize that this student had been raised in a household where children were never permitted to challenge their father or any authority figure. When the teacher wrote "Why?" in the margin, the student took that to mean "Why would you say something like this?"—in other words, why are you saying such nonsense? Naturally, then, the student thought that the only reasonable way to fix this problem would be to change it and say something different. This mutually frustrating situation came from a significant difference in beliefs about reasoning—the teacher has a belief system that expects everyone to reason freely and openly, in a climate where "Why?" is a question expressing genuine interest. The student has a belief system that some people are much smarter than others, and those who are not so smart ought not to assume their ideas are acceptable. In the student's experience, "Why?" is a challenge, questioning your competence. (This teacher is now careful to write "Explain" instead of "Why?" in the margins of papers.)

How do we act in accordance with Canada's commitment to a "cultural mosaic"? How do we honour differences in language and culture? Should we also adapt the way in which we go about reasoning, and the type or amount of evidence that we seek before we accept a conclusion? These are challenging questions without agreed-upon answers. The rest of this chapter offers discussion and suggestions, not conclusions.

Dealing with Significant Differences in Reasoning Behaviour

What can we add to our existing understanding of good reasoning to help us work effectively in situations where people disagree on reasoning? As always, we want to be neither undercritical (too passive) nor overcritical (insisting too rigidly on perfect accord).

In dealing with disagreements about when and why to reason, and what reasoning will count as acceptable, some people believe that reasoning is the same for everyone everywhere. These people argue that anyone who falters in reasoning, or fails to understand others' good reasoning, simply has not been educated well enough or is in some way deficient in rationality. Other people believe that each culture, subject area, and gender has its own distinctive reasoning behaviour and values and that we should not impose the reasoning standards of one group on another.

This leaves us to deal with a number of open questions about selection of responses and reasoning standards in different contexts. Is it fairer to treat every person the same, or fairer to treat each person within a system that he or she fully understands and that honours his or her moral principles? If a person is not persuaded by logical reasoning of the type we've set out in Chapters 5 and 8, is that person following a different legitimate pattern of reasoning, or is he or she simply irrational?

You saw two examples in the Introduction. A Russian study in the 1930s found that older residents of Uzbekistan would not give any answer to a logic puzzle if the subject matter involved things they had not personally seen, such as the colour of bears in the far north or the rainfall on mountains they could see in the distance but had never visited. It became clear that they held very strongly to a principle that prevented them answering. One man, repeatedly asked by the researchers to give an answer to the puzzle, finally burst out, "Look, if a man was sixty or eighty and had seen a white bear, and had told about it, he could be believed, but I've never seen one and hence I can't say. That's my last word. Those who saw can tell, and those who didn't see can't say anything!" (Luria 109). A younger man, standing beside him, volunteered that the answer to the logic puzzle was that the bears were white, yet the older man would not change his answer. For this man and many of his contemporaries, the only evidence that can be used in reasoning about what can be experienced is direct personal experience. The words of others or hypothetical rules are simply not enough to justify drawing a conclusion. The man is clearly capable of logical reasoning. Consider his first sentence, "Look, if a man was sixty or eighty and had seen a white bear, and had told about it, he could be believed, but I've never seen one and hence I can't say. "Taken together with his principle that a person cannot speak about what has not been directly experienced, this is a good argument to certainty, concluding that he cannot answer the question.

The second example from the Introduction illustrated a similar difference in reasoning practice. In Hamill's study, speakers who were fluently bilingual in English and Navajo gave different answers to the same question depending on which language it was asked in. "You are tall or you are not tall" is true if said in English, false if said in Navajo.

It is counted as obviously false in Navajo because traditional Navajo beliefs include a principle that overrides logical consistency. The principle in this case is that it is not possible to assert anything about the person to whom you are speaking (Hamill). What is interesting in this example is that the test subjects could move between two different types of reasoning practice depending on the language they were speaking. If you have studied French, you might find a similar but less restrictive linguistic principle in play. In French, you are expected to make the logical connections in your reasoning clear and explicit, by using all the logical connection words, such as *parce que* ("because"). In English, you can leave the connections ambiguous or implicit by connecting your premises with nothing more than "and."

Recognizing Differences in Values

The differences we are considering are differences that affect our reasoning practices. The study of argument acceptability does not take us all the way to showing how we deal with differences in the acceptability of reasoning in general. The differences are considered in argumentation theory—the study of argument, persuasion, and the uses of argument in different contexts.

You will know if you have encountered people who place a different value on reasoning than you do when you find yourself in a situation in which either they will not discuss a topic at all or they meet your attempts to discuss the topic with anger, silence, or indifference.

It helps to realize that these differences often run as deep as differences in principle—in fact, they can be caused by differences in principle and can be as slow to change. The differences may come from cultural beliefs about whether reasoning and disagreement are valuable or not. The person may come from an upbringing that did not welcome questioning and independent thinking, as described above in the case of the student who had been raised not to ask "Why?"

We must also recognize that not all situations can be resolved using reason. For instance, as mentioned earlier, people under stress will not reason as clearly as when they are calm and healthy. If you know that stress is a factor in the person's behaviour, reducing the stress or working around it will be the priority.

Similarly, if you encounter a person whose responses seem bizarre or absolutely unaffected by anything you have said—he or she seems not even to have noticed your words—you should consider the possibility that that reasoning is not the right approach. Perhaps you need to learn more about each other first. Perhaps the person needs a wise counsellor, not a debate partner.

There are also people who seem willing to engage in reasoning, but their answers are hard to follow or seem illogical and unconnected to what's actually been said. These people may be thinking in a different way, so what seems obvious to them does not seem obvious to you.

Responding to Differences in Values

How can you respond effectively to reasoning behaviour that is different from your own? In many of the situations described above, it becomes tempting to throw up your hands and declare, "They just won't listen to reason!" Yet reasoning can still help. What can we add to our existing understanding of good reasoning to help us work effectively in these situations? The same reasoning skills that have guided us through arguments can also be used to guide us in argumentation. The previous chapter showed how to decide *what* you might say. Now you can move on to consider *how* to present what you want to say.

If people seem to be capable of reasoning but clearly disagree with you about when and why they should have to give reasons, there are a number of procedures that may help you to deal with the differences.

As with our practical responses, we want to be neither undercritical (too passive) nor overcritical (insisting too rigidly on perfect accord). A first step in designing procedure is to step away from the why of reasoning and look at the who, what, when, and how of the context.

Who will respond to reason? Is it worth reasoning with a three-year-old? Can you still reason with your grandmother who has had a severe stroke? Can you reason with your father, who believes that he is the authority in the family?

What topics may be discussed? Is it reasonable to discuss how much money people make when you're out for an evening with friends? Is it permissible to discuss the supernatural with people who believe in ghosts and are afraid of what they can do? Can you discuss a disappointing grade with a professor, or can you only make a formal appeal if you are dissatisfied with the marking scheme?

When and *where* is it acceptable to engage in discussion? Can a firefighter question an order to go into a burning building? Can a witness ask questions in court? Can a guest at a wedding stand up and argue that the couple is not suited to each other, at a point in the ceremony where the officiant formally invites people to "speak now" if they have reason to believe the marriage should not go ahead?

How can the setting and format of a conversation be altered to improve the chances of good communication? Do you want to discuss treatment with your doctor while you're sitting on the examination table wearing one of those paper gowns that hang open at the back? Do you want to discuss your grades with your professor who is busy gathering up books to rush to the next class? Do you want to discuss changes to a charity's donation priorities casually, over coffee, or formally, at a meeting?

Being Flexible in the Face of Inflexibility

When we consider the answers to these questions, we are faced with two difficult challenges. First, the beliefs and values that guide what will be considered respectful and appropriate communication do not change quickly. If you must deal with someone who has a very different approach to communication, it's not likely either of you could change quickly enough and completely enough to satisfy the other.

Second, the beliefs people want to have respected are not always the beliefs we are willing to respect. Consider, for example, how difficult it can be for a man who believes deeply in equality, especially between men and women, to sit comfortably among men who think women have no opinions worth listening to. Consider what a challenge a woman faces when she has to work with such men if her job requires her to make them listen. Consider the challenges a young person faces getting older people to take advice or follow orders.

To deal with these challenges, we have to consider that we may need to negotiate not only what the outcome of the discussion will be but also how we will communicate. We look for ways to make everyone feel properly heard without any of them feeling that they have been forced to concede a belief or position they are not ready to concede.

Sometimes, too, we have to acknowledge that in some situations respectful discussion is not appropriate and in other situations not even possible. A junior police officer can't engage in respectful discussion with a senior officer about what to do next when they are in the middle of responding to a robbery in progress. There may be times when it is more appropriate simply to lay down the law or to act without discussion. Good reasoning involves recognizing when a situation requires an uncritical or authoritative action, and when it is possible to revisit the situation and discuss how it might be handled better another time.

One of the best examples of adapting reasoning behaviour to accommodate cultural differences has been in the justice system in northern Native communities. For example, a judge may sit on one side of a square of tables with everyone else seated and with the elders of the community also at the table as participants. The elders may participate in sentencing through sentencing circles, which can provide support to both offender and victim. This is much more egalitarian and less adversarial than a traditional courtroom setting, with a judge presiding from above. Involving the elders and giving them a say in sentencing represents a considerable change in who is entitled to join in the reasoning.

The appeal to the community and the reminder that this approach works to reduce crime reflect deeper differences in reasoning than courtroom layout. The changes in the justice procedure for northern communities reflect an attempt to build a mutually acceptable structure that fits two very different sets of principles and reasoning behaviour.

Similarly, and more recently, there has been a move to a restorative justice approach in the schools, with active attempts to deal with children's conflicts not by punishing or blaming but by encouraging mutual respect and by taking a problem-solving approach in which children themselves play a role as peer mediators.

How to Approach Difficult Questions and Sensitive Issues

What happens when the differences run deeper still? There are many open questions and unanswered puzzles in this area. In this next section, we will make a start on the basic questions you will need to consider. You may find these questions very challenging indeed. Approach them as open questions, rather than looking for right answers. These are not questions for which we already have clear correct answers—that's why we need reasoning!

It's true there are experts with training in some aspects of how to deal with people in difficult situations. For example, counsellors, labour negotiators, police officers, and others have specialized training in several aspects of these concerns. If you have worked in retail or service jobs, you might yourself have had on-the-job training in how to handle angry or disruptive customers, which covers some aspects of procedure. Life experience alone can give you expertise you may not realize you have. (Have you raised a teenager or been one? The mix of emotion and reason in teenage years challenges most of us in handling disagreements effectively.)

However, even the experts are realizing that there are many complexities for which they don't yet have answers. As immigration has increased, and as globalization has sent more and more people around the globe to face "culture shock" as they try to do business in other countries, there has finally been active investigation of the difficult puzzles that used to be left to professional diplomats. How can a Canadian female executive do business in Muslim Saudi Arabia? How do Sikh immigrants to Canada, raised with all the benefits of arranged marriages, handle their children's immersion in Canadian culture and their active interest in choosing their own marriage partner and even in marrying outside their culture?

Clearly, this debate overlaps into the area of rights. What right do you have, as a member of one culture, to impose your values about reasoning on a member of another? Sentencing circles and other innovations in the justice system are good examples of the attempt to deal with these difficulties without being either undercritical—thinking that it is not possible to bridge the gap—nor overcritical—insisting on imposing one preferred approach on everyone.

What follows, then, is not a test of your current abilities but an open door into thinking through how you might approach some of these situations, and what the advantages and disadvantages of different approaches might be. These are all situations in which any action you take could cause reactions you didn't anticipate. Which action you try is going to be less crucial than your willingness to look for feedback on how your actions are coming across and to learn quickly from the feedback. We'll be looking at feedback in the Postscript.

Meanwhile, summon a sense of adventure to approach the questions below.

Who

Many people have sharply defined expectations about who is permitted to reason. Behind most of the expectations are attitudes about power: typically, those who can give orders are those who must reason, whereas those who must follow orders have no need of reason. Correspondingly, if no one has a right to give orders because everyone is equal, then everyone can—and should—reason.

If you are dealing with someone who thinks that reasoning is the exclusive right of authorities or their designated advisors, you may find yourself treated as a subordinate who has not earned the right to question. If you are the one in a supervisory role, you may find that subordinates expect you to act as an authority and do all the reasoning and decision-making for them.

At the other extreme, some people believe that because we are all equal, we can and must discuss every decision, however small, with everyone affected, and we must not proceed until we have reached a decision by consensus. (You probably know where you fall on this spectrum; you might be surprised to find how strongly you feel about it.)

These beliefs run deep and change slowly. If you do not want to settle for expectations imposed on you, you have two main options. You can explain why it is important to you to give or get reasons and why you are willing to wait for a time and place that the others consider suitable. Alternatively, you can appeal to an intermediary whom you trust, someone in a position to be listened to by others.

EXERCISE ## Choosing Who Should Speak

In which of the following situations would you approach the person directly, by yourself? In which of the situations would you go as one member of a group? In which would you ask someone else to be your spokesperson? Explain your reasoning.

*1. You are in your early twenties, still living at home, and you want your parents to accept you dating people who are not of your culture or religion.

2. You are a female employee at a golf course that requires its employees to wear short, tight shirts on "men's nights" at the club. The shirts are too revealing and too uncomfortable. You want the middle-aged male manager to reconsider the outfits.

3. You've worked as hard as you can on a term paper and done what (in your opinion) is your best work in the course. When the grade comes back, it's a full letter grade below your average so far this term! The professor for this course is popular with some students, but you personally find him or her intimidating.

What

We vary as to which topics are considered public and which are considered private. Some people will defend their lifestyle; some will not discuss it except with their most trusted intimates. Some people consider it enjoyable to argue about religion; others consider their faith not open to question.

If you want to persuade people to discuss a topic that they are not easily able to talk about, and you have a good reason to raise that topic with them, you might be able to lead them into discussion by making sure that you offer only welcoming responses to what they say. You might start with questions about neutral, impersonal topics, then ask for opinions (but not expect explanations), and only gradually turn the conversation to more challenging topics or to asking for reasons.

If it's the other way round and you are expected to discuss something that you do not want to discuss, but you need to try, you might seek assurances of confidentiality. You could seek intermediaries whom you trust, or people who must maintain confidentiality: lawyers, counsellors, doctors, social workers, and priests. These people often have training in dealing tactfully with uncomfortable topics.

EXERCISE 12.2 ## Framing the Topic

1. How might you open a discussion on the topic of drug use and abuse with
    *a. a friend whose use of alcohol is worrying you
    b. a young teenager
    c. your grandmother, whose attitudes strike you as intolerant

2. With whom would you raise the following topics, and why:
    a. money worries: you are running very low and may need to borrow money
    b. health problems: you've got a problem that embarrasses you
    c. beliefs: you're starting to question your faith (or lack of faith)

When (and Where)

Many people find it inappropriate to be expected to respond rapidly in discussions. They may want time to think; they may want to hear other people speak first; they may want to demonstrate that they are giving proper attention to your ideas; or they may want the debate postponed to a more appropriate occasion or transferred to some other location.

Generally, it is unwise to put yourself in a position in which you or other people need a chance to think, but in which an answer is expected right away. Can you set the timelines out and agree on them before you discuss the topic? Can you agree on a convenient location? Do they want to be on home ground, or do they want to be able to consult someone by phone, take breaks, or have a library nearby? Can you ask when a response could be ready?

EXERCISE 12.3

The Right Time and the Right Place

When and where would you suggest a meeting for the following scenarios?

*1.   You need to meet with your landlord to ask for repairs to your kitchen.

 2.   You want to propose to your partner, who is not as romantic as you are.

 3.   You want to ask your boss for time off that you would not normally be entitled to.

How

Who may speak, and in what order? Who is seated, and where are they positioned? Must topics be dealt with systematically, one by one, or can the discussion flow back and forth through many topics? All the issues raised by "who," "what," and "when" find their expression in the "how" of structuring a discussion.

Generally, those who want to demonstrate or protect power and decision-making authority will want to stand, or sit higher than everyone else, or sit in isolation, facing everyone else—perhaps behind an impressive desk. They may speak first, and last, and interrupt at will.

Those who want to demonstrate respect and a willingness to defer to authority may reduce eye contact and choose lower or inconspicuous seating. Cultural differences will make a difference to how far apart people want to sit or stand.

Those who want to maintain an egalitarian atmosphere will sit (or all stand) in a circle or at right angles to one another, often avoiding desks and tables; they will speak in turn and avoid interrupting.

You may be able to make some easy changes that help the discussion to be comfortable. For example, suppose a doctor or a lawyer offers you a chair directly facing the desk. This allows you the opportunity to confront him or her, but also makes you run the risk of feeling intimidated, since doctors and lawyers are typically confident and direct in their speech. You have the option to swing the chair to a right angle with the desk so that you are still equal but less confrontational. If a teacher or pastor is standing while you talk, you might ask the person to sit instead, explaining that it makes you uncomfortable if he or she stands.

Other changes require negotiation and draw us back into considering the cultural and behavioural backgrounds that influence our practices.

EXERCISE 12.4

Helping Discussion Flow Smoothly

How would you organize discussions of the following issues?

*1.   Whether your sports team should commit to an out-of-province event

 2.   Whether a cigarette company should be permitted to sponsor a student art competition

 3.   Whether your board of directors for a volunteer organization should include volunteers on the board

Key Points in Review

- You'll need to give as much attention to procedure as you have done to content. Whenever you need other people's involvement and cooperation, you must be able to speak with them in terms all of you will understand. Mutual respect is important.

- Culture, background, and temperament produce major differences in the value that people place on reasoning itself. These differences in value produce significant differences in behaviour.

- You will know if you have encountered people who place a different value on reasoning than you do when you find yourself in a situation in which they either will not discuss a topic at all or meet your attempts to discuss the topic with anger, silence, or indifference.

- To approach some of these challenging situations, consider the advantages and disadvantages of different approaches. Avoid being either undercritical—thinking that it is not possible to bridge the gap—nor overcritical—insisting on imposing one preferred approach on everyone. Which action you try is going to be less crucial than your willingness to look for feedback on how your actions are coming across, and learn quickly from the feedback.

Part 4
Summary

Making the Best Response

Knowledge, if it does not determine action, is dead to us.
— *Plotinus*

Action and Response Overview

Action carries you forward. It turns your beliefs from insights to involvement. In this part you have seen how you might choose the wisest action and how to handle some of the complexities of presenting your choices. Responsible action engages you with other people and their needs, values, and preferences. Responsible action is a matter of negotiating the most reasonable way to respect yourself and respect others.

Part-Ending Exercises

Comprehension Questions: Review

1. What does it mean to be neither undercritical nor overcritical?
2. What do you need to take into account when setting priorities?
3. How can context influence how you respond to an argument?
4. What do you need to think about when trying to decide how to respond after an evaluation?
5. How might your response be influenced by the beliefs of the people you deal with?

Application Exercises

1. What is the most helpful feedback you've ever received? Explain why you found this response useful.
2. Take some examples from your argument collection and construct a response to each of them. Choose the context of your response yourself.
3. Choose two or three arguments with different perspectives on the same issue. Evaluate each one separately, and then compare the arguments to each other. Based on your evaluation, offer a constructive response that will help make progress in the discussion of this issue.

Postscript

Moving On: Learning from Feedback

■ Perspective

In Chapters 10, 11, and 12, you looked at how to prepare responses appropriate to the situation or the arguments. But even the best plan typically doesn't guarantee its success. Depending on what happens when you try it, you may need to reconsider whether you correctly identified the problem, issue, or opportunity in the first place, or whether you need to re-define it and try again. You need to give, and get, useful feedback. This chapter ends the book by starting the next cycle of critical thinking—how do you use what you've learned so far to do even better next time?

■ Scenario

You're in a new job that involves a considerable amount of customer service. After the first day, your supervisor told you to be more outgoing and chat with the customers. For the last week, you've been trying to make a point of chatting and being friendly with each customer. Now the supervisor tells you that you're spending too much time talking to the customers and you need to be more efficient. What do you need in order to figure out what you should do next week?

■ Key Question

What information do we need to move forward?

Feedback: Standards for Guidance

What is feedback? **Feedback** is anything you observe, or anything said to you by others, that reveals whether something is working well. A failing grade on an essay and a burst balloon are both examples of feedback—something went wrong somewhere.

"Feedback" is the common name for the responses we are supposed to learn from. The word doesn't often have the positive connotations it is supposed to have. Think of feedback, and you often think of the performance review that was unflattering, or the present you chose so carefully that was received with no real joy, or the joke that fell flat. We don't often think of the compliments we received, or the good grades, let alone think of the insights we got from suddenly seeing a situation as others saw it. We tend to think of feedback as something that we receive passively, something that is given to us whether we want it or not, instead of as something we actively set out to find, or something we would plan for. Worse yet, as the opening scenario for this chapter shows, we often receive conflicting feedback that seems to point us in opposite directions. How can we turn negative or confusing feedback into information we can use?

So far in the book you have been developing your skills as the person doing the reasoning and offering feedback to others. This chapter turns the tables and looks at what happens when you are on the receiving end—when you are dealing with the consequences of your own reasoning, or when you are receiving feedback from someone else. This chapter will focus on choosing your own feedback: how to plan for it, how to recognize it, and how to use it wisely.

First, we need to remember that critical thinking is a cycle. It circles back on itself to use its results to help move forward. Remember that an argument is only good if it stands the test of time and repeated scrutiny, so it may need repeated scrutiny. For example, when some municipalities banned smoking in public places, including restaurants, many places that could not provide completely separate smoking facilities found they either lost business or had crowds of employees smoking around their entryways. Revisiting the ban provided less extreme, more workable solutions, such as heated outdoor areas for pubs and restaurants, sealed smoking rooms in airports, and covered areas for smokers' breaks outside office buildings and stores.

To be sure we get good results from our reasoning, we need to set good standards for feedback. It must be

- what we need,
- in the form we need it,
- when we need it.

In Chapter 11, you saw what feedback you could give on reasoning. In Chapter 12, you saw what goes into figuring out who should give the feedback, and when, where, or how, they should give it. In this Postscript we'll look at how you can plan for and use feedback yourself.

Planning for Feedback

Planning for feedback is a challenge—not so much because we don't really want feedback but because it forces us to think very clearly about what our objectives are. We may not have articulated any objective more clearly than "I want to do a good job on this" or "Please, just let me stay below the radar and not be noticed." A round of applause might do nicely to prove I did a good job; no feedback at all might do nicely to show I didn't get noticed. Does that really meet my needs?

To see that we do need and do value more specific feedback, consider settings in which we are much more actively engaged in getting feedback. If you're learning a new craft, such as painting, or a new physical activity, such as weight training, then you engage actively in some experimentation with techniques. When you're learning to paint, you experiment. What happens if you blow paint through a straw? What happens if you squeeze it from an eye-dropper? You try various techniques for applying paint to paper, looking eagerly for the results, so you can find out which effects are possible and how you might create the desired effect when you come to plan a complete painting. Similarly, as you learn to use weights, you may experiment with body position, shifting your arms or your balance slightly to find out where you feel the pull in your muscles. Are you getting the stretch across the chest? Is the effort coming from your thigh muscles or your back? You need to learn from physical sensation whether you are targeting the right muscle groups for each exercise, and you do that by noticing what you feel each time.

These are examples of actively seeking feedback. In these examples, we are not interested just in vague general feedback, such as "Doesn't that look pretty?" or "See how much weight I can lift." We are interested in the differences that will help us later, the connection between what we've just done and what we might need to do in future. If I hand the draft of an essay to a friend to read, I probably don't just want to hear, "It looks fine to me." I probably want the answers to specific questions, such as "Could you tell what my main point was? Did the reasoning flow properly or are there gaps in places?" When I hand the final paper in, I don't just want a B all on its own at the end of the paper—a grade with no comments. Even if the grade is my main concern at this point, I want some idea of what made this better than a C paper and what kept it below an A, so I know what I might do the same and what I would change on the next assignment or in the next course. Ideally, I also want to know more about what I said—if I thought I'd come up with interesting ideas on the image of "the west" in literature, or a clever argument about why Aristotle could have been so confident and yet so wrong about how many teeth women have, then I want some response to my ideas themselves. Am I on to something here, so I can develop my ideas and see where else they lead? Or have I over-looked or misinterpreted some of the evidence? Where do I go next if I want to prove that our education system doesn't really promote indi-vidual development or even good citizenship, it just promotes middle-class consumer values? How can I critique the excessive deference paid to experts such as doctors and lawyers?

The more clearly we define what we want to learn from our achievements, the easier it is to get the information we need—the feedback we want. It even becomes easier to deal with the conflicting feedback we may get. Consider the scenario at the beginning of the chapter. If you have a new job, you do want to know if you are doing things right. You probably had so much to absorb that was new on the first day that you might not have been able to stop and ask whether you were handling customers correctly. After you receive the feedback that you need to be friendlier and to interact more with the customers, you could take a more active role in exploring the feedback. Can the supervisor give you an example of what would be a good customer interaction? Are there specific things you should remember to say? (Any job involving sales often has a very detailed script of things to say, and precise ways to say them so that they sound natural and yet still encourage the customer to make purchases.)

Taking the initiative to get more specific feedback might be enough to make your next week easier. But suppose that you did go ahead doing your best to interact more and the supervisor said you were wasting too much time talking to customers. Or similarly, imagine you wrote an essay that the professor handed back for a rewrite because it was too wordy and the assignment asked you to be brief. When you hand it back in again, this time the professor says it's not detailed enough. Now what? Can't they make up their minds?

With conflicting feedback, you may need some of the strategies from Chapter 12 to find a way to handle any further discussion, especially if the person giving you feedback is in a position of authority. The underlying principle, though, is still one of using reasoning to find a way through. What might be going on that could account for the conflicting feedback? There are two likely possibilities. One possibility is that the situation has changed. Perhaps the week you were practising talking more to customers was a week when the store went from too quiet to too busy. Suddenly people are back from vacation and crowding the store for back-to-school supplies. The skills you need to use when the store is quiet are not the right skills to use when the store is busy. But perhaps there has been no obvious change in the situation. Certainly, in the second scenario of an essay that was first too long and then not long enough, the assignment hasn't changed, and neither have the expectations of the professor. The second possibility, then, is that there is a skill you don't yet have, or a distinction you don't know how to draw between "too chatty" and "not chatty enough" or between "too wordy" and "too brief."

If the situation has changed, you can improve the feedback by asking what the priorities are now and how best to meet them. If the situation has not changed but your changed performance still is not acceptable, you can improve the feedback by asking for more specific information on what chatty means or what brief means in this context.

This brief discussion of conflicting feedback illustrates the principles that help you get and give feedback in general. As a good reasoner, you need to take an active role in getting feedback that is specific enough to help you, and that means you need to know what the priorities are and what options you have.

These final questions on feedback can end one cycle of critical thinking and begin the next:

1. How can we tell if we have correctly identified and dealt with our concerns? What feedback are we looking for?

2. How do we deal with the feedback once we receive it?

EXERCISE   **P.1**

Planning for Feedback

For one of the following situations, design a plan or checklist for collecting information to give you feedback. To help you, look back at Chapter 1 for guidelines on preparing checklists.

*1. You've written a paper that you hope will make a good starting point for a final term project. What feedback do you want so you know how you can develop the paper?

2. You have an elderly relative living with you, and the doctor has suggested that more physical activity is essential. You've agreed to make sure your relative does move around the house more during the day, but you're gone at work most of the time. How could you confirm whether your relative really is getting the extra exercise that's needed?

3. You've changed your diet, and you know that it may take some time for any improvement to show up. What could you keep track of so you have the best chance of knowing whether the new diet is working, or whether it's not making any helpful difference?

4. You're learning how to cook—perhaps for the first time, perhaps to learn a new cuisine or a new technique. How might you experiment with new dishes to become more confident that you are mastering the methods?

5. You have begun to learn a foreign language, and you have finally become confident enough to engage in conversation with native speakers. What feedback will you look for to check that you are using the language correctly?

Offering Feedback

When you are the one giving the feedback, not the one getting feedback, it is essential to remember that the other person is entitled to plan for the feedback. What feedback does the person want to have? What does the person need at this point? Put yourself in the other person's shoes first.

Imagine you are the one seeking feedback. If you give your essay to someone else to read and get nothing but the typos highlighted and suggestions for correcting your grammar, you would be frustrated if the essay was in an early draft and what you needed was comments on the ideas. You can fix the typos later; what you would want to know is whether the ideas that seemed so clear to you are equally clear to a reader. Conversely, if you're already committed to what you've said and the deadline is fast approaching, you may not want any criticism of the ideas but only a check for typos. If you've planned for feedback, you can specify what you need. You can say, "Don't worry about any typos, I'll catch those later. Please tell me whether the ideas make sense," or "It's almost done; I'd just like you to check for any typos or grammatical errors I may have missed." Turn these insights around if you are the person being asked to give feedback. You can be equally thoughtful and ask, "What kind of feedback would you like at this stage? Are you most concerned about how it comes across, or are you happy with what you've said and you'd like me just to check for typos?"

Even in more formal settings, where you are the person supervising a trainee or giving a performance evaluation, offering helpful feedback means finding out what the person wants to know, not just deciding what you want to tell them. What are the priorities for them? These matter as much as what the priorities are for you. They can't work on everything at once. It's hard for people who are anxious about their performance to take in everything they're being told. A trainee may want to know what he or she is doing right, before thinking about what still needs to be improved. "You're doing an excellent job of greeting customers with a smile and a helpful suggestion. Now that you've mastered that, I need you to work on being faster when you ring up the sale."

Similarly, if you are the teacher, coach, nurse, or doctor bringing your expertise to bear, you need to know what your students, players, or patients are concerned about. They are not simply passive recipients of your ability to develop skills or treat ailments. For them to improve their performance or to recover, they need to take an active role. To take an active role, they need to get the feedback that works for them to make sense of what's going on. "Why can't I use a calculator on this assignment?" "Why can't I play centre?" "Why do I need to be in hospital overnight?" Answering these questions is not simply a matter of recognizing their priorities as well as yours. It is an opportunity to think critically about how things look from their perspective. Why would they ask that particular question? They may see the task, the goals, or the situation very differently from the way you see them. If you are to work with them for your mutual benefit, paying attention to their feedback requests is an important part of understanding their approach.

Finally, as a friend or advisor, you may find yourself being asked for feedback on difficult personal decisions—problems at work, problems in relationships, personal crises. It's very tempting in these cases to think you're being consulted for your personal wisdom and expertise. They've come to you because they think you can help—so you step right in to help. You offer advice, solutions, even practical support such as money or a place to stay. Generous as this is, it's a last step. It's not a first step, and it's not feedback. First, the person needs to tell his or her story, and you are the designated audience. Probably the best feedback you can provide is to be an active listener, as described in Chapter 1. Listen first, and let the person see that you heard and understood. The feedback the person most likely needs is just to hear in another voice the words that were so important to say. In these situations, it has a distancing or silencing effect to say in advance, "What help do you want from me?" or even to say it immediately after the person has spoken. Only after the person has heard his or her own words again in a different way will it be time to move forward by asking what role you might play.

EXERCISE   P.2

Offering Feedback

How might you offer feedback in the following situations?

*1. A young child is showing you a bright red scribble on drawing paper.

2. You are a medical specialist. A patient has been referred to you because tests showed some anomalies. The patient is clearly anxious. In your professional opinion, there is nothing to be concerned about.

3. You've recently been promoted to video store manager. Several of the part-time employees are older than you are and don't seem happy taking direction from you. One in particular is very slow to respond to your requests.

4. You're coaching a children's soccer team, and the child who has been in goal wants to play a different position for the rest of the game.

5. You've just been handed a rough draft of a report by a new employee. It is full of typos.

Recognizing Feedback

The main challenge with feedback is recognizing when we've got it. This isn't always easy. In a business or professional setting, for example, feedback can be indirect or missing. You turn in the report by the deadline—and you hear nothing more! Does that mean it was fine, or has it simply been buried on someone else's desk, or was it so useless they simply discarded it? You would need to know your own organization to know how to interpret the silence. Very often, silence is good news—you certainly would have heard if there was a problem, so you can safely assume that the report was fine. Sometimes it does mean nothing has happened yet, and you had better check—it may be coming right back to you with major changes just when you least expect it.

Some of the feedback you get will be exactly the feedback you planned for. You'll ask the right questions and get answers that help you. You'll set up a checklist to gather data, and you'll be able to use the data to interpret how well things went. You'll release your model rocket and it will go straight up in the air instead of fizzling on the launch pad the way it did last time.

Other types of feedback are thrust upon us—the performance review at work, the grade to prove we completed the course, the sudden thumping from a flat tire we forgot to check before we started the car trip. This kind of feedback will be covered in the final section, Using Feedback Wisely.

In this section, we will look at the kind of feedback we don't always recognize as feedback. This comes in the form of information we hadn't planned to look for, or reactions we weren't expecting. The skills needed to deal with this feedback are really the same as those used in Chapter 1 to do open-ended observation.

One classic example may help you see how important it is to stay open to this unexpected feedback. Consider the anxiety most people feel about unintentionally acting in a way that counts as harassment. How careful must they be to prevent their innocent actions being misinterpreted? A casual hand on the shoulder, a hug for a child, a compliment on looks, a cartoon on the office door, a joke at the expense of some race or group—all these can cause offence. But the key element of harassment is not the single action by itself—it's whether you learn quickly enough from the feedback. A sudden stiffening of the shoulder under your hand? Time to move the hand. A stunned silence at the punch line of the joke? Don't tell another one. A complaint by your boss, reported to you, about the cartoon? It's off the door and back into a private space. If you respond quickly and appropriately to the feedback, you are not guilty of harassment. Harassment is demonstrated by a blindness or indifference to the feedback—hugging everyone, even the people you can feel resisting, or arguing you have a right to display your cartoons in a public space and tell the jokes you want to any audience, and if people don't like it, that's their problem.

The important element here is to notice the reactions in the first place. How did this person respond to your hug? Has there been a complaint about this cartoon? Then, before you react in your turn—"What's her problem?"—you stop long enough to pinpoint any relevant differences between this situation and others like it. Do people generally respond warmly to your hugs? What's happened when other cartoons have been on your door?

When you think about the differences you notice between this situation and others like it, you're more likely to realize that you can and do learn from unexpected or unwanted feedback. Consider a different, but related example. You have just changed jobs or schools. Where you came from, it was normal to hover outside the door of the boss or the instructor you wanted to see. If the person is busy with someone else, you wait nearby until the person is free. Now, however, in the new place, you've been waiting for just a few minutes near the door of someone you need to see, when suddenly the person stands up, comes to the door, and says, "Please go somewhere else. It's incredibly rude to hang around right by the door like that." You are taken aback. You meant no disrespect at all. As you walk away, feeling misunderstood, it dawns on you that you haven't actually seen anybody else standing casually in the hallways. You hadn't even realized that the halls were usually empty, because it hadn't occurred to you to think about it. Now it does occur to you that this is a different place, and it does operate differently from your last school or place of employment. Some differences you expected and set out to learn, such as how the phone system works. Other differences you didn't expect, like being criticized for waiting in the hall. But now you can put the feedback into a framework: organizations have "cultures," and there are more cultural differences than you had expected between the previous place and the new place. You are in a position to use the feedback you didn't know you were going to get. You can design more opportunities for additional feedback to help you. For example, you can ask someone else, "What's the best way to get in to see the boss? Do I need to make an appointment?" You can also ask broader questions about how things are done here. You can start to notice much more consciously what differences there are between this place and other places you're more used to. Do people interrupt each other or not? Do people exchange casual greetings in the halls, or do they hurry along meeting nobody's eyes?

Please notice that getting this feedback doesn't automatically mean you turn from your ways to theirs.

As you've just seen in Chapter 12, critical thinking does include negotiating differences where they arise. A problem may be occurring not because of *what* you do or say, but because of *where* and to *whom*. The behaviour you consider normal may be normal for a different group of people in a different place. The previous place liked an "open-door, wait-till-I'm-free" atmosphere. The new place likes a formal, "make-an-appointment" atmosphere. The rights you want to invoke may apply to your *personal* conduct and *personal* space, but not to your *professional* conduct or a *public* place. The cartoon's fine behind your door where only you can see it, but not in a public space where anyone can see it and where you are responsible to your employer for conveying the intended impression to customers and clients.

It is a separate question whether you will or should conform to what is expected just because it is expected. Again, you use reason to examine what is at issue here for you and for others, what your priorities are, what values are important to uphold, and what makes the best sense in the circumstances.

EXERCISE

Recognizing Feedback

How might you identify and explore the feedback available in the following situations?

*1. You speak a foreign language well enough to manage all your daily interactions while you're living abroad. However, you notice that native speakers don't seem particularly happy to talk to you. They will either switch to your language, or they will end conversations very quickly.

2. You've tried three times to set a date to get together with a person you'd like to know better. The person seems to want to get together, but has never been the one to suggest a time to get together, and on each of the three occasions you've tried to set a date, the person has had other commitments.

3. You provided the music for a party. During the party, people keep coming up to you to compliment you on the music. Some of them like particular tracks or artists, some of them just like the mood of the music. You're a bit puzzled—you just put together a compilation of music you had in your collection.

4. You got an A on your essay, "What does it mean to be good?" You're amazed. This was your first assignment for an introductory philosophy course, the one you took because it was the only elective that fit your timetable. You're in the aviation program, and all the rest of your courses this term are mathematics and business. You aren't getting As in your other courses.

5. As you're watering your houseplants, you notice one plant has got new leaves coming out, but another plant beside it has dropped some leaves.

Using Feedback Wisely

Feedback is intended to make a difference to your next performance, on the same task or a different task. Think about police officers debriefing after a robbery, firefighters debriefing after a forest fire is finally extinguished, coroners or medical personnel reviewing an unexpected death. These debriefings or critical incident reviews are not about assigning praise or blame. In all these situations, the discussion of exactly what was done, and whether it was good enough, is intended to make sure the people involved can do better next time. Under stress, they must rely on their training to help them act responsibly and effectively. There isn't time to slow down and think things through. Afterwards, though, there is time to look back and see what went well and should be continued, and what could have gone better. Can they improve on what didn't work well, without risking any deterioration in what did work?

Sometimes the feedback is an end in itself—an academic paper you slaved over for many, many hours gets a B grade. Perhaps you're thrilled; perhaps you're bitterly disappointed. Either way, that's the grade and you have to move on to the next assignment. Sometimes, even if you'd rather not have to, you are expected to revise the paper on the basis of the feedback received. How do you rethink, not just rephrase?

Your key aim in dealing wisely with the feedback you receive is to use it for a specific purpose.

For example, you might already know you need to check, confirm, adapt, or perhaps develop further what you have done so far. Does the carburetor need yet another tweak? Is the bicycle seat still a little bit too high for you? Was the birthday cake a big hit, so now you can retire the cake pans for a while? Can you improve your skills? Can you develop ideas further into more interesting applications? Can you apply what you've learned to helping others? These examples are all instances of using feedback to develop your personal knowledge or skills.

You might also use feedback to recognize problems or differences between you and others. Do your co-workers always resist your suggestions? Are you uncomfortable having to frequently ask for help? Are you struggling with your courses? Is there no way to adjust your work schedule for a bit more flexibility? These are examples of feedback indicating there is a mismatch between your expectations or needs and the situation you find yourself in. Will you change or will you leave? These examples illustrate how feedback plays a role in rethinking the situation you find yourself in.

Finally, as in the example of firefighters or police officers, you might use feedback for accountability. A firefighter who feels badly that the crew didn't get there in time to save more of the house before it went up in flames may be relieved to hear that more experienced firefighters feel just the same, and there really isn't any way to improve the practices. A police officer who engaged in a high-speed chase that ended in a crash may welcome an investigation that sets new, firmer guidelines for when to start a chase, reducing the officer's need to assess each situation personally, and reducing the chance of public criticism of the decision to pursue.

EXERCISE **P.4**

Using Feedback

*1. How would you make best use of the feedback about what happened in the following situation (a) if you were the manager of the shopping mall, or (b) if you were responsible for the ambulance service? A person collapsed with an epileptic seizure at a shopping mall. The mall manager called 911, and was told an ambulance would respond. Twenty minutes later, the ambulance still had not arrived. A mall employee was able to take the person to hospital in a private car. Debriefing after the incident discovered that the two ambulances that were on call were both responding to other emergencies. The third, a backup ambulance, was in for repairs and unavailable. ("Ambulance no-show puts service under review," *Vancouver Sun*, February 12, 2005, B10)

2. How would you use the feedback available in the information about the following situation if you were (a) a member of the board of directors of the charitable group, or (b) a resident of Sri Lanka near the coastline damaged by the tsunami? A charitable group responds to the tsunami on December 26, 2004, by collecting clothing, shoes, and bottled water and shipping them to Sri Lanka. Shortly afterwards, a newspaper article reports a survivor as saying, "Oh, no! More clothes. . . . We're not beggars. We don't need these hand-me-downs." (Shimale Senanayake, "Tsunami victims smothered with useless items," *Vancouver Sun*, February 12, 2005, A10)

Use feedback to take the opportunity to reflect on where you have been and where you might go. For example, think of some of the best feedback you ever received—perhaps from a coach, a co-worker, or a friend. Why did you appreciate it? Remembering how valuable it was, you can think ahead to how you might help others learn similarly valuable lessons. Or think about a project you enjoyed doing. Your enjoyment and satisfaction is feedback to guide you toward new opportunities. Where would you go next, if you had a chance to develop the project further? What new ideas would you explore? What could you say now that didn't occur to you then? Remembering what worked, yet seeing the work again once you have developed further gives you a different perspective, a different level of insight into what you are capable of.

Different perspectives and different levels of insight are the joys of reasoning well. We hope that this book has helped you gain new strengths in reasoning that you can apply in your own life.

Key Points in Review

- A solution to a problem or a plan of action is only as good as its results. This means we need to plan for feedback.

- Feedback is anything you observe, or anything said to you by others, that reveals whether something is working well.

- Your key aim in dealing with the feedback you receive is to check, confirm, adapt, or perhaps to develop further what you have done so far.

- Your key aim in offering feedback to others is to address their priorities, not just your own, and to give the feedback when they are ready to receive it.

- Feedback enables us to gain insights and to adopt a fresh perspective.

APPENDIX A

Answers to Selected Questions

Introduction

EXERCISE I.1 ## Sample Situations Calling for Good Reasoning

1. Your first step is probably to look back at the rows of plants you have just put in. Is the spacing even, or did it get wider as you went? Even a small spacing error can add up to a significant difference in the number of plants needed. If you have some plant knowledge, you may be able to figure out what the spacing should most likely be, and measure to see if you got it right. However, if none of these checks helps, you will have to ask for help. Thirty plants are too many to waste. It is reasonable to interrupt a busy person when you have done the most you can safely do on your own. You have shown you are acting reasonably if you can say, "I checked the plants and they seem to be spaced correctly. I have thirty plants left over. Was that expected, and what should I do with them?"

EXERCISE I.2 ## Opening Up Possibilities

1. You are careful not to assume that your friend is relaxing while you do all the hard work. You consider that your friend might have a good reason to stop and take a break. You consider your own needs—are you ready for a break yourself, or would you find it easier to keep going? If you are concerned that your friend might be taking advantage of you, you stop and sit down with your friend long enough to double-check how long the move is expected to take and when you can say you've done your fair share of the work.

5. As a good reasoner, you consider how likely it is that this job is legitimate and worth doing. Yes, there are jobs that pay "$$$$$," but do any of them require no previous experience? Commission sales or piecework such as stuffing envelopes or delivering flyers are examples of jobs that could be done with no experience, and might be profitable for some people. Can you imagine any other jobs that might need no experience, and do they suit your abilities? Next, "in your spare time" sends a signal that this is at best part-time work, suited to people who are not depending on this as their only source of income. Would that meet your needs, or would it simply cut down on the time you had available to find other work? Finally, "Call 555-8694" with no other identifying information presents a puzzle. Why would an employer stay anonymous? Are they not proud enough of who they are, or are they not a legitimate business at all? If you call this number without knowing who is at the other end, you may be so desperate for work that you're not going to worry about working conditions or pay.

EXERCISE **I.3**

How Intuition Fits In

Answers will vary. A sample comparison between two people might look like this:

Person A doesn't have any strong intuitive feelings at all. A likes to see "hard information": fact sheets, budgets, written proposals, packages on shelves that can be picked up and examined. A likes to be able to see and compare several options before making a decision, otherwise A feels the decision is rushed and can't be trusted.

Person B has had some bad experiences by trusting reason instead of listening to "gut feelings." B stayed in a relationship too long, suppressing feelings that it wasn't working. B accepted a job offer that everyone agreed was a terrific opportunity, in spite of B's own feelings that it wasn't really B's kind of job at all. Sure enough, within a month B could hardly stand to go into the office, and had to quit.

A, however, does listen to other people's strong gut feelings, when A knows they can be trusted. B is willing to ignore mild gut feelings and will at least try new things if other people recommend them.

 EXERCISE **I.4**

Thinking about Responsibility

Sample answer for responsibilities in scenario 1 from Exercise I.1.

a. As an employee of a gardening service, you have a professional responsibility to do the job to the best of your ability. This will include being responsible enough to show some initiative while also following orders accurately. One of the most challenging professional responsibilities we all face on a new job is finding out how we are expected to balance independence and obedience in this particular workplace. In addition, you have a personal responsibility to do your best at a job you have agreed to take.

b. The leader of the landscaping crew has a responsibility to ensure that the job has been done correctly and that all members of the crew are given correct instructions and can do the tasks assigned to them.

 EXERCISE **I.5**

Overview of the Critical Thinking Cycle

Answers will vary. Thanks to Trevor Yee, who contributed this example, which discusses something that was handled well at work:

Observing: I was a floor supervisor at a store. The district manager saw employees on their break smoking near the front door. The district manager banned employees from smoking outside the front door of any store in the district. The employees at our store came to me to see if I could help. They were upset because at night there was nowhere else safe to smoke. In the daytime they could use the loading dock, but at night there was no one to open the heavy door. I checked the employee manual to see how we were expected to accommodate employees' preferences, and I talked to some nonsmokers to see what they thought would be fair. I went to the district manager who had ordered the ban on smoking at the front door. I explained what the problem was, and I asked if employees could return to the front if they promised to stay well away from the entrance and to remove their aprons and name tags before they went out. Then they could be safe, but customers wouldn't know they were employees. The district manager agreed.

Investigating: I'm only a floor supervisor, but the store manager doesn't mind me taking the initiative to solve problems. The district manager doesn't come by our store very often, and this isn't the first time there's been a policy set at the district level without considering how it affects the different stores.

Evaluating: I think this was a good way to handle the situation because I knew the employees and the store, so I was in a good position to figure out a solution. A compromise like this might not be perfect, because customers could still recognize some staff by their faces and might still have a bad impression of the store. But if the employees couldn't smoke at all during their shifts, they would be upset and they'd show it in their work. I know our store manager's priority is making sure we offer good customer service by helping people quickly and cheerfully, so I think my solution helped the store keep running smoothly instead of letting the problem get bigger.

Responding: Next time a situation like this comes up, I think floor managers should be encouraged to see if they can help instead of passing the problem straight on to the store manager. I also think that there should be a trial period for new policies, so each store has a chance to tell the district manager what their problems are before the policy is fixed.

EXERCISE **1.6** ## Starting with Questions

Why am I doing this now? It's an assignment to help practise the questions. It's worth a try to see if they make any difference to how I'd normally read.

How might this make good sense to that person? Buchanan has a very low opinion of university education. How could he have come to hold such an opinion? He's taught in the college and high-school system, so either he's had frustrations there and he thinks universities are the same, or he's had good experiences in his own teaching but seen students get less out of universities than they expected. He's taught in the subject areas he's criticizing, so maybe he's seen courses change in a direction he considers "dumbed down." It's interesting that he criticizes the universities, not the students; he doesn't say the students are less well prepared for university—he blames everything on the courses. So perhaps he has a higher opinion of students, and he thinks their education should prepare them to fill jobs that meet "social needs." The more universities seem to drift away from job-related practical skills, the more people like Buchanan will think universities are not giving good value for the tax dollars spent on them.

The best thing to happen next for the discussion in general might be for someone to write to the newspaper with a contrasting view, to open up the discussion. If the reply is to be taken seriously by Buchanan himself, the writer had probably better be from a background like his own, so he'll find the writer credible. For myself, the best thing is just to watch the newspapers to see if anyone does reply, to get a sense of how many other people are as strongly anti-university.

Chapter 1

Reflecting on Objectivity

Comprehension

1. a. *Not objective:* the person has already decided against taking a stand, regardless of whether that is reasonable.

   b. *Not objective:* the speaker has already formed an opinion and is not open to change.

   c. *Objective:* the speaker is weighing personal preferences fairly against additional information.

   d. *Not objective:* the speaker has already made a personal judgment about the value of the essay.

   e. *Objective:* the speaker is describing features of the essay that should be equally evident to any other reader.

Observations or Judgments?

1. *Judgment:* The speaker has already decided what speed is "too fast." Another speaker might observe the same driver and judge the speed as reasonable.

2. *Observation:* The event and time are noted. Any observer could give the same details.

3. *Observation:* The speaker is reporting his or her own feelings, not including any judgment as to whether the feelings are appropriate or desirable.

4. *Judgment:* The speaker is drawing a conclusion about a relationship based on an observation of the people standing together.

5. *Judgment:* The speaker is drawing a conclusion about how life must be now, based on what is known about the past.

Practising Purposeful and Open-Ended Observations

Sample answer for question 1:

Purposeful observation: Contents of room for insurance purposes: Two lamps, replacement value $40; one room-sized rug, value unknown; desk, value $250; chair, secondhand, value unknown; etc. Contents of room for painting a still life: the room is quite dark, with just a glow from under the desk light. The desk is a warm golden brown where the light hits it, and so is the rug. Outside the range of the light, the desk is a dull brown and the rug is almost black, etc.

Open-ended observation: The room really isn't very well lit. There are only the two lights, and one of them doesn't shed much light. It's a comfortable place to work, but maybe a better desk light would be a good idea.

EXERCISE 1.4 Generating Accurate Observations

1. a. Not accurate, though as an estimate it's close. A standard pop can holds 355 mL, so two cans hold 710 mL—less than a litre (1000 mL). Three cans would do it.

   b. Not accurate: 2.5 metres is tall even for an adult male.

   c. Answers will vary according to city and year.

EXERCISE 1.5 Observing Word Choices

1. The person who speaks is likely to be less angry than the person who pounds the table.

2. The poetic phrasing of (a) suggests the writer is painting a picture in words, wanting you to see the sight and reflect on it. The prosaic phrasing of (b) suggests the writer simply wants to report that they saw an unusual sight.

3. Sentence (b) uses an uncommon word, "nugatory," which means "completely unnecessary." Unless the speaker of (b) is talking to academics, the hearers are not likely to understand what's been said. The speaker of (a) wants to be understood; the speaker of (b) either doesn't want to be understood or wants to appear superior by having a more impressive vocabulary.

Written Assignment

Part A

Universities are wrong to complain they do not have enough funds to meet societal needs.

About one-third of university and postsecondary college course offerings are of no apparent value and do not meet intellectual or practical standards. There are many examples, most in the social sciences and humanities area: for instance, Women's Studies, or Peace and Conflict Studies. Many traditional areas of study have been limited in scope and difficulty so they cover only simple Marxism and other ideologies that are not reputable.

The postsecondary institutions have probably simplified their courses because they needed to. About half the applicants for postsecondary education are seriously under-prepared.

EXERCISE 1.7 Careful Reading and Written Reporting

Sample: Article 1 (page 47)

In "Give no notice of cataclysmic asteroid, scientists told," David Derbyshire reports the opinions of Geoffrey Sommer of the Rand Corporation, who spoke at a meeting of the American Association for the Advancement of Science. Sommer believes that it would be better for politicians not to warn the public if an asteroid were found to be on a collision course with Earth. Sommer claims that advance warning of the end of the world would create "unnecessary panic." It would bring "chaos" to the streets, rioting in the shopping malls, and send the economy spiralling out of control. Sommer notes that there are no plans for civil defence and no studies of how to deflect such an asteroid out of harm's way. Sommer believes that if a deadly impact is inevitable, then "ignorance for the population is bliss."

Derbyshire reports that there are approximately 2,000 asteroids orbiting the sun in paths close to the earth. Approximately 1,100 of these asteroids are thought to be two-thirds of a mile (1 km) long, big enough to damage humanity if they collided with the earth. Spaceguard, an international collaboration of asteroid-tracking scientists, has tracked 650 possible asteroid threats. None have so far been on target to collide with the earth within 200 years.

Chapter 2

EXERCISE

Argumentative vs. Non-argumentative Persuasion

Answers will vary, but typically the non-argumentative persuasion will include emotional appeals and vivid, engaging language.

EXERCISE

Identifying Arguments and Non-arguments

1. Non-argument—neutral report of information about obtaining stem cells from a human egg.
2. Non-argument, presenting information to raise questions in your mind as to how dogs should best be dealt with in public parks.
3. Argument, which concludes that obesity does not result from individual choice (indicated by the question and answer at the beginning of the passage). The remaining statements are offered to support that conclusion.

EXERCISE

Identifying Indirect or Counter-Premises and Conclusions

Sample: From Chapter 8, Item 1, "Berry falls into regulatory crack"

Indirectly-stated premise: "Rather than being seen to be innocent until proven guilty, the EU policy essentially condemns saskatoon berries to exile until proven innocent." Direct version of premise: instead of assuming the saskatoon berry is safe unless proven unsafe, the EU policy presumes the berry is unsafe until proven safe.

Counter-argument: The argument as a whole is a counter-argument to the European Union's position.

EXERCISE

Understanding Structure

3. Group diagrams may vary depending on how each group identifies and labels the premises. The diagrams should all show the same conclusion, and groups should be able to explain their diagrams to each other. A sample is provided below.

1. We should be more concerned about our RCMP officers than about muskrats.

2. RCMP officers claim that muskrat hats are very effective in the cold weather.

3. RCMP officers spend hours at a time in sub-zero temperatures.

4. The muskrat is a very common rodent.

5. Thousands of people, many of them Aboriginal, make a living by trapping animals.

6. The use of muskrat hats should not be questioned. (1, 2, 3, 4, 5)

7. The use of muskrat hats is being questioned by urban animal rights groups who are misguided by emotion.

8. Cancellation of the Ontario spring bear hunt has lead to some black bears roaming into cities and towns.

9. Cancellation of the Ontario spring bear hunt has lead to some rural residents being afraid to walk in the woods.

10. Ontario police chiefs say that bear nuisance calls are too common.

11. The decision to cancel the Ontario spring bear hunt was wrong. (8, 9, 10)

12. The decision to cancel the Ontario spring bear hunt was due to pressure from urban anti-hunting groups who are misguided by emotion.

---

13. Urban people who are misguided by emotion should not make decisions that have a big impact on rural people. (6, 7, 11, 12)

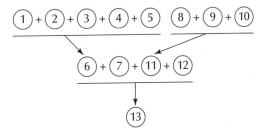

EXERCISE 2.5

Distinguishing Separate Arguments

Oberg's argument:

Learning Minister Lyle Oberg concluded that he was compelled to ask Alberta's four universities to write letters to the editor concerning the essay written by Premier Ralph Klein. His reasons were that the issue was "very, very serious," since questions had been raised about the integrity of the Athabasca University professor who gave Klein a grade of 77 percent for his essay, which had been taken largely from the Internet without proper attribution. Questions about the integrity of the professor were, in Oberg's opinion, a direct challenge to Alberta's postsecondary institutions.

EXERCISE **2.6**

Reporting a Written Argument

See the sample answer for Exercise 8.4 (page 374) for a report of "Berry falls into regulatory crack."

EXERCISE **2.8**

Converting Arguments to Standard Form

Standard form, question 1.a:

1. I could only marry a person my parents like.
2. My parents don't like John.

_____

3. I can't marry John.

Standard form, question 1.b:

1. My best friend has smoked pot every day for twenty years.
2. My best friend is a hard worker, a good father, and a good friend.

_____

3. Marijuana should be legal.

Standard form with sub-arguments, question 2.a:

1. I either pay back the money I owe my brother or I pay my phone bill.
2. If I pay my brother, my sister will find out.
3. If my sister finds out, I'll have to pay her the money I owe her.
4. So I can't pay my brother. (2,3)

_____

5. So I'll pay my phone bill. (1,4)

Chapter 3

EXERCISE **3.1**

Resolving Vagueness and Ambiguity

1. *When politicians have debates they are just playing games.* Loaded phrase: "playing games." The phrase "playing games" in this context implies that political debates are for entertainment or show, and do not have a serious outcome.

2. *They hunt for criminals with no remorse.* Ambiguous. Is it the criminals who have no remorse, or do the people who hunt them hunt remorselessly?

3. *My husband is babysitting our children tonight.* Loaded word: "babysitting." They are his children too—is he looking after them as a normal part of his parenting responsibilities, or is he doing something that a parent would normally hire a caregiver to do?

EXERCISE 3.2 ## Constructing Definitions with Examples

1. *Accident:* An accident typically covers events that were not intended and usually were not foreseen. Knocking a glass off the table with your elbow is an accident because it is not intended. Breaking your ankle by losing your balance on a step is an accident. In both cases, perhaps you should have realized you were hurrying or were too tired to pay proper attention to your movements, but typically we do not expect ourselves to pay complete attention in this way. In contrast, knocking the glass to the ground to cause a distraction is not an accident even if you hope it will look like one—as you move your elbow to knock the glass, you fully intend it to fall. Breaking your tooth by biting down on a jar top to open it is not an accident if you know your tooth is fragile and you should have realized there are safer ways to open a jar than risking your teeth.

   By comparison with these examples, Paul Willcocks is being too extreme in saying no car crashes are accidents. He might be right that some of them are caused by mistakes that could reasonably have been avoided. However, picture a car accident in which an inexperienced driver applies the brakes too hard at a point on the road where the guardrail is too low and the car skids off the road into a creek. The cause of the severe damage to the car and its passengers is a combination of the actions of the driver and the actions of the highways department that built the guardrail. Neither party would have intended to cause a crash, and it is not clear that either could have foreseen the likelihood of this crash.

 EXERCISE 3.3 ## Testing Claims

1. *If it's worth doing, it's worth doing well.* Universal generalization. Any exception will show the rule is invalid. (Many people find it hard to see counter-examples to this one.) Test it:

   It makes sense for building your own house, repairing a car, and raising a child.

   It doesn't make sense for sweeping the garage floor (do you really need it spotless?) or drawing a map to your house for friends (if they can follow your directions, does the map need to look elegant, too?).

4. *Farms are unsafe workplaces.* Non-universal generalization. Test it: Look for accident rates on farms. Accident rates by themselves won't tell you whether the farms are any less safe than other workplaces, such as forests (for foresters) or city streets (for police), so you need to look for accident rates in other work-places to see how farms compare. Testing should confirm the generalization.

 EXERCISE 3.4 ## Interpreting a Task

1. Before you take on a long photocopying job, you'd need to know what the deadline was, and how urgent this task was compared to other duties you

had. To estimate how long the task would take, you'd need to know how many reports per box, how long it took to remove the staples from each report and how long to run each one through the copier. You would also need to know whether you could have enough uninterrupted time at the copier, or whether you would have to make sure other people had access at regular intervals. (If you were uninterrupted, a task like this could take as much as eight hours.)

5. Thanks to Birgit Isaak, Colleen McCarty, and Trevor Yee for these guidelines on running a small sandwich store while the manager is on vacation:

Presumably, if you're being offered this responsibility, you already know some of the basic procedures related to opening and closing the store, and the standard procedures for safe food handling and storage. Your main aim is to be sure you know how to handle issues that you have not yet had to handle on your own.

When is the manager leaving and returning, and is there a contact number for emergencies? You need to know exactly when you are on duty and whether you can reach the manager.

Have food orders been put in for the next week, and where are supplies ordered from? You don't want to run out of food.

Has the scheduling for the employees been done, or are you supposed to do it? You need to know if there are any considerations related to scheduling that you need to be aware of, such as whether two new employees should not be scheduled together, or whether some employees need time off for classes. You also need to know how you can reach employees and who to call first if someone is sick and must be replaced for a shift.

Are there any appointments you need to make or take care of? For example, are the floors or bathrooms being professionally cleaned or equipment being serviced? You may need to be available outside normal opening hours.

Do you know the alarm code for the store, and do you have all the keys you need? Do you know the procedures to follow in case of emergencies, and do you have contact numbers for service people in case of breakdowns? You need to know how to handle the unexpected problems that might arise.

Are there any questions you need to be able to answer concerning methods of payment, use of coupons, and so on? You need to be able to deal with customers' offers to pay by cheque or requests to honour expired coupons or competitors' coupons.

If there is a problem with a customer, can you do anything reasonable in your power to rectify it, or must you ask the customer to wait until the manager returns? You need to know how much authority you are expected to exercise. Similarly, if an employee has a problem with a customer, is the employee expected to handle it or are you expected to step in?

How can you deposit money in the bank? You need to know how to handle the money that would normally be taken to the bank.

Chapter 4

Finding a Place to Start

1. To get good used sports equipment, preferably free, to supply a youth drop-in centre, sample starting points would be these: (1) Ask anyone who plays a sport if they know where there are good used equipment stores. (2) Check eBay to see how much used equipment costs and what's available. (3) Ask people with older teenagers if their children have any outgrown equipment they would be willing to donate.

4. To find out what regulations you would have to comply with if you wanted to put an above-ground pool in the backyard of a private house in your municipality or township, sample starting points would be these: (1) Telephone directory pages covering municipal government, for general inquiries or the planning department. (2) Friends or neighbours who have pools (note that you would be wise to consult neighbours about your plans so that you can address any concerns they may have). (3) Department of Fisheries and Oceans may need to be consulted if there is any chance your pool will drain into a ravine, creek, river, or lake that is an important habitat for any species. Ecological balance can be altered by rapid runoff and by chemicals.

Research Ethics

The key constraints on research involving humans are minimizing risk, maintaining human dignity, ensuring free and informed consent, and protecting the privacy and confidentiality of subjects and their information. To ensure free and informed consent, there must be no rewards, incentives, or threats to motivate subjects to participate; there must be a clear and complete explanation of the procedure and its effects; and the subjects must be competent to give consent. Notice that the conditions for free and informed consent are also conditions for good reasoning.

Investigating Numerical Information

Are the numbers plausible? For most people, the numbers are likely to be neither plausible nor implausible. Investigating for studies that show the number of left-handers in different societies may turn up very few results, and many of the results are likely to be reports of the same study described here.

One report drawing on the same source, "A Sinister Advantage," December 9, 2004, http://economist.com/science, gives some additional numbers from the report: the Yanomamo of South America have a rate of 4 murders per 1,000 inhabitants, compared to 0.068 in New York. Raiding and warfare are said to be central to Yanomamo culture.

Since the overall argument here implies that left-handedness is genetically favoured in these societies, we can also look for data on whether left-handedness is genetically determined. In Stanley Coren's *The Left-Hander Syndrome: The Causes and Consequences of Left-Handedness* (Macmillan, NY: Free Press, 1992), Coren cites his own research and a combination of data from other studies to question whether left-handedness is genetically transmitted: all the results he found indicated that if neither parent is left-handed, the child's chance of being left-handed is about ten percent and is the same if the father is left-handed. If the mother is left-handed, the chances rise to twenty percent, and with two left-handed parents, the chance of the child being left-handed is around thirty-five percent (Coren 85–87). Although he doubts that genetic transmission of left-handedness may be likely to account for the percentages of left-handers, Coren does acknowledge a connection to violence: he notes that a study of 9,125 children born in Copenhagen showed that by the time the children reached eighteen, strongly left-handed boys were more than twice as likely to have been arrested once than were the right-handed boys (Coren 180).

 EXERCISE 4.4

Investigating Imagery

In the Rogers cellphone ad, the viewer is positioned outside the car, and slightly above the eye level of the couple in the car. Since it's most unlikely anyone could stand in this position without being noticed, the viewer is a "fly on the wall," not a participant in the scene. The female is facing the viewer, and her smile invites the viewer to identify with her: playing games on a cellphone is fun. Her position on the driver's side of the car, and her ability to tolerate the male's kissing and cuddling while still doing what she prefers suggests she's meant to be seen as "in control" of the situation, which young adult viewers would be likely to appreciate. What is not seen is the male's face. The viewer has no chance to see whether the male is aware of his partner's lack of interest. Is he perfectly happy to be allowed to carry on regardless of whether his partner is enjoying what's going on? The image might convey to cellphone users that a cellphone with game capacity is at least as much fun as any of the casual summer relationships one might have. It is not clear whether she, or he, would be better off with just the cellphone instead of the other person.

 EXERCISE 4.5

Investigating to Increase Understanding of Images

2. Common images of luxury include gleaming metal surfaces, classic architecture, few people visible in the picture, and people dressed in formal wear. Common images for everyday products include indoor scenes (especially kitchens), bright colours, and people interacting happily with each other.

 EXERCISE 4.8

Standards at Work

Answers will vary depending on what job is chosen. One example is given here:

Punctuality to the minute is expected in television control rooms; it is not required in lifeguarding.

EXERCISE **4.9**

Choosing Personal Responsibilities

2. For example, you're tall and you like to do things carefully: volunteer to take down the decorations. You prefer to chat while you're working and you don't mind doing routine jobs: volunteer to wash dishes or move the furniture.

4. Your responsibilities include being sure you can meet your obligations related to work and school. If you don't have alternative transport, you had better take the car to a garage. If you can fix the car, how skilled are you at this particular task and do you have the right equipment? If you cannot do it safely enough, again, it would be better to take the car to a garage.

EXERCISE **4.10**

Academic and Personal Responsibility

1. For an example, see Bishop's University's Policy on Academic Integrity at **www.ubishops.ca/administration/INTEGRITY**

   This policy includes prohibitions on copying material without quotation marks; submitting as one's own work written in whole or in part by another individual; submitting in whole or in part work for which the student has received credit in another course, unless the permission of the instructor has been obtained; and helping another student plagiarize.

2. Answers will vary. The sample answer that follows uses the two articles on assisted suicide in Chapter 11.

   I chose this topic because I have always wondered how a person can face living with the prospect of constant pain and loss of ability to function. It hits home personally: I saw my father deteriorate after a series of strokes, yet insist on continuing to live alone until he died in a fire caused by his own pipe. The topic is also relevant to my academic interests. I'm studying philosophy because it deals with these difficult questions.

   I searched on the Internet using Canadian Newsstand and the search terms "euthanasia—opinion." These articles were suitable choices because both articles were published within the last year, and they both seem to cover assisted suicide in general instead of just responding to particular cases in the news. I have also seen other articles by Peter McKnight, and he often writes on ethical issues, so he may have some expertise in this area. I can show that I have met standards for academic responsibility because I can produce other articles I found in the same search if needed, to show I didn't simply take these two from anyone else. The articles are too recent to have been used by anyone in a previous version of this course, so I can't copy any earlier assignment. There are other people in the class who chose the same topic, but we are encouraged to discuss our topics with each other.

Chapter 5

Recognizing Goals: Arguments to Certainty, Probability, and Possibility

1. a. Argument to certainty.

    b. Argument to possibility. This is one interpretation; the speaker seems open to other possibilities.

    c. Argument to possibility.

    d. Argument to probability.

    e. Argument to probability: "high risk" is mentioned.

Recognizing Different Types of Reasoning

1. a. Deductive reasoning: the rule about speed is being applied.

    b. Inductive reasoning: the behaviour of the robins now resembles their behaviour in the past.

    c. Inductive reasoning: the results of experiments are being applied to the population as a whole.

    d. Conductive reasoning: the accumulation of facts are being used to justify adopting the dog.

    e. None of the four named categories: this reasoning relies only on an appeal to emotion, which is discussed in Chapter 9.

    f. Analogical reasoning: Heraclitus' example is used to compare humans to rivers.

2. Example from Chapter 1. In "Give no notice of cataclysmic asteroid, scientists told," Sommer's reasoning includes an example of deductive reasoning at the end: "If an extinction type impact is inevitable, ignorance for the population is bliss." Therefore politicians should not notify the public of the impending disaster. What might be a deductive step earlier, where Sommer claims that a warning of the end of the world "would" bring chaos to the streets, is more likely an inductive argument that this is the most probable outcome.

Checking Argument Patterns

1. a.

    If P then Q

    P
    _____

    Q

    Valid

b.

> If P then Q
>
> Not P
> _____
> Not Q

Invalid: My mother may be upset for some other reason.

c.

> If P then Q
>
> Q
> _____
> P

Invalid: The road might be slippery from black ice.

EXERCISE ## Recognizing Successful Patterns of Reasoning

1. Neither. Mariko could be there for some reason other than a party.
2. Deductively valid.
3. Deductively valid.
4. Neither. It is possible that some elephants are not scared of mice, and Dumbo may be one of them.
5. Neither. Dumbo may be a common name for other animals besides elephants.

EXERCISE ## Identifying Implicit Premises

1. 1. All students must go to class.
   2. You are a student. (implicit premise)
   _____
   3. You must go to class.

2. 1. If there is a will, there is a way.
   2. There is a will. (implicit premise)
   _____
   3. There is a way.

3. 1. Mark is a hard-working and intelligent person.
   2. All hard-working and intelligent people are sure to succeed. (implicit premise)
   _____
   3. Mark is sure to succeed.

EXERCISE ## Completing Standard Form with Implicit Premises

1. 1. Violent video games promote violence as thrilling, enjoyable, and an immediate response to certain stimuli.

2. All video games that promote violence as thrilling, enjoyable, and an immediate response to certain stimuli are creating a generation of violence addicts. (implicit premise)

3. Violent video games are creating a generation of violence addicts. (1,2)

4. If violent video games are creating a generation of violence addicts then violent video games need to be completely eliminated from our society. (implicit premise)

---

5. Violent video games need to be completely eliminated from our society. (3,4)

2. 1. All people who have experienced both physical and intellectual pleasures would agree that intellectual pleasures are superior.

2. If all people who have experienced both physical and intellectual pleasures agree that intellectual pleasures are superior, then intellectual pleasures are superior. (implicit premise)

---

3. Intellectual pleasures are superior.

Chapter 6

EXERCISE 6.1

Recognizing an Issue

In "The case for banning pit bulls," the main issue is whether to ban pit bulls. The topic discussed is the danger of dog bites. The main concern is the disproportionate number of injuries caused by pit bulls. The arguer's position on the issue is that the breed should be banned.

EXERCISE 6.2

Identifying the Crux of the Debate

1. The crux of the debate is whether members of a political party must not disagree too strongly in public. It is not freedom of speech in general they disagree about, only the freedom of speech of members of the Conservative Party. It is not whether the Conservative leader should be the one to check the speeches; the problem would remain whoever checked the speeches.

EXERCISE 6.3

Recognizing Alternatives

1. a. An immigrant who is committed to Canada might
     i. transfer money to Canada and invest in Canadian enterprises
     ii. take an active role in helping other immigrants adapt to Canadian life
     iii. volunteer to help with campaigns for candidates for municipal, provincial, or federal government
     iv. join organizations devoted to protecting the environment

2. An assumption made by Kosick in the letter on page 197 is that only those who understand French or English will understand what they should know

before voting in Canada. An alternative is that members of linguistic minorities are as well informed as anglophones and francophones about Canada, about voting, and about the political issues they should consider when voting. This alternative is plausible because there are news media across the country that provide information in a variety of languages.

Chapter 7

EXERCISE **7.1**

Checking Sources

1. c. Thanks to Kerri Leeper for the research reported here. Sample answer: A report by Portland General Electric supports Homeswest's claim: on average, energy-efficient dishwashers use 6 gallons (24 litres) less than washing by hand (**www.portlandgeneral.com/home/energy_savings/ ways_save/app_wind_walls/dishwasher.asp?bhcp=1**). An article titled "Have a Holly Jolly, Energy-Efficient Holiday" in *Home Made Simple Newsletter* (**www.homemadesimple.com/kitchen/holly_jolly/shtml**) says that hand-washing dishes uses between 9 and 24 gallons (36 to 96 litres) of water, compared to 6 to 10 gallons (24 to 40 litres) for dishwashers. The sources are consistent in their information. They also show that the main variable is whether the water is left running for any length of time during hand-washing. If hand-washing is done in a full sink with minimal rinsing, and if the dishwasher is an older model or is not run with a full load, there may not be a significant difference between the two methods.

2. b. Walking in Normandy, Henry Geunter must have dipped his foot into the Atlantic Ocean—the Pacific Ocean is half a world away. He was the chosen delegate of the Royal Canadian Medical Corps (a group of people), not the core (the centre or heart of something). There is a river Orne in Normandy, and the Royal Canadian Medical Corps was with the 4th Division of the Canadian Forces. Henry Geunter's name may be misspelled: Guenter is a much more common name, and there are no Geunters listed in the telephone directory for Abbotsford.

EXERCISE **7.2**

Credibility of Internet Sources

Life span of moose.

Site 1. **www.adfg.state.ak.us** Moose "rarely live more than 16 years in the wild." Alaska government site. No source cited, but article on website credited to authors Robert A. Rausch and Bill Gasaway, with revisions by Charles C. Schwartz, 1994.

Site 2. **www.env.gov.nl.ca/snp/Animals/moose.htm** Moose live 20 years or more. Salmonier National Park, Newfoundland, site. No source given for information; no author credited.

Site 3. **www.smouse.force9.co.uk** Moose life span 15 to 25 years. Site established by a private individual inspired by a vacation in Norway. Link to World Wildlife Federation. No source given for information.

The sites are listed in order of credibility. The Government of Alaska website named the authors of the article. A Google search of the authors' names turned up additional articles by the same authors on other topics related to Alaska, and presumably the authors could be contacted to find their sources. The same information about moose credited to the same authors appears on an unrelated website. Giving information that makes it possible to search for the original sources puts this site ahead of the other two.

The second site is also a government site, and a national park should presumably give accurate information. However, no source is given so there is no easy way to check whether the park generated its own data or whether it relied on an accurate source.

The third site clearly signals that the person who set up the site has no personal expertise. This individual may be relying on accurate information from the World Wildlife Federation but does not indicate this. The life span given for moose (15 to 25 years) seems to cover the maximum range given on other sites checked (16 years on the Alaska site to 27 years on www.muskokawildlife.com), making it seem least likely to be linked to direct studies of moose.

As a side note, if you're wondering how they can tell the age of a moose, the biologist Kristine Boutaites, moose biologist for the State of New Hampshire, is quoted at www.mooseworld.com as saying you can determine the age of a moose by observing the tooth eruption and the wear on the moose's lower jaw.

EXERCISE ## Credibility Check

(Based on sample answer given in Exercise 4.3.) The two sources chosen were "A Sinister Advantage," December 9, 2004, http://economist.com/science and *The Left-Hander Syndrome: The Causes and Consequences of Left-Handedness*, Stanley Coren, Free Press, Macmillan, NY, 1992. Discrepancies: The article from *The Economist* website is consistent with Highfield's article; it gives some additional numbers from the study by Faurie and Raymond and gives numbers with more precision. For example, it gives the murder rate among the Dioula as 0.013 murders per 1,000 people, where Highfield rounds the rate to one one-hundredth per 1,000 people. The information in Coren's book is consistent but not directly comparable; it does not give any murder rates by population. There is a possible conflict between Coren's information and the other sources since Coren indicates left-handedness is not clearly an inherited trait. Both sources are credible. The article is from a reputable magazine and appears to quote the study fairly and consistently with other sources. Coren has done his own research in this field and is a qualified psychologist. On the basis of this assessment, there is no clear reason to doubt the information in either source.

EXERCISE ## Recognizing Different Standards for Acceptability

Example: philosophy

■ No generally required sources. Papers written for courses may have instructions to consult specific sources—for example, papers on specific philosophers should consult original works by those philosophers or specified secondary sources. Citation format is typically MLA.

- A survey of original sources and recent secondary sources is required for upper-level and graduate papers discussing current topics. Many lower-level papers in philosophy discuss perennial topics and require no literature survey.

- There are no recognized authorities in the field you must be able to quote with approval. You may be expected to know and be able to quote Plato, Aristotle, Descartes, Wittgenstein, and other prominent philosophers, but you are not required to agree with any of them.

- To complete an assignment you may be required not to do any research, as demonstrated by the scenario in Chapter 2. If research is required, it is typically to read an original source such as Aristotle for yourself, or to trace the progress of a topic through recent academic publications.

- You do not have to be an expert in the field before your opinions are welcomed in an argument. If you can present a well-reasoned argument to support your opinion, your argument is welcomed.

- This field does accept personal opinion when backed up by argument.

EXERCISE **Checking Acceptability of Information**

2. *Example of college financial aid office categories:*

Education expenses (by semester)

Tuition and fees

Books and supplies

Living expenses (by month)

Rent

Food

Utilities (phone, hydro, cable, heat)

Transportation (bus/car)

Miscellaneous (clothing, laundry, entertainment)

Notice that, under these categories, it is not clear how you should classify long-distance transportation, such as flights to your home province if you moved away for school. Would it come under Transportation or Miscellaneous?

The minimum expenses anticipated in each of these categories in 2004 were

Tuition and fees: $1,024 to $1,300

Books: $523 to $1,700

Rent: $350 to $500 (shared accommodation off campus)

Food: $150 to $200 (per person)

Utilities: $130 to $200

Transportation: bus $24, car $200 (gas/insurance)

Miscellaneous: $200

Note that the figure given for Miscellaneous makes it seem unlikely that this category is expected to include anything other than discretionary expenses like those mentioned—clothing, laundry, entertainment. It does not appear to allow for non-discretionary costs such as dental care or prescription drugs. The figures are given as "minimum" expenses. Does the allowable amount change for a loan applicant who has health problems? (For example, the expected amount for food seems to anticipate that some applicants are single while some are supporting families.)

Example of bank categories:

> Housing Costs
>
> Daily living (groceries, childcare, pet expenses)
>
> Transportation (car/bus)
>
> Personal (clothing, hair, miscellaneous spending)
>
> Health (prescriptions, dental expenses, vitamins)
>
> Entertainment (cable, movies, lottery)
>
> Recreation (sports equipment, team dues)
>
> Vacations
>
> Savings
>
> Monthly payment on debts
>
> Other expenses (payroll deductions, miscellaneous)

Notice that there are more categories here, and it is assumed your lifestyle may include vacations and owning pets, but there is no category for education expenses. The bank does not indicate in its public material what it expects as anticipated expenses in each category.

EXERCISE 7.6

Considering Relevance and Sufficiency

1. Suppose you are wondering whether to eliminate caffeine from your diet. You would want information on what caffeine does in the body, since it has helpful as well as harmful effects. You would want information on whether any of your own health conditions or lifestyle choices make caffeine more or less risky for you than for the average person. You would want some information on how you personally seem to react to caffeine. Given information from reliable sources in all these areas, you should be able to weigh the risks and benefits of continuing to consume caffeine against those of giving it up. You should also be able to estimate accurately your risk tolerance: if you decide to change your consumption, are you willing to tolerate the risks involved?

2. For the same example, your friend would want all the same basic information you would. Your friend would want to see the information personally rather than take your word for it. The information may add up differently for your friend, who may have different health and lifestyle characteristics and may have a different level of risk tolerance.

Chapter 8

EXERCISE **8.1**

Evaluating Relevance and Sufficiency

1. Including hobbies and interests on a job application varies according to the type of job. Strictly speaking, your hobbies and interests are not relevant grounds on which an employer should be making a decision about your suitability for a job. (One notable exception is an acting résumé, where your ability to ride a horse, ski, skateboard, swing a golf club, handle a parrot, or talk knowledgeably about brewing beer will be as crucial as your appearance in indicating your suitability for specific parts.) Most often, a list of hobbies and interests serves as a "conversation starter"—something to ask about in an interview to help you relax and perhaps find common ground with people in the organization. However, this has negative as well as positive applications. Your hobbies may be a positive indication that you are a more well-rounded and active person than your work experience suggests, or your enthusiasm in discussing them may be a negative indication that your heart is really in your life outside of work and you will hate being cooped up in an office or store. If you do list hobbies or interests, you want to choose only those that are clearly relevant to performance on the job you are applying for—for example, listing canoeing on a job application for a camp activities director. In contrast, volunteer experience is almost always relevant because it indicates your skills. It can confirm how much you enjoy doing certain kinds of work, and it can show that you are capable of responsibilities you have not yet had a chance to handle in paid employment.

EXERCISE **8.2**

Testing Relevance and Sufficiency

Sample: "Berry falls into regulatory crack," Randy Burton, *StarPhoenix* (Saskatoon), June 5, 2004, A2. The conclusion is that it is absurd for the European Union to consider banning the saskatoon berry.

1. The tone of the article strongly indicates that this is meant to be an argument to certainty, not just to probability. Burton appears to argue that there is no reasonable concern the European Union could have over the safety of the saskatoon as a food item. Consequently the argument needs to use reasoning that shows that the conclusion is either guaranteed or is so probable that no competing conclusion is worth considering.

2. Whether the information provided is consistent with your background knowledge will depend on where you live. If you have enjoyed saskatoon berry pies or jam in the prairie provinces, or have had them as a gift or purchased them from a store, then you will know that they are regarded as a choice, edible berry just like the more familiar blueberries or raspberries. You may also know that there are closely comparable European berries available here, such as lingonberries and cloudberries.

3. The argument does contain premises suitable for an argument to certainty: for example, "The ruling stands natural justice on its head"—an appeal to

moral principle. It also makes universal claims about the saskatoon berry: "There's not a thing wrong with [it]," it is not a "novel food" in any sense. Are there assumptions that have plausible alternatives? This will be crucial to an argument to certainty, since even one plausible alternative that has not been ruled out will call the conclusion into question. One assumption that might create a problem is that the food safety review process will be long and costly: that it is "obstructionist," and by implication completely unnecessary. The plausible alternative is that the Europeans are as well aware as Canadians that saskatoon berries are safe, but that they are obliged to be consistent in applying their rules and that it is reasonable for them to insist on having the testing on record.

4. Based on the investigation just completed, the argument at this point remains unproven. It does seem likely that there is no cause for concern about the safety of saskatoon berries as a food item. However, the real issue may be a matter of principle—are there good reasons for the European Union to be seen to be consistent in applying its food safety tests, and are its tests reliable? The single example of the saskatoon berry may not be enough to undermine the reasonableness of the testing process.

EXERCISE **Checking Indefeasibility**

1. Only (c) can defeat the argument, by showing that the glass you are about to drink from cannot have been tampered with; (a) does not affect the probability of the conclusion, because it does not reduce the chance that your drink may have been tampered with by accident or as a prank, and (b) does reduce the probability of the conclusion, but not enough to defeat it. We don't know how the people at the party might have been influenced by what they have heard from elsewhere.

2. None of the arguments can be defeated by this information. The employee could be sick and be shopping for medicine, which is consistent with (a). The universal claim in (b), that people who are sick always stay home, is false, so (b) has already been shown to be a bad argument. The more cautious non-universal generalization in (c) gives us grounds to investigate the employee's health further, but the employee's shopping is not conclusive evidence of sickness or of health.

EXERCISE **Report and Evaluate an Argument**

Here is a sample answer for argument 1, page 253.

Report: In "Berry falls into regulatory crack" (*StarPhoenix* (Saskatoon), June 5, 2004, A2), Randy Burton concludes that it is absurd for the European Union to consider banning the saskatoon berry until it has been tested for safety. There is no reasonable concern the European Union could have over the safety of the saskatoon as a food item. The saskatoon has been used by First Nations for thousands of years as an ingredient in pemmican. Princess Anne was to be served saskatoon berry sauce with roast bison at a formal dinner in Regina shortly after Burton's article was written. The berries grow wild, and though there are about eight varieties, they all come from the wild and have been cultivated domestically. There is no such thing as a genetically modified saskatoon. According to Grace Whittington, co-owner of Riverbend Plantations in Saskatoon, the berries are versatile and of value to the Europeans who are looking for new flavours and new products. The berries even have some pharmaceutical benefits, because they contain anti-oxidants that can be extracted and used in capsules or sprinkled on food. Manitoba has already been exporting saskatoons to Europe, and Europe represents an important part of the market in Saskatchewan's search for diversification.

Burton considers that given the obvious safety of saskatoon berries, Europe's insistence on testing them as a "novel food" is absurd. It "stands natural justice on its head." It is not a food safety issue but "obstructionism" linked to European "paranoia" over genetically modified foods. Proving that a saskatoon has been safely used for a long time is a "long and costly" process under regulations. Prime Minister Paul Martin ought to raise this issue when he next meets with the leaders of the G8 nations for an economic summit.

Evaluation: Burton does seem to have sufficient evidence to show that saskatoon berries are safe. The jam is for sale in stores and at craft fairs across the country. However, the main issue here is not the safety of the food but the reasonableness of European policies that require testing and approval of any "novel food." These policies apparently require non-European natural food as well as genetically modified food to be tested. Burton has assumed the food safety review process will be long and costly: that it is "obstructionist," and by implication completely unnecessary. The process might be fast enough not to delay further imports from Manitoba or Saskatchewan. Even if the process is long, and if the Europeans are as well aware as Canadians that saskatoon berries are safe, it may be that it is more important for them to be consistent in applying their rules and that it is reasonable for them to insist on having the testing on record.

The argument at this point remains unproven. Burton's aim with the argument has been primarily to use the saskatoon berry as an example of how European regulations may be unreasonably hampering trade with Canada. It does seem likely that there is no cause for concern about the safety of saskatoon berries as a food item. However, the real issue may be a matter of principle—are there good reasons for the European Union to be seen to be consistent in applying its food safety tests, and are its tests reliable? The single example of saskatoon berries may not be enough to undermine the reasonableness of the testing process.

Chapter 9

EXERCISE **9.1**

Comparison of Arguments

Squeegee kids

1. The key area of debate is the main issue: whether squeegee kids create a nuisance that needs to be dealt with through legislation.

2. There are no useful points of agreement between the two letters: while they do agree that "public nuisances" should be restrained by legislation, they do not agree on the main issue that squeegee kids are a public nuisance.

3. Thompson's letter on behalf of the Safe Streets Coalition assumed that if legislation was in place, people would have effective protection from aggressive behaviour because police would be able to respond and deal with it. Hawirko's claim that the behaviour of squeegee kids is not aggressive enough to be concerned about is illustrated only by how they have responded when he has given them money. So Hawirko has not established that it is equally safe to refuse to give them money, and Thompson has not established that if panhandlers are aggressive, police will be able to respond quickly enough to help. Both extremes remain open for consideration: perhaps people can safely refuse panhandlers, or perhaps panhandlers can become sufficiently aggressive that people will be harmed before police can intervene.

4. What we still need to know is whether and how panhandlers of all kinds can safely be refused. This will indicate how risky it is to encounter a squeegee kid. We also need to know what kinds of preventive measures are possible to reduce aggressive behaviour on the streets in general: for example, what is the success rate of outreach programs that put street people in touch with local services, compared to programs that offer panhandlers newspapers to sell, or police foot patrols? This will indicate whether measures other than legislation have more promise.

EXERCISE ## Assessing Numerical Information

1. "Cruise Clampdown Critical": The numbers are certainly relevant: waste products in the ocean are a likely source of pollution. A check of several websites turned up closely comparable or identical information, much of it apparently provided by an organization called Oceana. The website **www.northamerica .oceana.org** gives the following figures for a ship with 3,000 people on board: 30,000 gallons of human waste; 255,000 gallons of "grey water" waste; 7,000 gallons of oily bilge water; and 7 tons of garbage and solid waste. Another source, **www.serconline.org**, gives the following figures based on a ship with 5,000 people on board: 1,000,000 gallons of "grey water"; 210,000 gallons of sewage; 35,000 gallons of oily water; and 50 tons of garbage. Both sites give additional information on how the pollutants affect the ocean. It looks likely the author of the letter relied on the information from the Oceana site.

EXERCISE ## Assessing Imagery

Example: Don't let your child go to sleep in the dark.

The intended effect of this advertisement is to inform and persuade the audience that reading helps children learn and grow, and that reading to children is part of good parenting.

The image appears natural and unaltered. It is relevant to the intended effect: the child is absorbed in the book that is apparently being read by the adult who is just visible in the background.

The lighting on the child's face is reflected from the book, as if the child is basking in the glow of a good story. The pages of the book and the face of the adult form a protective circle around the child. A black-and-white photo may seem less realistic than a colour photo, but it does convey the idea that reading to a child is a simple, straightforward process with a clear benefit.

The image does succeed in supporting the intended effect of the advertisement. Reading to a child is shown as an absorbing process, simple to do, which enlightens the child both literally and metaphorically.

EXERCISE 9.5

Evaluating Choice of Sound and Choosing Appropriate Music

1. The song "I'm a Survivor" works well in a Habitat for Humanity advertisement (sponsored by Whirlpool appliances) in which Reba McEntire acts as spokesperson. The lyrics of the song and McEntire's no-nonsense, "down-home" voice support the compassionate yet practical appeal of houses built by and for low-income families.

EXERCISE 9.6

Evaluating Emotions as Reasons

These exercises should generate some different answers and discussion. The purpose is to practise applying the criteria for mistaken appeals to emotion. Sample answers:

2. b. This is an argument that may be seen as appealing to fear because the speaker is threatening to quit his job. The argument has at least two different interpretations. If we take the conclusion as explicit, the conclusion is "I deserve a raise." In this case, the premise that evokes emotion ("if I do not get a raise, I will have to find a job elsewhere") is irrelevant and the appeal to emotion is a mistake. The speaker's threat to quit does nothing to prove that he deserves a raise, and the listener's fear about losing an employee is not relevant to whether or not the employee deserves a raise. On the other hand, if we take the conclusion as the implied conclusion "You should give me a raise," then the claim that the speaker will quit is relevant. The worry about losing an employee can also be a relevant emotion if the context is one in which the employer wants to encourage employee retention or continue to employ the speaker.

   c. This argument is appealing to the reader's pity. The conclusion is that the reader should give generously to the Children's Fund. However, there is no indication that the Children's Fund is a charity that will in fact help the children. The premises about the terrible poverty of the children are relevant, and the emotion of pity can also be an emotion that is relevant to your decision about whether to give to charity. But the emotion and the stated premises are not sufficient reasons to give to this particular charity.

EXERCISE 9.7 Identifying Practical Options

Suggestions for reducing water consumption:

1. Encourage people to adopt water-efficient showerheads and flush toilets
2. Ban lawn sprinklers and car washing
3. Promote drought-resistant landscaping

Chapter 10

EXERCISE 10.1 Personal Emergency Preparedness

1. *Observation:* cellphone, credit card, cash, maps, blanket, car first-aid kit, bottled water, energy bars, pen and paper for messages, flares or safety triangles, jumper cables, spare set of keys, flashlight.

   Investigation: first-aid training, lifeguard experience, self-defence training, credit card numbers stored safely at home, phone numbers for emergency contacts.

   Evaluation: Typically, people are slightly but not seriously under-prepared. They are well prepared for transportation breakdown and winter weather; reasonably prepared for theft or loss of valuables and work; and under-prepared for crisis situations such as their own or someone else's ill health, unexpected violence, fire, or earthquake.

   Action/response: Usually the highest priority to improve preparation is to acquire knowledge such as first-aid training.

EXERCISE 10.2 Setting Priorities

1. My partner and I agree our home is well protected against fire. It's one level, with easy exits and a sprinkler system. We experience power outages, but we've bought flashlights and a camping stove, so we are better prepared than we used to be. My priority would be an alarm system as protection from theft or intruders. My partner is more worried about water damage from the sprinkler system. The pipes burst in the house next door to us one winter and caused extensive damage to all the walls and floors. Insurance covered the costs, but the house was uninhabitable for months while the repairs were done. One possible cause was that the water pressure was too high for safety—apparently this is quite common in houses in our area. Our priority in the next week would be to get cost estimates on alarm systems and on water pressure testing to see which would be more affordable.

EXERCISE 10.3 Risk Management

1. See **www.cmhc-schl.gc.ca/en/bureho/reho/yogureho** for tips about rental agreements.

Each province and territory has its own legislation to cover the following: collecting and returning deposits, requiring postdated cheques, changing locks, permitting landlord entry to the property, managing sublets and assignments, renewing and terminating leases, rent increases, withholding rent for repairs, giving notice, handling disputes such as late rent payments or eviction, and allowing pets or smoking.

A rental agreement should cover all the following:

- the names of the landlord and tenant(s), and emergency contact information for landlord and tenant(s)
- the address of the rental property, the monthly rent, and whether it includes utilities, parking, or cable
- when the rent is due each month, the amount and terms of the deposit, and the security or damage deposits if applicable
- which repairs are the responsibility of the landlord and which must be done by the tenant at the request of the landlord
- the term of the rental period, the notice period required for terminating the tenancy, conditions under which the landlord can terminate the lease, rules for subletting, allowable rent increases
- specific restrictions or permissions such as pets, boarders, smoking, or waterbeds
- terms for resolution of disputed matters such as late payment, damage and repair, etc.

EXERCISE **10.4** **Responding Appropriately**

1. *Three possible constructive responses:*

   Say nothing and just sympathize.

   Ask the friend to role-play the interview to show me what happened.

   Ask the friend for more detail on what happened, to see if the interview really did go well.

   The third option is best. Maybe the interview did go well, but the friend simply lost to a better candidate. Getting more detail on what happened in the interview will make it easier to tell if there might have been a problem. This seems like the best first step, because if this friend really is inclined to talk, he or she probably will want to talk out the situation at greater length just to get all the feelings out. The second-best option is the role-play, even if I have to talk my friend into trying it, because practising interview questions is one of the best ways to relax and come across well in an interview.

Chapter 11

EXERCISES  **11.1-3**

Sample responses to a good argument, an unproven argument, and a bad argument were provided in the chapter on pages 307, 311, and 316.

EXERCISE 11.4

Making Recommendations

Sample based on Exercise 6.2, question 1

The crux of the debate about checking the speeches of Conservative Members of Parliament was whether members of a political party must not disagree too strongly in public. The problem was not whether the Conservative leader should be the one to check the speeches, but whether anyone should. The first recommendation would be to check Conservative Party principles, to see if they have anything in writing to indicate that elected Members of Parliament must not disagree too strongly in public. If there is something in writing, the party can enforce it. If there is nothing in writing, there may have been discussions or precedents that can be appealed to. If there is no guidance already in place, the dispute shows the Conservatives that they are not all of the same mind on this issue, and the issue needs to be debated, using whatever process they normally use to reach agreement on principles they will abide by.

Chapter 12

EXERCISE 12.1

Choosing Who Should Speak

1. A young adult living at home who wants his or her parents to accept him or her dating people who are not of the family's culture or religion might be wise to choose an older relative or family friend to raise the subject. The spokesperson can stay calmer and may be more credible in being able to see both sides.

EXERCISE 12.2

Framing the Topic

Thanks to Shirley Phillips for this answer on how you might open a discussion on the topic of drug use and abuse with a friend whose use of alcohol is worrying you (question 1a):

It's most important that the approach doesn't come across as accusatory, as this will shut the friend down immediately. So the trick will be to make an observation of the problem behaviour: "I notice that you've been drinking more than usual lately. Is something going on (going wrong)?" Or the question could be even less threatening, such as: "What's up?" Depending on the relationship, this may open the door to more discussion. It's possible, however, that the drinker will be quite defensive about the drinking habit and may just refuse to discuss it.

If so, another way the problem could be addressed is the "back door" approach. The friend could start with an example, either personal or another friend they both know, and tie the example into what the friend is doing. Again, this may or may not work depending on how defensive the drinker is.

The important point is that any attempt to open a discussion must be based on observable behaviour or else the friend will be able to deny any problem drinking. The questioner must have enough evidence to back up the claim before confronting the friend.

If the drinking friend offers a denial such as "No, there's nothing wrong, I'm just having some fun," then the questioner will need to have more evidence that obviously shows that the drinking friend is not really having fun—such as loss of driving privileges, speeding tickets, lost friendships, or trouble in relationships. This shows the drinker that his or her idea of "having fun" is not really fun at all, but actually painful.

EXERCISE 12.3

The Right Time and the Right Place

1. When meeting with your landlord to ask for repairs to your kitchen, you will probably want to meet in the kitchen so the evidence for the repairs is clearly visible to both of you. If there is no comfortable seating in the kitchen, you will want to have seating nearby that you can move to, in case either of you feels rushed or pressured trying to negotiate on your feet. The timing of the meeting should have both of you at your best—a weekday morning rather than a Friday night, for example. You may also want to allow for a preliminary meeting to assess the situation before negotiating repairs, since one or both of you may need time to research options.

EXERCISE 12.4

Helping Discussion Flow Smoothly

1. The discussion format may depend on the size of the team or club that must make the decision. The smaller the group, the more likely it is that discussion will flow best if everyone is in a circle and everyone has a chance to speak. For a larger group, this may be impractical, and it may be best to have a chairperson at a table facing the audience, to lead discussion and keep it moving. In either case, it would be helpful to send information out in advance for people to think about, so that they can come prepared with possible questions, advantages, and disadvantages.

Postscript

EXERCISE P.1

Planning for Feedback

1. Here is a sample checklist:

   ✔ What aspect of this paper interests me most?

   ✔ What can I learn from developing it?

   ✔ Who can give me helpful feedback on this topic?

   ✔ Who is the audience for the final paper, and what will be important to them? (For example, the expectations for the final paper may require you to change the format of the paper, reorganize the sequence, or expand some sections.)

   ✔ Is there additional information I will need to collect? Where can I find it?

EXERCISE **P.2**

Offering Feedback

1. Even young children usually want more feedback than just "That's lovely." "Tell me about it" is probably a necessary first step—offering the chance to discuss it is already a form of feedback, showing you consider the drawing worth discussing. Once you know what the scribble represents, you might offer to write a title for the drawing, if the child wants a title; you might accept it as a gift if the child wants you to take it; or you might put it on the fridge, if the child wants acknowledgment that this drawing is important.

 EXERCISE **P.3**

Recognizing Feedback

1. The feedback here is that something about your language use or conversational style is not working for the native speakers. To explore the problem, you might consult a non-native speaker who is more fluent than you are, to see if you are making any errors in your language use that might be causing misunderstanding. You might also consult a native speaker you do feel comfortable with, to ask what the customs are for conversation. Are there some topics that cannot be raised, or some conversational practices—such as interrupting—that are considered rude? You might also ask whether people in that country welcome a chance to practise your language, or consider it more polite to speak your language if they can. Perhaps there is no problem with your use of their language, but they have not realized you would prefer to practise it instead of using your own.

 EXERCISE **P.4**

Using Feedback

1. a. As the mall manager, you may find it useful to use the feedback to review the effectiveness of your mall's current emergency procedures. For example, were there employees trained in first aid who could arrive immediately to tend to the customer who collapsed or did you have to wait for the ambulance? Did you have any other safe transport you could call on, besides a private car? How effective were the procedures followed to deal with customers in the mall who witnessed the person's collapse and who either got in the way or tried to help? Did the mall follow up with the person who collapsed, or the person's family, and is there anything else you need to do?

   b. If you were responsible for the ambulance service, you now have at least one situation with three simultaneous emergencies where every minute counts. You do have three ambulances. There are two key uses of the feedback from this situation. First, you can discuss with the organization that funds the ambulance service whether this situation still falls within acceptable service guidelines. Are there any backup options you could call on, such as a volunteer fire department that can also respond to emergencies? Second, you can review the ambulance service schedule—given past experience in the area, is there a way to match the service schedule to when there is least demand for an ambulance?

APPENDIX B

Supplementary Reading for Selected Topics

Chapter 1

On Emotions

Damasio, Antonio. *Descartes' Error: Emotion, Reason, and the Human Brain.* New York: Avon Books, 1994. Damasio argues on biological and neurophysiological grounds that emotional awareness and competence are essential to adequate reasoning. Reasoning divorced from emotion will be inaccurate.

de Sousa, R. *The Rationality of Emotion.* Cambridge, MA: M.I.T. Press, 1987.

Ekman, Paul. *Emotions Revealed.* New York: Times Books, 2003.

Greenspan, P. *Emotions and Reasons: An Inquiry into Emotional Justification.* New York: Routledge, Chapman and Hall, 1988.

On Reasoning Difficulties

Baron, Jonathan. *Thinking and Deciding.* Cambridge, Eng.: Cambridge University Press, 1988. An overview of the psychological studies of reasoning and decision-making, including a review of the characteristic errors people make in reasoning tasks, and how we might deal with decisions involving moral and social dilemmas.

Chapter 6

de Becker, Gavin. *The Gift of Fear.* New York: Dell Publishing, 1997. How to recognize and interpret signals of danger and respond appropriately; the role fear plays in avoiding assault or abuse.

Chapter 8

Mayer, R. E. *Thinking, Problem Solving, Cognition.* 2nd ed. New York: W. H. Freeman & Co., 1992. A good overview of studies revealing the processes involved in different types of thinking and the characteristic behaviours and errors that occur in each.

Piatelli-Palmarini, Massimo. *Inevitable Illusions: How Mistakes of Reason Rule Our Minds.* Toronto: John Wiley and Sons, 1994. A short but useful overview of the major results in research on human errors in reasoning and why these errors may be inescapable.

Chapter 9

On Decision-Making

Brams, Steven J., and Alan D. Taylor. *The Win-Win Solution: Guaranteeing Fair Shares to Everybody.* New York: W. W. Norton & Co., 1999. Provides a method of dividing property or goods between people in an equitable way. It shows how contentious issues can be settled by a mathematically and morally defensible way of constructing shares of "equal value."

Chapter 10

Brown, Marvin T. *The Ethical Process: An Approach to Controversial Issues.* 2nd ed. New Jersey: Prentice Hall, 1999. A generic, step-by-step decision process for identifying and weighing the ethical dimension of a decision.

de Bono, Edward. *Six Thinking Hats.* London: Penguin Books, c. 1985. A structured way to cover six different perspectives on a problem, from objective analysis to emotional reaction. This is one of the more popular and widely used of de Bono's many titles.

Russo, J. Edward, and Paul J. H. Shoemaker. *Winning Decisions.* New York: Currency/Doubleday, 2002. A sampler of recommended processes ranging from purely intuitive methods to precise mathematical methods, including useful references to research that supports their advice. Not all procedures work for all decisions. The authors offer a philosophically sound method for testing the limits of any rule or procedure you are expected to apply.

Chapter 11

On Reasoning That Includes Statistics:

Burbidge, J. *Within Reason.* Peterborough, ON: Broadview Press, 1990.

Kahneman, D., P. Slovic, and A. Tversky, eds. *Judgement under Uncertainty: Heuristics and Biases.* Cambridge, Eng.: Cambridge University Press, 1982.

Chapter 12

On Cultural and Personal Differences in Reasoning Behaviour

Brody, Hugh. *The Other Side of Eden.* Toronto: Douglas & MacIntyre, 2000. An examination of how the language of the Inuit is interwoven with their relationship to the land they live in, and a comparison of how hunter-gatherer societies such as the Dene and Inuit differ from agricultural societies.

Goldberger, Nancy, et al., eds. *Knowledge, Difference, and Power.* New York: Basic Books, 1996. A collection of papers discussing the impact of theories that women reason differently than men. The same authors originally published *Women's Ways of Knowing,* which argued that women do reason very differently than men. This book presents refinements of the original theory, multicultural responses, and practical examples from different disciplines and professions.

Ross, Rupert. *Dancing with a Ghost.* Markham, ON: Octopus Publishing Group, 1992. A non-Native lawyer's account of his own exposure to and gradual recognition of the significant differences between Native and non-Native ways of experiencing the world.

Tannen, Deborah. *The Argument Culture: Moving from Debate to Dialogue.* New York: Ballantine Books, 1999.

GLOSSARY

Abstract: Removed from particular and specific examples.

Acceptable (information): Information that is most likely accurate.

Accountable: Required to perform to a particular standard, or being expected to justify one's actions.

Ambiguous: Describes a sentence, phrase, or word that can be interpreted more than one way; it is not clear which of the possible meanings is intended in the particular context.

Analogical reasoning: An argument that uses a claim of similarity between one thing and another to draw conclusions about one of the things being compared.

Anecdotal evidence: Evidence in the form of anecdotes about personal experiences.

Argument: The attempt to defend a claim by offering one or more other claims as support for it.

Argumentation: All the different social practices that involve the presentation of arguments; the practice and study of arguments.

Argumentative persuasion: Attempting to convince a person to believe or do something by presenting them with an argument.

Assumption: A claim for which there are plausible alternatives that have not yet been ruled out by evidence or argument.

Assumptions of principle: Beliefs or values that are not universally held.

Bad argument: An argument that has one or more unacceptable premises, and/or has irrelevant premises, and/or has insufficient premises, and/or is not indefeasible.

Biased person: A person who assumes that one particular view is right and does not or cannot produce enough support to show that his or her views are any better than those that he or she criticizes.

Certainty (arguments to certainty): Arguments with the goal of establishing that their conclusions are certain. An argument to certainty is successful only when its premises establish that the conclusion is either necessarily true or so highly likely that doubting its truth would be pointless.

Claim: A thought expressed as a declarative sentence.

Code of ethics: A formal expression of the moral obligations of members of a profession.

Cogent argument: An argument for which, if assuming the premises are true, the conclusion is *probably* true and the probability that the conclusion is true is not so high that doubting the truth of the conclusion would be pointless. Competing conclusions are possible, but less likely or less important.

Conclusion: The claim supported by other claims in an argument.

Conclusion indicator words: Words that signal a conclusion is about to be expressed.

Conductive reasoning: Reasoning that accumulates information as a way of supporting its conclusion.

Conflicting examples: Examples that are incompatible with the claim in question.

Consistency (of information): Information that is the same throughout a source and from source to source.

Context: The background and setting against which a communication or other event takes place.

Contraries: Competing statements that cannot both be true at the same time.

Counter-considerations: Premises that point away from the desired conclusion and support a different conclusion.

Credible (information): Information with a source that it is reasonable to rely on.

Critical attention: Noticing details with the goal of furthering your understanding of a situation or issue.

Crux of the debate: The key point of disagreement.

Deductive reasoning: Reasoning that deduces the truth of one statement from the truth of another statement or statements to show that the conclusion is the *only* possible option.

Deductively valid argument: An argument for which, assuming that the premises are true, the conclusion is necessarily true. That is, if the premises are all true, the conclusion cannot possibly be false.

Dysphemism: A negative expression used in the place of a neutral or positive expression.

Empirical data: Evidence we collect by observing, investigating, and measuring in the actual world.

Equivocation: Bad reasoning that is hidden because a single (ambiguous) term in an argument is used in two different ways.

Euphemism: A positive expression used in the place of a neutral or negative expression.

Evaluating in context: Using specific expectations, standards, needs, or goals to judge whether an argument, an action, or information is suitable for its purpose.

Fact-checking: Confirming information you already have by consulting an authoritative source or by comparing several reliable sources to see if the information is consistent.

Feedback: Anything you observe or are told by others that enables you to determine what worked well and should be continued, or what worked poorly and needs to be improved or changed.

Generalization: A claim about groups of people, things, events, or characteristics.

Good argument: An argument with premises that are all acceptable, relevant, sufficient and indefeasible.

Implicit premise: A premise that is not clearly stated, but must be part of the argument if the reasoning is intended to follow a deductively valid or cogent argument pattern.

Indefeasibility: An indefeasible argument has met the criteria of premise acceptability, relevance, and sufficiency and there is no other background information that would show the argument fails. It is a standard that is relevant only to arguments to probability.

Indirect arguments: Arguments that make their point indirectly, by asking questions, hinting at a point, omitting some points, or using humour or sarcasm instead of plain statements.

Inductive reasoning: Reasoning that relies on known examples to be good predictors of what is true of other examples of the same type.

Inference: A logical move, deducing the truth or probable truth of one statement from the truth of another statement.

Issue: Subject of discussion.

Layered arguments: Arguments with premises that have been supported by further argument.

Loaded word: A particularly controversial or offensive word—one that smuggles in certain assumptions about what the word describes or represents.

Main issue: The central, unifying topic of discussion.

Multicultural context: Any setting in which people have different cultural traditions and expectations, and may have significant differences in beliefs and values.

Neutral person: A person who has no opinion on the topic, or has heard arguments on both sides of the topic but does not yet favour either side.

Neutral presentation of information: Information presented in an objective, nonpartisan fashion.

Non-argumentative persuasion: Attempting to convince someone to believe or do something without presenting them with an argument.

Non-universal claim: A claim about less than all members of a category.

Objective: Not allowing personal bias to limit what is observed.

Objective observation: Occurs when the observer does not allow personal bias to determine what is observed. The objective observer reserves judgment until observations are complete.

Objective person: Someone who is willing to fairly consider all points of view including reasons against his or her own point of view.

Open-ended observation: Observation without specific goals in mind; observation to generate questions rather than to answer them.

Plausible (argument): An argument to possibility that has consistent premises, the combining of which makes the conclusion possibly true.

Possibility (arguments to possibility): Arguments with the goal of establishing that their conclusions are possible. A successful argument to possibility combines consistent pieces of information to show that its conclusion is possible.

Premise indicator words: Words that signal a premise is about to be expressed.

Premises: Claims that are offered as support for another claim.

Principle of charity: When there is more than one way to interpret a word, phrase, sentence, or situation in general our interpretation must be the most reasonable given the context.

Probability (arguments to probability): Arguments with the goal of establishing their conclusions are probable, as opposed to certain or simply possible. A successful argument to probability is one where assuming the premises are true makes the conclusion *probably* true, and the probability that the conclusion is true is not so high that doubting the truth of the conclusion would be pointless.

Purposeful observation: Observation with specific goals, typically to answer specific questions.

Quantifier: A word that tells you "how much."

Reason: Anything that motivates, causes, explains, or is used as a rationale.

Reasoning behaviour: How reasoning is indicated in practice—expressed freely or not expressed at all, expressed unemotionally or with emotion.

Relevance (of premises): Describes premises whose truth has some evident connection with the truth of the conclusion.

Relevant evidence: Information connected in a causal or explanatory way to the topic under investigation.

Report of an argument: A clear presentation of the conclusion of an argument and all its supporting premises, designed to help a reader or listener better understand the argument.

Standard form: A point-form arrangement of the premises of an argument where each premise is numbered and each numbered premise is set out on a separate line, with the conclusion at the bottom of the list.

Standardization: Conversion of an argument from its original prose form to the point-form list of a standard form.

Structurally valid: An argument is structurally valid if assuming that the premises are true makes the conclusion either necessarily true or so highly likely that doubting its truth would be pointless.

Structure of an argument: The way in which the premises are connected to support the conclusion.

Sub-argument: An argument that supports a sub-conclusion.

Sub-conclusion: The conclusion of a sub-argument that is in turn used as a premise to support a further claim.

Sub-issues: Topics that are raised as relevant to the main issue.

Sufficient (premises): Premises are sufficient to establish a conclusion when they present enough reasons to make the conclusion rationally acceptable. The premises *taken as a whole* must provide enough evidence to give the level of support for the conclusion required for that type of argument.

Supporting examples: Examples that are consistent with the claim in question.

Testimony: Information provided by a person or written source that can reasonably be assumed to have direct knowledge or to have appropriate expertise.

Type of reasoning: The way in which one or more premises are linked to support the conclusion.

Universal claim: A claim about all members of a category.

Unproven argument: An argument that has met the conditions for relevance and sufficiency but not yet for acceptability or indefeasibility and on which we suspend judgment pending further information.

Vague: Imprecise word or sentence.

Well-structured argument: An argument that uses the structure required to give the level of support needed by its conclusion.

WORKS CITED

Associated Press. "Tsunami Boosts Natural Disasters Toll." *Vancouver Sun* 18 Feb. 2005: A15.

Basset, Brian. *Adam@Home*. Comic strip. 22 Nov. 2004. http://www.ucomics.com

Chambers Dictionary. Edinburgh: Chambers Harrap, 1993.

Damasio, Antonio. *Descartes' Error: Emotion, Reason, and the Human Brain*. New York: Avon Books, 1994.

de Becker, Gavin. *The Gift of Fear*. New York: Dell Publishing, 1997.

Dixon, John, and Phil Bryden. "Charter Does Not Preclude Immigration Reform." *Vancouver Sun* 10 Sept. 1999: A23.

Ekman, Paul. *Emotions Revealed*. New York: Times Books, 2003.

Hamill, James F. *Ethno-Logic: The Anthropology of Human Reasoning*. Champaign, IL: University of Illinois Press, 1990.

Hume, David. *A Treatise Of Human Nature*. Ed. L. A. Selby-Bigge. Book I. Oxford: Oxford University Press, 1973.

Ignatieff, Michael. *The Rights Revolution*. Toronto: House of Anansi Press, 2000.

Joyce, Amy. "'Rent a Guinea Pig' and Other Weird Requests." *Vancouver Sun* 6 Mar. 2004: E3 (reprinted from *Washington Post*).

Kovalick, Jody. "Sand on Stage: Minimum Weight, Maximum Effect." *Technical Design Solutions for Theatre: The Technical Brief Collection*. Ed. B. J. Sammler and D. Harvey. Vol. 2. Woburn, MA: Focal Press, 2002.

Longman Dictionary of Contemporary English. London: Longman Group, 1978.

Luria, A. R. *Cognitive Development*. Trans. M. Lopez-Morillas and L. Solotaroff. Ed. M. Cole. Cambridge, MA: Harvard University Press, 1976.

"Making Migraines Less of a Headache." *Well Informed*. Pharmasave Healthnotes newsletter. Sept./Oct. 2004: 1.

Ross, Alex. "Sound and Vision: Glass's 'Koyaanisqatsi' and the art of film scoring." *The New Yorker* 27 June 2005: 102-04.

Spalding, Derek. "Veteran dips into history one last time." *Times* [Abbotsford] 18 June 2004: 17.

Spector, Norman. "Tiptoeing Around the 'T' Word Stirs a Fuss in the Media." *Vancouver Sun* 24 Sept. 2004: A17.

Sun, Shuyun. *Ten Thousand Miles Without a Cloud*. London: Harper Perennial, 2003.

Thompson, Bob. Letter. *Times Colonist* [Victoria]. 7 Sept. 2003, located on www.canada.com.

Wallis, Claudia, and Kristina Dell. "What Makes Teens Tick." *Time* 10 May 2004.

Willcocks, Paul. "The Seatbelt Solution to Saving Young Lives." *Vancouver Sun* 13 Mar. 2004: C6.

INDEX